PIANISTS AT PLAY

Interviews, Master Lessons, and Technical Regimes

by DEAN ELDER

KAHN & AVERILL, LONDON

First published in the UK by Kahn & Averill in 1986
Copyright © 1982 by The Instrumentalist Company

Reprinted 1989

British Library Cataloguing in Publication Data

Elder, Dean
    Pianists at play: interviews, master lessons and
    technical regimes. — 2nd ed.
    1. Piano playing — Personal observations 2. Piano
    playing — Manuals
    I. Title
    786.1'092'4

    ISBN 1-871082-10-2

Printed by Halstan & Co. Ltd., Amersham, Bucks., England

CONTENTS

PREFACE

For fixing a locked door, there is nothing like a key. I was fortunate to have 89 keys handy when seeking access to the artists in this book.

Of that number, 88 were ivory so-to-speak, and I like to think that in the beginning my own loving association with the keyboard helped persuade these pianists that their words would be understood. As I became known and word got around that interviews with me were pleasurable, artists became accessible.

Nevertheless, I am often asked how I got started. The answer lies in the fact that besides my having perhaps a certain gift and expertise for interviewing, one of the century's great artists happened also to have been my most influential and inspirational teacher. Just the mention of Walter Gieseking seemed enough to convince my subjects that the right questions would be asked. Gieseking was my 89th key.

I would never have reached Arthur Rubinstein, one of the first great pianists I interviewed, had he not known I had studied with Gieseking. Even so, credentials or no credentials, I was not going to interview Rubinstein without campaigning for the privilege.

It wasn't that Rubinstein was resistant, just terribly tied up. Of course, once his interview appeared other doors flew open — Gina Bachauer's, Rudolf Serkin's, Alicia de Larrocha's — but that didn't make the route to Rubinstein any less like the yellow brick road, full of twists, uncertainties and, of course, promise.

At the end of that road was certainly no fraud. I must say, however, that the great man, besides being very much a man of the moment, exuding charm, seemed also greatly egoistic, gratuitously inflicting any number of cuts upon his colleagues during our two hour talk.

Rubinstein shared at least two qualities exhibited by most of the other pianists — punctuality and good manners. Usually over a hotel house phone the artists would invite me to their rooms, not one minute before or after the appointed hour. Jeanne-Marie Darré came downstairs to meet me. Claudio Arrau, Lili Kraus, and Rudolf Serkin invited me to lunch when it should have been the other way around. Thus, at precisely noon April 12, 1969 Rubinstein's warmly welcoming bass-baritone came over the hotel phone.

"Come right up."

"Thank you."

"Thank *you*."

I had known Rubinstein's playing most of my life. One of my 78 rpm's was a Rubinstein recording and of course I had heard him many times in recital. Indelibly, I remember his playing the Brahms Concerto in B♭ with the New York Philharmonic when, during the slow movement, the announcer interrupted the broadcast: "Ladies and gentlemen, Pearl Harbor has been bombed!"

In January 1968 I called Max Wilcox, Rubinstein's RCA record producer, whom I had known since our student days at Columbia University Teachers College. Max said he would show copies of *Clavier* to Rubinstein at an appropriate moment. "Let's hope he's interested. Your kind of interview would certainly make a fascinating article." At a party, Max told Rubinstein about me and the great pianist agreed. But agreeing and the eventuality were a long way apart.

Rubinstein played his 1968 spring tour and returned to Europe. Max proposed we wait until he returned to America in the fall. In October Max gave me Rubinstein's Xeroxed USA performing schedule of 37 concerts for the 1968-69 season. It was obvious an interview would have to be sandwiched between Pittsburgh and Philharmonic Hall recitals in January or between Princeton and Carnegie Hall recitals in February, if not later.

On January 14, 1969 I wrote to Mr. Rubinstein at the Drake Hotel, again requesting an interview, enclosing copies of my Darré and Arrau interviews which had recently appeared. Max called two days later to say January and February were out, but to telephone late in March.

I did. Mrs. Rubinstein answered, saying many people were trying to see Mr. Rubinstein. "One man is writing a book on Cortot. He wants Mr. Rubinstein's recollections. And he is trying to write his own memoirs. . . . Today he has this, tomorrow that. . . . He is playing in Washington on Saturday, April 5th, with the New York Philharmonic on Tuesday, April 8th. The interview would have to be at 12 on the 7th. Telephone on the 6th in the afternoon or in the evening to confirm," she said.

I suppose I should have been gratified to have received a specific date but the conversation, a portrait of an almost-always unavailable artist, made me uneasy. Disoriented, too, judging from my next action.

In what was surely unusual for the Rubinsteins, I called back with the news that the interview was off. I would be going on vacation. Rubinstein would have to wait for my return.

I came to my senses the next day and telephoned Mrs. Rubinstein saying that I could, after all, fit Rubinstein in. I would adjust my vacation schedule, that was all.

"Now the 7th wouldn't be possible," she said. "Mr. Rubinstein wants to practice for his engagement with the Philharmonic on the 8th. The interview will have to be on Friday, April 11th, at 4 p.m. We are not leaving for Europe until the 12th. Call about 10 a.m. on Thursday to make sure no plans have changed. He plays in South Carolina on the 9th and has said he will attend a young pianists' recital on the 11th. Yes, four o'clock on the 11th is the only possible time."

On March 29th, I sent a confirming letter to Mr. Rubinstein. On Sunday, March 30th my family and I left on vacation during which time I assembled, consolidated and revised enough questions for a hundred interviews. Although I seldom follow predetermined questions, preferring to let the muse take its course, I intended to be ready.

I returned home on the 9th. The next day, I put in a person-to-person telephone call to Mrs. Rubinstein. A man answered the telephone. "This is Mr. Rubinstein's secretary," he said. "Who is calling?" Mrs. Rubinstein was on the telephone at almost the same time. A back-and-forth banter ensued between the two of them which I had come to realize was par for the course.

For what seemed like the tenth time, I heard Mrs. Rubinstein improvise, parry, fend: "Tomorrow isn't possible. Mr. Rubinstein played last night in Columbia, South Carolina," (which I already knew and had wondered how he could be back and ready for an interview at 4 p.m. the next day). "The morning flight was cancelled, so he won't return until this afternoon."

A *Pantalon-et-Columbine*-like drama took place between a screeching Mrs. Rubinstein and the secretary. I caught snatches: "My God, he'll kill me if I do that," I heard Mrs. Rubinstein exclaim.

"Can you come Saturday?" she said. "At 12 o'clock. You see he has to see a man about taxes later. Twelve is the only possible time."

By then, I will admit, the changes in appointments had got to me. Would I or would I not interview Rubinstein?

I had my doubts up until Rubinstein's "Thank *you*" that Saturday.

If in their discipline and manners the great pianists seem cut from the same cloth, they are strikingly dissimilar in other ways. The chain-smoking Darré with her deep speaking voice, the irresistibly charming Martha Argerich, the "motherly" spontaneous Novaes, the warm and hospitable Serkin, the determined Alicia de Larrocha who could conclude a festive evening with a rendition of "Auld Lang Syne" — each artist was or is thoroughly unique and inspiring.

But this is not so much a book about personalities as about music. For all of its biographical details and anecdotes, *Pianists at Play* is first and foremost a reference work on piano playing. It includes some of the best master class lessons (given not by entertaining salespeople, as is too often the case, but by artists on the order of Jorge Bolet who said some very important things about Schumann's *Kreisleriana*) and technical regimes. The Adele Marcus technical regime has been used all over the world. The interview with Badura-Skoda on the Schubert Sonatas has been used in classrooms in the Soviet Union.

Rubinstein's ideas on interpretation, how Gina Bachauer practiced Hanon, Gieseking on Debussy and Ravel, Guiomar Novaes' opinions of her recordings, Ravel's advice to Gaby Casadesus, Arrau on Beethoven, how Serkin practices scales, Argerich on Horowitz, Lili Kraus on Mozart, tempos, style, technical suggestions, pedalings — the index is a dictionary of ideas, a compendium on piano playing.

I would like to thank James Rohner, publisher, and Dorothy Packard, Christine Nagy, and Lee Yost, editors of *Clavier*, for publishing my work, my wife for her help and understanding, and various managers and PR people. I am also deeply appreciative of the many people throughout this country and abroad who have expressed their admiration both in person and in letters, wanting these interviews to become a book. Most of all I want to thank each and every artist for the privilege of sharing his or her time and invaluable opinions with me. The hours I spent with them have enriched my life immeasurably. Never before has the world been blessed with so many marvelously equipped pianists, both young and old.

Dean Elder
Dix Hills, New York
June 1981

INTERVIEWS

Artur Rubinstein

As Artur Rubinstein escorted me into the drawing room of his New York hotel suite (the concert grand piano prominent in the foreground), he pointed to a large profile photograph on the stereo set: "Just look at that beautiful, long, wavy hair, with the sun shining on it. It is a waterfall! When they told me it was my eight-year-old granddaughter, I couldn't believe it . . . "

And I couldn't believe, from his appearance, his speech, or his manner, that Mr. Rubinstein was 84 years old. I was immediately impressed by the smooth texture of his skin, the gleam in his twinkling blue eyes, his nice smile. His conversational English was mixed with foreign accents and syntax. He was wearing the red sport jacket and tie he wore for the Boris Chaliapin TIME magazine cover painting of him.

". . . and over here," Mr. Rubinstein continued, "this framed inscription and gold key I got in Columbia, South Carolina, where I played night before last. Do you suppose this key is really gold? No, it couldn't be; it's not heavy enough. But I was terribly touched by their giving it to me. It reminds me of the story of Reisenauer . . .

"There was this pianist, Alfred Reisenauer, a pupil of Liszt. He played a big concert in Germany. After the concert, the people in charge asked him backstage, 'Would you prefer a fee of 1,000 marks or a medal?' 'How much is the medal worth?' asked Reisenauer. 'Twenty-five marks' was the reply. 'Then,' said Reisenauer, 'I'll take the medal and 975 marks.' " Mr. Rubinstein puts you at ease at once.

Max Wilcox, Mr. Rubinstein's RCA Victor Record producer, had arrived, and the three of us sat down to talk, Mr. Rubinstein smoking a cigar.

Approach to Interpretation

"Mr. Rubinstein," I began, "Bernard Gavoty, music critic of the Paris newspaper *Figaro*, says in his book about you: 'there are two ways of visualizing music: either revelation of what it implies or transmission of what it expresses.' What do you think of this statement?"

Mr. Rubinstein straightened suddenly. "Well, I think both ways of visualizing music are possible," he said, "de-pending on the importance of the work we are performing. We are sometimes required to be the composers, to reveal what a composition implies, especially if the composition is not very important. There are certain compositions which become more important by the interpretation of a very great performer. For example, there are lovely pieces by Moszkowski and Liszt. Liszt himself played better than his compositions asked for. Ysaye, the great Belgian violinist, could make the Vieuxtemps Concerto sound better than it really was. And Casals played a Fauré Elegy so beautifully, it made me cry. But if we look at the music, we see these compositions are not important.

"On the other hand, other compositions are the great masterpieces by the revered masters, the great composers, to be served by us only as intermediaries, as a sort of link of better understanding between the composer and the public. We must transmit what these great compositions express. It is our gift to be able to transmit to an innocent and ignorant public. I mean ignorant in the French sense: *J-ignore* in French means simply 'I don't know it.' The public doesn't know the work. So both approaches — the revelation of what music implies and the transmission of what music expresses — are possible."

"Do you ever approach interpretation through extra-musical means," I asked, "putting the mood or character of a work into words, describing a passage in words?"

"Describing a passage in a literary way, I would say no," Mr. Rubinstein replied. "A passage doesn't mean a literary way but a work often strongly suggests a literary meaning, even some works of Chopin.

"Chopin was terribly reluctant to admit the importance of literature, a great enemy of literature's having any connection with music. And that probably was the reason he didn't have the admiration he should have had for Schumann, who was Chopin's great friend and admirer. You know that Chopin openly didn't like the proclaimed link between literature and music which Schumann professed all through his career.

"But of course Chopin *was* influenced by a literary theme, by literature. We know that very well. The only time he admitted something of this sort was when he wrote about the Larghetto from his F Minor Concerto: ". . . out of love for that stupid girl in Poland who sang very well but sometimes out of tune.' "

Max Wilcox interjected: "Mr. Rubinstein, you have mentioned to me that you have a sort of personal story in mind as you play certain works of Chopin, the A Flat Major Ballade for example."

"Well," Mr. Rubinstein replied, "when one hears one's self, you know, one is so influenced by the vision of something. The idea I have in mind when playing the A Flat Ballade is not an idea I had myself. Not at all. There is a drawing by Aubrey Beardsley, the English artist and illustrator, inspired by the A Flat Ballade. In the drawing Beardsley put a lady, wearing a very long black velvet dress, riding a white horse in the old fashion with her feet hanging sideways, as the ladies rode in those times. The dress was long, long, long. Behind her you saw a sort of bad weather, a nasty day. And that was all. So of course, I thought the thing was a rendezvous of love.

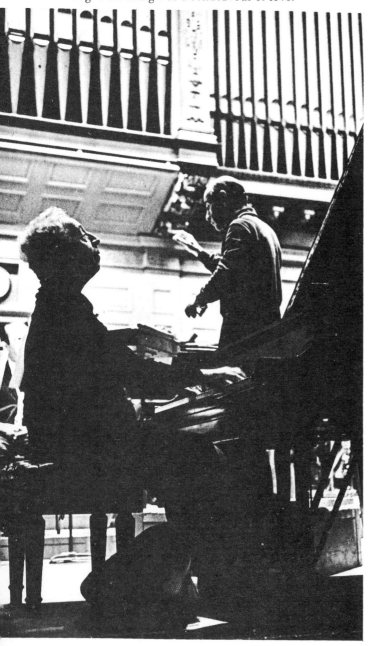

Rehearsing with Erich Leinsdorf.

"The beginning of that Ballade is a question and answer: 'Are you coming tomorrow, where can we meet?'

'Yes, I might do it.'

And so on. The whole thing is question and answer until it stops and becomes, with the second theme, the hopping of the horse." And Mr. Rubinstein sang in his suave, thick bass-baritone:

"And Aubrey Beardsley drew this; he shows the horse hopping. It looks it."

"I thought that theme was Ondine," I protested.

"No, a horse," Mr. Rubinstein continued. "It is a theme you might use, orchestrated, to accompany a beautifully dressed horse, with a lovely cavalier with a top hat, or a lady rider, in a circus. This theme would sound much better than what they usually use.

"And the works of other composers, too, often suggest a literary meaning. Debussy supposedly gave the titles to his Preludes after he had written the pieces. They say Schumann did too, but I don't quite believe that. Schumann was of such a literary bent of mind, he must have had certain ideas in mind. He composed his own feeling — Florestan and Eusebius and so on — that was his mood.

"I was playing Debussy's *Poissons d'or* the other day when suddenly my daughter, Alina, had tears in her eyes. 'The poor little fish,' she said. In the beginning of the piece you have this nice little fish, in the sun, swimming around, chasing, playing with the fisherman's bait, jumping around in the water. And there comes the moment where it is caught:

It tries to wiggle and can't get away. And the same theme of the beginning becomes tragic; the last section becomes tragic, a terribly sad story. You can play the piece absolutely to the point, right exactly according to the story. 'The poor little fish.'

"You see Debussy was very fond of water; he loved rivers, fountains, the ocean, and the sea, *La Mer*. He proclaimed that in letters. He was terribly attracted to water, contrary to myself. I like mountains; I don't like the sea at all. It bores me stiff. Many times I was on boats. I sometimes went to Argentina by boat, and I don't think I even peeped out at the sea. I stayed always inside the boat. I'm not sick of course, but I never gave a look to the sea. Never. I read books, went to bed, ate a lot, and so on. You couldn't get me to the deck to look at the blue water or what have you. Never in my life did I sit out on deck wrapped in blankets."

La Grande Ligne

Rubinstein often plays in blocks, in groups of notes. He is more interested in the sweep or élan in such pieces as the last movement of the Appassionata Sonata or the Chopin Revolutionary Etude or D Minor Prelude than he is in trying to make every note clear.

I told him I had always admired *la grande ligne* in his playing. "Details are so completely a part of you," I said, "you can kaleidoscope. You have said you would rather miss a few notes than play by phrases instead of as a whole."

"Well, you see," he answered, "preferring to miss a few notes to playing in a small way is something not quite due to my own character but to my great impression of the much older, great pianists of my youth — Messieurs Eugene d'Albert, Ferrucio Busoni, a man called Conrad Ansorge; there was a man Edouard Risler, the French pianist, you know. They did not play carefully like nowadays. Of course I accuse this careful playing of today — and this will amuse my friend, Max Wilcox, very much — to the fact that pianists are terrified they will not play so well as on their records.

"Because, you see, thanks to Wilcox the records come out fine, faultless, whereas in the concert, pianists might miss one or two notes. So pianists today are terrified and are concentrated on the perfection of the performance. And as a result they sometimes lose the line of a composition, because delineating *la grande ligne* requires a certain vision. Inspired is a stupid old-fashioned word which doesn't convey much, but still it is valid. You have to be inspired. There is a concert where you are inspired and a concert where you are not inspired. There is no doubt about that; I know that very well. I come out of a concert and I know that that was an *inspired* concert; I was under the spell. Another time I have to finish a concert because I signed a contract and have to play it. There is nothing to do to it. I can't help it."

"Inspiration for you is intuitive, almost unconscious," I said. "You don't plan."

"NO, no, no, never plan," he replied vigorously. "I couldn't plan; I am a born improviser. Again I think I learned this improvisational approach from my elders, my precursors. Even as a legend I heard so much about the playing of my namesake, Anton Rubinstein, who certainly must have been a fantastic pianist, a genius of a pianist. Even my pedantic and pedestrian professor, Heinrich Barth in Berlin, with whom I studied from the age of 8 to 15, who wouldn't pardon me anything — he wouldn't let me use the fifth finger instead of the fourth, 'Ah lazy dog, devil, the fourth finger,' he would say; he was pedantic to the last degree — had a bust of Anton Rubinstein, who played all the wrong notes in the world, who never practiced, who wrote his unnecessary music day and night. And yet Anton

Aubrey Beardsley's drawing (sepia wash) to illustrate the Chopin A Flat Ballade.

Rubinstein played so that Professor Barth couldn't get away from it.

"For me Anton Rubinstein's approach was something out of this world. His approach put me on that road, you understand. I let go. I preferred to let the people feel what I had in my heart, what I had as a temperament, what I felt about the rhythm of it, the go of it, the intention of the composer.

"To be absolutely careful not to miss A flat, or to touch a note next to it, or to touch two notes together because that right away involves clinging to the piano, being minuscule, small-minded, instead of going to it, damn it, the big chord must be struck because I need it. It is the big climax of the phrase; I must get it. Never mind if I miss one or two notes. The big line is the thing, and it seems to convey the right thing to the audience. Otherwise I would have been pushed from the concert podiums years ago. The public wouldn't stand for it. I think I am the champion of playing wrong notes, but I don't care. And the public doesn't seem to care much.

"You know the other night when I played the Mozart D Minor Concerto with the New York Philharmonic, I missed a few things, a few notes; I was nervous. I had a fine rehearsal with Mr. George Szell, but he makes me a little nervous, a little tense in the evening. He was tense so I became tense too. And of course that makes you a little bit self-conscious and I missed one, two, or three things, but for me this didn't matter much. For all in all it was a nice performance, a lovely performance, a beautiful performance, big, big, big line and so on, full of life, full of passion, full of everything."

Max Wilcox interrupted: "Mr. Rubinstein, may I ask you a question? There is one thing that I notice about your playing which always impresses me. Say there is a development section and then there is a theme that returns. Many people return self-consciously, or abruptly, to the theme again. They chop the sections. But you have a way, if you make a retard before the return of the theme, you make the retard a measure before and then go into the theme very naturally, very smoothly. Everything is blended smoothly together."

"You see," replied Rubinstein, "there are actually two things I try to follow: one thing is this sort of inspiration of the composer who doesn't think of the gallery, of the concert audience, of anything else but the piece he wants to write, which he has in his mind and his heart. The other thing is my feeling that what is behind the letter of the notes means everything. Maybe those pianists whom you blame for not returning smoothly to the theme and whom you quote now, maybe they are for the sheet of the music, for the indications there, being true to the letter. For me, playing by letter means nothing; it is what is behind the letter that means everything."

Musicological Details

In one instance Mr. Rubinstein has disclosed a musicological detail which helps him feel correctly what is behind the letter. He has said that the melody of the middle section of the Chopin B Minor Scherzo, the B Major *molto piu lento* section, is based on the Polish Christmas carol, 'Lulajze Jezuniu.' Thus this section should be played underlining the melody as follows:

and not as so many editions, such as the Paderewski, print it and so many pianists play it:

But for the most part Rubinstein relies on his instinct. I asked him about the ending chord of the B Major Nocturne. "You play the ending chord major and not minor as in the so-called authoritative editions," I said. "What is your feeling about this chord?"

"In the Debussy edition of Chopin, which I like," he answered, "the B Major Nocturne ends with a major chord. In Chopin one shouldn't discuss such things. Chopin changed his works constantly from the first edition, with each edition, with his pupils' editions. He was selling his works to Wessel in England, Schlesinger in Paris, and Probst in Germany at the same and separate times. He made changes in the volumes of his pupils. But I play the major chord because the minor chord weakens the ending; it weakens the whole theme."

"And what about the dotted rhythms in the Chopin Polonaises?" I continued. "Many players play the ♩. ♪ rhythm ♩. ♪ and ♪♪♪ as ♪♪♪ in the Polonaises, the Military for example. Is this a Polish tradition, is it connected with the Polonaise rhythm, or is this, too, something you feel personally to make the music more alive?"

"This is all rather in the dance of Poland. Each Polonaise requires another approach to it," he answered.

Chopin Rubato

"What is your feeling about Chopin rubato, Mr. Rubinstein?" I asked. "Should it be calculated, should it be free, should there be a basic rhythm? Have you at one time worked out rubatos, gradations, nuances?"

"Rubato is always a tremendously open question," he answered. "Only in the first six or seven Mazurkas does Chopin mention or write rubato. He never writes rubato in any major work. He saw the bad results of it. Rubato too should be felt instinctively; if you have the right instinctive feeling, your rubato will be right. Not as some American crooners sing without any feeling for the rhythm. But as Fred Astaire, who happens to be a wonderful musician, sings. When he sings songs of Cole Porter, Gershwin, Berlin, he never misses, from my point of view, a natural, instinctive rubato.

"I remember hearing Madame Callas singing Norma, and it was not the best time of her life. But when she sang the first big aria, Casta Diva, she sang so divinely that, as a compliment, I said to my wife, 'she sings as one plays the piano.' That too was instinctive rubato."

Memory

I asked Mr. Rubinstein about his memory, whether it was mainly photographic and aural. "My memory is mainly photographic," he said, "inherited from my father. When I play, I turn the pages in my mind; I even see the coffee stains. My knowledge of the architecture of a work, how it is built, helps too."

Practice: His Own Exercises

Piano playing being instinctive for Rubinstein, I knew he probably had never had to practice much, that he probably had never concerned himself much with pure exercises. Yet I had read he would sometimes play scales in thirds under his hat while watching a film, or make a little exercise on the piano before a concert. And before he played the Beethoven Fourth Concerto on the Hurok Presents television program, the camera showed him doing muscular-movemented finger warmups.

"What were those exercises?" I asked. "Have you always done them?"

"No, I don't do anything always," he laughed. "But I did discover one thing. I always had an allergy, an absolutely furious allergy to exercises, to exercising on the piano. I loathed the Messieurs Czerny, Clementi, his *Gradus ad Parnassum*, and so on. I always found my own exercises which were much more valid, more practical, and I would always practice my own exercises. Tell that to the young people.

"You see we all have different fingers, different bodies, different minds, different brains. We are different, aren't we? We are three men sitting here; we are absolutely different in many ways: we wouldn't approach the piano in the same way; we wouldn't put our fingers to be comfortable on the piano in the same way; we wouldn't sit the same way on the stage, and so on.

"Yet for quite a long while, some quack pianists — not quack doctors — have pretended there is such a thing as the Leschetizky method, the Philipp method, or what was it, the Matthay method. Methods are sheer, stupid nonsense. A real professor would be a great man, or is a great man, if he knows how to discern in every young talent its capacities and incapacities, its possibilities and impossibilities. This is the great gift of a Master, no? A real Master will tell one man to put his fingers straight on the piano because that gives him good results and another man to squeeze his fingers like claws because that gives him the same good results too, that the fingers are meant to be used this way and that way and give one man different pieces from the other and so on.

"And that brings us to my own exercises. Instead of losing hours by playing all sorts of exercises like Czerny, Cramer, or whoever it is, I always have used, as my chief exercise, obstacles in every composition that I have played or am playing still, because these obstacles are my own shortcomings.

"I have seen little girls, age 10, who had hardly started working on the piano, who played a little passage — which I could never dominate in my whole lifetime — as if the passage were child's play, which it was, but who couldn't play three proper bars of an Andante of Mozart which I could play in my sleep.

"There's a place in the Concerto in B Flat of Brahms, in practically every Chopin piece, in the Ballades, the Scherzos, the Etudes by all means, and so on — there are always moments where I am stuck by something which is difficult for me. So I often start my work on the piano, if I have to play a program having nothing to do with these obstacles, by exercising passages in other works which are difficult for me." And he sang, from the Brahms Concerto in B Flat, "Tada-deedee-tadum, tada-deedee-tahdum, tahda-deedee-tahdum," making finger motions in the air:

"Or, in the Brahms Concerto in D Minor:

"Or, in the Chopin A Flat Ballade:

"Or, the last part, the Coda, of the F Minor Ballade:

"Or, the middle of the F Minor Concerto, which is very difficult:

"I know young pianists who smoke a cigar while practicing, who put it away and puddle-luddle-luddle, exercise their fingers, paying no attention to what they are doing. There is nothing to the music. And right away after that in the melody which is very easy,

"they fall flat on their back; they are nothing. You see, that's it."

Wanting to know about his earlier practice methods, I said: "Mr. Rubinstein, I have read that in 1934 you took your family to a mountain cottage in southeastern France, rented an old upright piano and set it up in a nearby stable. Often playing by candlelight, you worked for three months, working as much as nine hours a day, polishing technique and repertory. How did you practice? Can you remember details that might help young pianists, students, or teachers?"

"That is a complete untruth that I practiced nine hours a day," he said. "There is always the exaggeration of interviewers. But to answer your question . . . there were two occasions in my life, two moments in my life, when I practiced really seriously. Once when I left Berlin for good and didn't know what to do with myself — I was then 16 years old — I spent the summer with a friendly family in the mountains in Poland, scared to death of my future. I was at loose ends, completely in a state; I didn't know what to do with myself. I got to Paris later, but I didn't know what would happen at that moment.

"So there was a piano in the living room where I spent half of the night building up repertoire. That was the beginning of every work I ever played in my life. I went through 150 compositions in the *embryon*. I did know then by heart all the concertos and sonatas that I play, all the pieces of Schumann, Chopin, Liszt, and Brahms. Everything, but as *embryon*, unfinished business. Then when it came to a concert, I tried to finish the work, more or less, less rather than more.

"Then came the second moment in my life when I practiced seriously. I was in a mood somewhat *rebellieux*, rebellious, which reminds me a little bit of the young men now who make a big revolution. They don't want to work anymore; they don't want a profession; they don't care; they say everything is rotten, and so on. And yet they don't build up anything new. They don't have any other plans.

"Well I was in that mood as a pianist. I said 'to hell with pianists. It's not interesting to be a pianist; it's a small thing to be. I want to live. I am a man with vision. I don't want to be a slave of the keyboard; I don't want to clean the keys of the keyboard.'

"I disdained the very existence of the most celebrated pianists. I said 'there's nothing to being a concert pianist, a piano pounder that's all. I am a musician. I feel music in me nobly. When I sit down to play some chamber music thing or when I think in a cafe of the Beethoven violin concerto, or if I play a symphony of Brahms, or if I take in some Mass of Bach, and so on, I am the noblest creature in the world because I feel music fully, nobly, wonderfully, heavenly, and so on.' I felt proud but completely aloof from the piano-playing business.

"Then I married. And suddenly I had another person called Rubinstein, not only Rubinstein but Mrs. Artur Rubinstein. I became reluctant to the idea that someone might meet my wife after my death and say, 'your husband was a lazy bum, never worked anything at the piano. With his talent he could have become a really great pianist.'

"That did something to me. So after my first daughter was born, one year after our marriage, we went to a little bungalow, a little villa up in the Savoy mountains in France. I had an upright piano brought up there. And as there was no possibility of putting it in the villa because I would wake up the whole household, I had it put in a stable. This stable wasn't even a garage. We used it for our little car we had there.

"I had to put up candle lights, and there to my great relish, again as in the previous mountain resort, I started practicing. I became a bit vain about this practicing because people from other villas used to sit on the grass to listen. After a while people were aware that somebody was playing there in this stable, and I saw sometimes 25 or 30 people lying around on the grass, listening."

"You were one of the first summer festivals," quipped Max Wilcox.

"Well this was the thing," Rubinstein continued. "But my practicing didn't go to extreme limits. If I played two hours, three hours, four hours, that was the limit. I never saw myself playing all day or all night. No, no, no. Don't let's exaggerate.

". . . So I became conscious of re-becoming a solid pianist. I entered into the syndicate, the masonry, the club, or whatever you call it. From then I slowly made progress. I played more and more conscientiously. And then Max Wilcox forced me to pick up lots of foul places because the playing had to come out on the record. I wanted to hire a dozen young pianists to help me out, but Wilcox wouldn't stand for it.

"I know you are a music teacher as well as a pianist," said Mr. Rubinstein, "and that *Clavier*. . .at least I read the tremendous lesson by you on Madame Jeanne-Marie Darre. . .but giving exact details of how I practice is a very difficult thing. You see I practice each and every piece from a different angle; I use other means for every piece. I don't play or approach my hands, my pedals, my head, or anything in a Brahms Concerto the same way as in the "Romance" from a Mozart Concerto. How can you even think of it when I play dee, dah, dah, dadadadada:

My fingers are involved in a completely different way than they are in Brahms, for example. They are committed to something which I never use in Brahms. Brahms doesn't want it, doesn't need it.

"So how I practice details, I would have to detail every little piece that I play. But I think it would be enough if you said that I approach technically, from the point of view of practicing, of getting the piece perfected or programmed, that I approach every piece from a different angle. I am sure of that. Chopin passages I play with another feeling, with other fingers than a Schumann passage. And regarding the variance in details from one artist to another, whether a certain virtuoso scale should be pedaled as this artist pedals it or that one, I think all artists are right if they can convince you."

Mrs. Rubinstein had entered the room. As I got up to leave, I asked the Rubinsteins if they remembered a concert in Zurich I'd heard. "Mrs. Rubinstein," I said, "as you came out of the stage doors to take your seat in the audience, wearing an extremely high-feathered *chapeau*, the conservative Zürchers, who don't wear hats at a concert, stood *en masse* and ah-ed."

"Then they must have liked my hat," she laughed.

"And you, Mr. Rubinstein," I said, "broke a string."

"Did I break the string because of the hat?" he asked.

Fine

Into Scarlatti without warm-up

Study with Gieseking

DESCRIBED AS "one of the greatest pianists of all time" (*Fasquelle Music Encyclopedia,* Paris, 1958) Walter Gieseking was the legitimate follower of such keyboard giants as Liszt, Buelow, Sauer, Lamond, and Anton Rubinstein in that he played with great feeling yet with controlled rubato, clear phrasing, and exact touch and even tone on each note.

For the nine years immediately preceding his death in 1956 at the age of sixty-one, Gieseking taught master classes in Saarbruecken, Germany, which at that time was under the control of France. These *classes de perfectionnement,* as they were called, were held for three or four days each month in the State Conservatory, situated on a hill overlooking the city. Every year there were eleven or twelve principal performers, former pupils of such well-known teachers as Arrau, Bauer, Casadesus, Cortot, Fischer, Kempff, Rosina Lhevinne, Marguerite Long, Yves Nat, Carl Seeman, and Carlo Zecchi. Gieseking's linguistic abilities enabled him to conduct the classes in German, French, English, and Spanish.

The large classroom contained two grand pianos—a Bechstein (later changed for a Steinway) and a Bluethner. Wooden chairs lined three of the walls; behind the pianos was a bay of floor-to-ceiling French doors. Playing several large works, each pupil performed in front of the others. Some could hardly wait to get to the piano; others became extremely nervous. Gieseking himself once remarked, "If you can play in this class, you can play anywhere."

He was a large, powerful man; electricity seemed to emanate from him as from a dynamo. It was unnerving to see him stride into the underheated conservatory, brush the snow off his ungloved hands and sit down to play Scarlatti immaculately. Listening to a performance he would become so engrossed that, during crescendos, his face would turn red, and he would breathe heavily and deeply.

He possessed a photographic and aural memory that was perhaps unparalleled in our time; it is said that he played in public works that he had read through only once. Furthermore, he could play the left-hand part of any passage from memory. He was a fantastic sight-reader and could and did sight-read anything. His curiosity about new compositions was intense, and he immediately played such works as the concertos by Bartók, Malipiero, Menotti, Pijper, and Roussel better than the pupils who had labored over them for some time. When a student performed a concerto, he played the orchestral parts, always without score of course. What he played, just using those phenomenal ears of his, excelled all existing piano reductions.

Although Gieseking was sparing with praise, each pupil felt a sense of freedom and the existence within himself of some quality which the master particularly admired. As one of them expressed it: "Musically, I had with him a feeling of freedom quite independent from 'nerves.' True, we have had the 'trac' in the Saarbruecken classroom much worse than in a concert in front of three thousand people. But Gieseking was for me the absolute communication. I knew that I was taken musically exactly for what I was. I was there to do what I could, to be what I am, and I was sure to be judged the right way." When satisfied, Gieseking would say: "Yes, it's about like that" or, "That's not bad; Yes, you can play that in concert" or, "It seems to lie well for you." One girl felt she had received the highest accolade when, after performing the Liszt E flat Concerto, the master turned to her smiling, "*Eh bien,* it's a beautiful concerto, *n'est-ce pas?*" When bored with pupil, piece, or performance, he would say almost nothing.

To him, the cardinal sin was to play in a self-willed manner, ignoring the intentions of the composer. At one stormy session he told a pupil:

Liszt knew exactly what he wanted, and it's not necessary to change a single note . . . I don't want anyone in this class to be a copy of me; but this is not my way of making music, and if you still feel that you want to play this way even after being here and hearing these students and hearing me play, then play it that way and go out and fight the battle with the critics and public . . . You must not take the work of a great master and throw it around and tear it to pieces . . . What do you mean, "You have to have something to say?" When you play the music of other people, *you're* not supposed to say anything . . . I think Rubinstein would play this piece (the B minor Sonata) very well.

In the classroom, Gieseking displayed a youthful freshness not observable on stage, where he appeared older and more serious. Through lesson after lesson his tremendous vitality never left him; at the end of the evening when everyone else was exhausted, Gieseking was ready to hear still more. On one occasion my wife, Carolyn Elder, had played an entire recital program for him. At the end of the lessons on all the works, which had taken most of the day, she was exhausted. "Now," said Gieseking, sitting back relaxed, "some encores."

After the day's classes, he often went to Radio Saarbruecken to record until late at night and was disappointed if all the pupils didn't come to listen. At other times, as many pupils as could be jammed into the family automobile would be driven to a restaurant where the circle would reassemble. After-dinner divertissement often consisted of the master's playing finger patterns on the table to see who could guess first. One could expect anything from *Scarbo* to *Tea for Two* followed, perhaps, by one of his puns: "Ah, pie for *pie*-anists!"

Tenets of his teaching

1. Exactness. Playing "exactly what the composer wrote as beautifully as possible" was Gieseking's artistic principle. He didn't look for "secrets" between the lines; the clear revelation of the exact text was his secret: "One has only to be able to read notes correctly, but that is beyond most performers."

2. Rhythmic precision. Gieseking placed great importance on rhythmic precision. In the opening of *Carnaval,* for example, Schumann clearly delineated two kinds of upbeats: ♪ | ♩ and ♪ | ♩ . The first six-measure period and its repetition begin with an eighth-note upbeat as do the next three four-measure periods, but after that the eighth-note upbeat becomes a sixteenth. Most artists make no real distinction, but Gieseking demanded that one be able to *hear* this difference.

3. Tone and melody. To Gieseking, melody was instinctive; his ear demanded a singing tone, a tone that would last, with other parts pianissimo.

Ex. 1—BRAHMS *Intermezzo,* Op. 117, No. 2   Ex. 2—GRIEG *Erotik*

"Always the melody beautifully singing; all the other notes pianissimo."

His conception of beautiful tone was important to his school of playing. He instinctively disliked percussive tone. In discussing a famous pianist, he once remarked: "Yes, he plays very well; but, you know, my tone is better." He constantly reiterated the importance of a full-voiced, uninhibited singing melody. The most important note was always the first note, the beginning note of a theme, a motive, or a phrase. "This should be brought out, so that even the least-knowing listener will know that *here,* from the *first* note, something is beginning."

Ex. 3—SCHUMANN *Kreisleriana* meas. 17

"The tied *d* is the first note of the melody."

Ex. 4—BEETHOVEN *Concerto No. 4* meas. 105

"The tone must sustain."

Ex. 5—BEETHOVEN *Concerto No. 4* meas. 170

"The melody immediately beautifully singing."

4. Phrasing to make melody communicate. This was achieved to a unique degree by Gieseking's phrasing in details and in "big line."

Ex. 6—BRAHMS *Sonata in F Minor,* Op. 5, Finale meas. 140

"At the entrance of the 'hymnus' theme, make three decrescendos—the first for two measures, the second for two measures, and the third for four measures. It must be very singing despite the pianissimo. Each phrase should begin a little bigger. No crescendo as marked in the third phrase."

For the melody beginning in measure 47 of Schubert's Impromptu in A-flat, Op. 90, No. 4, his recommended phrasing was as in Example 7.

Ex. 7—SCHUBERT *Impromptu,* Op. 90, No. 4 meas. 47

5. Concentration. "Do not allow yourself to wait until a second time to play better. You must concentrate the first time. In practicing, never play two notes that are not perfect. When you want to play in a certain way, you should be able to do it immediately through concentration. You don't have to practice at home. Concentrate right now, so that you can play the way you want."

6. Technique. "The weight of the arm should be behind the fingers. . . . Practice scales first with firm touch, then fluttery pianissimo scales with very small motions to quicken the fingers. . . . Scales must be perfectly even. . . . Good exercises for the fourth and fifth fingers are the first two of the Clementi *Gradus*. . . . You must not play with your fingers but rather with your ear, so that if a piano requires more or less weight, you can give it. . . . When you can play a simple five-finger exercise *à la* Tausig-Beringer, transposed through all the keys, well and evenly, then you can play the piano!"

But what Gieseking understood by equality and evenness was for most mortals an unreachable goal.

7. Practicing musically. Gieseking practiced almost exclusively on the recital stage. Having no technical problems when rested and feeling well, and being able to play from memory after having heard or seen a composition but once, it was difficult for him to understand in others the necessity for long, "repetition" practice of technical passages. However, he did believe in practicing musically. In Beethoven's Sonata in A flat major, Op. 110, he insisted, "The recitatives have to be practiced!" A pupil made him angry by saying he had practiced a piece technically but not yet musically. "What kind of difference is that? As though every dynamic and every nuance must not be produced simultaneously by a technical means!"

Interpretive ideas on various composers

Bach. Gieseking's Bach tone was cembalo-oriented (non-legato) or organ-oriented (legatissimo). The Gigues of the Fifth French Suite, the First and Third Partitas, and the Second and Sixth English Suites he wanted staccato; such passages as measure 148 of the Concerto in D Minor (Ex. 8), he wanted "legatissimo sixteenth notes, no rests, like an organ."

Ex. 8—BACH *Concerto in D Minor*

meas. 148

All dynamics in Bach should be a degree lower, never more than mezzo forte, because the instruments were quite different . . . The voice structure must always be clear . . . This music must be subtle, nothing done to it that the listener can say, "Ah, here is a crescendo." . . . The melody must not be colorless, not so much due to tone as from little subtle phrasings . . . Make four-note figures, V-I cadences, little accents, and sequences clear to the listener . . . Play with terraces of dynamic levels . . . Feel the rhythm inside yourself all the time and keep it steady and pulsating.

Beethoven. He considered Beethoven a Classicist who, towards the end of his creativity, bridged over into the Romantic, rather than a Romanticist bridging over from the Classic period. "Pedal in Beethoven for the first time from Op. 10, No. 1. Before this, one may not use pedal as tone-effect."

In spite of the fact that he adhered scrupulously to the *Urtext*, he was not averse to the Buelow edition of the last sonatas, which he found ingenious and stimulating. Only, "One must not exaggerate Buelow's directions but rather only intimate and always compare with the *Urtext*."

Brahms. Brahms was one of Gieseking's favorite composers, and he was masterful in his suggestions on how to bring out the beauty, sadness, and melancholy found in much of Brahms's music.

Intermezzo in B Flat Minor, Op. 117, No. 2 (See Ex. 1): "Begin modestly, not the full effect immediately, and then gradually let it develop from itself. Pedal on *each* beat. Every movement which is too much and too fast destroys the mood of calm and sadness of this piece."

Ex. 9—BRAHMS *Intermezzo,* Op. 117, No. 3

meas. 6

"After a certain sinister tension has been developed in the preceding phrase, the second phrase comes like a sigh of relief, an exoneration. Play this second phrase more expressively, with more color, and the basses with more tone and held back a little. This Intermezzo must not become too slow and must have pronounced lamenting character in its main parts."

Mozart: "Mozart should sound spontaneous, as if you are having a good time. . . . Mozart conceived his music for pianos which did not have anything approximating our damper pedal. . . . As clarity is of extreme importance, play almost totally without pedal. To keep the melodic line pure and clear, but at the same time to keep the left hand from sounding dry, play legatissimo, i.e., hold down the notes with the fingers in Alberti basses, etc."

Ex. 10—MOZART *Sonata in F Major,* Andante

"Always move forward; beautiful tone, without dryness . . . only melody—clear, pure, and expressive—the left hand very light, legato and even . . . without pedal, the Alberti basses held down, very legato, very even."

Schumann. One often heard from Gieseking the words "tender, excited, full of expression" in connection with the music of Schumann. One pupil related:

I started to play the Sonata in F Sharp Minor. I thought Gieseking, as the master of nuance and "piano," disdained passionate outburst. But through his impatient and ever-increasingly inflamed shouts, I changed my mind. He drove me into such a *furioso* that I pounded away at the piano enraged and inflamed with anger. He seemed completely unaware of my anger, and only when I had reached a state of emotional outpouring did he seem somewhat satisfied.

Such experiences were not infrequent for pupils performing the *Fantasy*, *Kreisleriana*, or *Carnaval*.

Fingering

Gieseking used a great deal of *"en face"* fingering, i.e., playing the fingers in regular order rather than going under with the thumb. For the difficult fortissimo left-hand arpeggios, measures 122 and 123 of Debussy's *Toccata* (Ex. 11): "Keep the hand together for power; use this fingering; jump with the thumb."

Ex. 11—DEBUSSY *Pour le Piano*, Toccata

meas. 123

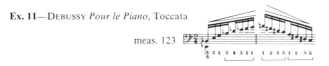

Sometimes he advised rather unconventional fingering. In the first movement of the Mozart Concerto in D Minor, nine and eleven measures before the Reprise (Ex. 12): "Use three after four to assure the crescendo to the *e* or the *f*."

Ex. 12—MOZART *Concerto in D Minor*

meas. 243   meas. 245

When power was needed, he often recommended avoiding the fourth finger. In the first movement of Beethoven's Concerto No. 1, measures 199 and 211 (Ex. 13): "Finger this chromatic motive 121235 in the left and 532121 in the right hand. Don't use the fourth fingers; they would give a weak sound." Or, at measure 240 of the last movement of the Schumann Concerto in A Minor (Ex. 14): "Finger the left hand 53211; use the strong fingers for power."

Ex. 13—BEETHOVEN *Concerto No. 1*   meas. 199   meas. 211

Ex. 14—SCHUMANN *Concerto in A Minor*, last mvt.

meas. 240

He preferred rapid repeated notes played with the same finger. In the opening repeated *d* sharps of Ravel's *Scarbo* (Ex. 15): "Play them all with the same finger, no change of fingering, just minute-motion vibrating of the second finger supported by the third." Or, in measure 4 of the first movement of Beethoven's Sonata in E Flat Major, Op. 7 (Ex. 16): "Do not change fingers in the opening left-hand repeated *e* flats except to facilitate reaching the first chord.

"If you can play in this class you can play anywhere."

You see, it sounds better." And again in measure 24 of the first movement of the "Appassionata" (Ex. 17): "Don't change fingers on the left-hand repeated e flats."

*Ex. 15—RAVEL *Scarbo* — meas. 2

Ex. 16—BEETHOVEN
Sonata, Op. 7 — meas. 4

Ex. 17—BEETHOVEN
Sonata, Op. 57 — meas. 24

Many times he wanted the same finger used on successive notes to achieve even weight and tone. For example, in Debussy:

*Ex. 18—DEBUSSY
Minstrels — meas. 58

"Use the third finger of the right hand on the repeated notes for power and evenness."

*Ex. 19—DEBUSSY
General Lavine — meas. 29

"Play these sixteenth notes with the same finger."

Ex. 20—DEBUSSY
Pour le Piano, — meas. 254
Toccata

"Use the third finger in the left hand for power."

*Ex. 21—DEBUSSY
Des Pas sur — meas. 34
la Neige

"Stroke the descending quarter notes tenderly, *pppp*, all with the fifth or all with the fourth fingers, the arm completely relaxed, and hold pedal."

In *ff* and *sff* upper voices, Gieseking sometimes took the whole hand sideways and struck the key with the length of the fifth finger reinforced by the other fingers. A classic example: the *sff* accents in measure 12 of Debussy's *Golliwogg's Cake-Walk* (Ex. 22).

*Ex. 22—DEBUSSY
Golliwogg's — meas. 12
Cake-Walk

Pedaling in Debussy

Gieseking's general rule: "Often the pedal sign in Debussy is the bass note." This may result in long pedals held for several measures or even pages when the harmony remains the same—in the Prelude of *Suite Bergamasque*, measures 52-56 (Ex. 23): "Don't change pedal for four measures;" in the Prelude of *Pour le Piano*, measure 71, where the

sixteenth-note *d-e* trill begins (Ex. 24): "Hold the pedal when possible, according to your instrument and hall, to the Reprise, measure 97, *almost two pages!* It is all one whole-tone harmony."

Ex. 23—DEBUSSY
Suite Bergamasque,
Prelude — meas. 52

Ex. 24—DEBUSSY
Pour le Piano,
Prelude — meas. 71-97

Or, in the fourth from last page, measures 166-186, in *L'isle joyeuse*: "Pedal for the entire page." Perhaps the most remarkable long-pedalings were in *Voiles* (Prelude No. 2, Bk. 1). "After measure 15, change pedal only at measures 42 and 48. Then in the last three measures, new pedal on each beat to keep the final third, *c-e*, clear."

Of course, in these long held pedals, it was important that melodic notes be brought out, non-harmonic notes of the melody played softer than harmonic ones, everything else weaker. For example, in measures 28 and 29 of the Prelude of *Suite Bergamasque* (Ex. 25): "You can pedal through each two beats, if you play the top *d* sharp more *pp* than anything else in the first two beats and a little more on the *g* sharp than the *c* sharp, *d* sharp, *e*, *f* sharp in the third and fourth beats. Blur so there is a nice sonority."

Ex. 25—DEBUSSY
Suite Bergamasque,
Prelude — meas. 28

On the other hand, he often recommended very little pedal. In *Des Pas sur la Neige*, for example: "The pedal is only for connecting, for nothing must grow hazy, dissolve, or merge." Or, measures 32-35 of the Prelude of *Suite Bergamasque* (Ex. 26): "Clear, very little pedal, nice legato."

Ex. 26—DEBUSSY
Suite Bergamasque,
Prelude — meas. 32-35

For the ending three measures of *Clair de Lune* (Ex. 27) he suggested this special-effect pedaling: *"Una corda* for the first two measures, all quiet, nearly like a metronome; then *tre corde* for the last rolled chord, rolled from bottom to top, without delay. Otherwise, it sounds dull, flat."

Ex. 27—DEBUSSY *Clair de Lune*

Gieseking died in 1956, but the tenets of his teaching and the inspiration of his personality still live through his pupils, many of whom are teaching and performing throughout the world. Walter Gieseking will long be remembered by them as a great man, a kind man, and a consummate artist.

Jose Iturbi

interview
November 24, 1964

An interview with the famous pianist, conductor, and former Hollywood star, discussing

- **His Approach to Piano Playing**

- **The Importance of Exercises**

- **Some Pianists of the Past**

"Yes, Mr. Elder—Yes, I'll be delighted to talk to you about my approach to piano playing. Can you come to my hotel tomorrow afternoon?"

Jose Iturbi was playing with the American Symphony Orchestra. That evening, in Carnegie Hall, as I listened to his interpretation of the Mozart Concerto in D minor, I was particularly impressed by his individuality and his communicative, compelling tone. He remained physically relaxed as he played, but it was always apparent that he was listening intently. The next morning *The New York Times* noted he had "played with a personal authority and independence that were refreshing. There was drive, a lovely soft tone, an elegant tossing off of phrases...."

The next afternoon, pipe in hand, Mr. Iturbi greeted me in the large sitting room of his suite. Before getting into his approach to piano playing, Mr. Iturbi answered a few questions about his beginnings in music.

"No, I was not a concertizing child prodigy," he said. "I never believed in it and I still don't. But I have been told I played little tunes when I was three. I don't remember. In order for me to reach the keyboard of our upright piano, my parents used to put me on top of two or three music books. My father was a piano tuner, but not just a piano tuner; he was a piano technician and could build pianos. I still remember asking him one day what the pedals were. I also remember my first piano lessons, when I

was five years old. I studied first with a lady, Maria Jordan, in my home town of Valencia, Spain. My parents did not have to make me practice.

"When I was about nine or ten," Mr. Iturbi continued, "I played for the famous pianist Emil von Sauer, who was in Valencia playing a concert. He found certain qualities in me and suggested I play a semi-private recital in Valencia so that I might obtain a subsidy from the proper authorities to continue my studies in Paris. At the Paris Conservatoire my teacher was Victor Staub. I graduated in 1913; and as I received the highest first prize of anyone in all the graduating classes, I was chosen to play at the graduation exercises in the concert hall. Gabriel Fauré was then Director, and I played his *Theme et Variations*. I have a copy, which I treasure highly, of the published edition of this work on which Fauré himself wrote in certain corrections."

Three Chief Elements in Piano Playing

In Mr. Iturbi's view, three principal elements in piano playing are the Approach to Interpretation, Melodic Playing and Phrasing, and the Training of Muscles Through Exercises. In our lengthy but relaxed discussion, he stated his basic philosophy of the pianist's artistry.

The Approach to Interpretation

"In answer to your question about the Approach to Interpretation," said Mr. Iturbi, "I would suggest the following: Take a piece and study it. Study thoroughly its form and spirit. After that, *play it!* Play as you feel, but respectfully, not arbitrarily. And please don't just talk about it. There is the intellectual type of artist who discusses compositions only through analysis, anatomy or dissection—the so-called intelligentsia approach. This approach is, to me, too pedantic. There are conductors, for example, who say *my* Beethoven Fifth or *my* Eroica, who think they have a philosophic or intellectual idea for every note. They *cherchent midi a quatorze heures* (they look for noóntime at 2 p.m.).

"I don't believe in interpretation through intellect only. I insist on a happy meeting of intellectualism and intuition. It has to be fifty-fifty: intellectualism vis-a-vis intuition. If it is only intellect, No; if it is only instinct and intuition, No. It must be both.

"Know your solfeggio and your musical forms. When you know these and have studied a composition well, your inspiration will come through this strainer of analysis. As a teacher, Yes, you must talk construction, forms of music. But as a performer, through crystallization of the previous analysis, No. In performance the supreme and indispensable elements are Soul, Heart, and Feeling.

"One proof that interpretation is a combination of intellectualism and intuition—that there is not only *one* correct way to interpret—is that when you hear recordings of great pianists of the past, you realize that few interpret that way today. I know of two great pianists of the past who were excellent composers and conductors. Yet when they sat at a piano

they took great liberties: one played one hand before the other; they both added chords and arpeggios. You will listen to these old recordings and, in a few cases, in certain passages, you will listen with horror because of the tremendous liberties they took with a composition—liberties we would not dare take today.

"True," Mr. Iturbi continued, "some people are born with a personality and with a magnetism. We cultivate, develop, and learn. But these are not the reasons why every pianist plays differently, why there is such a thing as an individual interpretation. Every pianist plays differently because of the principle of *humanity:* we change; our receptivity changes; we are human.

"Our change in receptivity is what I mean by humanity—why styles of playing change. For example, when I listen to a recording I have made, I never say 'It is pretty good.' I always say either that it is too fast or too slow. The record didn't change. I have changed. My receptivity has changed. Or, to state it differently, when I am in a hurry the red traffic light takes a century to change. At other times it changes too quickly. I don't even have time to light my pipe. My receptivity changes according to my nerves or state of mind, according to whether or not I am in a hurry."

Melodic Playing and Phrasing

The preceding evening, when he played the Mozart Concerto in D minor at Carnegie Hall, Mr. Iturbi allowed himself a bit of individuality which added interest. In the piano's second theme in the second movement, he played the entire theme (twenty-eight measures!) without the left-hand continuo octaves. He kept his left hand off the keyboard (Ex. 1).

Ex. 1 Romanze

He played much semi-staccato, six-teenth-note passage work but with pedal so that it sounded "legato." He often started a melodic phrase with full tone, almost an accent, and then diminuendoed, ending with beautiful soft tone (Ex. 2a)—a school of melodic playing which is different from those players who phrase according to the up and down movement of the line (Ex. 2b).

Ex. 2a Allegro   Ex. 2b Allegro

When I mentioned this interpretation, it launched Mr. Iturbi into some ideas about phrasing.

"To know how to phrase," he said, "study the *neumes.* I mean the ancient *neumes* of the ninth to the thirteenth centuries. By *neumes* I mean the syllables of the music and how they should be accented or unaccented. I wouldn't say, 'Mr. Eldrrr, how *are* you?' Yet, when you see the way some composers mark the slurs in their music, it is fantastic!

"Read d'Indy's *Formes Musicales.* This may sound pedantic but if you study this book your phrasing will be all right. To repeat—if you don't study the *neumes* thoroughly your phrasing will be off. First we study solfeggio, then the *neumes.* Next comes the phrasing. Then you can use your intuition and instinct. You have a sound basis for what you do."

Training Young Muscles Through Exercises

Jose Iturbi has firm convictions that technique is the *sine qua non* of good piano playing. He has evolved a work and practice regimen that maintains and develops technical skills, resulting in a synergistic readiness that reduces the need (after years of hard work!) for excessive practice.

"Many pianists," said Mr. Iturbi, "practice their technique through compositions. I do not believe in this theory. I *think* technique. I compare technique to money in life. It sounds prosaic. Now if you have the technique, you can buy anything you like. If you have good taste you buy good things. If you have bad taste you buy bad things. Every individual has his own theory.

"So I studied yesterday after the concert. I came back here to clean a little bit the technique, to put the muscles back 'in place' again. In playing tennis, billiards, and other sports, we use a perfect logic but not in playing the piano technically.

"For me, you must first build up your technique through exercises, with some Bach and Mozart, of course, and then afterward practice with other compositions. What exercises? Czerny above all, also Cramer and Moszkowski. Practice the first

Czerny study of the School of Velocity (Op. 299), or for that matter the Dexterity (Op. 740) too, *very slowly,* moving each finger up and down exactly right. This lifting of the fingers is simple: As one finger goes down, the other comes up. Of course you have to know from the music just what the fingers have to do, what touches are required.

"You have to know, like the athlete, how to train your muscles. In wrestling and boxing—I am talking purely muscles—wrestling is tightening and boxing is percussion. Sometimes certain colleagues, violinists, brass and woodwind players as well as pianists, play *mf* because they get tired. You have to build up endurance. You expand every day. When you build up technique, you don't have to practice so much, but if you don't practice, your technique degenerates. And remember I am talking technique because I know the answer: *to serve and express music.*

"From the standpoint of technical perfection, there is an expression that is awfully dangerous: 'He isn't a great technician but he keeps a great line.' I will give you one example. In a big passage, say in the "Revolutionary' Etude (Ex. 3) of Chopin, you hear the right hand—'*la grande ligne*'—but what is going on in the left hand and in the interweaving parts? Certain pianists play the right hand with *Schwung* but every note in the left hand is not there, or is 'artistically' hidden.

Ex. 3, Key of C minor

Chopin Etudes

"And speaking of the Chopin Etudes," Mr. Iturbi continued, "in my opinion there are two which are impossible to play: the Op. 10, No. 2 in A minor and the Octave Etude, Op. 25, No. 10 in B minor. In the Op. 10, No. 2 (Ex. 4), the right-hand sixteenth notes must be fast, even, clear, precise, articulated perfectly."

Ex. 4

Mr. Iturbi illustrated, making his fingers move in imitation of the sixteenth notes. His hands are fleshy with much-worked fingers, with particularly wide stretch between his third and fourth fingers; though the fingers seem short, the hand is quite wide.

"To get every note perfect," he explained, "precise and fast against the 'pizzicato' notes in the same hand (and he made the conductor's motions for sharp, exact, pizzicati strings)— I think is impossible.

"In the Octave Etude (Ex. 5)," he continued, "pianists just put down the pedal, but to play every octave perfectly and at the same time to hear the inner notes is impossible. Remember in these Etudes I want to hear the notes in between and the notes regular in the indicated *Allegro con fuoco* tempo.

Ex. 5, Key of B minor

"And even the Etude in A minor, Op. 25, No. 11 (Ex. 6), is about impossible too. You can keep it up for a few pages, but for eight pages, who can *really* do that?"

Ex. 6

Sound Study: Sound Technique

"If you study well," he concluded, "you will *know*. In my dictionary the word *invention* doesn't exist. In my dictionary the word is *discovery*. Electronics, infra rays, and so forth, always existed: they did not invent them; they discovered them.

"There are no secrets. You just have to know solfeggio; you have to know how to read notes correctly; you have to discover. Study well, get equipment, then launch yourself. Don't do too much analyzing, too much dissection of rhythm apart, phrasing apart, big line apart. Of course we study certain pages, but if you don't have the technique before, you are never complete."

Pianists of the Past

"Of the pianists who recorded before LP," Mr. Iturbi said, "for me there are two who would still be considered great, who would still stand up today: Josef Lhevinne and Rachmaninoff.

"But you can't say this pianist or that one is the greatest. You can only ask if whatever he brings you or plays at the moment, 'Is it good, Is it great?' You either like it, yes or no. (I do not belong to the legion of profound or very cultured people who admit only two points of view: their own and the wrong one.) You can't say, 'I liked what he just played, but I don't know if he can play the thirty-two sonatas of Beethoven. The greatness of an artist depends upon how beautifully he has just played, not whether he has the greatest repertoire or is the greatest natural talent.

"You can't compare Gieseking, Rachmaninoff or Lhevinne. Great pianists are like great painters. Who is the greatest? Van Gogh, Cezanne, Renoir, Matisse, Velazquez, Bracque, El Greco? Do you analyze how many paintings El Greco painted and compared to what?

"It's the same thing with likes and dislikes of compositions. You can't say *why* you like a composition. I once went to a concert of an excellent conductor. He conducted a composition which I found beautiful. He asked me, 'How did you like the composition'? 'I liked it very much,' I replied. He said, 'Why?' I discontinued our brief conversation at this precise point. You find people who, regardless of what you play in a concert, with not excessive tact, often ask why you didn't play something else. Why? In the final analysis— why??"

The afternoon (including refreshments) had been fun. Just as I was leaving I asked Mr. Iturbi about his home in Beverly Hills, where he has lived for many years. "Many of us have lived there," he said. "Several years ago Horowitz, Hofmann, Lotte Lehmann, Stravinsky, Rachmaninoff, Bruno Walter, Heifetz, Piatigorsky, and others all lived there or spent the summer there.

"I can tell you an amusing anecdote about the Hollywood Bowl concerts. One reviewer said, when summing up one of those years: 'We had a wonderful season, especially if you consider that they were all local talent!' "

Guiomar Novaes in the vestibule of her home

Guiomar Novaes

interview December 23, 1970

Great pianists are instinctive, spontaneous people with extraordinary musical memory (photographic, surprisingly often), unusual hands, and an unquenchable passion for playing the piano. Not all master pianists are great sight readers, but they seem all to have or to have had absolute pitch: Arrau, Bachauer, Backhaus, Casadesus, Cortot, Edwin Fischer, Gieseking, Gilels, Godowsky, Hofmann, Horowitz, Iturbi, Kempff, Lili Kraus, Lhevinne, Novaes, Rachmaninoff, Richter, Anton Rubinstein, Artur Rubinstein, Schnabel, and Serkin, for example. Despite such common characteristics, pianists' personalities seem unpredictably and amazingly different.

In a rare interview, Guiomar Novaes, the great Brazilian pianist, proved no exception. I met her first, backstage at Philharmonic Hall — where she had come to congratulate a colleague — and drove her to her hotel. (Because of the taxi strike she was going to walk the eight long blocks in the howling wind, sleet, slush, and snow!)

About a week later in her hotel apartment, she greeted me warmly and then sat down, propped with a pillow on the sofa, ready for our interview. A modest, motherly woman ("Won't you have some cookies? They are for you. Just one?"), she seems to think more with her eyes, ears, and instincts than with her intellect. She speaks English slowly with Brazilian accent, in a mezzo voice with a "used" singer's quality and delicate upward inflections, and laughs spontaneously and frequently.

At one point my spurring made her really laugh: "I think it is disagreeable to talk about ourselves, don't you? When I think of all these details of the reviews, of the public, and all these things, I say sometimes 'How do I have the courage to go, with my nature as I am, to play for these people?' If I would think of the reality of the career, I would never do it."

Family and Birthplace

But "do it" she has, most of her life. She was born in the town of Sao Joao da Boa Vista, Brazil, near the metropolis of Sao Paulo, of Manoel da Cruz and Anna (De Menezes) Novaes.

"My mother raised 11 children," Madame Novaes-Pinto (as she prefers to be called) reminisced. "I was the third from the youngest. My mother, who married too young, felt everything deeply. People used to call her the century 2000 because she was alert in everything — singing, working. She was very poetic and liked to be out admiring nature. I remember she used to put us to bed at eight o'clock, so we could get up to see the sun rising.

"While we took breakfast she read beautiful things 'to inspire us to study' and educated us in a big discipline. After breakfast she went to church. She played the piano, she sang (before she married she sang in a church choir), she had a beautiful voice. Naturally she was so busy with the family she didn't even think of becoming a performer. But she was artistic by nature and could have been anything she had chosen."

"Your family lived in Sao Paulo. How did you happen to be born in the town of Sao Joao?" I asked.

"I was born in Sao Joao by coincidence. As my maternal grandparents and the only uncle I had — my mother's brother — lived in Sao Joao, my mother was anxious to visit them. So she went to Sao Joao for a visit and a vacation. And she loved the place so much — that lovely, picturesque spot with its view of the mountains — that she stayed six years. She said those six years were the happiest of her life, that she never met an unsympathetic person. The people were so lovely, so happy-looking, so hospitable, so kind, so educated.

"My father was a coffee commissioner and a newspaper man. Later on he brought his business to Sao Joao in connection with the business he had in Sao Paulo. He wrote a sonnet to each of his babies when it was born. Both my parents were very artistic by soul and by heart."

"What is the region of Sao Joao like?"

"Sao Joao is in one of the best parts of Brazil for coffee-growing. It is there where we grow our best coffee, which we call 'Bourbon.' We used to have a monarchy and our Emperor, Dom Pedro II, came from a Bourbon family in France with a Portuguese lineage, Braganza. We in Brazil are more or less 80% Portuguese descended. And this coffee is still called Bourbon. The land of coffee is a special one, of a rare purple color. We have only a few places with this kind of purple land color."

"Were any of your brothers or sisters musical?"

"Yes, they were musical but they went more for literature. My mother, having so many children, thought of their future and made them study well. She wanted them to be educated so they could have a career. We were a lively family."

Beginnings at the Piano

"When did you begin to play the piano?"

"In kindergarten when I was four. I don't remember very well but they say I was playing by ear everything I heard — marches for my colleagues, improvisings, and so on. At home we were so many brothers and sisters, that the last of us were brought up mostly by the oldest sister. She took piano lessons and maybe I watched her play. I was so little I don't remember."

"Do you remember when you learned to read notes?"

"I learned before I was seven. From four to seven I stayed at the kindergarten, helping. I was the official pianist (laughter) for marches and things like that. When seven, instead of going into the first grade, I stayed to be taught to read and to write in the kindergarten. They didn't want me to go because they needed me.

"At one of the festivals, I conducted all the children's songs. And I remember at that time I had the inspiration of composing a waltz which I named 'Kindergarten.'"

"When did you begin piano lessons and who was your first teacher?"

"I had a few lessons from a teacher whom I don't remember. When I was seven I played for Luigi Chiafarelli, a most exceptional, perceptive, deep teacher. We were at the home of a friend, a pupil of his. He put me in another room while he played notes on the piano to test my ear. As I said note by note well and he liked my playing, he accepted me. I had lessons from him as well as from two of his assistants. One of them, Antonietta Rudge Miller, a Brazilian of English descent, taught me once a week. And then Chiafarelli came to my home each Monday at seven o'clock in the morning. He prepared me for the weekly class he gave in his home where his pupils played for each other for two or three hours."

"Where had Chiafarelli been trained?"

"He was a contemporary of Busoni in Italy. When Busoni went to Germany to study, Chiafarelli went also. Chiafarelli left a wonderful class of piano teachers in Sao Paulo and was the first there to make his pupils play all the Beethoven sonatas, all the Bach Well-Tempered Clavier, all the classic and all the romantic literature. He used to go to Europe every year to keep in contact with everything best in Germany and Italy."

"You first appeared in public when you were seven?"

"I was nearly eight. I played a Beethoven Sonatina, the G Major. It's funny I never repeated any more that Sonatina. I should make a recording of it as a souvenir. Time flies by so quickly, we hardly have time to live nowadays, as you know."

Novaes heard her first concert — a joint recital by Pablo Casals and Harold Bauer — at the age of eight. When she was 11, the year her father died, she performed Gottschalk's difficult "Variations on the Brazilian National Anthem." And when she was 13 she went to study in Paris.

Study in Paris

"Why did you choose Paris?" I asked.

"It is a long story. My mother had a friend — a lovely, religious woman (at that time people were strict in practicing religion; we all went to Saint Cecelia's church) — who had known me since I was very young and who looked upon me with great friendship and attention. She knew what I did in the kindergarten and asked me to play the harmonium in church. (I became the organist at the Sunday morning mass, improvising the accompaniments for the children to sing.)

"This lady, who visited her sister in Paris nearly yearly, used to say, 'You have to go to Paris to have the *conservatoire* prize.' And when I was 13, she took me.

"Our boat arrived at Le Havre one or two days late because of a storm. I remember we arrived in Paris on Saturday, the 13th of November, 1909. Chiafarelli

Guiomar at the age of six

20

At fifteen — already a concert pianist

had a constant correspondence with Isidor Philipp about music, and had recommended me to Philipp. So, we went right to Philipp's home.

"'You have to hurry up,' he said. 'Today is the last day of the enrollment and the first examination is in two days!'

"It is amusing that I was the last to put my name on the contestants' list. There were 388 contestants and only two vacancies for foreigners, 11 vacancies altogether."

The Momentous Day

"The day I was chosen I played the Bach Prelude and Fugue in C Sharp Major from Book I of the Well-Tempered Clavier, the Liszt Paganini Etude No. 4 in E Major. What more? Oh yes, the Chopin A Flat Ballade and part of Schumann's Carnaval. They asked me to repeat the Ballade in the second examination. Fauré, Debussy, Moszkowski, and Lazare-Lévy were in the jury."

Who discovered that letter by Debussy in which he writes of your playing for the jury?"*

"This letter was found about 15 or 20 years ago — many years after I was at the *conservatoire* — by André Caplet, the conductor. Caplet orchestrated and edited some of Debussy's works. Later, A Brazilian newspaper man, who went to Paris every two or three years, always searching for novelties, heard there was an interesting letter written by Debussy about a Brazilian person. So he looked up this letter and wrote about it."

*Debussy wrote: "She has all the qualities for a great artist, eyes that are transported by music, and the power of complete inner concentration which is a characteristic so rare in artists."

Study with Philipp

"What was your study with Isidor Philipp (1863-1958) like?"

"Philipp was an extraordinary pianist, a very interesting composer, and a wonderful, devoted pedagogue, a big friend to his pupils. He corrected what his pupils did wrong but allowed each pupil to have his own personality. You know his technique, don't you — the Phillipp-Pichna, the stretch exercises, the scales, the octaves, the trills?* He had a wonderful technique himself. Unfortunately, he was old and tired when he came to the United States; he should have come much earlier."

Beginning of Career

Upon graduation from the Paris Conservatory at the age of 15, Novaes received the *Premier Prix*. For her final examination *"la petite Novaes"* played the required sight-reading piece by André Messager (1853-1929) and the second Ballade, in F Major, of Chopin. She made her Paris concert debut the next year playing with the Chatelet Orchestra under Gabriel Pierné.

"How did your career begin?" I asked.

"In Sao Paulo, as soon as I became known as a child who played the piano, I was asked to serve as pianist at the festivals. I gave concerts in Sao Paulo and Rio. In Paris I played in Philipp's public pupil recitals several times. As soon as I finished my studies at the *conservatoire* I was invited to play a recital in London. And after this recital I was asked to play with orchestra (Mozart Concerto in D Minor) at Queens Hall, Sir Henry Wood conducting. Afterwards I was invited to go back several times. So began my career."

American Debut

"Do you remember your American debut at Aeolian Hall in 1915 and how it came about?"

"More or less, yes. In Rio there was a prominent newspaper man, Dr. Jose Carlos Rodriguez, who had lived in New York for ten years. A very talented boy — he was 21 when he first came here — he came to the attention of the society and the press people and became popular.

"Then he went to London. He heard there was a Brazilian girl who studied in Paris and so forth, but he never heard me. When I was in London, he was in Paris; when I was in Paris he was in London.

"But finally he heard me play a Chopin recital in Rio. And as I was playing, he had the inspiration to invite me to give a recital in New York. So, a month later I came with my mother and him to New York. He arranged for me to play at Aeolian Hall. I was 19.

"As Dr. Rodriguez had good relations with the Brazilian Embassy in Washington, D.C., several prominent people attended my debut. Among them was a New York society lady, Mrs. G.F.D. Lanier, who founded The Friends of Music. One of those talented brothers — you might remember the name — Paul Draper, was a friend of Mrs. Lanier. He had heard me in London and said to her, 'I will take you to a concert of a pianist I heard in London.'

"Mrs. Lanier came backstage to ask what I was going to do after that concert. 'I go home now,' I said. 'Why are you going home?' she asked. You should give a second recital.' And she invited me to her home for the following Sunday. It was a most interesting reception of artists and interesting people. She offered to sponsor my second recital by taking all the boxes.

"After the second recital — I had a good public; I think everyone who came to the first recital came to the second — Mrs. Lanier took a manager for me. He advised me to give a third recital three weeks later. So, I gave the third recital and had a sold-out house."

"Why have you concertized more here than in Europe?"

From my home to Europe was always a terrible journey, although naturally now with the airplanes it is not so difficult. Then too, things changed. I lost my friends in London and Helene Chaumont, Philipp's assistant, in Paris. Madame Chaumont was an amazing musician, the teacher of Magaloff, of De la Vrancia, a very fine Roumanian pianist, and of many others. Philipp came here. There were the two wars. And my husband, who worked with his brothers in an office as an architect, could travel with me only during the two or three months of his vacation."

"Did Sigismond Stojowski (1869-1946) have an influence on your development?"

"Yes. When I arrived here I played for Paderewski. I wished to play for someone to have advice about programs. Paderewski advised Stojowski. I admired very much Stojowski's musicianship and knowledge. He wrote beautiful compositions. Do you know his 'Vers l'Azur?' Incidentally, I also played my programs for the great Alexander Silotti."

How Piano Playing Has Changed

"How has piano playing changed since your youth?"

"I think they play much faster now than when I learned. When I recorded the Beethoven Emperor Concerto in Bavaria, — you can't imagine how wonderful the orchestra was — it was so amazing that Jonel Perlea, the conductor, always gave a faster tempo and the orchestra always went back. In Germany even today they never play as fast as in any other part of the world. They are conservative; they keep the old-time tempos. Don't you have that impression? I had very much so."

Inspiration from Nature

I knew that as a young student Madame Novaes had thought of becoming a painter. "Do you think of nature as you play?" I asked.

"Very much . . . the colors of the sun, the sky also. Wherever I am I search for sunsets. This is natural for everyone who loves nature. I don't know if I put the colors and atmosphere of nature into my playing, but I do my best to think about them. All the time, especially in the romantics, no? In the classics also. Beethoven is full of everything. He described nature so directly. In the *pastorale* symphony, you are seeing everything of nature.

"Last week on television I saw two paintings by an English painter which amazed me. Both were nature. One was of a yellow color, deeper than I had ever seen before, with gradations to almost hazel at the bottom. The other was of a very striking dark blue — not so dark and not so light — but a very special color of blue which impressed me deeply. These paintings were exactly like the impressionists in style. I was curious to see who had painted them and was astonished to learn they had been painted 130 years ago. Imagine it. I said, 'How is it possible that that English painter, Turner, had in mind a school of painting which developed 100 years later!"

"Do you see images of nature, or do you think of colors?"

"I think especially of the colors of nature, the colors of the sky, the sunset. For instance, every day in Rio de Janeiro we have a spectacular sunset with its reflections in the bay. And I always do my best to be free at that hour to contemplate. When Coquelin Aîné, the greatest French actor at the beginning of this century, first came to Rio he was so flabbergasted by our nature, so inspired by our sunrises and sunsets that for the rest of his life he came yearly to spend his vacations. France has a beautiful, a very special coloring in the sky which is always light. Did you notice? Light blue, light rose, everything light. England is more grey but also very light. But in Rio the colors are vivid.

"I spent part of last summer in Petropolis, a city north of Rio. I had been in Petropolis several times before but this time I had more time to search nature and to know more things. And imagine, Mr. Elder, I discovered *six* kinds of flowers that I didn't know before. I visited a place near the mountains, over 1,000 meters above sea level, devoted to the orchid industry. You go up, up, up to this place in the middle of the highest part of the mountains and there is this huge panorama of orchids: over 600,000 plants. I thought, Is this reality? or am I dreaming?"

"Petropolis is named after our former Emperor Pedro, who liked to live there. It is an amazing place, so beautiful, so high, with a lovely climate. In Sao Paulo we are also up in the hills — nearly 900 meters above sea level — but we are just 40 minutes away from the seashore by car."

Programme

Chaconne, transcribed by Busoni. . Bach

Sonata, Op. 31 No. 2 . . Beethoven
    Allegro
       Adagio
          Allegretto

Intermezzo A major / . . . Brahms
Capriccio B minor \

Carnaval, Op. 9 . . . Schumann

Two Etudes
Three Preludes . Chopin
Scherzo, Op. 20 B minor

Concert Etude, G flat major . Moszkowski

Program for New York Debut — at twenty

Interpretative Ideals

In 1916 shortly after Guiomar Novaes's New York debut, Harriette Brower wrote in her book, *Piano Mastery*, Talks with Master Pianists: "Technic in Novaes's case is an 'art in itself.' No problem seems too difficult; all are flawlessly mastered. Imagine strings of pearls, large and small; in each string the pearls are exactly the same size, round and perfect; such are her scales. Her *glissandi* ripple up and down the keyboard with a perfect beauty and smoothness that the hand of no other pianist within memory has surpassed. Her chords are full and rich, her trills like the song of birds. The listener sits aghast at such absolute mastery, and marvels where this girl has acquired such consummate technic. He marvels still more at the interpretative genius, which seizes upon the inherent meaning of the composition, finds its poetic, emotional message, and is able to present it with such convincing, overwhelming conviction and appeal." I asked Novaes what *she* felt are her special qualities as an artist.

"I don't know my qualities," she answered. "I only know my faults. But tell me what my qualities are because this interests me very much. I was never asked that question before."

"As I go on I'll try to mention a few of the special qualities *I* find in your playing," I said. "When you play what are the things you strive for most?"

"Well, I want to be obedient to the text. I do my best to read as the composer wrote, how he wanted his works to be played. I think that is the duty of all of us who wish to play the piano."

"What do you strive for technically?"

"Naturally I have to prepare everything, but when I am in public I never think of technique. I just play as I feel, as I think I should play, without any preoccupation with this and so on. I let myself go and give my mood of the moment which I think is much better than calculating. We have to be broad in giving what we are feeling and doing. Inspiration and intuition are the most important qualities of an artist."

"Do you strive for any special kind of tone?"

"No, I just go as I am feeling, Mr. Elder."

"The older generation of pianists — Rachmaninoff, Hofmann, Gieseking, Horowitz, Rubinstein, and yourself, for example — were or are easily recognizable," I said, "but many of the younger pianists sound alike."

"That is what I think. I was going to tell you. This generation plays more or less all the same. You don't feel their personality. Do you know why?"

"Perhaps today we don't live enough with nature," I said. "Perhaps the world has become too much the same, placing emphasis on conformity and machine-like perfection."

"Yes . . . and I have the impression the younger generation is very anxious to play fast," Novaes continued. "The faster the young pianists play, the happier they are. I see this at contests where I am invited to watch. When one of the younger pianists plays for me, I say 'Control yourself a little in the tempo; go ahead and put yourself on but don't go too much because that is not the style we are looking for.' "

Chopin Interpretation

What is the style we are looking for? Throughout her career Guiomar Novaes has been famous for her individual and communicative Chopin playing. "What is your interpretative approach to Chopin?" I asked.

"I read the life of Chopin. He suffered so much that when I am studying I cry sometimes. I say 'Why did this poor soul suffer so much for us to play his music?'

"But at the same time he must have been a happy person because they say he liked only himself. Schumann loved and admired Chopin, but Chopin didn't care for Schumann. After Chopin's death it is reported they found the Schumann Concerto wrapped up just as Schumann had sent it. Chopin hadn't even had the time or curiosity to look at it!

"I was sorry for Schumann to hear that because I love the superb Schumann. I also feel sad about *his* life. My God, how he must have suffered, always that hallucination of ideas he had in his head!

"This suffering in the lives of Chopin and Schumann touched my nature very much. You must be the same because we artists, without wanting, live with what we are doing. Don't we? When I had the privilege of hearing wonderful actors in London and Paris, I noticed how they lived their parts. And we pianists do the same thing: we are actors without knowing we are actors."

"I listened last night to your recordings of the Chopin Nocturnes," I said.

"Oh! They are very bad. I must make them again — especially the G Major which I was not prepared to play. I even had to read it because I hadn't had time to look at it before. You know how it is — they set the day and the time you have to play this and that. For me it is a sacrifice to have the day and the hour set. I wish I could go any time I am more inspired. I am sure you and your wife — you are artists — you are the same."

"My wife is more that way than I am."

"You are more disciplined. Then you can do much more because today we have to be very disciplined in every way. Everything goes straight forward."

"I find in those Nocturnes," I said, "that you emphasize reflection, nostalgia, serenity, and a certain deep feeling."

"Maybe too much sadness and serenity, isn't it?"

"Not at all."

Melody Playing

"Mme. Novaes, how do you color a melody, according to the rise and fall of the phrase, pianistically, or do you approach a melody according to its structure?"

"All together! I think of these things all together and I don't know how they go on afterwards. I prepare everything, hoping it will go as I wish I could play. But I am never satisfied. So it is difficult to say how I approach a melody."

"I think some pianists contemplate a melody," I said. "For them the melody is a certain mood or atmosphere whereas with other pianists, the melody is something that sings from within. I find this latter approach more communicative and warmer. Although I admired the playing of Lipatti, for example, it didn't really move me. His playing was perfect in many ways but perhaps too formal."

"Because he was a great musician, a great talent,"

Madame Novaes replied, "you think he should have been more communicative, more lyric, that he should have sung more, that he should have gone more with the phrasing of what he was doing. You admired his playing but it didn't move you. Yes, I understand."

"Do *you* sing a melody inside yourself as you play? I ask because I believe a teacher's approach to melodic playing is very important in guiding the student," I said.

"Yes, I feel very much so. I think it is very important for the pianist to sing the melody inside himself as he plays. Singers and violinists can have great success without accompaniment. They can move people deeply with only the singing tone, the line they express, and how they phrase.

"But maybe melody playing comes natural to me because I never have the preoccupation of thinking only of the melody. I think of everything — the chords, what the left hand has to do and so on. And naturally I like very much to have everything clear. For example in playing a Bach fugue, each time the theme comes we must give it its different sound; we must give everything its own quality and hear all the voices. It is my ideal to hear everything I am doing."

A Novaes Trademark

"I think one of your trademarks — rarer today than it used to be — is the bringing out of secondary voices. During intermission at a concert you played at Hunter College, I heard a young man say, 'She finds melodies where no one else does.' I find your way of bringing out secondary voices beautiful and individual. For example, in the Chopin Nocturne in C Sharp Minor, Op. 27, No. 1, eight measures from the end, you bring out the descending tenor thumb notes in the left hand:"

"I do my best to reach everything. When we make a cake we put all together what we want to taste — everything we are going to eat. This is not a comparison but it just came to my mind. If you waste those beautiful notes, it seems to me incomplete. I am sure Chopin would have loved to do it himself that way."

Pedaling

"Your pedaling too is individual," I said. "Sometimes you use less pedal than is usual. For example, in the Nocturne in G Minor, Op. 15, No. 3, many pianists hold the pedal for three measures and similarly throughout this section. You pedal short, observing the rests."

"I believe that Chopin wished always a breather in the third beat, which brings more character to the phrasing."

"Or, to cite another example," I continued, "in the Nocturne in F Minor, Op. 55, No. 1, you play the second notes of the basses a little staccato, letting the pedal up, more staccato than is perhaps usual. Rubinstein holds pedal for each two bass notes."

"This staccato you mention, making the second notes of the accompaniment a little staccato, is just a question of accent — a little accent in the basses — which sounds so logical and important.

"Again I'm asking," I said, "because these are things that pianists used to do which younger pianists mostly don't do. Maybe that's one reason why the younger pianists tend to sound so much a-like."

"Why do you think they don't do these things nowadays?" Novaes asked. "Years ago piano teachers were strict about every sign. I don't know if today they are the same."

"But to return to the pedaling of this Nocturne — sometimes I play so much with pedal I get tired of hearing so much pedal. I begin to play without the pedal. To me maybe this arrives instinctively. I am always in search of beauties in the accompaniment, following the line of the phrases. It is so natural, musically speaking, to underline the melody, especially in the Nocturnes."

Practice

"How did you practice as a little girl and during your training years?"

"Very little. I have had a versatile life: I have had my family; I have been interested in many things. At the *conservatoire* I used to play four or five hours. Before an examination I sometimes had the privilege of studying six hours. But this happened very seldom because I had other things to do — French language and so on. Naturally I dealt with Phillip, Pichna, Cramer, Czerny, Bach Preludes and Fugues and similar approaches while a student. Nevertheless, I didn't have much time to make technique.

"If it is necessary, I do the technique in the passage. I have never been concerned with exercises since I was young. It seems that technique was natural to me. Piano playing has never been a struggle."

"There are people who say they practice six, seven, or eight hours a day. I look at them astonished. Maybe they have much to prepare; this is natural. But I never have practiced so long; I wouldn't have the patience. I like to play one hour or an hour and a half and then look at the sky to see how it looks, and then come back again to work."

"How do you practice when you are preparing for a concert?"

"Just the same. What I think I have to work, I do. But I am not all the time at the piano; this tires my mind, myself. I like to change."

"Once before a Town Hall program, the newspaper reported you on the stage going through the Waldstein Sonata slowly with the metronome."

"Yes, maybe I did because I didn't want to lose my tempo, especially in the first movement. Maybe when we are nervous we never know what will happen. Maybe my companion was supposed to watch the metronome to see that my tempo was just so."

"Then you just warm up a little before a concert?"

"Yes, I warm my fingers. If I am nervous I review pieces; if not I don't. I know everything by heart."

Memorization

"How have you memorized?"

"Very naturally; I have never forced my memory. When I began with Chiafarelli, on Monday morning he gave me a piece, explained it, and said 'Play this by heart Thursday.' I had to obey."

"Is your memory strongly aural or photographic?"

"Both. I like to look at the music very intentionally."

"Then you see the music when you are playing?"

"Oh yes, very much so. I have photographic memory. And you? What is your memory like?"

"I have a little photographic memory; I see the page I'm on and some of the notes but unfortunately not all of them. My memory is aural and then I memorize the structure, harmony, and fingering of the piece, noting as many details as possible."

"I do the same; I do everything necessary to memorize, doing my best to keep in mind every detail I read."

"Have you ever read a score and then played the work in concert without playing it on the piano?"

"Yes, the Fourth Beethoven Concerto. I had received a cable from Mr. Philipp that I had to play the Beethoven Fourth in less than two weeks. I was terribly nervous when I got that order, so I took the score and read it while going from Lausanne to Milan and from Milan to Paris on the train. When I arrived in Paris it was easy for me to play it. I don't remember if I played it without touching the keyboard, but I had the music in my mind."

Recordings

"What do you consider your best recordings?"

"It is difficult to say. I'm never satisfied with them. When I finish a recording I listen to it attentively and if I'm not satisfied I ask to repeat it certainly. And then after a time when I hear it, I am sorry because I feel 'Well I should have done this and that and so forth.' Art is so infinite and each time we change, don't we?"

"Then you don't have favorites?"

"I would have to hear them, but I never find time. I am waiting for a day when I can sit and listen to them to see which I think is the less bad."

Mme. Novaes today

"For instance, when I made the Waldstein for Vox I was in a hurry to do something. It was a beautiful Sunday morning. There was a lot of snow outside and as soon as I got to the studio I warmed up my fingers and said to the technician 'Let us try once the Waldstein Sonata. I will not stop until the end.' You know it was not necessary to play a second time. I played a second and a third time, but the first time — when I played without any interruption — was the best.

"Maybe I also recorded the Schumann Symphonic Etudes in one take. How you record depends also on your preparation. There are so many details you have to do before. Our lives are full of details. Many details make up the end result."

Performances

"Do you remember performances in your career that pleased you most?"

"No, I never thought of this. Sometimes there are recitals that maybe I played better than others. My friend tells me that the last recital I gave in Rio last year was the best she has ever heard from me. And then I began to think: Why? There is always a reason for it, isn't there?

"My daughter thought my performance of the Schumann Concerto with the New York Philharmonic under André Cluytens in 1957 was the best I have ever done. I felt I did well. She is very musical, very talented, my daughter. She's my best critic. My son is also a very artistic soul and has evinced talent as a decorator."

Humorous Events

"Do you remember any humorous events in your career?"

Novaes' Brazilian colonial style house, designed and built by her architect-husband, Octavio Pinto.

"Oh yes, many things. I was telling the other day — this is not funny for other people, just for myself — of an incident that happened here when I was young. I had an engagement to play in Newark, New Jersey, on that Sunday series. But my contract didn't say evening or afternoon; it just said Sunday, the date, recital, Newark.

"I went to a leisurely lunch with a friend. Afterward my friend said, 'Let's take a ride to see how the hall looks.' 'Yes, let's go,' I said, 'I'd like to see how the piano will be for tonight.'

"As we approached the hall, I saw two men running toward us, 'What's the matter with you Madam? The concert was supposed to begin at three o'clock and it's nearly four.'

"'Don't say the concert is in the afternoon. I am new here; I am a foreigner. I never expected to play in the afternoon because I always play in the evening.'

"'Another pianist is playing Caesar Franck while waiting for you to come,' he exclaimed. So I changed my dress in five minutes, went out, and played.

"Then there was this man in a suburb of Philadelphia who had many dogs. He invited me to play a recital in his home on a Sunday afternoon. Again I went with a friend. At the station there was a Rolls Royce waiting for us. As we approached the gate to the castle-like mansion, I saw many dogs. I thought his having so many dogs was very queer.

"And when I entered, the host, Dr. Barnes — he invented a well-known medicine for the eyes — said, 'You don't have to change your dress; the concert is just for my wife and myself.' I could see paintings from the doorway all over until up the stairs. There was a banquet-sized dining room and two big living rooms, one with two Steinway pianos. A large collection of clocks — small, large, big, tall, everything — all were stopped.

"'What lovely dogs you have,' I said. 'They were so nice.'

"'I put them outside so they wouldn't make noise when you play,' he said. 'And I stopped the clocks because I don't want to hear any ticking or striking while you play.'

"'What do you want me to play?'

"'Anything you like, but play some Beethoven. I am very fond of Beethoven.' So I played some Beethoven for an hour or so.

"Two months later he invited me again. It was the same scene: the dogs outside, the clocks stopped. I thought it was very eccentric, don't you think?"

We both laughed hard. As I was preparing to leave, Guiomar Novaes gave me some motherly advice: "Keep practicing, Mr. Elder, even if only two hours a day. That will keep up your technique!"

"Une Bavardage" with the French Pianist and Composer

interview January 9, 1970

Robert Casadesus

"To make a good *carrière* of pianist, you must be ready to play the Chopin Etudes before you are 15 years old. Because you have all technique there, and after that you can play what you want. But after 15, after the muscles are *plus fort* — stronger — it is impossible."

Robert Casadesus, the affable, modest, five-foot-nine dean of French pianists, and I were discussing piano technique. Monsieur Casadesus was emphasizing the necessity of beginning early. In New York City to play a piano and violin sonata program with Francescatti, he had met me in the comfortable conference room of Steinway Hall. After opening amenities — *"Je suis enchanté de vous voir,"* he said — we began our discussion by my asking of his own early beginnings:

ELDER: *I, of course, have read biographical material on you, Monsieur Casadesus, but I would like to hear in your own words when and how you began to play the piano.*

CASADESUS: When I was three and a half, my grandfather gave me a violin, which I broke. I didn't want to play the violin; I wanted to play the piano. And my aunt, who was my first piano teacher, started with me when I was four years old. I don't remember when I played the first piece, you know.

ELDER: *You had three uncles who were musicians?*

CASADESUS: Yes, and my father, who was an actor, was also a musician. He was *compositeur* for light *musique*.

ELDER: *Louis Diémer (1843-1919), who succeeded Marmontel at the Conservatoire in 1887, was a famous teacher, having many well-known pupils. When did you study with him?*

CASADESUS: I became a pupil of Diémer when I was 12 years old. After he heard me he said, "Next fall you must go to my class in the *Conservatoire*." So, I entered the Paris Conservatory in October, 1911. I stayed only nine months because I got the first prize the first year.

ELDER: *In nine months?*

CASADESUS: Yes, I got my first prize when I was 14, in the spring of 1913.

ELDER: *And you had studied with your aunt before that?*

CASADESUS: Yes, she was Mademoiselle Simon, a wonderful teacher, but nobody knew her. She was a pupil of Marmontel, a very famous teacher; and I studied with her until, I must say, I was 30 years old. Each year I went to the country in Normandy, to play something for her; and she also heard my son, Jean. Her teaching was absolutely wonderful, and she was my real teacher. Diémer was a good teacher, but I learned much more from her.

It is difficult to call her school the French school because she was an old girl. For her, the best music was Schumann. She taught me the way to play Schumann; and for the technique, too, she was very careful.

Diémer and Saint-Saëns

Diémer gave the first performance of the Franck *Variations Symphoniques* which were dedicated to him. And he was a very close friend of Saint-Saëns. I remember I played in Diémer's class one of the Saint-Saëns *Six Etudes for the Left Hand*. Saint-Saëns wrote these etudes for the best pupils of Diémer. We were 12, so Diémer made the choice of six.

I was, what you call in French, *chouchou*, the teacher's pet; so Monsieur Diemer gave me the sixth study, the "Bourrée Pour la Main Gauche," the best piece of the set. I played it for Saint-Saëns, but I never spoke with him. And I never heard him play, unfortunately.

Edouard Risler (1873-1929) was a pupil of Diémer. Did you hear Risler?

Risler was a wonderful French pianist and teacher. His *specialité* was Beethoven. About 1906 — it was very early — he played the 32 sonatas of Beethoven. Afterwards Schnabel did, Backhaus did, but Risler was the first.

I remember hearing Risler in concert when I was 12 or 13. He played Beethoven sonatas with Lucien Capet, the violinist. Capet had a famous string quartet for years and years.

One has heard more about Philipp and his pupils than about Diémer. Who were Diémer's best pupils?

The best pupils of Diémer were Risler, Cortot, Yves Nat, and me. Diémer also had a very good Spanish pupil, now teaching in Madrid. Incidentally, I got my first prize in the conservatory the same day as Iturbi. But Iturbi was not a pupil of Diémer; he was a pupil of a pupil of Diémer — Victor Staub.

And I believe you both played the Fauré Variations as your examination piece.

Yes, the same day. Iturbi was 17; I was 14. We were 18 in the competition, and everyone had to play the same work. Fauré was in the jury. At this time, Diémer taught only men. Now the classes are mixed. And Philipp taught only women. Cortot too.

Didn't Madame Casadesus also study with Diémer?

Yes, she was the last pupil of Diémer; she studied with him the year he died. But she studied especially with Risler and also with Moszkowski. Moszkowski taught privately in Paris.

I read that you met Madame Casadesus in Diémer's class, that you had brought in a two-piano concerto of yours, and the two of you played it.

That's right, but it was just a piece for two pianos, not a concerto.

Francis Planté (1839-1934)

Did you know Planté?

Yes, yes. He was wonderful.

Do you know the International Piano Library issue of his recordings?

Yes, and it is very interesting because we saw him maybe three months before he recorded the Chopin Etudes which are on this LP. We spent the whole afternoon with him from 2 to 7 o'clock p.m. And he played many things: the Chopin Etudes, the Barcarolle, the Mozart Concerto in D Minor with my wife, and the Liszt A Major Concerto with me. It was a wonderful afternoon.

And at this time he was 93! He played with wonderful legato, never brilliant. He played the Chopin Etudes as I imagine Chopin played them.

Did you notice what he says after the C Major Etude on the recording?

No, what does he say?

When he goes up and misses those notes at the end? I think he says, "Merde."

(laughter) That's good! But he didn't miss those notes when he played for us; it was absolutely right.

First American Appearance

Do you remember your first American appearance, in 1935 with the New York Philharmonic?

Yes, I remember I played the Mozart *Coronation Concerto* with Mr. Hans Lange, conducting. Toscanini was in the hall and came backstage in the intermission and said to me, "Will you play with me next year?" And I played the Brahms *B Flat Concerto,* and he asked me at the same time to play a Saint-Saëns Concerto. And that is a wonderful story — because you know when you are young, you don't know things about your own country: I had never played Saint-Saëns before that. For the young man of 35 or 40 Saint-Saëns was a minor composer. About this time I talked with Ravel about Saint-Saëns, and Ravel said to me, "But the best concertos for piano are those by Mozart and Saint-Saëns, not Beethoven or Brahms."

And when the conductors noticed my first performance of the Saint-Saëns *C Minor Concerto* — it was my first performance with Toscanini — they asked me for two years to play only Saint-Saëns. No more Beethoven, no more Mozart, only Saint-Saëns. It was my *punition,* my punishment, for not having played Saint-Saëns for 15 years.

You made up for lost time.

Yeah, yeah, yeah. But I still play this concerto; I recorded it with Bernstein. It's a very good concerto. And now the Soviet pianists are playing Saint-Saëns.

How have you been celebrating your seventieth anniversary?

Dont' speak about that . . . but I am not too old.

Of course not, but I though maybe you had planned some special concerts.

No-o. But I received wonderful letters from conductors. I have a collection of congratulations from Klemperer, Stokowski, Steinberg, Bernstein, Kondashrin who was a boy when I played in Moscow.

When did you play in Moscow?

The first time in 1929, two performances with orchestra, without conductor. And one time in 1932 and one time in 1936, and no more since.

Did you meet any Russian musicians?

I met Shostakovitch, Katchaturian, and a wonderful teacher — one of the best piano teachers — Felix Blumenfeld. He came from Germany, but he was in Moscow at this time. Horowitz and Simon Barer studied with him. And I met Horowitz's father in Hakov, in the country.

Teaching Your Own Children

There are three professional pianists in your family: Madame Casadesus, your son Jean, and yourself. And I believe your other two children play too. What are your feelings about musicians teaching their own children? Peter Serkin didn't study much with his father; Gilels hasn't taught his daughter; and Alicia de Larrocha doesn't teach her children.

I think it is much better for children to study with someone in the family. My son, Jean, was a pupil of my wife. She taught him, but each month he played for me as an examination. My wife is more patient than I am. And her teacher was her mother in the beginning, like me with my aunt.

And you never had any problems in teaching your own son?

Never! Sometimes I said to Jean, "You must change; you must go to Serkin or to someone else." And he said, "No, I prefer to stay with you."

But it doesn't always work that way. Sometimes children don't want to study with their parents, or musician parents don't have sufficient time to teach their children.

Sometimes yes, I can understand. But no problem with my family. Three days ago, we played a concerto for three pianos, and no *problème.*

Pianistic Objectives

Your playing has been characterized as having elegance, sparkling technique, and objective clarity. How would you characterize your aims in piano playing?

First comes the sound, not the technique. And then, as with Planté, the legato; don't make the piano too percussive. And *égalité,* evenness, is very important. I can say the French school, but it's not true. You have no French school, no German school, no Russian school. You have good school or bad school.

When I was studying at the Conservatoire, Doyen, Lazar-Lévy, and Yves Nat all seemed different to me. And Cortot's school was completely different too.

Absolutely. Perlemuter, too, is different. But I think Doyen, Lazar-Lévy, Perlemuter, Cortot, Risler, Nat, me — we were all fond of the *touché,* the touch. And good pedaling, not too much pedal, which is very important. I call the pedal, *le cache-misère;* I don't know if you say this in English.

I guess we don't say hide the poverty; we say hide the faults.

Good, is good.

Do you believe in a lot of articulation?

Not too much, not too much. To acquire some brilliance — velocity of the fingers — the best is Czerny. He was Hungarian, not German or Austrian. That is very interesting, because now if you hear Hungarian pianists, they carry on the tradition from Czerny. Is good tradition. Very clear, and very brilliant too.

But in balance you have the teaching of Philipp, coming from Chopin. Philipp wrote his exercises, using the chord of the diminished seventh. Chopin wrote to a pupil or friend that you should practice exercises on the position of the diminished seventh chord. He said also that the B major scale is the best position for the hand. C major is one of the most difficult scales because you have no black keys.

The Philipp exercises, such as the following, are wonderful. But not too much, only 10 minutes a day.

If you do them too much, you can get a stiff wrist which is not good for piano playing. And the Brahms exercises, the same. They are wonderful exercises for extension, but the teacher must be careful about the amount of time the pupil spends on them. You can play scales and arpeggios thirty minutes a day, but not the Philipp or Brahms exercises.

Marguerite Long believed in a lot of articulation.

That's true. Too much. Because she played very well, but she played dry, very dry, the contrary of the legato about which I spoke to you. Her playing was brilliant, but not *artistique.*

It's interesting to get your ideas on the French school's not stressing articulation so much, because many people think that the French school — and as you said there is no one French school — stresses primarily strong finger articulation.

Yes, but we spoke about Lazar-Lévy, Cortot, and the others who did not go in for strong articulation. Landowska, on the piano, was like Madame Long, but not on the harpsichord. And Landowska's articulation on the piano came from the harpsichord. To play the harpsichord you need much articulation, but it is wrong to use this technique on the piano.

Some pianists and critics think you should play the opening of Ravel's "Ondine" with much articulation.

No, absolutely not. Those opening right-hand figures should be played very close to the keys. But, I must tell you, I read your article on Rubinstein. He said the *sotto voce,* pianissimo, legato octave passage in the first movement of the Brahms *B Flat Concerto* and the coda of the Chopin F Minor Ballade were two of the most difficult passages for him. Is the same for me. I did not know that. I am very proud because we have not the same feeling for certain things. But for me, too, these two examples are the most difficult on the piano.

It seems he finds jumps and double notes his difficulties, never just finger work.

Yes, is absolutely true. Each time I have to play the fourth Ballade — and him too — we are *nerveuse.* We are never sure if it will be good or not. And we practice every day the same spot for forty or fifty years, and when we have to play it in public, we have *le trac* — stagefright.

Scarlatti

I would like to ask you about your interpretative approach — or technical approach for that matter — to various composers. Your early 78 rpm recording of Scarlatti sonatas was highly esteemed. How do you approach Scarlatti?

For me, Scarlatti is the most difficult music to play, especially because you always play it at the beginning of the program. It is always difficult to start with Scarlatti, or Rameau, or Mozart, because you are not warmed up.

More difficult than Bach?

Ah yes, because Bach is not the same; you can play Bach closer to the keys. Scarlatti you must play fast, leggiero, like jugglers. At the time I made those 78 rpm recordings, it was difficult because you couldn't repeat a small part. It was 4 minutes 25 and no more for one side. If you missed something on the fourth minute, you had to do the whole thing over again.

I remember, during the time of 78 rpm recording,

I was recording the Mozart *C Minor Concerto.* The concerto took seven sides, and I was to play something of Mozart for the eighth side. I played the Gigue in G Major, and I started eight times — I was very nervous I must say — and Goddard Lieberson from Columbia Records was there and said to me, "Go have some coffee." And after the coffee, I played the Gigue again and it went all right. It was the ninth time. Now it is easier to record because you can cut and splice, but you don't get the human performance.

Do you use pedal in Scarlatti?

In general no; very, very light sometimes. And in Rameau too.

Do you imitate the sound of the harpsichord?

No; imitating the harpsichord is difficult, because on the modern piano it is not the same. But I play exactly what Scarlatti wrote. Some people add notes which is not good.

Mozart Trills

Musicologists say the trills in Mozart should begin on the note above; but most great artists begin them on the main note because they sound better. How do you feel about this?

Sometimes your taste tells you to start on the upper note, sometimes not. If you have a line that goes to the top, with a trill on the middle note, I think it is better to start the trill on the note above, because to do otherwise would break the melodic line:

But when you come from a jump, it is better to start the trill on the note:

This is what I think, but it not the law. Different people have different taste. I remember Schnabel many times began the trill on the principal note, not from the note above.

Beethoven

You are playing Beethoven piano and violin sonatas with Francescatti. What are your Beethoven interpretative ideals?

I think the best Beethoven interpretation comes from using the Kalmus edition, the Urtext edition,

and playing what Beethoven asked. You are sure then to be on the truth.

Chopin

What about Chopin interpretation, the old schools versus today's playing?

You know Chopin loved Mozart more than any other composer. It is difficult to say you must play Chopin like Mozart; but regarding style, clarity, and taste, you must play Chopin like Mozart.

Chopin is not often played that way.

Unfortunately. For years Chopin has been the most betrayed, deformed composer. I don't want to use the word *romantique* because *romantique* is very good. *Mais, on joue Chopin manièré, morbide, comme la musique d'un malade.* (But Chopin is played in a mannered, morbid way, like the music of a sick person.

In a more mannered way today than formerly?

The same. I can see this in the competitions. I am always surprised to see the little girls or boys play Chopin with bad style, bad feeling, and too much pedal of course — but that is *le cache-misère*.

What would you say constitutes a good style of Chopin playing?

Play as Chopin wrote, with personality maybe, but not change of tempo. The beginning of the first Ballade is Largo and Moderato afterwards. But you have many bad interpretations of this first page, with changes of tempo. Chopin asks for Largo; you must play it Largo and not change everything.

I sometimes think the introduction of this Ballade is the hardest part to play.

Absolutely. And remember after the Largo, you have: and many people play:

Why? I don't understand this bad tradition.

In the introduction, the first note is marked pesante, then you diminuendo as you go up . . .

Yes, yes, and then you have silence, very big silence. And then you have:

and not:

Why do people play it this way?

When I hear pupils do that, I give them zero. For me, it is wrong, wrong, wrong, wrong. You know — everybody should know — if the composer puts a slur between D and C, he means like an appoggiatura, as in Mozart, as in Beethoven. People who do the opposite, I call anti-musician.

After the introduction, many people play accelerando, fortissimo. But if you look at the music, it is not that. You have passion; you have appassionata, but you shouldn't change the text or play false accents. It is difficult to respect the text of the composer.

Schumann

When I was studying in Zurich, I heard you play the Schumann C Major Fantasy in the Tonhalle.

You were there? . . . The Fantasy is perhaps the best work of Schumann, but it is too long for the public. Why? Because today's public wants more brilliance maybe. People prefer very brilliant Schumann, and the Fantasy is *in-time*. People prefer *Carnaval* and the *Etudes Symphoniques*.

Even after they know the Fantasy?

Maybe they don't know the Fantasy, because pianists don't play it enough.

Bach the Most Difficult to Memorize

How do you memorize?

That is difficult to say, but I must say immediately that Bach is the most difficult to memorize. Bach and Fauré are very difficult to memorize. When you have to memorize the preludes and fugues, you have to repeat, repeat, and repeat. The finger memorization in Bach is difficult.

In practicing a Scarlatti sonata or a Chopin etude for many hours, you don't need consciously to memorize. They memorize themselves. Whereas, the Bach preludes from the *Well-Tempered Clavier* can be difficult to memorize — the C Major or the F Sharp Major, from the second volume, for example:

Naturally all fugues are difficult to memorize too, but you have the fugue style — the entrances and so on — which is a help. But in the preludes you don't have this help.

On the other hand, Beethoven — except for the adagios — is not difficult to memorize. You can learn fast . . . In general, I think the only way to memorize is to repeat and repeat and try to play by memory afterwards — after a long time.

Practice Regime

How do you warm up?

Each morning I play a scale, a Philipp exercise, and an arpeggio for about 30 minutes — 30 minutes of pure technique — and then I start to practice.

Have you played a lot of Czerny?

In my youth, I played Czerny; and after Czerny, in the Diémer class, we had wonderful etudes — more difficult than Czerny — Kessler. Now he is forgotten, but Kessler's etudes are very good. So are those of Moszkowski. Cramer is good, but maybe he is a little old-fashioned now.

Especially in the "School of the Virtuoso, Opus 365," you have Czerny studies for Beethoven, Chopin, Schumann, and even Brahms . . .

Yes, and Mozart too. You know Czerny knew the Scarlatti sonatas very well. It is interesting for a Hungarian at this time to have known the Scarlatti sonatas.

. . . And the nineteenth Czerny study in Opus 365 is an exact model of the Chopin Chromatic A Minor Etude from Opus 10.

Yes, and I don't know if Czerny wrote that after Chopin, or Chopin after Czerny. It would be interesting to know.

I tried to look that up once. Czerny lived from 1791 to 1857, Chopin from 1810 to 1849. In 1831, when 21, just after he had composed the Opus 10 Etudes, Chopin visited Vienna and met Czerny who was 40. So, I think Czerny probably wrote his Opus 365 after having heard Chopin and seen his Opus 10. Moscheles (1794-1870) wrote a chromatic etude, Opus 70, No. 3, which could also be used as preparation for the Chopin.

I think Beethoven was very much influenced by Czerny. Surely, in the last sonata. Maybe Beethoven asked Czerny, "May I write this passage or not?" Especially in the fifth Concerto, maybe Czerny showed some trick to Beethoven.

Where in the fifth Concerto?

Near the end of the first movement. In the music, you can see the *piu facile* version. It's lovely; it's

lovely. But nobody now plays it; they play the double-note version. And I'm sure maybe Czerny said to Beethoven, "You can write tadatadatadatada." As Brahms, in writing his violin concerto, asked Joachim many things and Joachim would say, "This part is impossible," or "this way would be more playable."

Do you think of certain passages you've found especially beneficial to practice?

You have to practice all your life the beginning of the Beethoven *Waldstein* Sonata. The beginning of the *Appassionata* is very difficult. In the beginning, measure 14 — pumpumpum, tadadada — Beethoven wrote for one hand. Afterwards editors arranged the passage for two hands, but the result is much better, more difficult but much better, with one hand, as Beethoven, perhaps, asked Czerny and then wrote.

In other words, you should play the division of the hands in Beethoven exactly as Beethoven wrote. The beginning of Opus 111, for example:

Absolutely with the left hand. It's the same principle. Many people play the two opening octaves — pumpum — with two hands, but it's not the same. You can say to me, "It's not important because Beethoven was deaf when he wrote that;" but, nevertheless, it's much better for one hand.

How about in Schumann? Many pianists divide the left-hand chords of the Adagio in the "Fantasy," using two hands instead of one:

Play it as Schumann wrote it. Absolutely.

Symphonic Etudes

A pupil of yours told me you add octaves in the left hand, third and fourth measures from the end, of Variation VIII (Etude X), of the Schumann "Symphonic Etudes." Do you add the octaves for power and sonority?

Casadesus plays the left hand in octaves on the repeat

I do; I must confess. Maybe I am wrong, but I think it is much better. You must play the octaves, but don't play them like Prokofieff — not hammered. For the music is still in the right hand. I think the octaves are much better, the second time.

You know Schumann omitted the Etude III and this one from the second edition. Look at the German edition and you will see they are not in the second edition. I heard Clara Haskil play this work without those two etudes. Schumann did not say he cut them out because they were too difficult, but perhaps that was the reason.

Would you like them cut?

No — aw. And you know the posthumous variations are wonderful. Some artists play the whole thing — Cortot did sometimes and also Rosenthal — but it is difficult to insert them. I am never happy with the result. Especially numbers 4 and 5 are wonderful; number 5 is absolutely like Fauré. The posthumous variations are very good Schumann. I'm surprised Cortot does not mention the second edition; I think the Peters edition is better.

Imitating Other Instruments

Do you think orchestrally or imitate other instruments when playing the piano?

In playing sonatas with Francescatti, which I play tomorrow, you have some parts in the right hand in answer to the violin. The violin has a wonderful melody, and this melody is repeated by the piano. I play this part like oboe, not like piano. If I play like a piano, the sonority is not good, is too dry. If you think about oboe, the sonority is clearer. A good oboist never plays hard; he doesn't play dolce, but he plays piano. In the *Fifth Symphony:*

That is real oboe playing. In some parts you imitate the bassoon, or the horn. For me it is a joy to think about the orchestra — good orchestra, of course.

You have examples of imitating other instruments many times in the Mozart concertos. Sometimes the oboe plays and you must play like him in the repetition or before. But you know the piano is a *bad* instrument! If you put your finger on the A, the sound is not like the oboe or the clarinet or violin. It is always a hammer. You must be careful about the hammer on the piano, because the piano is hammer — *Hammerklavier. C'est un piano à marteaux.*

One of the wonderful things about the piano is that you can imitate other instruments.

Absolutely. And you can imitate the organ too, except for the pedaling. You must play Bach, except for some parts of the Partitas, always, always with legato. On the other hand, in Scarlatti, although you have some legato, it is generally staccato, leggiero. It is Italian.

Debussy

Did you know or meet Debussy?

No, but I heard Debussy three months before he died. It was in Paris, in the Salle Gaveau, a charity concert during the first world war. He played some songs for Madame Ninon Vallin. It was absolutely beautiful. Beautiful sonority and pedaling.

At this time I thought it was the way of Chopin. Years later I heard Bartok play — not the big, *sauvage* Bartok, but the *Mikrokosmos* — in New Brunswick, New Jersey. His playing reminded me of Debussy.

Was Debussy playing on a beautiful instrument?

Yes, and it is very interesting that Debussy wrote all his music on a Bechstein. And if you play Debussy on a Bechstein, it is easier to play because the composer was thinking on a Bechstein. And Ravel composed all his music on the Erard, a French piano which we have no more. It had exactly the same construction as the Steinway. If you play Ravel on a Steinway, it is easier than on a Bosendorfer, which is also a good piano, in Austria.

Do you find the American Steinway the same as the German Steinway?

No, American Steinways are more dry; the German Steinways are less percussive.

Ravel

Did you know Ravel?

Ah yes, I knew Ravel between 1922 and 1930. We played together on tour in Spain, Switzerland, and France, starting the program — it was very interesting — always with *Ma Mère l'Oye.* Ravel played the top part, and I played the bass.

For the second part of the program, Madeleine Grey — a great interpreter of Ravel — sang some Ravel playing the accompaniments. For the third part, I played either *Gaspard de la Nuit* or *Miroirs.*

After intermission, Madeleine Grey sang again. And to finish the concert, I played the trio with my uncle, Marius Casadesus, and the cellist, Maurice Maréchal.

The first time I played for Ravel was in Paris. I played *"Le Gibet"* from *Gaspard de la Nuit,* and he said to me: "You bring out harmonies which pianists usually don't do; I can see you are a composer." I was very proud about that.

Was Ravel a good pianist?

I must say not too good because his playing was stiff. He tried to play his *Sonatine* for some friends; it was impossible for him to play with a nice touch. He wrote some glissandos in fourths and thirds in *"Alborada del gracioso"* which are very difficult because if you do them too well, you can scratch your finger. But Ravel could do those glissandos. Maybe the stiffness in his wrists and fingers made it easy for him to play them. For many pianists they are impossible to play. For me, impossible. I played "Alborada" for Ravel and told him, "These glissandos are impossible." And he said to me, "No *problème.* Play what you want."

Do you find having the hands on top of each other so much, difficult in playing Ravel?

Yes, it's difficult. I think that Debussy's music for piano comes from Chopin, and Ravel's from Liszt. It is not the same technique. The Liszt technique, although more brilliant, is easier than the Chopin technique. If you look at the Liszt Etudes and the Chopin Etudes, the Liszt appear more difficult than the Chopin. But they aren't. The Chopin Etudes are very difficult. It's similar with the Paganini Caprices for the violin.

What do you think of this statement: "Debussy continues the work of the great classicists in his preoccupation with the questions of musical structure and development; whereas Ravel is primarily interested in sound textures." Or stated otherwise: "Ravel starts with a sound effect; whereas Debussy starts from musical motives."

That is true. But I don't know if Ravel wrote his music for the effect. But I must say it is more brilliant than Debussy. I said a few moments ago that for me Debussy comes from Chopin, Ravel from Liszt. And if you go further, Debussy comes from Couperin, Ravel from Rameau. You see the difference? Couperin is absolutely different from Rameau. Couperin is more *discrète,* more *interior,* whereas Rameau is always *exterior.* Two big musicians but one was not timid. For me, Couperin-Chopin-Debussy is the same line and Rameau-Liszt-Ravel is another line.

That's very interesting. To continue with their compositional differences. . . it has been said that in Debussy, the pianist is required to solve technical problems that arise out of compositional experiments; whereas, Ravel starts with the instrument and the player's technical capacities and builds his music around these considerations. For example, in "Scarbo" did Ravel think of the spooky sound of the chromatic scale in parallel major seconds first, or the fingering which makes the playing of the scale possible?

I think he thought of the fingering first. But something else that is interesting: The first pieces of Debussy — the Sarabande, the Toccata, and so on — are not in the style of Franck but they are in a piano style which was a little old-fashioned. Then when Debussy saw the first Ravel compositions — *Jeux d'eau, Sonatine,* and *Miroirs* — he changed technique; he was more on the side of Ravel. That is an influence of Ravel on Debussy. On the other hand, Debussy's new harmonies influenced Ravel. You have many harmonies in Ravel's "Ondine," "Scarbo," and "Gibet," which come from Debussy's "Reflets dans l'eau," "Hommage a Rameau," and "Mouvement." And these Debussy pieces were written three years before Ravel's. You can see the *rapprochement,* the interrelation.

Printing Errors

Usually editions which correct printing errors do not appear until after people who knew the composers are dead. Do you think of printing errors which Ravel mentioned?

In "Ondine" the octava signs were omitted in the white-key glissando:

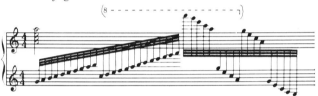

And on the first page, the right-hand figure in measure 4 should remain the same. Ravel told me that is a mistake. But if you see the photostat of the manuscript, you see that Ravel wrote it wrong. I spoke with Badura-Skoda about that. When I played "Ondine" for Ravel, he said, "Continue the same kind of figure to measure eight, to the last line."

I saw the latest printing of the Debussy Preludes; they corrected the last part of "Feux d'artifice." The Tuheeudum should be in the bass clef, not in the treble. But we waited fifty years to get this correction. Fifty years! And maybe Debussy did not see the mistake. Sometimes when the composer revises the print — Chopin did too — he forgets.

Casadesus Composition

Mr. Casadesus, besides being a world-renowned virtuoso, you are also a composer of great distinction, having composed seven piano concertos, 24 preludes, 4 piano sonatas, 2 sonatas for violin and piano, concertos for 2 and 3 pianos and orchestra — over 64 works in all. Is there an easy piano piece of yours suitable for CLAVIER to publish?

To commemorate the birth of my third grandson, Carter Rawson, I composed a piece on the letters of his name. And because he was born on the 16th of July, the day the American astronauts departed for the moon, you have in the middle of this piece — glorifying the landing on the moon — very discreetly:

It is only two pages, a sketch, not for a child but not difficult to play, and I think it will be suitable and better than other things such as my *"Enfantines"* which Durand has in Paris. I think I will give it to you.

●

Our *bavardage,* as Monsieur Casadesus modestly called our dialogue, ended just as vivacious Madame Casadesus arrived. We chatted a few minutes in French, and then said *"Au revoir."* One week later, I received *"Berceuse Lunaire,"* Op. 67, No. 4 — an original copy in Mr. Casadesus's own hand. With the manuscript was a note which I have translated from the French:

Cher Monsieur,

Here is the small piece of which I spoke to you. I'm not keen on its being printed. Instead, I would prefer that the manuscript — which is very clear — be reproduced in "photo-copy."

I was delight to make your acquaintance and to chat — *"Bavarder"* — with you . . .

1,000 sympathiques souvenirs
ROBERT CASADESUS

CLAUDIO ARRAU on
The Beethoven

Claudio Arrau, during the interview, trying to find the exact words.

"*That is for me like the red cape for the bull*," exclaimed Claudio Arrau, when I asked him his views on rearranging hands to make certain passages easier in the Beethoven sonatas.

"Not out of pedantry," he continued, "but because when you play a passage written for one hand, with division of hands, it sounds different. If the composer wanted the passage to sound like crossed hands, he would have written it that way. I think leaving out notes and dividing passages between hands is a fundamental mistake: *the difficulty itself is from the composer*. He wanted to express something difficult and hard.

"For example, in Opus 31, Number 2, measures 161 and 162 of the first movement, play the arpeggios all with the right hand."

"This:

"Not this:

"And in the Appassionata Sonata, Opus 57, measures 227 and 228 of the first movement:"

"This:

"Not this:"

I had arrived twenty minutes early for my interview with Mr. Arrau in the music room of his home in Douglaston on Long Island Sound, New York.

One wall of the music room is a wall of books, in front of which sits a record machine, piled with records. Multicolored paperweights cover the table at one end of a black

Piano Sonatas

Performance Insights

interview December 1967

sofa; a large picture biography of Beethoven fills the book-rack at the other. Intricately carved African figures of various shapes and heights and shades of wood adorn the fireplace mantel. A collection of icons hangs, frame to frame, above a Virgil silent keyboard.

In the wing of the grand piano is a long coffee table, stacked high with books: among others, the paperback edition of Amy Fay's *Piano Study in Europe* and Richard Rosenberg's imposing two-volume *Die Klavier-Sonaten Beethovens*. Nearby on music stands are facsimile editions of Bach's *Inventions*, *Well-Tempered Clavier*, and Debussy's *L'apres-midi d'un faune*. A clavichord, more books, scattered chairs, and a few abstract paintings (including a puzzling blue, fish-in-water scene) complete the picture.

Mr. Arrau came in promptly. A short, dark, dapper man, friendly and urbane, he speaks with Latin accent, looking at you with searching, black eyes. After opening amenities, we talked, sitting on the sofa, in the center of the room.

I had planned to ask Mr. Arrau questions regarding his ideas on playing Beethoven's piano sonatas and the value of these works in teaching and study. Here are my questions, and Mr. Arrau's incisive replies.

Mr. Arrau, you have written that "the mighty 32 piano sonatas, constituting a veritable Bible of the keyboard, form a great arch which spans and encompasses Beethoven's life, from young manhood and hopeful beginnings, to full manhood and heroic struggle and victory, to completion, fulfillment and transcendent immortality . . ." What place do you feel Beethoven's "mighty 32" should occupy in teaching and study?

I think the Beethoven sonatas should occupy the most important place in teaching and study. They teach a young student almost everything he will need for other composers, too. Chopin should also be another starting point and, of course, Mozart.

Edwin Fischer has written that "in studying Beethoven's piano sonatas one encounters difficulties, questions, and problems the solution of which constitutes part of the entire artistic and human education of a musician . . ." I'm sure you agree. What are some of these difficulties, questions, and problems?

Yes, I agree with him entirely. Mainly, I would say the difficulties are the art of contrasts and espressivo, and then of course there are tremendous technical difficulties that sometimes seem to be almost beyond solution. As to what the Beethoven sonatas actually teach the student — they force him to take a stand, to form his own conception, and to decide what the character of the work is. I think many other composers one can play with some measure of success just by playing the notes, but not Beethoven. Beethoven asks for meaning in every note, in every phrase and rhythm; he forces the student to take a stand, to commit himself — something which most young people don't want to do.

Which Beethoven sonatas should be learned first? Do you agree the early ones are in many ways the most difficult?

Arrau: In many ways, yes; others have other difficulties as big . . . Start students with samples of the different aspects of Beethoven: Opus 2, Numbers 2 and 3; then give them Opus 10, Number 3; the *Pathetique;* and Opus 31, Numbers 2 and 3. Especially Opus 31, Number 2, the *Tempest,* is enormously important. Then give them Opus 53, Opus 57, and Opus 90 — and *then* one of the late ones. But don't start with the late ones. I see all these young

Demonstrating one of his points on his home piano.

pianists making their debuts with Opus 106 and the Diabelli Variations. They seem to want to take short cuts, to
skip and just start with the big things. How can anybody
understand the late sonatas or the Diabelli Variations
without knowing the whole line of Beethoven first in all
its aspects?

*In your recent Carnegie Hall Beethoven recital, I no-
ticed you use a lot of weight and relaxation in your technical approach. How do you teach this weight and relaxation?*

I show pupils the basic movements of piano technique:
1) arm and shoulder weight
2) rotation
3) finger action
4) combination of these three
5) pushing up from the wrist for chords, an accented
   note, et cetera and
6) vibration with high wrist.

They can invent their own exercises as long as they do
these basic movements. We start right away applying them.

Arm and shoulder weight

I never let pupils use the fingers alone. I always ask
them to use the whole arm with the fingers. I start first with
the big arm movements, just lifting the whole weight of
the arms and dropping the arms onto the keys. Raise the
arm high, let the entire weight of the arm fall on a very
firm finger, on a black key, for example. Most pupils cannot do it. Free falling of the entire weight of the arm should
be the most natural thing. But pupils keep the upper arm
and shoulder tight. The shoulder should be entirely relaxed and used — if you want a greater forte, use the
weight of your shoulders as well as the weight of your arm.

Rotation

I start with rotation, and then with vibration for octaves
and rapid staccato notes with big circular movements and
high wrist as in "Pantalon et Colombine" from Schu-

mann's *Carnaval*. All the broken octaves in the first movement of Beethoven's Opus 2, Number 3, also the difficult
broken chord in the development, and the left hand part
of the last movement where almost no one plays all the
notes are examples of rotation in Beethoven.

*How do you have students work on the broken chord
work in the development section of the first movement,
measures 97 to 109, of Opus 2, Number 3, which you just
mentioned?*

I start by having them do the rotation movement between each two notes very slowly, so they go all the way
in one direction and then in the other, so they develop the
sideward striking power, striking hard with the fingers,
turning the arm from the shoulder, gradually increasing
the speed.

In the last movement, you have this very difficult tremolo passage in the left hand. Once you can make rotation
motions naturally, this tremolo passage is no problem.
And there is no limit for speed either. Of course, the fingers have to be really developed.

Finger Action

As I said, I teach the big movements along with training the fingers, not just using the fingers. Having strong
fingers is the *sine qua non*; if you don't have strong fingers, you can't have the use of the whole arm. To develop
finger action, lift the fingers as high as you can, then strike
immediately down on the key, taking the arm along and
relaxing afterwards. I start students very slowly, of course.

*Students have difficulty getting enough speed in the
left-hand triplets of the last movement of Opus 2, Number 1.*

PRESTISSIMO

Piano playing is a many-voiced thing. Bringing out the
melody forte and playing the rest pianissimo came from
Paderewski, particularly. For me, the first movement is
more of a harmonic happening than a song. The melody
is important but not the only thing.

*At the end of the first movement of Opus 110, you
brought out the fugue theme contained in the alto voice.*

Beethoven has *marked it crescendo. I wonder why no one else does this.*

Moderato Cantabile
molto espressivo

I didn't bring it out because of the crescendo. I just discovered it, and so I bring it out.

(Editor's note: because of a make-up error, part of the copy on the preceding page was in the wrong order. Following is the question that prompted Mr. Arrau's comment that "Piano playing is many-voiced.")

To return to your recent Carnegie Hall Beethoven program: in the first movement of the Moonlight *Sonata you outlined the bass line, making it almost as important as the right-hand melody. Isn't this departing from scrupulous adherence to Beethoven's directions, more something a pianist of the Romantic school would do?*

(The answer to the question on speed in triplets follows:)

If you use only the fingers, it will sound mechanical — use the arm too. Use rotation on groups of three. Also you have the arpeggio movements which are different. Most of the work is done with the arm. Of course, you would have to practice it like an exercise too for the fingers. You have to develop the fingers and have them at your disposal. I also believe in practicing to a certain extent on the silent piano. But not too much. *I don't believe in disassociating the artistic and musical function from the purely muscular function.*

One should have very well-trained fingers at one's disposal but one should not always use just the fingers, except for certain things. I believe very much in weight-shifting to get the legatissimo, particularly in Chopin. Every passage must be like a melody and should not be played in a mechanical way.

I have heard that you make a point with your students about the use of the thumb on black keys.

I use the thumb a lot, for big skips, for very important notes where you cannot afford to hit a wrong note as in "Chiarina" from Schumann's *Carnaval.* I always fall on the thumb on the black keys. In the Beethoven Opus 2, Number 3 development broken chord passage, you have to use the thumb on A flat. There are many examples like that. The taboo against using the thumb on the black keys came from the old way of playing with just the fingers and a rigid hand position. Now we play with all this upper arm movement. It is easy to play on the black keys if you are relaxed all the way through. The passage from the *Appassionata,* which I cited earlier, where so many people rearrange the hands, is also an example of the use of the thumb on the black keys. This passage is not so difficult if you are relaxed and use rotation.

It is generally agreed not to extend Beethoven's alterations in his reprises, where his keyboard did not extend high enough. How about the downward places? You didn't play the low E at the FF *subito entrance of the second theme, measure 26, second movement, of Opus 2, Number 3. It seems·to me if Beethoven had had the low E, he would have used it here. One doesn't hear this* FF *subito as powerfully if played with the upper octave E. You don't agree? I ask because these places abound in the Beethoven sonatas.*

Whether or not to extend the compass of Beethoven's piano is a point *ad libitum.* As far as the alterations in his reprises are concerned, obviously in the reprises he changes something, and we know his piano didn't go any higher. But the changes that he made are so interesting and beautiful that we play what he wrote. But as I say, that is not a hard and fast rule for me. In the passage you cited, you are coming from a higher note and although it is sudden *ff,* when you play it as written you keep a certain connection to the bar before in the line of the left hand. Schnabel writes about these changes very well.

What do you think of Czerny's references in his piano method to Beethoven's performances?

Czerny is one of the very few sources we have on the way Beethoven played: there are also Schindler and Riess. Sometimes they contradict each other. But I still believe in taking into consideration Czerny's suggestions, particularly his metronome markings, which prove Beethoven's performances were not metronomical. I do not always follow one hundred per cent what he says in general, but at least I try to come close to his suggestions.

It should be said over and over again: *fight this absurd taboo against changing tempo in a movement* — this kind of metronomical playing that has become the ideal of so

Arrau in concert dress before the audience arrives.

many pianists. To hold, to tie down a titan like Beethoven to a metronomical performance — everyone who heard him play has said how he would exaggerate the rests, for dramatic expression. He would enlarge or shorten the rests, and he would change tempo within movements.

Besides perusing the original manuscripts and first editions, I know you prefer the Kalmus and Henle Urtexts. Let's discuss some of the other editions.

Liszt

The wonderful thing about the Liszt edition is that it keeps to the original text, keeping all Liszt's suggestions in small print so you know what he is changing, adding, and suggesting. It shows such an honesty towards the composer, and many of his suggestions are extremely interesting and inspiring.

Bülow

Bulow is inspiring, but use his edition with care because he changes a lot of notes and chords without saying anything about the changes. If you use only Bulow, you will sometimes do things that were not written in the Beethoven manuscripts and first editions. Bulow is extremely important to work through because he understood Beethoven's spirit and message more beautifully than almost anybody else.

Casella

Casella is uninspiring and dry and doesn't go into the core of things. He is occupied with unimportant details.

Schnabel

No, I don't really agree with his counting out rests. The rests should not be calculated: they should come from within; they should be different from performance to performance, according to the creative current that is happening. Otherwise, I think Schnabel's edition is marvelous. HIS edition did a lot to get teachers away from this taboo against elasticity of tempo. Putting the tempo down again every four or eight bars in the movement confuses sometimes. He put down too much, I would say.

Schenker

Schenker's edition of the four last sonatas is excellent. What I miss in the rest of his edition is footnotes.

I am myself bringing out a new edition to be published by Peters. It will take at least two years.

What edition do you find has the best fingerings?

I think it is very important to use the few original Beethoven fingerings that we know. The fingering is such a personal thing according to the build of the different hands. One should not stick to the fingering of any one edition. I think Schnabel's fingerings are very good, and the new Henle edition has excellent fingerings, too.

What about repeats in Beethoven?

I believe in repeats if the composer wrote down to repeat, particularly with Beethoven who had such a strong intuition. He would never write a repeat just for conventional reasons as Mozart would. In certain Mozart movements one could omit repeats, but not in Beethoven. You would destroy certain formal elements. In the last movement of Opus 57, it might be more effective not to take the repeat. But the repeat is such a strange repeat. Beethoven would never have put it down unless he had wanted the section stated again.

In certain places Beethoven used the pedal to veil the atmosphere in mist. What do you think about these Beethoven pedalings and pedaling in Beethoven in general?

In general, we use too much pedal in Beethoven. I think that the pedal in his early works should still be an event, be felt by the listener as an event. But adhere strictly to his *own* pedalings as he wrote them. An additional amount of pedaling one does anyway. When he writes in certain spots pedaling and nothing before and after, one should be careful not to use too much pedal before or after, so that Beethoven's own pedaling becomes an event.

Czerny writes something very interesting about the original pedaling in the first movement of Opus 31, Number 2. He calls it *hall* (resonance) pedal, this kind of sonority that stays in the air, that Beethoven wanted there.

RONDO
ALLEGRETTO MODERATO

Of course Schindler, or somebody else, calls it "spoken like a voice out of the grave" to give it an unearthly character.

About the Beethoven pedalings in the last movement of Opus 53, Schnabel used to say — he had a whole philosophy on it — that Beethoven wanted to have unity between tonic and dominant, "always letting the fundamental note sound, until the next fundamental note follows."

I think Beethoven also wanted something unreal like a sunrise, like something germinating. *L'Aurore* (sunrise) is so important; unfortunately this title is not used here. We don't use it, but in many original editions it says *L'Aurore*. Kleiber, the conductor, told me it was like the beginning of spring, the first germinating of nature, like indistinctness achieved by holding the pedal and playing as pianissimo as possible. Also the beginning of the first movement is like the first grass coming out of the soil, figuratively speaking. The usual thing we hear is so basically wrong.

Do you think some writers have overemphasized thematic relationships in Beethoven?

He probably didn't always connect thematically consciously, but the idea that things develop out of a little germ in Beethoven — that is, of course, a fact. For example, in Opus 2, Number 3 the germinal "turn" is used, changed, or transposed in all four movements.

ALLEGRO CON BRIO

ADAGIO

SCHERZO
ALLEGRO

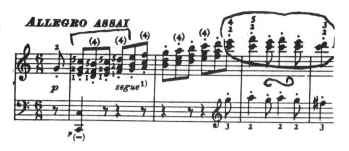

Whether he did it purposely or not, that is the way he composed. That is why his works have this tremendous unity.

Sometimes relationships between different sonatas composed close together have the *same* motives, as do Opus 109 and Opus 111. In Opus 109, the F#, G#, A#, B of measure 15 come back and forth, also in inversion at the Tempo Primo, and in the second movement too. In Opus 111, you have the G, A, B, C. Some time I want to play these two sonatas together to show these similarities — I would love to play them together.

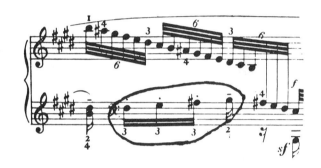

And last, Mr. Arrau: In your performance I felt you emphasized the robust elements of Beethoven's music, always pointing out the structure, an important harmony, what is going on in the music. But what about beauty of tone, beautiful singing-communicating melody as opposed to a more intellectual approach?

I don't think that beauty of tone is always important; it isn't a main point in Beethoven interpretation. I sometimes go to the point where I think certain things shouldn't sound too well or too lush. I think one should even include the possibility of rough sounds once in a while, as in Opus 106 or the Diabelli Variations. Beauty of tone is not so important as it is in Chopin, Mozart, or Debussy.

Beautiful tone may please audiences more, but that is not the point. *You are not supposed to please; you are supposed to stir!*

At Ease with Claudio Arrau

interview July 30, 1971

Driving to Claudio Arrau's 400-acre farm — his peaceful, summer retreat in the Vermont mountains — I had climbed gradually from the Massachusetts border about 100 miles, then climbed more steeply off the main highway, finally winding up a steep, dirt road. Signs in colored letters — CLAUDIO AR-RAU — guided me past maples, birches, and ever-greens, amidst a jungle of ferns and undergrowth.

Suddenly I came to a clearing and faced a long, white New England farm house with a large pond behind. Three basset hounds announced my arrival. The maid met me at the door and, speaking in Span-ish, led me to a large (about 20 by 16 feet) wood-paneled music room. There among colonial antiques,

I saw a white cat sleeping on a chair, a grand piano, a colorful Ecuadorian rug on the floor, and two South American abstract, Matisse-influenced paintings on the walls. Shelves of books lined one wall. Books and foreign editions lay scattered all over: on the piano rack, Schubert's posthumous B-flat Sonata; on the piano lid, Jarocinski's book on Debussy, the Baeren-reiter edition of the Liszt Etudes, and the Universal edition of the Schubert sonatas.

As Mr. Arrau and I settled into comfortable chairs, I remarked on his fine note-reading ability, for it is said that he could play at sight a movement from a Beethoven sonata at the age of four.

"Yes," he said, "I always played by reading the

music, never by ear. That was the strange thing. I taught myself to read music, and then I started sight reading. I knew music reading before I knew the alphabet."

How did you begin playing the piano?

I listened to my mother teaching and heard her play — she played very beautifully. She was the first inspiration, and then I taught myself. I had this tremendous urge: the only thing I wanted to do was play the piano, rather than play with toys. My family couldn't get me away from the piano; they had to feed me while I was playing. Even then I knew that playing the piano was the only thing I wanted to do in life.

You never went through the usual note-reading processes?

Not really. I must have taught myself somehow, although I can't remember the details. But I do know I could read all of a sudden.

You were an astonishing child prodigy, giving your first recital at the age of five, in 1908. What did you play?

I remember I played a few of the easier Chopin Etudes, and the Schumann *Kinderscenen*, and the Beethoven Variations on "Nel cor piu non mi sento." And I think a Beethoven Rondo and a Liszt Consolation.

Fantastic . . . What are some of the problems of being a child prodigy?

Mostly psychological. You have to work so hard. You have no time to develop in the normal way. There isn't time for playing with other children, for remaining a child.

Perhaps spending much time with other children has a negative influence by forcing conformity.

That's true. My mother took me out of school after six months because I couldn't practice enough. From then on, I had very good tutors. I never conformed then, and I never conform now. Not conforming is a disease with me.

Maybe one reason many young pianists sound similar is that they conform too much.

Absolutely. They're always together, they know each other, they're close friends, they play for and criticize each other. That might be one of the reasons there's a certain leveling of the whole generation.

You were a judge at the Marguérite Long contest in Paris recently and also in Vienna. What was your reaction to the playing?

These young people, many of whom were fine technicians, all used fast, loud sections merely to amaze. I said after the contest in Paris that they seemed to divide music into halves: one half — speed and brilliance, which has little to do with music — and the other half — slow playing, when they wanted to express feeling. Some of them were quite musical, but they used their musicianship only when they played slow, soft passages. The moment there was a fast, loud section, they used it for flash, hitting people on the head, so-to-speak. It amazed me, too, that when they had to play piano, they played pianissimo, bloodlessly, so you couldn't hear the shape of the phrase. They became sentimental, immediately using the left pedal for pages and pages. They didn't have sensuousness; passion never arrived.

Points on Playing

What is the principal problem in interpretation?

Coming as close as possible to what we know to be the intentions of the composer; and from that basis, taking your own flight of imagination. Interpretation is on the one hand serving the intentions of the composer and on the other hand putting the interpreter's own blood and personality into the realization of the text. These two things must be balanced. It is objectively wrong, for example, to play fortissimo where Beethoven wrote pianissimo and to call that interpretation.

I have said often, the test of interpretation is how wide and far the imagination can be made to range around the written text as is. It is as wrong to be paralyzed with awe of the text as it is wrong to act in an irresponsible way toward the demands of a composer. Based on the text, I go along with Mahler: "Music is not in the notes." He meant that the music is above, between, below the notes. Everywhere — even in the rests and sometimes especially in the rests.

You believe that tone should be different for every composer. Does this difference stem primarily from the dynamics?

The degree in forte, crescendo, decrescendo, sforzato, etc. is definitely different. For instance, a Beethoven fortissimo would be different from a Mozart or a Schubert. A crescendo would be more violent in Beethoven than in Mozart. Sometimes string quartets play late Beethoven with the same quality of sound as they do Tschaikowsky. The

Claudio Arrau has an extensive African collection that includes a few rare Benin bronzes.

tone in late Beethoven must be de-sensualized. The same kind of vibrato will not suit both Beethoven's and Tschaikowsky's music.

You have said that in a real melody "there shouldn't be two notes equally loud."

Yes, for there are never two notes equally loud in a sung phrase. A singer doesn't sing two notes on the same level but rather every syllable and pitch on a different dynamic degree.

Does the "no two notes equally loud" rule apply to Bach?

In Bach, there is the problem of the instrument. I played all the Bach keyboard works in twelve recitals in Berlin in 1935. Afterwards, I decided that the piano itself causes a performer to bring something to Bach that doesn't belong, that somehow sounds a little too worldly. Not that Bach doesn't have emotions, but they are different emotions — usually on the spiritual side. Take the *Chromatic Fantasy* — it's like a dialogue with God, with the Infinite. It is music for the glory of God, but it is never music between one human being and another.

How important is the beat in the rhythm of Bach as compared to the music of Mozart, Haydn, or Beethoven?

In Viennese classicism a group of measures becomes overly important; whereas in Bach, except in the dance forms, the bar line is much less important than in Beethoven.

Should an artist play principally for himself or should he always try to keep the audience in mind?

You should always project on an audience; you should never play just for yourself. But your first aim should not be to try to please the audience. You should give them what you have to give — the message of the composer through your own personality. It is always the composer's intentions and the deeper meaning of the work that counts most, not whether or not the performance pleases. The trouble with a whole generation now is that foremost they are supposed to please. Of course this attitude has to do with the whole musical setup becoming a big business. Nevertheless, you should develop resistance against following the commercial trends in interpretation. Commerce and art are two different roads.

What type hands are best for piano playing?

The stretch between the fingers is more important than bigness of the hand. And the fingers should be middle-size. If they're too long, they get in the way; curving them is difficult. They say of Brahms — my teacher, Martin Krause, in Berlin, heard him many times — that his very thick, wide fingers made him hit wrong notes, two keys with one finger.

How would you describe your hands, Mr. Arrau?

I have been lucky to have hands of the right size and proportions. The span between my thumb and forefinger is eleven notes, as great as between my thumb and fifth finger.

How did you practice as a child?

I practiced a lot, an average of nine hours a day, starting when I was 12 or 13. I practiced two or three hours a day on technical exercises — double thirds, double sixths, octaves, chords, everything. Later, I changed. I saw the danger in playing exercises: you dissociate the function of making music from the muscular function.

Do you believe that beginning students should practice exercises?

Oh yes, but later they should learn to enlarge their technique by overcoming the difficulties in the works they play. From that time on they should look at a passage — from Chopin or Liszt, for instance — as a fast melody, never mechanically. I no longer practice scales or arpeggios. I practice a difficulty as I find it in a work.

Do you practice the day of a concert?

I go through the program once, not strongly but sort of intellectually to freshen my memory. I never really practice; I never do more than two hours. The day before a concert I practice the difficulties but not too much.

You can play two hours and still be fresh for a concert?

Yes. Probably if I would practice six hours with involvement the day of a concert, I would be tired. I make a point not to expend my emotional strength — I'm not emotionally involved — so that when I start a concert I have a fresh approach, emotionally speaking.

Great pianists seem to have the physical ability to play long periods of time.

Being able to play a long time also depends on the way you play. If you play in a stiff way, then of course you will get more tired than if you play in a relaxed way, with no stiffness in any joint. As a young fellow, when I had to learn something quickly — an engagement to play a particular work, where I couldn't afford to lose the engagement — sometimes I had to practice 20 hours a day to get the work ready. I had the physical capacity to do this; I never tired physically from practicing.

How do you keep relaxed?

By sinking into, swimming, or floating in the music, letting myself be carried by the current so-to-speak. Let the tension happen; let the emotion flow. Then you will not cramp. When you cramp, you are still not one with the instrument: you are here, and the instrument is there. You should become one with the piano. That is why you should play with your whole body, the whole weight of the body going into the keys.

On the other hand, although I'm an advocate of physical relaxation, I believe in tremendous inner tension and feeling. Great piano playing requires you to have incredible emotional tension without getting physically tense. That seems simple, but it isn't.

How do you memorize?

First I play through the work without thinking of memorizing, until it's in the muscles. I have four kinds of memory: muscle, photographic, sound, and analytic. I use analytic memory last, after the work has gone into my body — my muscles, my ears, my vision. I advise students who have difficulty in memorizing or playing in public to use only one edition, to know exactly where things are on each page.

Do you see the notes when you're playing?

I see the page, but there's not enough time to see all the notes. I think the most important memory is the analytic. To know exactly what is happening — repeat this phrase, retard, modulate, know from

what key you are leaving and to what key you are going, know all the different voices, be able to play the left hand alone by memory, be able to play the separate voices in a fugue by memory — is to have an analytical memory that almost never fails.

Many talented people use the four memories you have mentioned without ever acquiring your tremendous repertoire. How have you accomplished this?

In general, acquiring repertoire is a question of not being lazy, and I've never allowed myself to be lazy. I've wanted to learn new things, to pile up repertoire, since I was a child. I have never liked to play the same work too much and have always tried to play as many different programs in a season as possible.

I understand that many of the great pianists of the nineteenth century had rather small repertoires, playing only the works they thought they played well. But, for the development of an artist, playing a small repertoire is not healthy in the long run. The more music an artist has in his mind, the greater interpreter he will become. When I started playing those complete cycles of Bach, Beethoven, Mozart, and Schubert in the 1930s, I wanted to become more acquainted with these composers' entire musical language — not only their solo piano works, but their chamber music, lieder, opera, works for orchestra, everything. Sometimes solo works, when compared with the chamber or orchestral music of a composer, become clearer.

Do you still learn new works?

Yes, I try to when I have the time; I don't want to get stale. I have been working on the Third Sonata

of Boulez. The latest thing I learned was the Carlos Chavez Concerto, a beautiful work.

What contemporary works, after Prokofiev's, do you think will become part of the repertoire?

This will depend upon the development of the audiences, which are changing tremendously everywhere. I can imagine a time, not too far away, when Schönberg's *Pierrot Lunaire*, let's say, will attract a big audience. His piano concerto is starting to become a repertoire piece.

Recommended Books

Of the newer composers, I like Luciano Berio and Krzysztof Penderecki. Of the older new composers I like Elliott Carter — his piano concerto is a major work — and Tippett — I consider his *King Priam* a masterwork. I was also tremendously impressed by the Zimmermann opera, *Die Soldaten*. Stockhausen can not be ignored. All of the newer music is a new experience. Rather than being afraid of the experience, we should welcome it. Something totally new, possibly having nothing to do with music as we know it today, could come of it.

What books dealing with problems in piano playing have you found worthwhile?

Of the recent publications, *"Die Kunst des Klavierspiels"* (Musikverlage Hans Gerig, Köln, 1967) by Heinrich Neuhaus, the teacher of Richter and Gilels, is quite good. Of the older publications, I like very much the books by Rudolf Breithaupt. I think you can still get them in secondhand book stores in Germany.

Do you agree with Neuhaus that "tone is the first and most important requirement of the interpreter?"

Absolutely not. Tone must be different for every composer. An artist should have the right sound for every composer. There is no such thing as an artist who has a beautiful sound. Yet there are many pianists who approach piano playing from the sound standpoint. Of course the individual interpreter's tone should vary, but tone should not be a conscious preoccupation. That approach leads to superficiality.

Sound should be at the service of interpretation to begin with. Take the trills at the end of Opus 111 of Beethoven. If these trills are played with only beautiful sound in mind, what have you? But if you have a cosmic vision in mind, all the beauty of sound should be there anyway.

There are certain things that shouldn't sound beautiful — things in Beethoven and Brahms that need a sort of rough sound, coarse at certain moments, whereas in Chopin or Debussy you can never have a coarse sound.

What other books would you recommend?

The Czerny book, *On the Proper Performance of all Beethoven's Works for the Piano*, (distributed by Theodore Presser in this country), is very important. Czerny gives metronome markings not only for every movement of the solo piano works but also for the piano-chamber and -orchestral works. You have to be discriminating; some things seem far-fetched. Czerny probably put in some of his own ideas, not only those of Beethoven. For example, Czerny says the last movement of Op. 31, No. 2 is supposed to have been inspired by the sound of a galloping horse

that passed by Beethoven's house. I can't believe that. The rhythm could have been inspired by the galloping horse maybe, but the movement became something completely different. It is far beyond merely galloping horses. It is a mysterious vision. The galloping horse idea would be more applicable to the last movement of Op. 31, No. 3:

Other books I should mention are the Cortot editions (published by Salabert). What Cortot wrote about Schumann and Chopin is also extremely important.

Die Klaviersonaten von Ludwig van Beethoven by Badura-Skoda and Jörg Demus (published by F. A. Brockhaus, Wiesbaden, 1970) is excellent for every sonata. The book on Beethoven, *Die Synthese der Stile*, by Hans Mersmann (published in Berlin, 1922) is very important. For years Mersmann was the head of the Cologne Conservatory. Unfortunately, German and French books on music don't get published in English very often. The Mersmann book should be translated into English at once.

In the old Kullak edition of the First Beethoven Concerto, there is a marvelous introduction. Schirmer left it out; it is only in the Steingraeber edition. It is really important to read on the style and performance practice in the time of Beethoven — the trills, the grace notes — there are many things to absorb.

I find *Musical Performance in the Times of Mozart and Beethoven* by Fritz Rothschild (Oxford University Press, 1961) important too. That's published in English. Hermann Keller's book, *Die Klavierwerke Bachs*, (published by Peters, 1950) is very good. Peters is supposedly going to print an English version; I don't know if they have.

And there's an important book on Debussy, in French, by a Polish musicologist, Jarocinski. He deals with the works, the life, the atmosphere, and the influences on Debussy. In English, I think the Edward Lockspeiser book, *Debussy, His Life and Mind* (published by Macmillan, 1965), is still the best on Debussy — not the short biography, but the two volumes Lockspeiser published more recently.

Mr. Arrau, what is your approach to teaching?

I look upon teaching as a moral obligation. I feel it is my duty to pass on what was given me, what I have to give. I do it with great love. I talk about the work, give a general idea, and then go over every detail. I have found that just telling students the general idea and the spiritual aspect is not enough. Even if you are very clear, they will not be able to apply what you say right away. You have to help them apply these ideas, but never by performing. The student, once having windows opened for him, must be made to go in on his own.

Mr. and Mrs. Arrau after a concert.

Have you found that students often become dependent upon you to go over every detail?

Yes, there are many dependent students. The teacher becomes a figure who knows everything, whom they can always ask. They become lazy and wait for the teacher to make the decisions on how to play something. Then there are the ones who know better than the teacher, who don't agree with anything you tell them.

Do you get that kind of pupil? And is it true that all who are chosen to work with you are given scholarships?

Once in awhile I get that type of pupil. I *want* pupils to question me, to ask "why." It's healthy when students want to be convinced. But some of them question issues just to assert themselves in front of the teacher. As for the scholarships, that is true. But since my teaching time is limited, I can accept only two or three students now a season. Occasionally I give master classes, as I did in the Beethoven year in Bonn.

In your Hunter College recital, the trilled variant section in the Chopin Nocturne in B major, Op. 62, No. 1, was an inspired moment. How do you conceive and how did you perfect these trills?

I try to give trills meaning according to the nature or mood of the work. Even the speed of the trill should depend upon the mood. At this point in the Nocturne, the mood is ecstatic elevation, a floating kind of thing. The trills dissolve the contours of the melodic line; you see the melodic line as if through clouds. Certain trills, as in the late Beethoven sonatas, must not be too fast. You hear people play Opus 111 trilling as fast as they can. In his late works, Beethoven arrives at a metaphysical language of expression where trills become a trembling of the soul. Something similar happens in this Nocturne, but not quite that elevated or transcendental. You don't decide on a definite number of notes or a definite pedaling. The pedal trembles, physically.

Advice on the "Appassionata"

Of those difficult, sudden fortissimo chords in measure 17 of the first movement of the Beethoven Appassionata Sonata, you have said that "getting sufficient power depends upon lifting the arm sufficiently before each chord."

Yes, and use the whole arm; avoid using just the wrist and the forearm. Use the arm as an entity, actually lifting. There are some chords that you push up, also using the whole arm.

Towards the second theme, which begins at measure 35, gradually get a little slower as a transition to the slower tempo. For the repeated E's, I would recommend the thumb with rotation. 2-1, 2-1, 2-1 is also good. The fingering is a personal question. The thumb, however, gives more of an agitato character and permits you to shade a little better; the agitato doesn't come out too mechanically. The thumb here is more advisable — if you can do it.

In the two bars just before the second theme, breathe a little before the right-hand chords in order to get more of this calming-down feeling. Then particularly before measure 35, a bigger hesitation is needed. The sound must seem to come from heaven, to be consolation in the middle of tragic turmoil.

The second theme has no upbeat. These four bars form a phrase that is one of the most difficult to play in the whole piano literature. It should not be given

too much expression, but on the other hand, it should not be too even; you must shade a little. In measure 36, there is a little crescendo, an imperceptible tarrying on the B-flat, and then a diminuendo on the following G, A-flat, and E-flat. The same thing occurs on the E-flat of measure 38; the tone is almost imperceptible. The listener only feels it as mood, not as distortion or rubato. Change the pedal often. Keep the tied-sixteenth and sixteenth-note rhythm as uniform as possible. This rhythm is basic and must be kept constant, somehow obsessively in this movement.

The forte in measure 42 after sudden piano must be wild, like an upheaval, a revolt. Measure 43 is so very passionate. If you sang it, you would make a little crescendo to the B-flat and then diminuendo.

The pianist must replace what can't be done on piano with something else. So wait a little bit after the A-flat before starting softly again.

The trills from measure 44 must be clear, not moth-eaten, and the *nachschlag*, or afternotes, must not be too loud in the transition from one trill to the next.

Do not play the run in measure 47 too fast. There must be in it something of the mystery of the beginning — *schleichend*, creeping, crawling. Inch your way. Don't rush; stay steady. All of a sudden you

shrink back, half paralyzed, expecting, in fear, a premonition of what's coming.

When in measures 53 and 54 the two voices come fighting towards each other to a head-on collision, the right-hand sixteenth notes must be as clear as those of the left hand. The left hand must not be light; it must be vigorous, heavy, strongly accented on each note. Crescendo the F-flats right into the sforzato.

In the middle of this turmoil, at measure 59, avoid getting faster. The sixteenths must remain steady, equally emphasized. Each one-beat figure starting in measure 61 is a kind of sobbing. Rhythmically, the three A-flats come a little later than written — but very little, or the effect will be exaggerated. Imagine that the three A-flat sixteenths are each a sob.

At his Virgil, a silent keyboard.

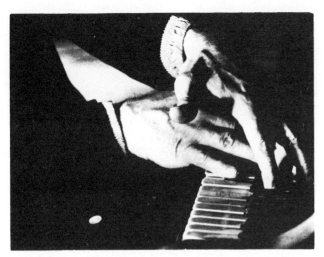

Again in the first movement of the Appassionata Sonata, you said that the fortissimo chords at the Piu Allegro "should not sound like 'filled' octaves." Other artists, feeling that the top notes of chords should be brought out even in fortissimo passages, might not agree with you.

For me, the middle notes of a chord are as important as its outer notes. I would play these chords as a unit with a rich sound of the middle notes, curving the middle fingers, so that they strike stronger. If there is a special voice in chords, it should be brought out, but that would be the exception. In general, chords lose their meaning if you play them like "filled" octaves, octaves with middle voices. You lose the idea of *zusammenklingen*, the sounding together of a group of notes.

The difficult contrary-motion octave passages in your Chopin F minor Fantasy were completely accurate. Any secrets?

I play them legato as written, using the third and fourth fingers. Usually they are played non legato, which is wrong and which I find makes them more difficult.

Do you play octaves from the wrist?

Never. I use shaking, vibrating octaves, even in such a piece as the Liszt Sixth Hungarian Rhapsody. There is no limit to speed with this kind of octave playing. Carreño used to play octaves this way. As a child I heard her play the Sixth Rhapsody many times; she played it in every concert. She also had this idea of relaxation and vibration which she got from Breithaupt. She restudied at a late age — I think she was about 50 — and changed her entire way of playing through Breithaupt. It was beautiful to see her arms; she wore sleeveless dresses, and there was never any stiffness anywhere.

Edwin Fischer said that "beat is vertical, taking no account of that which precedes and that which follows; whereas, rhythm is horizontal, the power which connects what precedes to what follows and also has a tension function."

That's very good. I would also say that "beat" is more mechanical than rhythm. One must not beat just by measures; the musical current should go through the bar lines.

There's the controversy as to whether the Scherzo movement of Beethoven's Op. 110 starts with an upbeat bar. Schnabel says no, Tovey and Fischer say yes.

I think it begins with an upbeat, counting by measures in groups of four.

Would you count the Chopin Scherzos by measures, in four-bar phrases — Opus 31, for example?

Not consciously. The Scherzos are very much in four-bar phrases. But I think counting them by measures would make you play too fast. I would prefer to count "one, two, three" very fast.

Do you think of rhythmic figures that often are not played precisely enough?

Sometimes figures are played too precisely. Rhythm should be very elastic, the notation of rhythm being only approximate. Otherwise, rhythm becomes motoric, which I hate. In such a rhythm as the fourth Variation of the Schumann *Symphonic Etudes*, a variation built mostly on rhythm — you should of course be very precise. But, on the other hand, there are cases in romantic music where the slight distortion of the rhythm will help the expression.

Tempo and Mood

What are some things to consider in establishing the right tempo?

You should always consider the fastest values and see where they fit in without having to force the musical feeling. In music such as the Appassionata Sonata the changes in tempo must never go beyond a certain range. You have the basic tempo and you have a range of deviation towards a faster tempo and towards a slower tempo — but only a certain range. Beyond this range is distortion, which cuts the whole thing in pieces.

There shouldn't be changes of tempo without transition. Never become a little faster or slower without a transition, never suddenly faster or slower unless marked. **And afterwards you should have the** basic tempo in mind. When you deviate you should be able to come back to the basic tempo again and again. It's like people's breathing: when they get excited they breathe faster and when they calm down they go back to their basic way of breathing.

As a rule, should gradual changes of tempo — ritardando, accelerando — begin not at the beginning of a phrase or a measure but a little later?

Yes. When a student sees ritardando, he is likely to become immediately slower. He should still be in tempo where it says ritardando and then gradually get slower. The same thing with accelerando: he should still be in tempo where it says accelerando and then gradually get faster. And crescendo doesn't always go with accelerando, or diminuendo with ritardando. Toscanini got angry when his orchestra rushed forward in a crescendo.

What is the difference between ritardando and ritenuto?

Originally, at least, there was a difference: a ritenuto meant a sudden change of tempo, ritardando a gradual change. In French it would be *retenu* and *en retardant*, in German *langsamer* and *langsamer werden*.

What are some things to aid your intuition and momentary feelings in transitions between one and the next piece, say in Carnaval, the 24 Preludes of Chopin, or between the movements of a sonata?

Put yourself into the mood of the piece and then figure out how much time you need to get into the next mood. Between movements you should completely stop sometimes, take a breather and then go on.

The Chopin Preludes are a unified cycle. These pieces belong so much together, by their succession of keys in the circle of fifths, that I think they should always be played as a cycle. They are organic, each prelude producing the next.

Pianists often rush loud, fast endings such as the ending of the Schumann Symphonic Etudes. Aren't such endings more effective when not rushed?

Definitely. Pianists used to play the ending of the *Symphonic Etudes* without rushing. Many today do this horrible rushing at the ends of pieces, instead of holding back to give more emphasis and a triumphal feeling.

The problem of repeats will probably always be with us. What would you do with the six repetitions of the "A" section in Chopin's Military Polonaise, for example?

I am for repetition because the composer must have had form, proportions in mind. Composers wouldn't have put repeat signs just for conventional reasons, except maybe in Mozart's and Haydn's time. If Chopin wrote a repeat, he really wanted it.

Do you do anything different in playing repeats?

The Germans write *"tüfteln,"* an out-of-way word meaning to draw over-nice distinctions, to go in for subtleties. You shouldn't figure out anything to do differently, but when you come back to the same idea, let your feelings or intuition hold sway: if you feel a little more vitality or variety the second or third time, then just let go. But don't do as some artists do, play the repeat with the left hand loud and the right hand pianissimo, or the other way around. That kind of thing I hate.

50

Do you vary the dynamics depending on whether you are repeating back to piano or going on to forte?

I leave something in reserve — in strength, power — for the second time, the actual ending.

Would you tell a student to end the third section of the Mozart Turkish Rondo forte when he is going to repeat forte, and end with diminuendo when he is going on to the next piano section?

No, not really. Making a diminuendo as transition to the next section would also be *tüfteln*. There is such a change of key and everything, I would finish strongly. This movement is conceived in sections, like terraces of sound, and shouldn't be smoothed out between change of key and dynamics.

Of course you would take the repeats when the first ending contains material not heard elsewhere in the movement, the first ending of the opening Moderato of Schubert's posthumous B-flat Major Sonata, for example?

Never omit such a repeat. The first ending has some of the best music in the whole sonata. This also applies to the Chopin B minor Sonata. Most of the time these repeats are omitted. I don't think I've ever heard a performance of the Schubert where the repeat was taken.

Myra Hess.

She did? Good for her.

And she played the movement slowly, too.

Good. This movement can hardly be slow enough, but neither the interpreters nor the audiences have enough patience. Audiences don't open up entirely to receive the music. If they wouldn't halfway listen and halfway think of other things, they would be happy to hear the start of this repeat again, this heavenly idea. Length is not a criterion. I hit the ceiling when I hear, "Oh, it's too long." Well, feeling it's too long is the fault of the listener; he hasn't got enough breath to listen. Certain composers, like Schubert, need time to expand. You violate if you cut things down.

Editions To Seek

What about your new edition of the Beethoven sonatas. Who will publish it and how will it be different from other editions?

Edition Peters, Frankfurt am/Main, the publishers, have done thorough research into early editions and original manuscripts. So as an Urtext edition, my edition will probably be better than those we have had up until now, even more accurate than Henle. For instance, Henle sometimes considers a bowing that is different the second time to be a neglect of Beethoven, correcting it to make it more logical. I've had arguments with Henle about that.

I think what we need is the original. Beethoven had the freedom of a titan: all of a sudden he changed a bowing. Why should he want it the same way every time? It's very much in line with his personality to make little changes like that. Peters and I have been corresponding, arguing about every little staccato mark and so on. From the standpoint of textual accuracy, my edition will be as authentically "Urtext" as possible.

I have added fingerings wherever needed; but I have kept Beethoven's fingerings wherever they are. There are very few of them. I have put one fingering for the average player, and then I suggested — not imposed — the one I use. I've kept the dynamic markings very strict: wherever there is nothing, I have added my own dynamic suggestions in brackets. I suggest my own markings, too, where there are stretches with no signs as to whether to play legato or staccato.

At the end there will be a separate book with my suggestions about interpretation, the character of every movement and of the whole sonata, and the character of the relationships between the movements. I give Czerny's tempi and mine. All trills and grace notes are in accordance with eighteenth century performance practice. The first volume is scheduled for publication in 1972 and the second, hopefully in 1973 or 1974.

I've noticed you play such movements as the last from Opus 7 seriously. You don't conceive this movement as essentially lighthearted?

No, not really. This last movement used to be called "the Loved One," with the consent of Beethoven. I think it should not be played too lightly, but in a feminine, friendly way. I look upon Opus 7 as one of the very first of the tragic sonatas.

Do you think there's humor in Beethoven?

That's a difficult question. I, personally, think that humor has nothing to do with music: humor has to do with words, music with emotions. People, through associations, find certain contexts in music funny. But I'm against speaking of humor in music, unless in an indirect way.

In the Chopin F Minor Fantasy, what are your reasons for playing the ending phrase of the second march theme, diminuendo?

It seems to me that one of the laws of Chopin's musical personality is that he bends before the climax. So, many times you should play the climactic tone, the highest tone, softer, whereas in Beethoven you go to the top, louder. Phrasing dynamically this way also has to do with masculinity and femininity. In that respect, Chopin's *anima* — the feminine side of the soul, in the sense of Jung — is very strong. This sort of femininity makes for the elegance in his music, elegance in the best sense of the word. You have to avoid squareness, even in the rhythm. Chopin's rhythm is approximate.

Do Chopin's pedal markings have less validity than those of Beethoven?

Chopin is not very systematic about marking pedaling; he writes one way and then another. He seems to be improvising. That is why I dare to advise doing something sometimes other than he wrote.

What edition shows his pedalings most clearly?

The Paderewski or Polish edition. I have been comparing it to the facsimile editions of Chopin's man-

uscripts, and sometimes the Paderewski edition makes little changes. But in general it is very accurate, as is the Henle edition. I don't think Cortot shows the original pedalings; he shows just his own suggestions.

When Beethoven wrote pedal, it was an event. He wrote pedal so seldom that you have to stick to his pedaling. But Chopin seemingly changed all the time through the manuscript and the French, German, and English editions. Markings that he wrote in pencil when he taught pupils differ too, proving that he kept changing. In other words, there's more room for improvisation in every respect in Chopin than in Beethoven. But when Schumann writes *pedale*, he wants quite a lot of pedal, with quick changes. He leaves the actual changing to the discretion of the player.

What editions are best for Schumann?

The early editions before Clara Schumann's edition. You can get them at secondhand stores in Germany. These editions differ in details, the tempi differing considerably from those of Clara Schumann. The Henle edition is also very good for Schumann.

What constitutes great Liszt playing?

Nowadays you need courage to go all the way in playing Liszt's music with tremendous pathos, expression, very exaggerated expression, in a theatrical way almost. So many pianists approach Liszt with the idea that he's old-fashioned; they start flattening him. Then he really becomes unbearable.

As in acting Schiller, the actors get ashamed and start speaking as they do in everyday life. Then Schiller becomes appalling, unbearable. So, in playing Liszt, you have to go all the way in dramatic expression, characterization, and contrasts. All passages should have expression. You have really to believe in Liszt in order to play his music properly.

51

You should adhere to Liszt's original markings. In the B minor Sonata, for example, on the third page, Liszt wrote crescendo, diminuendo, crescendo, diminuendo — and you never hear that:

Today's players don't seem to follow the original markings. You cannot be ashamed of emotion when you play Liszt.

Appreciation of Liszt comes and goes. Today in Germany there is little appreciation for Liszt. In Zürich, they don't even want you to play Liszt. But in Paris, London, and New York there is a growing audience for his music. Thank heavens.

How do you reconcile your views on Rachmaninoff's concertos with their great popularity?

The masses applaud these sensuous melodies. The tremendous amount of notes and the brilliant endings are very effective. I think, however, Rachmaninoff's music is more like show or movie music than serious music.

Speaking of applause, do you think it wrong for audiences to applaud at the end of the first movement of a concerto?

In my youth, the first movements were always applauded. When Arthur Nikisch, for example, conducted a symphony, there was always a big applause after the first movement. Or, after the first movement of a Brahms concerto, there was always applause. I think the composers counted on applause — you see these big, incredible climaxes in the Brahms D Minor, for instance. When I listen to the Brahms D Minor, I can't restrain myself. The natural thing is to burst out into applause. I'm sure the composers didn't mind because the audiences applauded all the time. The English started this "not applauding."

On the other hand, at the end of Opus 111, you should never applaud. In the Cardiff cathedral in Wales, I played four Beethoven sonatas, finishing with Opus 111. I have never been more happy in a concert than there — the piano is in the middle of the church. It was absolutely unbelievable, the impression, the feeling of having been in communion with a transcendental sphere. In such a case, applause would have brutally destroyed this feeling. I think one should put in the programs: Opus 111, no applause; the Brahms Concertos, you may applaud if you wish.

Records and Recording Sessions

You have made many, many records. What are some of the problems in recording?

You have to play slightly differently than for concerts. Some things you do in concerts are not good for recordings, the extent of rubato, for instance. If you play rubato as in concert, it might sound too much on records. That's one of the problems.

The other problem is the absolute necessity of flawlessness and the fact that you have to insert corrections if something has gone slightly wrong or if you are interrupted. It is difficult to fit the corrections in. In the early days of recording, you had to play four and one-half minutes flawlessly. There was no way out; you couldn't correct. So, trying to play flawlessly became a habit with me; I had to pull myself together so as not to play any wrong notes. Today, I imagine I am in the old times and pull myself together to get a flawless recording as long as possible. And then I'll insert only the absolutely necessary little corrections. Playing as long as possible also keeps the continuity and spontaneity, the current of the music alive. There are, of course, artists who record bar by bar.

Have you made recordings in one take?

Do you know the Liszt Concerto No. 1 with Ormandy and the Philadelphia orchestra? We recorded that in one take, without even one little correction. The slow movement of the Hammerklavier was also in one take. I think Opus 110 and Opus 2, No. 3 we did in one take.

You mentioned that if you played with as much rubato in recording as in concert, it might be too much. On the other hand, a pianist whose playing is too straight in performance might come off well in recordings.

That's true. Then there are people who want recordings that are just pleasing, that don't disturb, that you can listen to while reading a book.

Flawlessness is nonsensical in a way. Yet, if you hear a recording by a singer with one note out of pitch, and you hear it several times, you begin to wait for this out-of-pitch note. So you cannot have wrong notes in piano playing on records. Record producers are right in insisting on this. In a concert, however, flawlessness by itself doesn't mean a thing.

Which of your recordings are your favorites?

Perhaps the two Brahms Concertos — in the latest version with Bernard Haitink on Philips; the Schumann F Sharp Minor Sonata, the Humoreske, and the *Etudes Symphoniques* with the five posthumous variations; and my new Liszt recordings, especially the one with the sonata. But I never listen to my recordings. Once completed, I leave them behind.

Have you had any humorous misadventure during a performance?

In Cologne before playing the Liszt *Totentanz* with orchestra, I had forgotten to lock the wheels of the piano. During the performance — I was playing with much vitality — I noticed the piano moving towards the cellists. Then I saw the horrified faces of the cellists as they moved backwards. It was a funny situation until we got the piano stopped.

What final advice might you give students for solving problems in piano playing?

I would advise students and young artists to forget about the competitive spirit, which produces all the neurotic difficulties they may encounter later. I would advise young artists to remember that as individuals, as interpreters, they are unique. They have the small, big, or deep message which is their very own. The most important thing then is to fulfill themselves as personalities, in this case as creative personalities — to try not to please but, as the saying goes, "to do their own thing." ∎

Serkir

interviews February 25, 1970 and July 2, 1970

The Curtis Institute of Music in Philadelphia, where I first interviewed Rudolf Serkin, occupies a well-kept, four-story sandstone mansion on one side of sedate Rittenhouse Square. The entrance to the building is notable for its ornately sculptured, three-arched facade; the interior for its wood-paneled walls, oriental carpets, and paintings, as well as its intimate concert hall and more modern orchestra-rehearsal and practice rooms.

"The atmosphere seems more relaxed than at the Juilliard School or the Paris Conservatory," I said to Mr. Serkin shortly after he arrived.

"Don't be misled," he replied smiling. "We make the students work."

And work they do at Marlboro too, where Mr. Serkin had invited me to come to complete our interview. The Marlboro Music Festival is held on the campus of Marlboro College in the verdant, rolling valleys and hills of Marlboro, Vermont. Some of the white frame practice cottages and rehearsal rooms used for the festival's informal, high-calibered music-making are remodeled farmhouses. A large, high-vaulted, wooden, modernistic concert hall is the setting for the weekend concerts. More than seventy-five works, selected by the musicians themselves, are rehearsed each week; there are twenty-four grand pianos.

As a person, Rudolf Serkin is unusually polite, tactful, hospitable, and sensitive to other people's feelings and well-being. He has a pleasant laugh and a walk which is almost a run. His hand and fingers are heavy, with wide stretch between the fingers. It is quite a big hand — "Yes, I can strike the tenth, D to F-sharp" — and heavier than you would expect of a man his stature. His temperament shows itself in his quick, nervous movements, in his suddenly saying, "Let's do this!" or "No, don't do that!"

In Philadelphia we had lunch in an elegant, homelike private club; in Marlboro, in the large cafeteria where Mr. Serkin mingles with the visiting artists and students like the paterfamilias.

During lunch we talked of Switzerland:

SERKIN: You studied piano with Walter Frey at the Zürich Conservatory? I recently saw him; he is a fine pianist and musician . . . The Zürich Symphony is very good; their former conductor, Volkmar Andreae, was always wonderful to me . . . You heard Lipatti? . . . Did you speak Swiss German? Well, they won't let you. I lived a long time in Basel, and still the Swiss would laugh when I spoke Swiss German. The Swiss are very musical and Zürich is a wonderful city for concerts.

ELDER: I'll cut out the parts of our conversation about me.

SERKIN: *No-o*, bring them in. I think they make it more personal for everybody. Don't you think so? I would strongly feel that way. You can't bring in enough of the human.

We talked of Paris:

SERKIN: People say the French public is not musical. I don't agree. The French respond to every note; they know when you play really well. They are so artistic — if something unusual happens in a musical performance, they are there; they know it . . . When the Curtis Institute was looking for additional theory teachers, I asked Nadia Boulanger if she had any pupils she could recommend. She said she had three outstanding students. They turned out to be Americans, and all three are now teaching at Curtis.

ELDER: I studied counterpoint with Madame Honegger, wife of the composer, herself a fine pianist and teacher. For our counterpoint and fugue examinations, the secretary of the school locked us each in a room, with the piano taped shut. We brought our lunches and worked all day on our eight-part choruses, fugue, or whatever, turning them in when finished to the concierge. Do you have examinations like that at Curtis?

SERKIN: Well no, not yet. But that reminds me of an experience Toscanini told me he had in his youth at the conservatory in Parma. They locked him in his room to practice the cello. With no place to go to the bathroom, he went in his cello. Later, when he played for his teacher, the water came running out!

And we talked of miscellaneous things:

ELDER: Where did you play on your recent tour of Europe?

SERKIN: In Berlin I played a Beethoven concerto with the Berlin Philharmonic. The orchestra was superb . . .

ELDER: Have you ever played in Russia?

SERKIN: Not since the 1920s. I met Glazounov . . .

ELDER: Do you think it's good for students to listen to recordings?

SERKIN: Highly personal performances might be successful artistically but not help students much, whereas performances that respect the composer might help a great deal.

ELDER: Your son Peter has played a lot of modern music.

SERKIN: Yes. For example, he recently played the Schonberg Concerto, with Shaw in Atlantic City and other places. He's a greatly gifted pianist. Even if I am his father, I feel I can say he is the greatest talent I have encountered amongst the young generation. He's an amazing guy and only twenty-two.

In Philadelphia, after lunch, we talked in Mr. Serkin's large, cheerful second-floor studio at the Curtis Institute; at Marlboro, in his white, wooden-frame home near the Marlboro campus. I had planned to ask Mr. Serkin questions about his training, work habits, artistic tenets, and ideas on Bach, Beethoven, Schubert, and Chopin performance. Here are my questions and comments and Mr. Serkin's cooperative, interesting replies:

How He Started

Mr. Serkin, where were you born and how did you start to play the piano?

I was born March 28, 1903, in the little town of Eger, Czechoslovakia, which then was part of Austria. Eger, now called Cheb, is in the northwestern corner of Czechoslovakia near the north Bavarian German border. It's a beautiful, completely preserved town, with a big *Marktplatz* from the fifteenth century and the ruins of a beautiful old castle. A friend just sent me photos from there. I was born in one of those old houses.

I started to play the piano before I can remember. My father made me play. He was a singer and gave up singing to teach his eight children. He tried teaching all of us either piano or violin. I hated the violin; it was so close to the ear.

When did you first play in public?

In Franzensbad — I don't know its Czech name; it's a spa like Marienbad and Karlsbad, not farm from Eger — when I was five or six. I played little pieces of Stephen Heller from his *Trotzkopchen* ("Stubborn Little Head") and the Impromptu in E-flat major, op. 90, no. 2, of Schubert.

Do you remember the opus number of the Heller pieces?

No, but I remember there was a little poem next to the title of each piece, written in French, English, and German. I remember my father reading the poems first to me in each of those languages and then in Russian, as he was Russian. Unfortunately, I understood only German. I think these Heller pieces are still available, although I haven't looked. They were easy pieces for beginners; they didn't seem easy to me then, but I don't think they are demanding.

That's really something to play the Schubert E-flat Impromptu at five.

That depends on how one plays it. My performance probably wasn't at a very fast speed.

Where and with whom did you study after you studied with your father?

I was supposed to study in Prague, the nearest large city, but I was too young for them to accept me. About this time my father took me to hear a concert in Pilsen by the much beloved Viennese pianist, Alfred Grünfeld. I played for Grünfeld, who said I should come to Vienna to study with a friend of his — a great teacher — Professor Richard Robert. So my father took me to Vienna to study privately with Professor Robert, who really was a great teacher. I was nine years old. Professor Robert put me up with a family. I was studying, but I was very lonely.

In Vienna I met George Szell, also a pupil of Robert. Szell was an accomplished pianist, a virtuoso in those days; he had also composed symphonies. He and his family were very kind to me. We were almost like brothers; he was fifteen, I was nine. My friendship with Szell then and later has been something very special. I studied theory and composition first with Joseph Marx and later with Arnold Schonberg.

Do you remember your first concert in Vienna?

My first concert in Vienna was with the Vienna Symphony when I was twelve. I played the Mendelssohn G minor Concerto. Emanuel Feuermann played a Haydn cello concerto; his brother Sigmund, a Viotti violin concerto. And then the two of them played the Brahms Double Concerto. It doesn't seem possible that they played the Brahms, now that I think of it — they were so young. Feuermann was an incredible player, one of the greatest artists I have ever known.

Practice and Technique

How do you practice?

I'm old-fashioned. I practice scales and arpeggios that I might need but don't always use. I find practicing scales and arpeggios necessary because you need them all the time in varying degrees. In chamber music, you use fewer muscles than you do in big solo works; in certain chamber works you have to adjust to the other instruments — the cello, for instance, in the lower register or in any register. You use fewer muscles than you would in a big concerto as soloist or even in a solo sonata. So if you play chamber music one night and a solo recital the next, you have to keep in shape. You have to keep up a certain basic training.

I practice and have practiced long hours. After five hours I begin to get warmed up. I practice scales slowly and rapidly — never in-between — with expression: crescendo, diminuendo, legato, leggiero, staccato, in all keys, and in thirds and sixths. I work for evenness, control of the fingers, speed, and accuracy. The performer has a duty to practice scales in ways to assure the basic equipment he needs in performing music.

The other day Casals spoke about the importance of practicing scales and arpeggios on the cello to the students at the Curtis Institute. But scales, of course, are only one of the basic exercises. Everyone has his own exercises or studies. For instance, some people are born with fantastic, fast octaves. Unfortunately, I'm not one of those people, so I practice octaves to keep up the speed, a little faster than I would ever need. This is one of the things which I think is important in music as in sport — what Donald Tovey called "the athletic part of music" — the training to be able to play everything louder and faster than you will ever need, so you will have a generous reserve.

I had very good training. I had to study a lot of what you may call trash, but I am not at all sorry. I played a lot of Moscheles, Hummel, Thalberg, Kalkbrenner, and Liszt, but very little Czerny and no Hanon. My teacher also had his own exercises.

Josef and Rosina Lhevinne believed in holding the inside fingers curved in and back when playing octaves. Do you?

I should think this would depend upon your hand. If you have big fingers, they would probably hit the notes in between. Whether or not you hold the inside fingers curved would depend too on the speed. For the Tchaikovsky Concerto, it is probably very good for the fast octaves in the first movement.

I believe in a good system, a good technical upbringing, such as Madame Lhevinne's. But from there out, I believe in finding your own ways according to the piece you are studying and the way you are constructed. There are no two people alike. There is no end to the acquiring of technique. It goes on all your life. Sometimes I discover something — certain things open up — and I think what an idiot I've been all my life.

Do you think you can overemphasize technique, that too much emphasis on technique will kill musicality?

I don't think you can overemphasize technique, if you really love music. If you are really gifted, you can't practice technique too much — your musicality will still come through. This is the French and the Russian approaches. I don't know much about the German school now, but some German approaches used to be more emotion and deep feeling and not so much technique. But what good does it do to feel deeply, if you don't have an even trill in the

Beethoven G major Concerto?

At the Paris Conservatoire, I thought there was such an emphasis on technique and fingering in some of the classes that the musical instincts of the pupils were deadened, at least not developed.

I don't think you can kill musicality by emphasizing technique. On the contrary, I think you can't emphasize technique enough. After all, students can make music after their lessons; they are not prisoners of the conservatory. They have friends; they can go to concerts. They can hear almost any major artist in recital, not to mention recordings.

I don't like to say "emphasize" technique, however, because "emphasize" sounds apologetic. But I do think the listener is entitled to hear the right notes as far as it is humanly possible to play them.

I know that the French and the Russians give their players a first-class technical training — in theory too. When I read about the winners at the Moscow competition, I'm sure that the winners deserve to win. In the olden days the German school was very famous too, but what I mean to say is that emotional, deep feeling can't cover up poor technique.

Yet German school artists have had some of the world's greatest techniques and interpretative powers.

I don't know which artists you are referring to, but a great artist will be a great artist regardless of his school. His first training will not be so decisive.

To me there is more German school in Artur Rubinstein's playing — in his finger action, and in Mozart, Beethoven, and Schubert interpretations — than is generally realized. He did study with Heinrich Barth and live in Berlin from the ages of eight to fifteen.

But look, Rubinstein is a typical, international, great artist.

And Heinrich Neuhaus, the teacher of Richter and Gilels, studied with Barth in Berlin at the same time as Rubinstein. In reading Neuhaus's book on piano playing, I'm amazed how "German school" his teaching is.

Would you call it German school? I would call it typically Russian. See how far we are apart, though I suspect we aren't really.

I have thought of the Lhevinnes as being Russian school, and yet I wouldn't say they were like Neuhaus.

That's true, but maybe it's wrong to generalize, anyhow about schools of technique.

Memory

How do you memorize?

I memorize by remembering — unconsciously. After a while the work sticks. There is the difference between memorizing the work and memorizing its markings. You make a crescendo and you aren't sure if it is yourself or if it is what Beethoven wrote. You may think a lot of things are in the score that aren't. So you have to check your memory with the score.

Memory is no problem when I perform such works as the Bach Goldberg Variations, the Brahms Handel Variations, the Chopin Preludes or Etudes, the Beethoven Hammerklavier Sonata or Diabelli Variations, and the Reger Bach Variations. But you have to keep memorizing. There is so much music you don't get around to it all.

I play any work I want to perform without music, though I wouldn't feel anything wrong if someone plays with music, as used to be the case. I find it natural that Myra Hess played with the music; I didn't find it disturbing at all.

In the old days Clara Schumann — they all played from music I understand.

But if one doesn't need the music, why should one use it? I never had any problem; when I had learned a piece, I knew it. So I didn't need the music, so far at least. Let me touch wood.

Of course memory isn't all unconscious. Certain things one has to remember. You try to analyze pieces consciously. You can't perform any work without knowing its architecture.

What about finger memory?

Finger memory is irritating really, a dangerous, unreliable thing. With me it would be disastrous because I change fingerings constantly, at the spur of the moment sometimes, according to the piano, the hall, my disposition, how I slept, and so on.

Do you study away from the score?

You know how it is, the score studies you. You can't sleep; it follows you. I learned to enjoy this. In the early days when this happened, I thought I was kind of suffering. Toscanini once talked to me when I spoke about it: "That's not suffering; that's wonderful," he said. "Beautiful music; what better can you think of to have going around in your head?" Performing and memorizing of course go together; I can't separate them.

You can acquire a technique of memorizing, I suppose, page by page. But I can't talk about this kind of memorizing because it is so alien to me. I can't even imagine it. But I know there are students who try to memorize that way, phrase by phrase, and so on.

Interpretative Approach

Mr. Serkin, what is your interpretative formula or approach?

I think there is no formula for art, no specific interpretative approach. If you find a formula, art isn't art anymore. You may approach a Mozart concerto as chamber music; Rachmaninoff much less so. But you can't separate a chamber music approach from a purely pianistic approach.

With Pablo Casals at the Marlboro Festival.

Besides, I don't believe in one approach or technique; you need a thousand techniques for different composers, even for different works within a single composer. If you apply any single approach, technique, or "school," you limit your approach; you are misusing the great works of art.

Do you ever express the mood of a phrase in words?

I don't especially try to find words to express phrasing. For me, everything goes together: architecture, harmony, phrasing. Schnabel said of the third phrase of the second movement of the Schumann Concerto: "Free as a bird sings!"

His expression was very fitting, but more for him than for me. It would never have occurred to me to mention this, if you hadn't asked me. You don't mind if I tell you this?

Not at all. I asked because I knew you had known Schnabel, and Schnabel was almost a fanatic at expressing phrases in words, wasn't he?

Yes, I know that. Anything Schnabel did was so personal, really wonderful. I was one of the many pianists on whom he had a tremendous influence. I was fortunate; he was extremely kind to me.

At my first recital in Berlin — I was seventeen I believe — there were fifteen people in the audience. And Schnabel was one of them. He didn't miss one of my concerts, always coming backstage. He would tell me some pleasant things and some very critical things. I never forget how kind he was. Sometimes he was there for half an hour or even an hour, talking about the pieces I had played, why I did it this way, wouldn't it be a good idea to do it just the opposite, did I ever think about this, and so on.

Rubinstein told me: "There is a concert where you are inspired and a concert where you are not inspired . . . I never plan." Naturally, there's inspiration and intuition, but along with these things doesn't there have to be — when you have played the piano as much as Mr. Rubinstein has — certain basic things he believes in, and does over and over again, to make his playing always so similar?

Well, maybe he doesn't like to talk about planning. He wanted to stress, probably, the unimportance of planning, or of taking it as a matter of course. I think he is absolutely right about inspiration. Sometimes you simply are not inspired. But this is very difficult to talk about — the borderline of inspiration, being well prepared, and intuition.

Before Rubinstein played the Beethoven G major Concerto on television, the camera showed him doing muscular-movemented finger exercises, away from the piano, in the air. But when I asked him, he didn't want to tell me what those exercises were.

Maybe he's not aware of doing them. It's possible. I know Gieseking studied works without even using the instrument. Sometimes when he was young, he was able to go on the stage and play a piece he had never before played on a piano. He just practiced those pieces moving the fingers, without instrument. It was a phenomenon.

Tone

Mr. Serkin, every great pianist has his individual quality of tone, different from the tones of other great pianists. What are your ideals of tone?

I use whatever kind of tone I find is needed in the work I am playing. You shouldn't produce the same kind of tone in a Beethoven piece as in a Mozart sonata. Take the slow movement of the Beethoven G major Concerto you just mentioned — there is a certain sonority I hear inside and try to achieve. The first movement of the *Moonlight* Sonata requires the most tender, relaxed tone; the first movement of the *Pathetique* at times asks for a dry quality plus speed and drama. In a Chopin nocturne, naturally, I try to get the most tender sound I am capable of achieving; and if it's a piece of Bartok, I will aim occasionally for the most biting tone, whenever necessary. Sometimes ugliness is part of the expression of the piece. I personally hope and strive for the utmost variety of tone, rhythm, of everything.

Tone is difficult to talk about, because I don't think one knows oneself really what tone one uses. But what you say about individuality of tone is true. If a great artist touches the piano, there is something absolutely his own — you know who it is; otherwise, he isn't great. This I have heard all my life with Horowitz, Busoni, Schnabel, Rachmaninoff — I could list all the great artists I have had the privilege of hearing.

Great Performances

What colleague performances have moved you most deeply?

I couldn't know where to begin. I never heard Hofmann in his prime. Busoni, Schnabel, Backhaus . . . Horowitz made an unforgettable impression on me in Basel the first time I heard him, because I'd never even heard his name.

I was seventeen when I heard d'Albert in Berlin. I thought he was terrible; he wasn't practicing any more. I remember a little fat man running down the big stage of the *Philharmonie*, not taking a bow, just sitting down and going right into Opus 111 — crash, crash — with everything wrong. I was horrified. I expected the great d'Albert. But in his great time, he must have been fantastic in every respect.

Phrasing

Do you think big-line phrasing is more important for the Romantic than for the Classic composers? Is this why the so-called Romantic pianists were less successful in Bach, Mozart, and even Beethoven?

I don't think that last statement is quite accurate. You would probably call Hofmann a typically Romantic performer — he had a big, long, wonderful line in Beethoven. I heard him play the fourth Beethoven concerto in Europe. His phrasing was the most beautiful you could imagine.

I really believe in a unity in music. I personally don't believe too much in style; Romantic, Classic never had much meaning for me. Of course what phrasing comes down to is a matter of taste — good and bad taste.

A Bach cantata can be so romantic. And Brahms for me, is a classical composer. Some Mozart works, the slow movement of the A major Concerto, K. 488, for example — are romantic. I can't think of anything more romantic. Can you?

If a performance doesn't move you, it is a poor performance. But the phrasing and style is a matter of taste. Regarding romantic style or freedom in phrasing, we know that Mozart played freely: he wrote in a letter to his father about rubato, saying that his left hand didn't know what his right hand was doing. He knew what rubato meant — the same as Chopin — and it's not fashionable today to mention Mozart and Chopin in the same breath. For me, I could never feel much of a difference there. Maybe I have bad taste, but that's the way I feel.

Rhythm

You have a wonderful, forward-moving, exuberant rhythm, Mr. Serkin. What about accenting to give tension to Allegro movements, when to accent "one" and "three," when just "one," when every other measure, and so on?

Rhythm goes together with phrasing. But you can't bring rhythmical accentuation down to any recipe. Sometimes you think you have found something, and then what you have found fits only that one place. I like a really established basic tempo. I like the rhythm clearly defined as to whether it is in four or three, unless it is composed intentionally to confuse the listener. I am sure the audience feels the same way.

Books on Piano Playing

What books on piano playing have you found most worthwhile?

Neuhaus, the teacher of Gilels and Richter, has written a very interesting book about piano technique, published in Germany.* I found this book fascinating. It has examples of problems and how to solve them. Schnabel never wrote about piano technique. Busoni wrote illuminatingly about music.

Perusing Original Manuscripts

What value do you find in perusing original manuscripts?

First of all, you get the shivers to see the creation. Then you discover new things. Today, for instance, in looking at the first edition (the manuscript doesn't exist) of the Beethoven Sonata in E-flat, op. 7, I found certain phrasings not found in any edition today.

What edition is this?

The original edition, directly from Beethoven. I own it, but it isn't generally available. At measure 72 of the third-movement Allegro, to cite one small detail, Beethoven wrote, and I play, just two notes slurred. All the later editions have three notes slurred.

tions have three notes slurred. There are of course many more important things in the "Waldstein" and "Appassionata" Sonatas, of which we have the first editions as well as the original manuscripts — the message directly from Beethoven.

In the last movement of the *Appassionata*, near the beginning of the recapitulation, in measure 226, there is a retard in almost all editions.

Yes, the autograph, which is in the Paris Conservatory, shows that Beethoven wrote rinforzando, not ritardando as in the first edition. The ritardando is probably an error because there is no following a tempo. Right?

*Neuhaus, Heirich, **Die Kunst des Klavierspiels**, (Koln: Musikverlage Hans Gerig, 1967.)

Right, you already know. But I have a hard time giving up the retard. Some first editions mean a lot and some are unreliable, for Beethoven complains about many misprints. He wrote to Breitkopf: "You are nothing but a misprint."

Something even more important than this *rinforzando* is the marking on the last chord before the Allegro ma non troppo, the last movement. Beethoven says clearly in the manuscript: left hand *arpeggio* and right hand *secco*, which means dry. For many years I tried to get the crash fortissimo with just an arpeggio. But it is easy if you break just the left hand and crash in with the right:

And there is another important place — in the "Waldstein" Sonata. There is this long stretch of *sempre pianissimo*. In measure 257, all editions except the Henle have *espressivo*. But it is misread; the autograph says clearly, if you care to read it, *sempre pianissimo*, just the warning to keep soft. *Espressivo* would contradict this; it would mean louder.

Do you own original piano manuscripts besides the Brahms A major Piano Quartet?

How did you know I own that? I have some Reger manuscripts too. But I am not a collector; I am satisfied with the photostats. The Brahms manuscript was willed to me. It gives a marvelous insight into the way Brahms thought musically, because of the many corrections.

Beethoven Sonata Editions

On your piano, Mr. Serkin, I see the Henle, Craxton-Tovey, and Schnabel editions. I don't know the Craxton-Tovey.

The Craxton-Tovey edition of the Beethoven sonatas — I think it has been reprinted — is interesting because of what he has to say in the notes. Unfortunately, the text is unreliable.

Do you ever use the Liszt edition?

Liszt is very interesting because he doesn't add anything himself; he tried to do what the Henle edition is trying to do. I believe Liszt intended to publish the complete works of Beethoven, but I don't know if he finished the project. I have some of the volumes, published by an old firm, Wolfenbuttel. At home, for instance, I have a copy of the string quartets. Liszt is so conscientious that he didn't even correct some obvious mistakes out of respect for Beethoven, because he had no proof; he had no access to the manuscripts.

What do you think of the Henle editions, of which you have the most?

Dr. Henle, publisher of the Henle editions, is a friend of mine. Publishing these Urtext editions is an idealistic enterprise for him; commercialism is not involved. He is a steel industrialist by profession, and a very good amateur pianist, by the way. Of course he can afford it, but he uses his money to wonderful purpose; he really wants to make these editions the best possible.

He goes to much trouble. For instance, if he finds a different source — if he were to find the Opus 7 manuscript and it would be different — he would destroy all his stock and reprint it.

My only reservation is that he puts in fingerings; he and I disagree that people need fingerings. Besides the Mozart and Beethoven, there are also the Henle Schumann and Chopin editions. The fine Chopin editions are new. But again he suggests fingerings. The same with his chamber music editions and bowings. He tells me few people can find good fingerings themselves; they need fingerings. But if a pianist with a short hand does the fingerings, they won't fit a pianist with a large hand.

Your students, Mr. Serkin, are so advanced, perhaps they don't need fingerings. But I find young students do when learning their first Mozart and Beethoven sonatas.

Yes, but you are giving your own good fingerings, "spoonfed," for their individual needs and not the fingerings from someone you don't even know.

We have some fingerings from Beethoven and Chopin which are very interesting and unorthodox. Whenever the expression demands it — legatissimo, you know — Chopin would not hesitate to slide from a black key down to a white key with the same finger, as a violinist slides. The second finger slides down also, not just the fifth.

From the manuscripts you can understand things that Beethoven meant. He didn't hesitate to use the thumb on black keys, there is no doubt. He used the natural weight of the hand for the natural accent. He wasn't influenced by any hard and fast rules.

Do you know he wrote sketches for a piano method? Professor Oswald Jonas showed it to me years ago in Chicago. There were exercises for the whole fist, where the whole hand comes down. Everything is allowed which helps the music.

Bach Performance

Mr. Serkin, you have said "there is nothing more important for musicians than the intensive study of works by Johann Sebastian Bach, and for pianists it is particularly fruitful. I can't imagine an accomplished pianist who has not attempted to master Bach's piano works." What is your approach to Bach played on the piano?

I think you should approach Bach played on the piano with taste, with restriction of the dynamics from piano to forte. There can be abrupt changes from one keyboard to another, as on a harpsichord. Sometimes there are markings by Bach himself. Within the forte you can make many changes and colorings, but these changes and colorings should be within a limited dynamic framework.

Casals says music should be made with great freedom, not restrained — "Freedom is performing with honor." That is, play as freely as you want but always with honesty and not for effect's sake. If someone plays a lot of Bach and studies the cantatas — if he is a musical person — he will find out how to play Bach, at least most of the works.

I read that you acquired at auction a copy of the Goldberg Variations made by a pupil of Bach. You were surprised to discover that this copy was the nearest thing to Bach's authentic intentions in existence.

It is the only contemporary copy of the Goldberg Variations; the manuscript is lost. But we have the first edition, which was engraved, I believe, by Bach himself and his son. In the copy which I have, there are tempo indications only on the minor variations, Bach's having taken for granted a contemporary understanding of how the major variations would be played.

When you made one of your first appearances with orchestra, you played the Goldberg Variations complete as an encore!

That's true. I was playing in Berlin for the first time — with the Busch chamber orchestra in an all-Bach concert, in 1921. I was seventeen years old. At the end of the concert, because it had been a great success, Busch pushed me out, saying I should play an encore. "What shall I play?" I asked. "The Goldberg Variations," he replied, as a joke. And I took him seriously. When I finished there were only four people left: Adolf Busch, Artur Schnabel, Alfred Einstein, and me.

I have read that Landowska, after practicing the Goldberg Variations for forty-five years, gave their first complete modern performance on the harpsichord, in France in 1933. You had played them earlier on the piano?

Busoni and Bülow must have played them too. I had played them before the Busch concert, in Vienna in 1918, when I was fourteen or fifteen after one of Arnold Schonberg's seminars. He was unfamiliar with them.

A friend of mine made a wire recording of your wonderful Town Hall performance of the Goldberg Variations in the late 1940s.

Really? I have no recollection of that performance, except that I thought I was prepared. I prepared for it at least six to eight weeks, even though I had played them many times. I completely restudied them.

My students have worn out my copy of your Italian Concerto recording.

We had a terrible time making that recording in Prades, France, at the Casals Festival. Trains and buses would go by, making us stop all the time . . . I would play the last movement much slower now anyway.

Your tempo on the recording is about 146 to the half note. I've tried to play it that fast; it's darned fast, but I like it that way.

(Amidst great laughter) . . . I don't know what came over me. When I heard it recently I was aghast. I play it slower now, about 112 to the half note. I think you enjoy it more at this tempo.

I greatly admired your Carnegie Hall performance of

the big A minor Prelude and Fugue, which Bach later arranged for trio, and your Hunter College performance of the Capriccio on the Departure of the Beloved Brother. I think you're a great Bach player and that you should record more Bach — the Well-Tempered Clavier and the three big A minor works, which so few people even know, for example.

Thank you. And the Inventions — they're wonderful works — the Partitas, the English, and the French Suites. If I do record some Bach, it'll be because of your encouraging me.

I've played the A minor Fantasy and Double Fugue a lot. (Mr. Serkin played the fugue's first theme on the table, staccato.) You play the theme staccato? I played it legato à la Bülow. But now that I think of it, staccato makes good sense, contrasting with the legato, chromatic second fugue theme.

That's the wonderful thing with Bach. He can be played in so many different ways and still sound right.

Even the Swingle Singers or the Jacques Loussier trio can't hurt Bach's music. On the contrary, their recordings perhaps create interest for the real thing. What do you think of Rosalyn Tureck's Bach?

I've heard Tureck in Beethoven but not in Bach.

She plays fast scales staccato, the opening of the third movement of the Italian Concerto, for example, which you said you play slower than formerly.

I believe, generally speaking, that scales in Bach should be legato. There is the confirmation in the few markings we have by Bach. He writes staccato on some scales to indicate the exception. You shouldn't strive for pseudo-harpsichord effects on the piano. I find the harpsichord effective in a small room, but in general I prefer Bach played on the piano. If Bach had had our piano, he would have liked it. We should use our piano's resources, with a stylistically smaller framework, as I said before.

Do you find Glenn Gould's Bach eccentric?

Yes, but he's always musical and spontaneous.

Always? Did you read what he wrote in HIGH FIDELITY about piecing together several takes of the A minor Fugue from the first volume of the Well-Tempered Clavier to achieve a different approach to various sections of the fugue?

You're right there. I heard him in a BBC broadcast; he said ridiculous things, which made one mad. But then at the end he played, and everything was all right. I think he tries to shock. But I am really very fond of Glenn; he's, perhaps, in a transitory period, but I believe he will come out all right.

The Beethoven Sonatas

Mr. Serkin, you will play Beethoven's 32 piano sonatas at Carnegie Hall this season, the fourth of the eight concerts falling on December 16, the 200th anniversary of Beethoven's birth. What are the first things to consider in Beethoven performance?

Before you can begin to talk about other important things, you have to consider faithfulness to the text and personal involvement in the music, which we talked about in discussing Urtext editions and planning versus inspiration.

What about unified tempo versus changes and fluctuations of tempo in such movements as the first movements of the Waldstein *and* Appassionata *Sonatas?*

For any music, the pulse should remain unified, with a certain flexibility. In the *Appassionata* or the *Waldstein* Sonatas, I think a tempo that is not unified is a crime. I know that many musicians think it should be different, but I get confused when I hear a performance with a tempo that is not unified. There can be beautiful moments in such performances, but the end result sounds like a rhapsodic architecture, to me at least. The ideal would be to combine both: to play in time without making the listener feel it is in time. But that's not easy.

Toscanini compared a movement's tempo to a glove: the tempo has to fit the five fingers. If some spot doesn't fit, you are wrong.

Schnabel, too, certainly believed in unified tempo. He marked tempo changes in his edition to indicate a certain flexibility — that's all. He told me he didn't want anyone to play the tempo changes as he had marked them. He didn't mean different tempi; he meant give and take. Besides, later he disapproved of his editions.

There is a quote in George Marek's new book, Beethoven: Biography of a Genius, *which shows that Beethoven believed in unified tempo. Marek quotes Thayer as saying "that at a quartet performance, although Beethoven was so deaf he could no longer hear the heavenly sound of his compositions, with close attention his eyes followed the bows and therefore he was able to judge the smallest fluctuations in tempo or rhythm and correct them immediately."*

Yes . . . and I personally think that Beethoven was not completely deaf. I really do. It happens sometimes that people cannot hear speech, but they can still hear music. I have experienced this with friends. They were almost completely deaf, but when it came to music they could hear.

Mr. Serkin, I'd like to ask you about a few miscellaneous interpretative problems, which would be of help to students and teachers: Do you play the second phrases of Opus 14, no. 2, softer, louder, or the same?

I play them the same. Actually I phrase four bars.

In measures 15 et al. of the same sonata, do you play the first notes, the appoggiatura notes, or the second notes louder?

The first note has to be slightly louder, definitely, because it is a *Vorhalt,* an appoggiatura.

In the repeat of the exposition in the Pathetique *Sonata, why do you repeat the Grave introduction? You can argue that since Beethoven omits the Grave idea in the recapitulation, he wanted the repeat to start only from the Allegro; to repeat the Grave would make the exposition too long in relation to the other sections.*

I repeat the Grave introduction, first of all, because the music says to repeat from the beginning. There is no repeat sign at the beginning of the Allegro. Henle should not have put the repeat sign in.

The form is ABABACB Coda. You have A, the Grave; B, the Allegro; then A and B repeat. Then you have shortened A Grave, C the development, then B, and the Coda. Beethoven used the same form in the later quartets.

Regarding piano subitos — Ivan Moravec, the Czech pianist, said in an interview that the crescendo in measures 71 to 77 in the first movement of Opus 28 is a crescendo from pianissimo to piano, and not a crescendo with piano subito. He criticized Backhaus for making a crescendo "far above piano" and then pausing before the piano subito. Do you think he misunderstands Beethoven's piano subito markings?

Literally, on paper, he has a point. It is written pianissimo-crescendo-piano. But these piano subitos are one of Beethoven's most characteristic traits. I make quite a big crescendo and then play piano subito. Besides, when Beethoven wants a little crescendo, he makes a crescendo sign; when he wants a bigger crescendo he write *crescendo* as a word.

Then, Moravec criticizes Kempff for accentuating the third beats in the second theme: "a characteristic from the old school and slightly out of taste," he says. I would certainly play this second theme with emphasis on the third beats.

I would too. The third-beat harmonies are so beautiful, so strange. Opus 28 is one of the most beautiful of the Beethoven sonatas.

In the last movement of the Appassionata, *why did Beethoven mark the development and recapitulation sections to be repeated and not the exposition? I don't believe any other sonata movement is marked to repeat its second half and not its first.*

Beethoven wanted to balance the first movement in weight. Even if the last movement is played Allegro ma non troppo, as I try to do, it must be repeated. Beethoven demands the repeat: in the original manuscript he says in Italian *"la seconda parte due volte,"* "the second part twice."

Do you remember when you first learned the Appassionata?

I must have learned it rather late. I learned the famous sonatas such as the *Moonlight* and *Les Adieux* comparatively late. I am sure I was twenty-five or more.

However, I played the *Hammerklavier* Sonata at an early age. I probably played it terribly, but I played it. You can't start too young on such a work. I learned it in Vienna when I was sixteen or seventeen. Eusebius Mandyczewski, a teacher at the Vienna Conservatory, was there. I remember the look he gave me, saying, "You will play it well some day."

Martin Cooper, in his book, Beethoven, The Last Decade 1817-1827, *discusses the opening tempo of the* Hammerklavier *Sonata at length. Do you think Beethoven's metro-*

nome marking for the first movement should be followed?

I don't think so; I think somehow it got down wrong. But like many of Beethoven's metronome markings, it is hard to talk about because if you feel it, you think suddenly that Beethoven was right.

You know Czerny's book on how to interpret Beethoven's works. There are all the major works where piano is involved; Czerny gives metronome markings as he thought he remembered Beethoven played and performed them. In studying this book, I have been pleased because many of the markings are the ones I use. This is really no scientific proof; but if it confirms what you like, you think it's right. And certainly in the first movement of the *Hammerklavier* Sonata, I see no possibility to make it clear to the listener if you follow Beethoven's metronome marking of 138 to the half note.

Schubert Interpretation

Mr. Serkin, in your recording of the Schubert A major posthumous sonata, it seems to me you emphasize robustness, Schubert's proximity to Beethoven.

The A major Sonata is a gigantic symphony. When it says fortissimo, I try to play fortissimo.

Schubert has been called "the most otherworldly of the great composers."

Perhaps because of the last B-flat Sonata. Otherworldly can apply to Mozart too — the last B-flat Piano Concerto is kind of a stratosphere. In fact, otherworldliness can apply to quite a few late works of various composers, Brahms, for example. I don't mean that later works are any better necessarily than early works. But there is something very special in certain late works — the Beethoven Diabelli Variations and late quartets, the last three sonatas and string quintet of Schubert, and the last concerto of Mozart.

What do you strive for in Schubert slow movements?

For each type of slow movement, there is a different answer. Singing is what most of them have in common. Then we come back to phrasing. Singing and phrasing are probably the same thing. If you have a long breath you can get a bigger line.

What about subduing the accompanying parts of a melody versus a chamber-music approach, in the slow movement of the A major Sonata, for example?

If the lower parts are really accompaniment, I believe in subduing them. But the A major Sonata slow movement is different. I would compare it to a string trio. Musically speaking, there is no borderline between piano and string quartet.

Chopin Interpretation

In connection with rubato you mentioned you could never feel much difference between Mozart and Chopin.

Yes, Chopin in many ways is closer to Bach and Mozart than to the Romantics. For me, he is one of the greatest composers, something that the public doesn't always realize because the brilliance and sonority in his music perhaps sidetracks from its depth.

In Chopin interpretation, as in any interpretation, first you have to be faithful to the text. I feel certain liberties have got out of hand by tradition. Maybe Clara Schumann made a little rubato, and the next one who liked her rubato made still more. A lot of liberties today are, for my feeling, distortions. And I believe in the greatest liberties; there is nothing worse than a strait-jacket kind of music making.

We know that Chopin played his music rather disciplined. We know that because he told his students to play it strict. But again if it is a strait jacket, it is certainly the greatest crime against spirit, though it's very hard to put into words.

But sometimes you hear Chopin played with absolute distortions. If one bar suddenly lasts twice as long as the bar before and there is not indication at all by the composer, it distorts, it breaks the line. In other words, some students believe anything is allowed — "no holds barred," as they say in wrestling.

Teaching

Mr. Serkin, do you think great pianists have a moral obligation to teach, to pass down their traditions?

Yes, we have the obligation to teach whatever we have to give. Most great pianists have the desire. In Russia they all have to teach. Richter doesn't teach any more, but the others do. Horowitz enjoys teaching, if he gets the right student.

Humorous Moments

Do you remember any humorous incidents in your career?

Plenty, as you can imagine in fifty years of concertizing. Once I played in an open-air concert in Salzburg on a piano that had stood in the sun. When I started to play, a chicken flew out.

Another time, in Geneva, I couldn't practice in the hall the day of my concert because a ballet was performing. At my concert, in the evening, the piano sounded choked. As I continued to play, I saw something sticking out of the sounding board. So after the first movement, I quickly pulled the thing out — and it was the corset of a ballet dancer.

And still another time — when I was playing a concerto, the back leg of the piano cave in. I tried to keep on playing, even with the keyboard tilted dangerously. But the audience thought it terribly funny and roared!

Amidst laughter and handshakes, Mr. Serkin excused himself and rushed off to a quartet rehearsal. As I was leaving, my eye caught a plaque, lying on a chair, which reminded me of his farm near Marlboro, that his life in Vermont is not all music making. "To Rudolf Serkin in recognition of superior quality performance for outstanding achievement during the year 1966 as a producer of high quality milk for H. P. Hood & Sons," it said.

Lili Kraus...

Regal Lady of the Keyboard

interview November 30, 1969

Lili Kraus belongs to that breed of artists who make a concert an "event." Always gorgeously gowned, she is the actress-artist par excellence, exploring in words and in sound the gamut of music's heights and depths. Her long career includes early Parlophone recordings, wartime Japanese imprisonment, and recording the complete Mozart Sonatas and Concertos besides playing over 100 concerts a year. At 72 years of age she seems at the height of her powers, apt to outswim her hosts the day of a concert. And she is one of the warmest, most articulate, and compassionate human beings.

How would you describe the evolution of your career?

You know the biography — the facts are so rich that I could write a book. I am ever and again asked to do so, but so far I haven't had the time. Perhaps when I cease to careen over the face of the earth, I will one day settle down and write my autobiography.

But the essential details about my career are these: ever since I can remember — which goes back to age three — music was in my blood, in every fiber of my body and in every recess of my soul and spirit. I really manifested my musicality first through dancing. My mother told me that whenever I heard music, in the street or in the park, I danced.

There is a charming story by Gottfried Keller, the Swiss novelist and poet, called *Tanzlegende* which means the legend of the dance. In this story a little girl dances in front of the altar as her religious offering to Maria. She is caught, and the people accuse her of heresy. And then Maria comes down from the altar and folds the little girl in her cloak.

Like this little girl, I was compelled to dance whenever I heard music. Then when I was six my mother decided I should learn to play the piano. I really wanted to play the violin, but I am sure she was instrumental in the plans of the Lord as we all are. So the piano it was.

I am infinitely grateful to her because the piano is the only instrument except the organ that doesn't need the support of another instrument to produce polyphony. And if I recall how often I have heard violinists or cellists accompanied miserably, I am thankful this was not my fate. For perhaps I would have ended on the gallows for having murdered those accompanists! But I am not of a violent disposition, by the way.

Then I was fortunate in having the most all-around training imaginable. When I was eight, I was admitted to the Royal Academy of Music in Budapest (the normal age of admittance is 14), and I studied with a direct pupil of Busoni. Before I left the Academy I studied with Bartók and theory with Kodaly.

I went to Vienna when I was 18 and studied with a Leschetizky pupil who hasn't become famous because he lost his memory through shell shock in the First World War and couldn't perform freely. But at 23 he was head of the master class at the Berlin Academy, so you can imagine what kind of a musician and pianist he was.

I studied contemporary music in Vienna with Edward Steuermann, the friend and disciple of Schönberg. And finally, when I was already a full-fledged artist and had played with many orchestras, I studied with Schnabel. Schnabel then remained a life-long friend. Shortly before he died, he told me he considered me his only spiritual heir.

So from my 18th year I never ceased to play, to perform, to record, and to teach. I had my first pupil, who was five, when I was eight. And I had my next pupil, who was 45, when I was 11. I got this pupil through the Academy where the names, but not the ages, of the most talented students were on the blackboard. This lady was vastly astonished when she found at her doorstep a child, announcing in a tiny voice: "I am your new piano teacher." But we got along famously.

To this day I consider it both my privilege and my God-willed function to share all I was given and all I am able to impart — and that includes teaching as well. I would consider it a grave failing if I withheld the knowledge gathered in my life instead of having it carried forward by those I teach.

What pieces did you study as a child, and what did you play on your first recital?

The head of the Budapest Academy was Kálmán Chován, and we played his pieces predominantly. Then of course we played Jensen, Hummel, Bertini, the small Mozart pieces, and the Anna Magdalena Bach. On my first recital, when I was eight, I played two pieces from the Schumann "Album for the Young," that charming little Mozart minuet, and the little G Minor Minuet of Bach's from the Anna Magdalena book. My teacher took the pedal for me because my feet wouldn't reach.

Do you remember how you practiced as a child?

I remember very well. First of all I had on the one hand the good fortune, and on the other hand the ill fortune to have a mother who was exceedingly talented and musical but who had never studied music. In those days to be a singer was the next worst thing to being an old maid.

So, my mother, who understood music instinctively but had no idea about piano playing and had been thwarted in her own ambitions, centered all her ambitions on me. I could never really practice alone, carefree as I would have loved to do. I was always under surveillance but without expert advice.

Now this was a two-edged sword and a two-sided blessing: from the beginning my study was regular but somewhat hemmed-in. Later my mother's influence had one terrible disadvantage: when I was at the Academy I adored chamber music (Leo Weiner was head of the chamber music department), but my mother considered it a waste of time. And therefore I had to go unprepared to the chamber music classes when I would have loved to spend much more time on this literature.

Later on, however, when I was an artist I made up for lost time, for years having this duo with Szymon Goldberg. And the Kraus-Goldberg duo, as you know, was a household word.

How do you practice now?

I never think of my work as practice. Practice somehow has the overtone of going over and over things, hoping to get the tempo. My work is not like that. I call what I am doing solid work, and it consists of many types of activities. First of all, before I approach a piece on the piano, I have lived with it for at least months and possibly years. The literature is big enough to allow for that. Secondly, there are certain parts in a composition which immediately, long before I materialize them, are clear and want to be played. And that's it. For instance, big sections of a theme are often so clear in my head that I can play them on the piano without any trouble, but I might have to work for hours on a short shake. You remember the Opus 96 Sonata in G Major for piano and violin by Beethoven: it starts first with that shake on the violin and the piano answers.

When I recorded this work at the E.M.I. studios in London, I had the run of the place; they allowed me to come at any time. I remember I went there one night with my husband at 10 o'clock and left at one in the morning, and I worked on this shake and this shake only.

Now someone outside and uninitiated might think that I was demented, but I wasn't. This shake

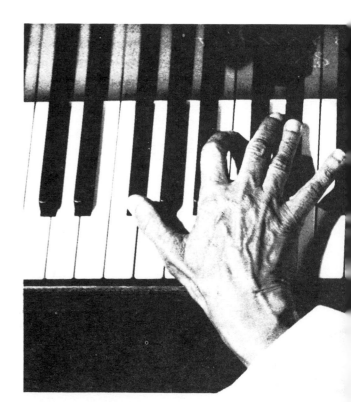

or trill had to speak in a certain way, and boy did I ever learn to play short shakes ever since! No trouble. So it works this way sometimes: one four-note section of a passage or 16 sixteenth notes might cause insurmountable difficulties. Why I don't know. The slightest difficult spot that "doesn't walk in the light before the Lord" casts its shadow on the piece. And such shadows had best be eliminated. I haven't worked on a scale, or octaves, or double thirds *per se* for 30 years.

In other words, you practice difficulties from the interpretative point of view.

Yes, always from that point of view. But of course for the interpretation to appear in immaculate truthfulness, technical supremacy is indispensable. Therefore, my practicing includes technical work and hard drudging drills all the time, but never divorced from the text. In the really great works of music even a scale has something to say. And I assure myself the luxury of playing only the great works of music.

How do you memorize?

Memorize — there again I don't know that word. By the time I can produce what I want to hear, by the time I am satisfied with the interpretation and it is technically correct, I have known it a long time by heart.

Do you have a photographic memory?

I have an excellent visual memory, but when I am playing I try to eliminate it because I want to remember with my ear, not my eye. I don't want to see the music but to hear it, to live it. I have to remember the sound and identify with the harmonic, thematic, rhythmic, and mechanical aspects so completely that I don't want to see the picture.

Does seeing the printed music hinder your hearing it?

Not exactly, but it might hinder my being carried beyond the page into the realm where I want to live when I perform.

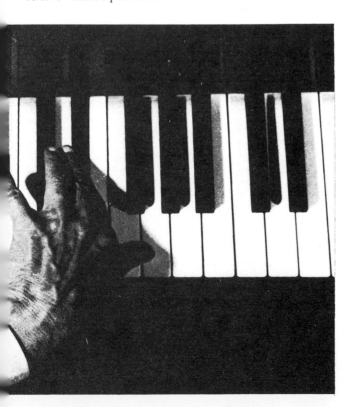

What advice can you give for memorizing?

I think that every musician when asked this question can have only one answer: the student or the artist must know the piece from every aspect — harmonically, melodically, and rhythmically. The harmonic life is the "key" in a classical composition. And then the student must analyze the piece formally and master it technically so that hesitation doesn't enter. But first and last, a reliable memory is possible only if an absolute identification with the piece in living experience has taken place.

However, even these "moorings" do not guarantee absolute security because such a thing doesn't exist. Even a man like Schnabel who could perform all the Beethoven Sonatas once simply broke off in the middle of the "Hammerklavier" and said, "Allow me to play another sonata. I can't play this one today." And it was a proverb that no concert of Cortot's ever took place without his getting stuck. To my best recollection Gieseking never had memory lapses, but he had a very special kind of memory.

So, my final point about memorizing is that almost no memorizing is 100% secure. Memory depends on the person, the performance, and the state of the person's nerves.

What is your approach to interpretation?

This is a crucial question. At my age this is the sum total of my life's experiece: that what you call a great interpretation must go far beyond not only the instrument but the music itself, and great music tries to manifest nothing less than the cosmos. This cosmos includes all that exists: the music of the spheres in all its appearances whether water, wind, bird, noise, storm, lightning, thunder, or the sweetest rustling of the leaf. Great composers like Bach, Mozart, Haydn, and Beethoven, of course, had such fine perception and heard these things within themselves so clearly they could give them immortal form.

In interpreting a piece you have to feel the entire cosmos; through endless research you have to penetrate to the core of the matter and then wed the spirit you find therein with your own into one indivisible whole. Otherwise, you do what Beethoven in one of his letters despised: "The interpreter must be absolutely faithful to the written text; he must neither omit nor add even an iota of what he sees. But if he does nothing else but this, he renders very poor service to music indeed." Now this quote answers exactly what I call "big" interpretation which is my aim and for which I live.

You once mentioned a particular performance as an example of Beethoven's quote.

Yes, this particular performance related everything about the music except its essence. It was correct, beautifully-rendered, and quite musical, but it was never sad, gay, impetuous, or playful. There was no sin committed against phrasing or against understanding of musical matters. But music goes far beyond that, and no more was forthcoming.

One of the wonderful things about music is that many approaches to interpretation are possible. Some critics, unfortunately, push just for one kind of playing.

Today's critics get their information mostly from gramophone records and from the contemporary output which is, except for a few exceptions, cut off from the great tradition.

Great music blossomed from a completely different source of information and inspiration than today's music. Those were not technological days. When Beethoven composed his "Pastorale," he could walk for 20 minutes out of Vienna and be in utter stillness, stillness filled with the music which existed in nature and in him.

When the great composers demanded "molto espressivo, molto cantabile, or andante amoroso," they meant that these should be the emotions of the players. If Mozart writes "amoroso," as he does for the second movement of his Sonata K. 281, he wants to hear the music filled with love.

It was Goethe, I think, who said "the hallmark of genius is love." If you don't have that love in you, how can you express it? If you have it but are afraid to express it, how can the listener receive this message? So I think that when an audience is thrilled for technical reasons, this thrill is on the surface. When listeners are moved because they have received the performer's emotional message, this is both elating and lasting.

Speaking of recordings, two of the first I ever bought were your Parlophone recordings of the Beethoven Eroica Variations *and the Mozart B♭ Concerto, K. 456.*

Oh you remember them! You know in those days there were only two papers in London that wrote about gramophone records in a serious way: the *Gramophone* and *The Statesman and Nation.* Edward Sackville-West of *The New Statesman* said, "Although the Schnabel recording of the *Eroica Variations* is really superb, I prefer the Kraus." Reading this made me shiver, very happy.

You have said it takes a lifetime to simplify, to find the essence of what is happening in classical music.

What I mean by "simplifying" is that the more concise the music, the more economic the means must be to bring the message across. If you really understand the message, you don't have to gild the lily. No dynamics or agogic effects other than what you would use to bring to life a Shakespearean text need be employed for clearest articulation and deepest emotional projection.

Take a piece like Mozart's *A Minor Rondo* which is his only composition with dynamic indications in almost every bar. With the utmost precision, Mozart writes to the sixteenth note where a crescendo will start. This kind of detailed dynamic notation doesn't exist in any other Mozart piece. So Mozart was particularly bent on giving expression to what he thought and wanted to be expressed. But if you take these dynamic markings at their face value and play actual *forte*, actual *crescendo*, actual *piano*, you break the piece into a thousand little bits. It took me almost a lifetime to

understand that all these markings are grades of expression and are only infinitesimal diminishments or infinitesimal augmentations to bring home the sense of the happening.

Now this is simplification because you bring it down to a minimum instead of blowing it up to a maximum. Not every piece is like this. Beethoven asks for a maximum *espressivo* when he writes *fortissimo*; but there again instead of bodily volume *per se*, you must reach a climax in keeping with the sense of the text. Open the bars. Let the music either soar or thunder, but not with a conscious effort to play a *fortissimo* for its own sake. In other words, the dynamics must be a result of your desire to bring the work to life and never a means to prettify, to diversify, or to make amusing or interesting.

Among today's great artists, you are perhaps the only one who prefaces the actual playing with commentaries. What is your feeling about expressing the meaning of a work in words?

Expressing the meaning of music in words is an easy task if you know the literature, for almost all composers at one time or another have put words to their musical symbols: Mozart in his operas, Schubert in his songs, Beethoven in his Mass, Bach in his cantatas. There is practically no composer who hasn't written abstract music, for example, Mendelssohn in his "Songs Without Words," that could not easily be paralleled in already-existing texts.

Now why is expressing the meaning in words so helpful? Because if someone has a completely wrong feeling for a passage, words will help. For example, in Brazil a very talented student of mine asked, "Oh, will you play that lovely, gay Mozart Sonata in A Minor?"

"The gay one? Which one do you mean?"

And then she sang like a bird, without a care in the world, the first theme of the A Minor Sonata, K. 310:

"You call that gay?" I asked. "Yes, it's very gay, isn't it, like a march?" she said.

Now even if one didn't know Mozart composed this sonata right after the death of his mother, and disregarding the revealing fact that it's the only sonata that bears the indication "Allegro maestoso" and one of the two minor-key sonatas in all the 17, one should still feel that this is an epitaph, a tragic piece. But okay, let's assume you don't. Then words can be of great help to describe what it all means. Schnabel used to improvise texts for almost all the music he taught, and his texts were extremely helpful.

Is smaller-unit phrasing more important for the classics and big-line phrasing for the romantics?

What is more important — to speak a whole sentence or to articulate syllables? The big line, of course, is absolutely indispensable. You articulate details to bring the whole sentence to life. The only reason for articulating in small units is to enable the big line to emerge. The big line is just as important to the classics as to the romantics; and for this big line to emerge and come to life, attention to detail is indispensable.

You seemed to conceive the Waldstein Sonata dramatically, more in the style of the Appassionata than in terms of something burgeoning, something having to do with nature and the sunrise.

Beethoven never called it the "Spring Sonata." This is a nickname given afterwards. I don't go along with this burgeoning, but I do imagine it as the first day of creation with the pulsating heart in the beats at the beginning where nothing has crystallized yet. This sonata is dramatic; and although spring is at times dramatic, I don't associate this sonata with spring.

You don't see the sun rising at the beginning of the last movement?

Yes, but that's not spring; it could be any beautiful sunrise. No, I don't feel it that way.

It bothers me that certain critics deplore what they call "the Dresden doll" approach to Mozart, saying Mozart should be played big, with lots of pedal.

Such an approach is of course utterly false. But it is important not to mix up two things: Mozart should be big in emotional content. It shouldn't have little or much pedal; it should have the right amount of pedal. As you know, the Mozart piano had two unconnected pedals. The left hand, therefore, could produce uninterrupted harmonies without interfering with the melodic line. But since we can't do this, I play the left hand, say an Alberti bass, with absolute legato by holding down the fingers. The left hand sounds swimming in pedal, but there is not a drop of pedal. The right hand is then free to move as it wants. In Mozart there should never be one moment that obscures a running passage or robs us of the harmonic continuity.

Mozart must have all the greatness of Beethoven, but with diminished means. The whole difficulty in Mozart is that you have to pretend a loud *forte*, and this pretence must come from an intensity, a relative strength, vitality, and dramatic power rather than actual body volume.

You mentioned in one of your concerts that the first theme of the second movement of Beethoven's Pathetique Sonata has an identical melodic line as the theme in the middle section of the second movement of Mozart's Sonata in C Minor. Did Beethoven emulate Mozart?

Both excerpts have the same climate, thought, and key relationship, and I would give anything to know whether Beethoven took the Mozart theme as a model or whether the two themes are a coincidental similar thought. Nobody will ever know for

sure. But certainly the Beethoven is an absolute replica à la Beethoven of the Mozart theme.

Schubert is sometimes called the most other-worldly of the great composers. Do you agree? Would you comment about playing Schubert?

Schubert, for several reasons, is terribly hard to play. He is the most unpianistic piano composer I know. It must be that he wasn't a piano virtuoso, like Mozart or Beethoven, and didn't care so much for piano sound. I would say he wrote against rather than for the piano, but when you master his writing, it sounds more pianistic than almost any other piano music, except perhaps that of Chopin.

The other-worldliness is perfectly true and is a very good description of Schubert — so other-worldly because genius in its most childlike form is other-wordly. Schubert's genius is not tinged by experience, artfulness, or acquired knowledge; it is a first-time emanation, not yet schooled.

The handful of friends that Schubert had are all agreed that he had a most childlike, innocent nature. He was utterly incapable of a lie, malice, or simulation. Indeed the miracle of his music is that, like his life, everything was a first-time happening, with the same freshness and new marvel of the child experiencing for the first time.

When I think of Schubert, my heart is so brimming over with love and compassion that sometimes I can hardly bear it. But loving and understanding him is not enough. He really does present enormous problems. In his music the harmonic life of the piece is more moved, rich, and irrational than in any other composer's music I know. To be constantly aware of all this and yet not betray that you are is one of the difficulties in playing Schubert. The other difficulty is to avoid sentimentality, because Schubert was never sentimental, and to be as passionate as was his heart, but without show.

I enjoyed your Chopin. It was good to hear Chopin played with fire, without the contours filed down. Do you play much Chopin?

I used to. Between my 18th and 23rd years I was known as a Chopin player. At that time my hair was very long, and I wore huge hairpins to pin it up. By the end of a Chopin program, the hair was down and the hairpins all around me — very romantic. I am sure people thought, "if that isn't the real Chopin, what is!"

I love to play Chopin and would play much more if it weren't for the fact that life is too short and I am asked to play other kinds of music as well. But I would like to make clear that Chopin is not so near my heart as these other composers simply for the fact that I need that cast of mind which includes the symphonic, polyphonic imagination of these other composers. Chopin was a piano composer *par excellence,* and somehow I am always hesitant to offer even the Chopin Concerti to an orchestra because the orchestra has so little to do.

What are some of the qualities of the great pianists?

Their qualities are as manifold as there are pianists. They should have application, passion, understanding, very likely technique. But the common denominator is indeed their involvement and identification with the music and the extent to which they can project this identification.

Should a great pianist have great passion for playing the piano?

No, for music. There is a great, great difference. From what I gather a man like Lhevinne — whom I didn't have the pleasure of knowing or hearing — had a great passion for playing the piano, but not for music. Horowitz is more triggered, luckily in a very demonic way, more by his desire to play the piano than by music, whereas with Schnabel it was just the other way around. Schnabel's first and last concern was the music which he eventually put into words through the medium of the piano. Backhaus was similar.

What are your ideals of tone?

That's a good question. There are singers, for instance, who have a golden tone, a gorgeous sound. But if this tone factor is the focus of their interest and not what the music wants to say, after awhile their singing becomes boring. A pianist, of course, yearns to produce the most beautiful, singing, unpercussive sound possible, and that is one's greatest challenge. On the piano, as you know, the individual note dies at its birth, but in great music, all kinds of sound must be found and produced. Harsh, percussive, impatient, pleading, anxious sound — all of this — must go into what you are saying because this is what the music says.

To be able to produce this great variety of tone you must have much more at your command than just the general use of color. You must have a million shades as needed to give the composition its due. I always use weight. Only the speed with which I make the contact on the key varies, and this safeguards the beauty and roundness of the tone because I never hit the key. Such increases or decreases in tone are produced always with the maintenance of weight, firmness of finger, but with varying speeds of contact.

I assume that conveying the content of the music is more important to you than imbuing everything with a certain kind of pianistic tone.

You are perceptive to recognize this. Striving for a certain kind of tone is not paramount with me. My absolutely first consideration is to express what the music says. ∎

Memories of Ravel

Gaby Casadesus

interview January 5, 1975

Gaby Casadesus and her husband, the late Robert Casadesus

"Don't slow down," Ravel said. "This is something very gay, gay, gay!"

Madame Gaby Casadesus was reminiscing about the time she played *Jeux d'eau* for Ravel. This vivacious woman, with her easy smile and large expressive eyes, was preparing for the Robert Casadesus Ravel Centenary Piano Competition at the Cleveland Institute of Music. She was also looking forward to her summer master classes at Fontainebleau and the Académie Ravel in Saint-Jean-de-Luz. "I started teaching at the Académie Ravel two years ago, since I knew I was one of the few musicians still living who had known and played for Ravel," she said. "Also, my husband had played much Ravel in recording, in concertizing, and in traveling with him."

A distinguished pianist, Gaby Casadesus, nee Gabrielle L'Hôte, — who studied with Marguérite Long, Diémer, Moszkowski, and Risler — continues to concertize as well as teach. She had recently played at the Kennedy Center and the Library of Congress in Washington and had also recorded the *Etudes* and the *Fourth Sonata* of her late husband for Columbia Records. "I try to do as much French music and the works of my husband as possible. I think that this is now my line of life," she said to me as we conversed in the elegant drawing room of the estate outside Philadelphia where Mme Casadesus was visiting her daughter's family.

Her lucid memories continued to effervesce, with very little questioning needed on my part. She spoke of how she first played for Ravel in 1919 in the salon of her teacher Mme Long. Ravel had been invited for lunch, after which Mme Long was inspired to ask pupils to play for the composer.

"As he was smoking a cigarette and having coffee," Mme Casadesus recalled, "I played *Jeux d'eux*." His comments, which appear near the end of this article, are still clearly etched in her memory, as are

the remarks he made when she played *Alborada del gracioso* as she was finishing at the Conservatoire in 1920, a year before she married Robert Casadesus.

"My husband met Ravel for the first time in 1922 when he played *Valses nobles et sentimentales* and *Gaspard de la nuit* in a concert of modern music at the *Vieux Colombier* in Paris. Ravel was so enthusiastic that he asked my husband to make some piano rolls of his music in London. Ravel was too out of practice to make all the rolls himself. My husband played the *Miroirs* and *Gaspard*, and Ravel played the easier pieces. I don't know where the rolls are. We never got them from the company, which was named Aeolian.

"Ravel did not have time to practice the piano. He said to me once, as we were having dinner in the Fournier home, 'I must practice. I want to play my new *Concerto* which I am writing for myself. Maybe I will go to Mme Marguérite Long for some technical exercises. I need them badly.' But in the end, Mme Long premiered the *Concerto* and Ravel conducted.

"During our week's stay in London to make the piano rolls, we spent a memorable evening in Mme Allevard's home. The concert that evening in her salon was marvelous. Ravel started with his *Sonatine*. Then my husband played some of *Le Tombeau de Couperin*, Mme Allevard sang some songs, and Jelly d'Aranyi and Hans Kindler (who became the conductor of the Washington, D.C., Symphony) gave the first performance in London of the wonderful *Duo* for violin and cello.

"After supper, throughout the night until early morning, Ravel asked d'Aranyi, a young Hungarian gypsy, to play some gypsy melodies. The girl was perhaps 17 or 18 years old, dressed with a Spanish shawl, and was a very remarkable violinist. Each time she stopped, Ravel asked for more.

"Upon our return to Ravel's house in Montfort l'Amaury, Ravel composed *Tzigane*. We saw the birth of this composition. I will never forget Ravel's excitement at hearing this gypsy music, and then afterwards rushing home to write. He was not only able to *enregistrer*, to record in his mind what he was hearing, but he was also able to recreate it after that. *Tzigane* is dedicated to d'Aranyi."

She spoke again of her husband who was the first to record all of Ravel's piano music. "My husband was also the first to give an all-Ravel program in Paris. Ravel was there. That was in 1922 at the Salle Pleyel. He played *Miroirs, Gaspard de la Nuit, Valses nobles et sentimentales,* and the *Prélude, Menuet, Forlane,* and *Toccata* from *Le Tombeau de Couperin.* Robert did not like so much the *Fugue* from *Le Tombeau.* Now that I am teaching the *Fugue,* I think it is interesting. All of *Le Tombeau* is very beautiful but not so outstanding as the *Miroirs. Le Tombeau* was written later in homage to Couperin.

"When Ravel was going to write his two concerti, he asked Mr. Durand of the Durand publishing house to send him all the Mozart and Saint-Saëns concerti. 'I want to have them when I write my concerti,' he said. I suppose he played them to see how they were made. His concertos, however, are very different from those of Mozart and Saint-Saëns. Nevertheless, it is interesting to see how he was impressed by something and then proceeded to create his own work.

"When we were traveling, Ravel often said, 'You have to work in composing, not just let inspiration come.' His works are all more or less in classical form although he did not call them sonatas. He did not compose in an improvisatory way as Debussy did sometimes. His concertos likewise are in classical form."

I commented, "Roland-Manuel wrote that 'Ravel made music as easily as an apple-tree grows apples,' and that 'in some compositions Ravel sketched out the whole composition, where he was going to have this or that key, before he put in any of the themes.'"

"I heard him say that every note was in his head before he wrote them down," replied Mme Casadesus. "So maybe when he was in front of the paper, the compositional process went fast. He said, 'I don't compose every day. I just think of composing.' He was a very bad sleeper. He was unable to sleep well for many years. He went to live in the country because of his insomnia. 'I have too much noise in Paris,' he said. 'I go too late at night with my friends. I want to retire in the country so I will be able to sleep and have a normal life during the day.' But he was unable to sleep there too. He composed during the night in his head. He was extremely careful of every detail.

"In certain ways he was a very nervous man. I remember his saying, 'Oh, it's too bad, I've signed a contract with Monsieur Durand. I have to give them two or three works during the year. I'm sure I will be unable to do it. The thought is driving me mad.'

"I attended the premiere of the *Chansons madécasses* in 1925 at the Hotel Majestique in Paris. Parny wrote the French translations of the Madagascar folk-song texts. The second of these three songs is more or less a cry, the exclamation of *l'esclave,* the slave against the white. 'Les blancs nous ont menti . . .' (The whites lied to us. We are not free, we are slaves.) After the performance, amidst the great applause,

Léon Moreau — a composer, I believe — shouted, 'I don't understand people who think the blacks are marvelous. Look what they are doing to our men at war in Morocco.' Some people were for Ravel, shouting 'Ravel, bravo Ravel, bravo Ravel.' Others were against him, shouting 'Bravo Moreau, you are right. It's a disgrace to compose such a piece.'

"I am sure Ravel didn't understand what was going on at first. He had written this work without any feeling about the war in Morocco. He had just become enthusiastic about this poetry written by a man who said the whites did not do what they should for the blacks. In 1910 Ravel had aligned himself with a group called 'Les Apaches' who were against the bourgeoisie. He had always been in advance of his time."

Ravel had a tendency to be somewhat retiring. "He did not like to answer questions, to talk about his work. For example, in London, if someone would ask 'What, Maestro, are you going to compose now?' — Ravel would say, 'Give me a cigarette, Robert, will you?' "

He was also uncomfortable with too much attention. "My husband and I were in Ciboure in 1930 when they were honoring Ravel by putting a plaque on the house in which he was born. First an outstanding team played *pelote-basque,* a Basque ball game, outside for an hour. Ravel, who was typically Basque, was very excited about the game. After that there was music and speech-making in front of the house. Ravel took my husband and me by the arm and said, 'Let's go drink something at the café next door. I don't want to be here. I hate this kind of official gathering.' Ravel didn't like being with a lot of people. He was shy in a way.

"So we had a drink and afterwards a big lunch. In the evening there was a concert in Biarritz. My husband played some of *Le Tombeau de Couperin* and with Ravel as usual *Ma Mère l'Oye.* Madeleine Grey sang the *Chansons madécasses,* and Thibaud played the violin sonata with Ravel." (See illustrating program and letter.)

"Ravel was always searching for something new. Around 1924, when we were crossing on the boat, he said, 'Oh, I can't do any more Ravel. I have to go ahead with something new. I can't write more works in the same style as *Daphnis et Chloé* or the *Rapsodie espagnole.* I have to change my style because time goes.' He would never repeat the successes of his life.

"He was fond of mechanical and exotic things. He gave me a Chinese doll. He had a mechanical bird in a cage which was made in Switzerland. What tune this bird sang I don't know. But he kept it on his desk when he was composing. He had a lot of mechanical things in his house. When you went to see him, he didn't want to speak about his music. He wanted to show you how these mechanical things worked.

"His father was an engineer, in charge of building the railroad in Spain, not a Swiss watchmaker as some people believe. His father was also a good musician. But maybe his grandfather was some kind of watchmaker because Ravel, in the way he composed so much in details, was like a watchmaker."

When asked if Ravel ever fell in love, she replied, "He was devoted to all his family — his mother,

Program of a recital given August 24, 1930, to celebrate the placing of a plaque on the house in Ciboure, where Ravel was born. Concerning it, Ravel sent a hand-written letter, dated August 1, to Casadesus. A portion of the letter is reproduced at right. The text, translated read:

Dear friend,

Mapou has sent me an eight-page letter with margins for the answers, requesting immediately the programs for the press. A little of the program must be scratched out. I've had to arrange this myself because of the rush.

Ma Mere l'Oye will be cut down to *Laideronnette* and *Le Jardin Feerique*. For you, I have removed *Alborada* of which Miss Lamballe dances a part — you know, up to the passage where people applaud prematurely.

I have therefore written *Jeux d'eau, Forlane,* and *Toccata* for you. Is that right? I would be most obliged if you would confirm this promptly by mail to Mapou — Mairie de Ciboure — especially since, facing this fearsome questionnaire, I may have forgotten something.

Thanking you in advance. See you soon. I will be in St.-Jean-de-Luz two days before the concert.

Gratefully yours,
Maurice Ravel

father, brother — and also to some close friends and children. *Ma Mère l'Oye* is dedicated to the two children of the Godebskis, a Polish family in Paris very devoted to Ravel. It is impossible to know what was between these people and Ravel. He was not willing to show his feelings.

"But he loved children, *la jeunesse,* youth. As soon as a child came into the room, he would go 'Ohahhh.' You can see his love of mechanical things and children in *L'Enfant et les Sortilèges* which starts with all the clocks, the playroom full of children. That scene typifies what he was."

I asked if he had long thumbs, as many people say he had. "I don't think his thumbs were especially long." she responded. "He was, however, very stiff in his piano playing. His stiff mechanism was strange considering that you need a very supple wrist to play the *Sonatine,* for example. Ravel used to do difficult techniques better than easy ones. I had the feeling that easy things were not easy for him.

"I think Ravel's not winning the *Prix de Rome* was bad for him. André Caplet got the first prize in 1901, the year Ravel missed getting it. First Ravel got the second prize. Then for three years, until he was 30 and too old to compete, he tried every year but never got the first prize. Caplet as a composer was more conservative than Ravel.

"I remember hearing Caplet and Ravel conduct in the Concerts Colonne. Caplet came out on the stage well-dressed in a formal jacket. Ravel, not wanting to dress the same, wore a gray suit and a colorful cravat. He was chic but eccentric in his dress. He never wore what other men were wearing. Ravel always went to the best tailor, the best shirt maker.

"Perhaps he dressed fastidiously as a reaction to his short, thin physique. Only his face, with its dark, closely-set eyes and clear complexion, was beautiful. Especially when he became white-haired, his face was as if from the time of Rameau — as in the beautiful paintings of LaTour, the eighteenth-century artist. Nonetheless, I think Ravel suffered from his short physique, from not being more athletic looking. He didn't say so, since his sensibility was very great."

Towards the end of his life Ravel began losing his mind. Mme Casadesus recalled that the aging Ravel didn't recognize anyone. "If he went in the street, he didn't know where he was. He was unable to write his name. He didn't recognize his own music. He would say, 'Oh, that is a beautiful piece,' not knowing it was his own.

73

"I heard the premiere in Paris of the *Concerto for the Left Hand* at the Salle Pleyel. Ravel conducted the performance by Paul Wittgenstein, an Austrian pianist who had commissioned the work after losing his right arm in the war. When Ravel came on stage I said, 'What has happened? Ravel looks ten years older than he did last year.'

"After the performance I called my husband, who was in Zürich, to tell him how terrible Ravel looked but also to tell him how beautiful the piece is. I said, 'You must play it as soon as it is free.' (Ravel had given Wittgenstein exclusive permission to play the piece for three years.) It is like *un chant du cygne de Ravel*, Ravel's swansong. We were always enthusiastic about this work.

"The year after this performance, Ravel lost his sanity. Everyone gave him good care. He stayed with his brother in Levallois-Pèreire, a suburb of Paris, instead of going to his own home in Montfort L'Amaury, and his brother was always with him. For two years he had a lovely, relaxed face without any sign of tiredness or worry. But when he shook your hand at a concert, you had the feeling he remembered nothing.

"It was the possibility that a tumor might be the cause of his trouble that made his brother decide on the brain surgery from which Ravel never recovered. Robert went to Ravel's funeral in Levallois. I did not go to the funeral myself. It took place the day before we left to come to America for the first time."

Mme Casadesus clearly recalls the comments Ravel made both times he listened to her performance of his compositions. We discussed *Jeux d'eau* first, which she had played in 1919, and then *Alborada del gracioso* which she played a year later.

Jeux d'eau

M. 1. "Ravel told me not to play too loud, to play the broken chords in an easy way, with a lovely touch. And he said not to forget the Henri de Régnier quotation at the beginning: '*Dieu fluvial riant de l'eau qui le chatouille,*' (A river-God laughing at the waters as they caress him). Ravel wanted the feeling of water falling on this kind of God, a *dieu des grècques*, a bronze statue at Versailles, someone with water falling over his body.

"Almost the first thing Ravel said was 'Don't slow down. This is something very gay, gay, gay!' He wanted the tempo rather formal, without ritardandi at the ends of phrases, always with this gay feeling of water all over the keyboard."

Ms. 13-14. "He wanted the dynamics kept soft for a long time. He did not want crescendo too soon. On the second page you will see crescendo, fortissimo, and forte signs. He did not want the fortissimo and forte to be too strong."

M. 26. "He wanted to save the big fortissimo, which is very strong, for the bottom of page three:"

Ms. 19-20. "Here he stopped me for slowing down the tempo, a normal tendency. 'Don't forget it is "*Dieu fluvial riant de l'eau qui le chatouille,*"' he repeated. 'Don't slow down.'"

*Gaby Casadesus confirms Ravel's desire that this music be played in rather strict, formal tempo. Younger pianists today tend to play Ravel with considerable rubato. For example, a young French pianist who has recorded the Ravel Piano Works for London, says "For me, Ravel is a Romantic. Each time you feel a letting-go, two bars later it is pulled back."—D.E.

Ms. 38-48. "In this passage which starts at measure 38, '*le chant un peu dehors,*' and continues through the glissando in measure 48, Ravel wanted the right-hand fifth-finger melody brought out all the way, but with no ritardandi."*

M. 75. "It is only near the end that you have the expression of a human being in front of this lovely fountain with the water running over the body of this God in bronze. Here Ravel marks, '*Lent, très expressif.*' And it is only for two measures that you have this sensitive, human expression."

Ms. 90-91. "Ravel wanted the end to die away, again *sans ralentir*. It is no real ending. It was unusual to end a piece for the first time like this.

"Ravel wanted me to play with a lovely technique, a Liszt technique, I would say — very keen, very clear. The most important elements are written for the upper part of the right hand, the part of the piano where the technique should be light and lovely as in Liszt. '*Jeux d'eau*' opened the way for the water effects which afterwards were so important in Debussy's music. Ravel wrote '*Jeux d'eau*' before Debussy wrote '*Reflêts dans l'eau.*'

"I had played '*Jeux d'eau*' in the class of Diémer who said 'Whew, it's a difficult piece! Are you sure you are playing all the notes?' Diémer was an old man then and did not know the piece. But he understood that we should play modern music."

I asked if Ravel wanted the melody brought out, with the water figurations kept very soft. Some pianists play the melody and the figurations, Czerny-like, almost equal in dynamics — an approach sometimes praised by critics but not the public.

"Such an approach ruins the beauty, the magic, of this music," Mme Casadesus replied. "You just have to look at the music. It is not difficult to play Debussy and Ravel if you follow the notation for nuances and pedaling. They were very careful in their markings. Chabrier started this trend. Chopin marked carefully, but not so carefully as Debussy and Ravel.

"Next to strict observance of their markings, touch is the most important thing. When I was in the class of Marguérite Long — I was 12 years old — and was going to play my piano examination at the Paris Conservatory, my friends told me not to play loud because Debussy would be there. Debussy did not like hard touch or strong keyboard jumps. He wanted the sound to come from you and from the keyboard, not from bounce. Ravel, on the other hand, was more inclined to ask for a lot of rhythm, especially in *Alborada del gracioso*. To Ravel, with his Spanish-Basque heritage, rhythm was extremely important."

Alborada del gracioso

It was 1920 when Gaby Casadesus played the second time for Ravel. Mme Long was presenting some pupils in concert in the Salle Gaveau and asked Gaby Casadesus, a former pupil who had won first prize in Diémer's class, to conclude the program. She played a comparatively new Ravel piece, *Alborada del gracioso*.

"*Alborada* is a marvelous piece, very new in piano technique. It's the only piece I know that is so rhythmical, yet so full of expression in the middle section. You can give much beauty in the tone in the middle section. It's a Spanish morning serenade. 'Gracieux,' I suppose, is playing his guitar and singing his love at the balcony of his *Belle*."

M. 1. "Ravel wanted the chords played close to the keys to sound like a mandolin or guitar, very crisp, quasi-pizzicato. He wanted the arpeggiated chords very dry."

M. 43. "He wanted these repeated notes soft and lovely. He was not a virtuoso but he did play these repeated notes very well."

M. 71 et al. "The melody for Ravel was more or less as you have in the third Scherzo of Chopin — the chorale theme interrupted with descending, broken-chord arabesques. I like students to practice the melodic phrases without the intervening chords, so they have a feeling of the respiration of the phrasing like a singer."

M. 74 etc. "He wanted the grace notes played on the beat, but without repeating the tied notes. If you don't start with a big accent, the vibration does not come through."

M. 75. "Ravel wanted these intervening chords very soft each time in bright contrast to the returning melody. He wanted the next phrase of the melody to return as if you had just taken a breath."

M. 126. "He told me to slow down slightly the group of four thirty-second notes marked *trés expressif*. He also told my husband either to slow them down or to start a little sooner — in any case, not to play them exactly in time. The basic tempo remains unslowed. He wanted the arpeggiated chords expressive, especially the syncopated chords."

M. 170. "He wanted the fingering 1, 3, 1, 2-5 on the last four right-hand notes."

Ms. 175-180. "Ravel could do these glissandi in thirds and fourths very easily. He said, 'I don't care how you play them. Play them in single notes, or with your nose if you want. I want the effect of glissando.' Some people work all their lives trying to play these double notes."

Ms. 180-181. "The decrescendo in the last double-thirds glissando was very important."

M. 195. "He wanted the fermata a little longer than I was doing and then to start in again pianissimo."

A Visit with Jeanne-Marie Darré

How the Distinguished French Virtuoso Stays at Concert Pitch

interview December 3, 1967

de la Grande Technique

Known for a number of years, only through her recordings, Jeanne-Marie Darré made her first appearance in the United States in 1962 with the Boston Symphony Orchestra. She has since toured extensively throughout the United States both as recitalist and orchestral soloist.

I first heard Madame Darré in 1948 in Zürich, when she played the Liszt B Minor Sonata in a recital in the *Kammermusiksaal*. A few years later my wife and I heard her play the Chopin F Minor Concerto at the *Palais de Chaillot* in Paris, and most recently, her brilliant Carnegie and Philharmonic Hall recitals in New York.

So I was delighted to have the opportunity to interview Madame Darré shortly after her spectacular all-Liszt concert at Carnegie Hall. In a leisurely Sunday afternoon visit at her Park Avenue hotel, we talked over a multitude of pianistic matters.

Jeanne-Marie Darré is a friendly, relaxed woman whose entire life is piano playing. She is pretty, white-haired, energetic, and has a nice sense of humor and an easy smile.

Paradoxically, this dainty woman is strong, with vibrant muscle from her shoulders through her arms, wrists and fingers. Her hands—much smaller than they seem on stage—are supple and muscular, with wide stretch between their short fingers. On stage she is *la grande dame formidable!*, but at leisure she is an amiable, expressive, electrically-charged charmer.

The gamut of our colloquy was wide: her early training, her teachers, her professional career, her opinion of various schools of playing, how she has acquired her formidable technique, herself as a distinguished teacher. I asked a series of simple, compound, and sometimes loaded questions (said Madame Darré, "I can tell you're a pianist!"). And always I got informative and forthright replies. Last, I asked for technical suggestions, ways of practicing *technique pure*, in certain passages in one of her chef-d'oeuvres: the *Paganini Etudes* of Liszt.

These extracts from this busy career, together with some occasional digressions, show how this renowned virtuoso stays at concert pitch for her performances, and still has time to be a sensible soul who enjoys friendships and social communication.

First Lessons at Age 5; First Concert at 15

Born July 30, 1905 in Givet, France, in the Ardennes near Belgium, Jeanne-Marie Darré began piano lessons at the age of 5. At 9, she entered the Paris Conservatory.

"I studied with Madame Marguérite Long from the age of 9 to 11 in the *classe moyenne* (intermediate class)," she said. "At 11, I went to Isador Philipp for the *classe superieure* (advanced class). My hand was very small and I had from Monsieur Philipp very good stretching exercises. I got the first prize at 13, worked two more years, and at 15 started for the career. My first concert was in Belgium with orchestra.

"I should tell you that you have to be very careful with stretching exercises. That is why I am very careful in speaking about stretching the hand. You have to be careful with stretching exercises because you can break a hand very fast. You don't need long fingers for playing the piano, but you need wide space between the fingers. I can play ninths but not tenths; I don't play the Ravel Concerto for the Left Hand because my hand is too small.

"I was athletic even as a child. All my life I have done *gymnastique* every day. When I was 7 or 8, I learned classic ballet and always did exercises with my legs and my arms. And I still do. I do *gymnastique* for 15 minutes every morning, and when I have time I go to dance because I like very much to dance."

Madame Darré likes to play concerts often, almost every night—a concert one day with perhaps one day's rest if there is much traveling.

"The day of the concert I think more than I play. And I like before the concert to sleep about two hours. I can sleep when I want. Sleeping is good for the nerves. If I don't have to travel all day, I practice in the morning for one hour or 1½ hours on technique, and I play all the program slowly. But sometimes I arrive two hours before the concert and only have time to try the piano. If I have only a half hour, I play technique on the piano and try some piece of the program."

She mentioned various places where she had recently played: Florida, Atlanta, Macon, Washington D.C., Baltimore, Philadelphia ("I like to play with Ormandy in Philadelphia; you have very good orchestras here"), Pittsburgh ("with Steinberg"), Ithaca, New Bedford, Boston, Texas, Tulsa, Kansas City, Hollywood Bowl, San Diego . . . "So, I've been getting an idea, traveling around quite a bit in this country."

Formidable Technician

"You know technique requires much work. For me, much work, enormous work: years of hard practice on scales, exercises, and études. I have practiced since I was five years old. And I work all the time, even now, more than ever.

"Some pianists play low, sitting on a low chair. But I like to sit high, not too high of course, and I play sitting close to the keyboard. For me, more important than position at the keyboard is to play technique with much articulation. I learned like that in France."

She illustrated "articulation," lifting the muscular finger high, striking hard.

"As I said, my masters were Madame Marguérite Long and Monsieur Isidor Philipp. I learned technique in this way. Especially Madame Long taught like this with much articulation. For technique, you have to play from the end of the hand, with just the fingers and the wrist. Cortot differed from Long and Philipp in that he played always with the arm too. To be sure, when you have to play loudly, you have to help with your arm and your shoulders. I never try to play fortissimo only with my hand; when I want power, I take it from the shoulders. But for the real technique — scales, et cetera — I play with only the fingers."

The form in Madame Darré's technique is extraordinarily clear. "When I practice slowly I raise my fingers high, keeping the fingers not in use high," she said, "but when I go faster, it is impossible to raise the fingers so high. So when I play fast trills, for example, I keep my fingers close to the keys because it is impossible to do otherwise.

In playing scales, the thumb movement is important. To pass the thumb under, I move just the thumb not the arm. Ascending, the hand is turned towards the right, descending towards the left, with the weight towards the thumb, the outer part of the hand high. My hand goes like that when I play scales. It was natural for me. I don't teach students to play like that. The form you use in playing scales depends on the hand that you have.

"In teaching scales I have the student play very slowly at first, with fingers raised high. In playing scales with the right hand for example, be careful with the thumb. Play slowly and don't turn the hand. When you play *a, b, c, d,* the thumb going under, don't turn the hand sideways at all when you play *d* with the thumb. And to master that, pupils have to practice very slowly at the beginning. And the same thing for the left hand: the hand must not turn."

Fingering

"You have teachers who have only one fingering and I think this is not good because fingering depends on the individual hand. Very often my students try to play with my fingering. One says it is very good; but another says he can't use it. They have different fingers.

"When my students come with a new piece I look at the piece with them. I say, 'I play with this fingering; try it.' And even if they don't know the piece I see if my fingering is good for them and if it isn't I *chercher,* I search for one or two others.

"When the teacher is a concertizing pianist, he sometimes uses fingerings which are good for concert but not good for a student whose technique still needs development. In the beginning scales in the Third Concerto of Beethoven, for example, many artists end the scale with the thumbs:

But students must learn to play the end note with the fifth finger because the fourth and fifth fingers are weak; they need developing. Students must first practice the scale with a strong fifth finger on this note. Afterwards in concert they can jump with the thumb; the sound is better with the thumb."

The Role of the Wrist

"For me *le poignet* (the wrist) has a role *très important* in piano playing. I use my wrist very much when I play. If I have a Nocturne of Chopin I don't play with my hand stiff. I use my wrist in playing the melody, making small, relaxed lateral, not up and down, movements. And I teach this to my students. The relaxed wrist is very important; *le jeu est plus souple.*"

Chordal Technique and Speed

I had heard Madame Darré play Beethoven's *Ruins of Athens* as an encore and noticed that she threw her arms down on the keys—almost like someone doing fast physical work—coming straight down with marvelous accuracy. I asked her about chordal technique.

"For me there are two principal kinds of chordal playing," she said. "*Fortissimo* chords you have to play with the hand and arm with down movement, especially with the forearm and down from the shoulders. Lighter chords you have to play from the wrist, practicing very slow so that the wrist has time to relift after the weight of the chords."

She illustrated practicing light chords, holding her arm motionless, striking down with the wrist, slowly lifting the wrist back up high, waiting between each chord.

"For staccato chords you must practice this way with the wrist. For big chords I work with the arm. Not too loud because if you practice too loud you become tired. I stay in *mezzo forte* when I practice. To get a good wrist I always say to my students when they find a staccato note in the music, 'Play it with the wrist.' " (And again she snapped her wrist down and up.) "If they practice 5 or 6 hours a day they practice very much the wrist. Or, for a staccato passage in the left hand, I have them practice slowly, playing everything staccato from the wrist. I like very much a supple wrist in playing the piano.

"For the working out my students have always to think about the wrist, and when playing slowly raising the hand high from the wrist. Of course if you play faster you have no time so the hand goes not so high. But you can get a very relaxed wrist with this method of practice. I learned that from Philipp. And especially all the octaves have to be practiced with the wrist, if you want to play very fast repeated octaves. If you have a developed wrist you can play them faster.

"Speed comes from music as well as from études," she continued. "Scarlatti and Mendelssohn are very good for developing technique. I like very much Mendelssohn and so you have so many nice pieces which aren't played much. I would like to play Mendelssohn; maybe I play some here. I like very much the *Variations Serieuses.*"

Horowitz Her Inspiration

"When I was a little girl in the conservatory I learned the Mendelssohn *Rondo Capriccioso* and afterwards the *Variations Serieuses.* I didn't like the *Variations Serieuses* very much. Later I heard them played by Horowitz in Budapest and for the first time I understood the piece.

"I was 22 when I heard Horowitz for the first time in

Budapest in 1927, and I said, 'that is the way to play the piano.' I have all his records and I always listen to them. For me he has been *la révélation* to the piano; he has been my inspiration.

"His octaves are what is marvelous in his technique. They seem like glissandi. When he plays Liszt's *Funerailles*, the left-hand octaves are so fast, like one note, and so clear. And I love to hear him play the Liszt Sonata. *Il est humain.*"

"Very introspective," I said.

"*Oui.* He can play something very soft, so soft it sounds like a dream, and suddenly it is something strong. He can play things so soft he leads you far away, and suddenly he gives an accent. The *contraste* I find marvelous in his playing. With many pianists you exhale pfff when they play; with Horowitz you hold your breathing. And he has such a wonderful crescendo. In my youth I heard him everywhere—Paris, Vienna, Brussels. But I did not hear him in concert for a long time now, maybe for 15 years.

"When I was young I heard Busoni, Saint-Saëns—I played his concertos with him; he was a very, very good pianist, having a wonderful technique—and Paderewski too. They were wonderful, especially Busoni. It was wonderful when he played the Liszt Paganini Etudes. But Busoni, Saint-Saëns, and Paderewski were all of an older generation.

"Later I heard Rachmaninoff and Gieseking too. They had wonderful, wonderful techniques, legato, and tone. Gieseking played Debussy and Ravel like a God! I shouldn't say this but there are no French people who can equal his playing. He loved French music very much. I heard him once in Paris playing the Bach B Flat Partita. I never will forget the Gigue; it was a dream."

Differences in French, Russian, and German Schools

"In my opinion, one has much technique in Russia and France. I suppose it is because the students in these countries work very hard. The Russians have much facility in technique; they are very strong and skillful in technique. I think the Germans, in general, play more with their mind. The French and Russians play more with explosion; their playing is more physical. I don't want to say that the French and Russian schools have no sentiment, but I think that the Germans are more concentrated, especially when they play Beethoven.

"For me, Beethoven is very German and has to be played by a German. I heard Schnabel, Bachhaus, and Kempff. I heard all the sonatas played by Bachhaus, but the most marvelous was Schnabel. The French and Russians can play Beethoven very well, but their playing is less concentrated."

I mentioned that one famous pianist I know, trained in Central Europe, intellectualizes the emotional aspects of interpretation, even such a tour de force as the coda of the Chopin G Minor Ballade. I wondered if Madame Darré's approach to such music would be primarily technical.

"This coda starts very *forte* but afterwards it changes," she said. "There is much expression in this coda, in all the codas of the Chopin Ballades. These codas express certain emotions; they aren't only technique. The first expresses *la douleur* (suffering), the second *le désespoir* (desperation), the third *une victoire, un triomphe*, and the fourth *la puissance* (power). These codas are not only notes. That is why it is so difficult to play them. You have to play them with a wonderful technique and also with expression."

The Artist as Teacher

As a professor of piano at the National Conservatory in Paris, Madame Darré is highly regarded and much sought after. I asked how she trained good pupils who entered her class, how many years they would have studied before reaching her class, did they choose her or she them, and how many years did they study with her.

"That," she stated, "depends on their ability. Generally the students have to study 6 to 7 years before reaching the conservatory. If a student starts at 5 and works *very* hard he can reach the Conservatory at about age 12. I have my own students and prepare them myself, but sometimes one year or six months before the examinations a teacher brings me a pupil. If the pupil is good, seems to me to be a good student, I take him. My students study with me about 4 or 5 years in the conservatory and afterwards too if they are good.

"They study everything with me—Scarlatti, Mozart, Beethoven, Schumann, Chopin, Liszt, Debussy, Ravel, Prokofieff, and some Bartok. And all year long, they study Bach Preludes and Fugues from the *Well-Tempered Clavier* and Chopin Etudes. All the lessons are in classes. Each teacher has 15 in his class—8 advanced, 4 intermediate, and 3 foreign students—meeting in groups of five, three times a week. This year I have an American, a very talented girl from Los Angeles, and in the summer I have many American students at the academy in Nice where I teach."

Technique Pure a la Darré

"If you want to get a good technique, perhaps you don't have to practice all the life, but in the beginning certainly you must practice about 3 or 4 hours a day on pure technique: scales, exercises, and etudes.

"In the daily practice of *technique pure* it is not only necessary to play regular scales but also scales in sixths and Czerny etudes too. There is one Czerny Etude, one of the best, which prepares you for the Etude in A Minor, Op. 10, No. 2 of Chopin.

Czerny, *School of the Virtuoso*, Op. 365, No. 19.

Chopin, *Etude in A Minor*, Op. 10, No. 2.

"You have the Etudes of Chopin but to play them well you already need a good technique. You cannot begin with Chopin Etudes. You have to play well enough, to be ready for them; you need all the other etudes first.

"First the student should study Czerny's *Petite Velocité*, Op. 636 and *Grande Velocite*, Op. 299. Then he should study Czerny's *School of Legato and Staccato*, Op. 335 and his *School of the Virtuoso*, Op. 365.

"The long etudes of Charles Alkan, the Moscheles etudes, and the Moszkowski *Etudes de Virtuosité*, Op. 72* for the two hands and those for the left hand alone, Op. 92 are very good. And there are very good etudes of Saint-Saëns for two hands and one for one hand too. The etude for the left hand is excellent."

Suggestions for Practicing Certain Passages in the Paganini Etudes of Liszt

"We play a lot of Liszt in Paris because *c'est de la grande technique*. All the Cortot Liszt editions are very good. I have the Peters edition of the Transcendental Etudes. For the *Paganini Etudes*, I have a very good edition but very

*Horowitz often played these as encores and has recorded No. 6 in F Major and No. 11 in A Flat Major.

80

Dedicated to Madame Clara Schumann.

Grand Études after Paganini.

Étude I.

Franz L.

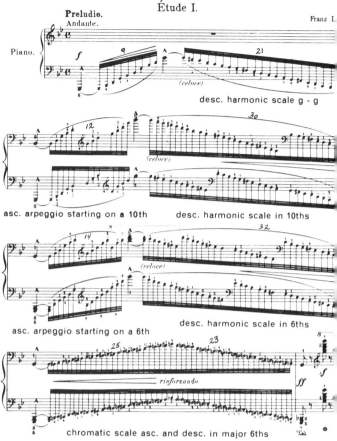

desc. harmonic scale g - g

asc. arpeggio starting on a 10th   desc. harmonic scale in 10ths

asc. arpeggio starting on a 6th

desc. harmonic scale in 6ths

chromatic scale asc. and desc. in major 6ths

old, a German edition, Breitkopf. I got it when I was in the conservatory and you can't find it now." *

Etude I

"I will tell the pupil to practice the first arpeggio in all the keys. I practice very much in modulations; it is good to play in all the keys. The pupil must practice this arpeggio in all the keys ascending and descending, and in rhythms and repeat a lot of times.

"For the scales the same. They are different notes but it is the same work. You have to play the arpeggios and scales in all the keys and always ascending and descending, not just the way it is in the music."

"To practice separate hands is very important. First the right hand, afterwards the left hand, and then together. Pupils have to play very slowly the first days and afterwards, if they play well enough, they can begin faster until the right speed is obtained. It is very important not to practice with wrong notes. It is why in the beginning it is very important to practice slowly. Because if you practice with some wrong notes, you play with wrong notes in performance. Playing has to be very, very clean."

Etude II

"Students have to practice these thirty-second-note scales very slowly. These scales have to be very even, equal. If you want to play them *pianissimo*, they must be practiced

*Twelve years after the first edition, Liszt revised the **Paganini Etudes,** publishing a second edition which he dedicated to Clara Schumann. This edition, Breitkopf & Hartel, 1851, is the one to which Madame Darre refers.)

slowly at first and *forte*, striking hard down into the keys, *bien enfonce dans le clavier.* You risk having holes if you practice first piano. After you practice these scales *forte*, then play them *mezzo forte*, then *piano*, and when you know them very well then play them *pianissimo*. But, I repeat, it is very important to play them first *forte*, striking hard into the keys."

Before plunging into the *Poco piu animato* section of this Etude in her Carnegie Hall recital, Madame Darre, a master at marshalling and controlling her physical resources, stopped an instant to wipe her brow with a handkerchief.

"You can't play this page if you're tired," she said. "I play all this page *forte* but I play all the octaves with my wrist. The octaves must be very relaxed and played with the wrist. They must be practiced slowly with the wrist, the arm motionless, the wrist snapping down and up. In a piece like this it is because I play relaxed with *souplesse*, (suppleness) that I have the necessary endurance. I always made exercises for the wrist. If you play from the arm the tone can become hard and you become more tired."

Etude III

"In the beginning of *La Campanella*, there are all these jumps:

It is good practice to play further, wider jumps, than you have to do in the piece.

"To develop an exciting trill in the middle section, measure 68, use both hands for the trill and practice very hard

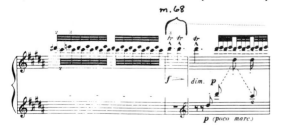

in rhythms, adding 2, 4, 6, and 8 notes between the notes of the trill:

After a long time, practice in equal rhythm. I play more notes than on the music because on the music the trill is very short. In concert the number of notes I play depends on my mood: if I have a good mood I play longer. It depends too on the piano.

"All the techniques have to be practiced first in *fortissimo* but not *piano* . . . Play the octaves on page 29, measures 110 et al *(con spirito)*, with the wrist:

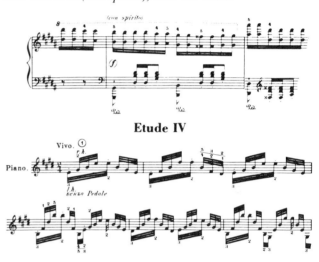

Etude IV

"First practice the left hand, going back and forth. When you practice a long time, all the life, you make yourself your technique, you make yourself your own way of practicing the difficulties first.

"If I have to practice a new piece, when I practice it for the first time, if I have a very difficult passage, the first time I try it fast to see where the difficulty is. And then I start working on this difficulty first. And so you should start to work slowly. I have tried this myself and for me it is a good thing because if you can't practice a long time every day, you have to practice the difficult things first. You have no time to lose. Practice the difficult things first; afterwards play the whole piece."

In her Carnegie Hall recital, Madame Darré's performance of 'La Campanella' had been so extraordinary, she received an ovation. *The New York Times* review had said, " . . . delicate, lacy traceries in the upper treble were truly phenomenal," and went on further to state, "Miss Darré separated the wheat from the chaff, as it were, and focused the listener's attention upon the unifying and important elements of these vastly ornamented musical structures. The entire recital was a triumph of virtuosity, concentration and taste."

To her, triumphant piano playing was principally a matter of hard work. The following day she would play the all-Liszt program in Philadelphia; the following week, Ravel, Prokofieff, and Schumann's *Carnaval*, "A completely different program," in Philharmonic Hall. I said that 'Paganini in *Carnaval* would not be difficult for her. She laughed *"Il faut donner l'impression qu'il n'est pas difficile,"* she said—you must give the impression it's not difficult."

Jeanne-Marie Darré

"Grande dame" of the French Piano

There is a dash of the Hungarian gypsy in the "grande dame" of the French Piano, Jeanne-Marie Darré, who in December 1979 celebrated her 60th anniversary as a performer with a gala concert at Carnegie Hall and who continues to perform and teach extensively. Since her debut in 1919 the flamboyant Frenchwoman, now 75, has been on the go, energizing and exciting audiences in her distinctive, spirited style. "They have music all through their bodies," she says of the gypsies, and the description suits her too.

Harold Schonberg has written that her playing represents "the French School at its best — sophisticated, rhythmically alert, intelligent, technically flexible and musically charming," and although her repertoire is large and varied, she has played a lot of Chopin and Liszt throughout her career. "After all, Chopin was half French." And as for Liszt, "I like Liszt because it's exciting and difficult, also perhaps because I often went to Hungary, almost all my life. I played in even the smallest places. Hearing the gypsies play in the country was fabulous." In fact, it was in Hungary that Madame Darré fully decided upon her life's course and since then Budapest has often been a base for launching her tours.

"Horowitz was really my inspiration," she recalls. "When I was 18 I was in Budapest, and my mother — naturally, because then one didn't travel alone — took me to hear Horowitz. I realized then that music and the piano were the most important things. I have many of his recordings at home. For me he is the greatest."

Last season New York, Horowitz' home, was the scene of another inspirational performance, this time by that still star-struck and still youthful woman. Madame Darré's musical style has changed over the years. "When you are young you don't understand the quiet aspects of music; that comes with age." No longer a fire-eating virtuoso, in recent recitals she has molded *cantilena* with an exquisite soft *legato,* always charged with unexpected colors, turns of phrase, or important bass voice-leadings.

Nevertheless, one of her trademarks, an infectious rhythm, remains the same. "I like rhythm very much," she declares in her startlingly deep voice. "I like people who play in time. Playing in time doesn't hinder making a rubato or playing with expression. But immediately afterward re-take the tempo and play in time."

Her personal style is as striking and colorful as ever. She still strides onstage like the athlete and dancer she has been, resplendently gowned in extravagant hues that offset her white hair. Perhaps, if she considers it warm, she'll fling her jacket to the side of the stage before plunging without any fuss into the performance. Her audiences seem to sense that here is an artist who loves to play, "no ifs, ands, or buts."

"I played the concertos of Saint-Saëns for the composer."

Melismata and *jeu perlé* passages ripple and cascade with breathtaking charm, the inner fingers doing most of the work. Make no mistake, this free spirit will take chances. From high above, the arms fall full force to th keys for *forte* chords. If she misses a few notes these days, *tant pis*. "I'll get the effect anyway."

One fears a little for a woman of her age to play with such tremendous energy; a chain smoker, she was quite ill in her 60's. She is a treasure, a link to Chopin and Liszt and a performer for Saint-Saëns, Fauré, Ravel, Busoni, Paderewski, and Moritz Rosenthal. One almost feels she must be protected from her own vitality.

A life not lacking in men (she is now married to conductor Fernand Oubradous) and physical exercise (she puts in 15 minues of gymnastics every morning and goes out dancing whenever possible) has obviously left her with stamina a gypsy might envy. Her recitals these days are, in a way, a celebration of strength as well as spirit.

No concertizing child prodigy — "It's dangerous to be a child prodigy — Jeanne-Marie Darré started to study at age five with her mother in Givet, France, in the Ardennes near Belgium where she was born, but did not make a big splash until she was 21.
splash until she was 21.

That May 28, 1926 performance of the five Saint-Saëns concertos with the Lamoureux Orchestra under Paul Paray was by all accounts spectacular, "astonishing the Parisian musical world," as one present, Maurice Dumesnil, has rcalled. The artist herself terms the evening "brilliant, more interesting than my debut recital when I was 14 at the Salle Erard. I had great joy playing those works the same evening without fatigue."

Behind that success stood Paris Conservatory teachers on the order of Marguérite Long and Isador Philipp, who guided her from age nine through her first prize at the age of 12 and her debut diet of Bach, Beethoven, Chopin, and Liszt. At 15 she played outside of France for the first time — the Beethoven Concerto No. 1 — and by 16 her career had begun.

"I played a lot in France, in London and in the English provinces. I continued playing throughout the years in almost all the countries of Europe and in North and South Africa. My fervent wish was to come to the United States. I came for the first time in 1962, making my debut in New York with Charles Munch and the Boston Symphony. It was a nice debut at Carnegie Hall and since then I have come often and played in many cities.

"I have no anecdotes," she says. "You know, we soloists are always alone. We travel alone. We don't have anecdotes like people who travel in groups."

On her life's journey Madame Darré has had some highly interesting company. "I've had much luck in my life to have been near these people who had been close to great artists like Chopin and Liszt," she acknowledges.

"In Budapest I knew Professor Stephan Thomas, whose students included Dohnanyi and Bartók, and who was one of the last pupils of Chopin. He gave me much advice about nuances. I played some Chopin Etudes for him. After I had played the Etude in 'Thirds,' he said that Chopin didn't play as fast as we play now. I had attacked the last descending run with an accent and he said, 'No, no. Chopin didn't like big accents in the Etudes.' He showed me how to make the *diminuendo*. And I remember he said Chopin had wanted the soft pedal used throughout the 'Harp' Etude and a rather slow tempo, also the 'Butterfly' Etude on the slow side.

"Also in Budapest I worked with Margit Vargas, the last pupil of Liszt. She showed me many things *extrêmement précieuse*. I knew some important personalities there like the Count Apponyi who was an intimate friend of Liszt. He spoke to me a lot about Liszt.

"I played the concertos of Saint-Saëns for the composer. He was very boorish, you know, not amiable. He said of me with his cross air, 'This little one, if she works, she will go far. If she doesn't work, if she stops now, all is lost.' Naturally, I was very happy. My *maître,* Philipp, was there.

"Ravel was a charming man. I was a little moved playing for him. I asked him, '*Mâitre,* how should one play your *Toccata*?' And he answered, 'As fast as possible, but so that one hears each note!' What he said stayed with me. I returned home and worked very hard to play it at that speed (Ravel's metronome marking is 144 to the quarter), and I've always told this to my students.

"When I played *Ondine* for him he said, 'It's very good but you cut up the melody.' And it was true. I was very young and didn't understand very well this story of Ondine. I had read the poem of Aloysius Bertrand but I was unable to understand this siren who tried to charm a man. Ravel explained the story very well for my age. 'You see this song in the left hand underneath the right hand which is like waves, this song must not stop for one second; this complaint must go right to the end, up to the moment where the man tries to seduce her. She says that it isn't possible because he loves a woman. At this moment the voice breaks. She utters a great laugh and disappears.'

"And I played his *Trio* for him. He gave me and my two partners some excellent suggestions. It is a magisterial, very difficult work. There are measures in seven and eight beats. And I can tell you something funny. This past summer I had projected to play Ravel's *Trio* at the Academy of Nice where I teach in the summers. I was going to play with two eminent colleagues, the violinist Christian Ferras and the cellist André Navarra. I started to re-work this *Trio* and thought, 'It isn't possible for me.' Two days later my camarade Ferras telephoned. 'You want us to play this?' 'Well,' I said, 'That depends.' 'My dear,' he said — he is much younger than I am — 'At our age one plays in four beats, not seven or eight!' "

Fauré she remembers as "very nice, very good, very

formal. He had a magnificent appearance. I played for him the Nocturne No. 7 — for which I won my First Prize — and a Barcarolle. He too gave me some good suggestions. His is extraordinary pianistic literature but the public doesn't appreciate it. It's intimate music, close to chamber music and a large hall impairs this intimacy. It's a great pity because Fauré was an incomparable musician.

"For Busoni I played a terrible transcription, the *Marriage of Figaro Fantasy,* which Philipp wanted me to play. Busoni was a magnificent pianist. I heard him play the fifth Beethoven concerto as well as a lot of Liszt. He had his own style naturally — different perhaps from what we're accustomed to hearing — but it was very beautiful. Particularly in Liszt he was great."

How She Practices

"If she works, she will go far," said Saint-Saëns — and Madame Darré has worked hard her whole life. She continues to begin her practice sessions with "lots of scales which many young people no longer practice. I can't open my piano in the morning without playing scales. I practice scales for one hour, playing four octaves at first with separate hands, then hands together. I play all the scales in descending order: I begin with C, connecting with the notes C, D, C, B to A minor, then F, D minor, Bb and so on. First I play all the scales with the fingering of C major; afterwards I play them with the standard fingerings.

"I practice scales in double thirds, double sixths, and octaves. I also work on scales in fourths which people seldom practice. If you play the Debussy Etude in Fourths or the scales in fourths in the last movement of Beethoven's Op. 101, for example, you should prepare the technique demanded in the pieces. So I amuse myself playing scales in fourths.

"As soon as I try a piano I begin with scales. It's instinctive."

"Then I practice trills with all the fingerings: one-two, two-three, three-four. You seldom trill with three-four, but just the same it's good to work the fourth finger. I trill most often with thumb-three. I even do exercises from time to time.

"After an hour on scales, I spend a second hour on about six Chopin Etudes to keep up the entire 24. Which ones I play depends upon my mood, or if I'm playing a program, or the piano. To play the first two of Opus 10, you have to have a good piano. And then there are those that are especially attractive to the public. Then I play the etudes of Czerny, Moszkowski, Alkan, but especially the Czerny *School of the Virtuoso*. If you can play the 60 etudes of *The School of the Virtuoso* up to tempo, you have everything. I play them all.

"If I'm on tour obviously I don't have much time to practice, but as soon as I try a piano I begin with scales. It's instinctive, even if I have only 10 minutes. I wake up my fingers. It's exciting to practice technique. I love it very much.

"One summer several years ago, I didn't want to play concerts for two months. During these two months I did only technique for about four hours every day. I was traveling enormously at that time during the regular season and didn't have time to work on technique as I wanted. So I took these two months, playing nothing but etudes and exercises, and it did me great good."

Madame Darré's labors have been somewhat aided by her gift for sight-reading, although she points out that even on this she worked every day for an hour. "My mother brought home from the music store all the music possible and she had me read through it an hour every day. It's a necessity to become a good sight-reader. If I receive music even of the style of Boulez or Stockhausen, I amuse myself by reading it to keep up my memory. I also spend 15 or 20 minutes every day playing a Bach prelude and fugue."

This small-handed *"grande dame,"* faintly obsessed with technique, who studied with the last pupils of Chopin and Liszt and who plays these masters as they may have wanted to be played, doesn't like to talk much about her own interpretations. "I like the music, try to speak to my public, and play as I feel." She is, however, outspoken in her praise for the "magnificent" younger generation, singling out Pollini, Argerich, and Bishop-Kovacevich.

One could understand if Madame Darré were to lessen her teaching, performing, and practice schedules. But she doesn't. "The life of a concert artist is a good one," she says. "I love my work."

85

LOTTE MEITNER-GRAF
LONDON

Gina Bachauer

"I Adore to Play the Piano"

An Interview with the Celebrated Greek Virtuoso

interview May 4, 1969

"Governments rise and fall, and the seasons change, but Miss Bachauer's playing remains a constant," wrote Harold Schonberg in *The New York Times* after Madame Bachauer's recent Carnegie Hall recital. "She represents the romantic tradition in piano playing — she, with her enormous technique, her big and penetrating tone, her love for the piano as a steed upon which to ride . . . Gina Bachauer continues to be one of the great pianists."

At a recent interview, wearing a long, pink, brocade hostess gown, Madame Bachauer, a stately brown-eyed brunette, five feet six inches tall, was extraordinarily gracious, considerate, and warm. For nearly 11 months in the year she travels all over the world, together with her husband, Alec Sherman, the British conductor, spending four and one-half to five months in the United States each year. Since her Town Hall debut in New York in October of 1950 Gina Bachauer has toured the United States for 19 consecutive years, and has concertized in over 500 cities.

She was born May 21, 1913 in Athens, Greece. Her parents were Jean Bachauer and Ersilia (Marostica) Bachauer. She has traced her paternal lineage back 400 years in Austria.

Early Study

Although her early piano study and musical development were fostered by the inherent love of music in her family, she explained in her relaxed speech, tinged with charming Greek accent:

"My father and mother were very musical, but no one in our family had ever been a professional musician. When I was five years old, Emil Sauer, a famous pupil of Liszt, came to Greece to give a recital. And my father, who went to all the concerts because he adored to go everywhere, asked me if I wanted to hear the recital of Emil Sauer.

"I said, 'Yes I want to go.'

"And he said, 'But will you behave?'

"I said, 'Yes, I will try.'

"In any case, the recital of Emil Sauer was the first concert I ever heard. I don't remember — I was very young at the time — but it seems I was very much impressed with the people, with this man who played in such a wonderful way. And when we left the theater, I told my father that playing the piano is what I will do in life; I will become a pianist.

"When we got home my father said, 'Now you go to bed, you sleep, and everything will be all right tomorrow morning.

"But the next day I said again, 'I want to become a pianist, I want to become a pianist, I want to become a pianist.'

"So in the end my parents bought me a piano, and I started to have lessons from a lady who lived near our house, who was giving piano lessons to children. And I must say that until the age of nine, I was just playing like every other child, without showing that something better could be done.

"But when I was nine years old I had a very big luck. Woldemar Freeman, a truly remarkable Polish pianist, came to Greece to give recitals and to play with the orchestra. He fell in love with Greece and a beautiful Greek lady. So he made Greece his headquarters, traveling from there to give his concerts in Europe and everywhere else.

"Besides concertizing, he started giving master classes in the Athens Conservatory. And that was something really wonderful because besides Freeman's Master Classes, we had the great luck to have Mitropolous as conductor of the orchestra. Every great artist came to Greece to play; musical life in Greece was at its peak.

"One day my father, wanting to know if it really was wise for me to go on with my piano playing, took me to Woldemar Freeman. Freeman heard me play and said, 'Yes, I will work with her.' So I worked seriously with him, finishing my studies at the Athens Conservatory when I was 16 years old, winning the Gold Medal in 1929."

Study with Cortot

"Because Woldemar Freeman, who had been a pupil of Busoni, had a German technique and approach, he wanted

me to go to Paris to work with Cortot. He wanted me to hear French music and to work with a master who was a great specialist in French music.

"I never quite agreed with Cortot's exercises for piano," said Madame Bachauer in answer to my question about Cortot's editions, "because he had a peculiar hand. His exercises helped him very much but didn't help his students. But I find his edition of the Chopin *Etudes* extraordinary; if the Chopin Studies are worked as he suggests, the results are extraordinary. I would certainly advise every student to try the Chopin edition edited by Cortot. It is one of the best that we have."

Study with Rachmaninoff

Gina Bachauer studied with Cortot for three years at the *Ecole Normale de Musique* in Paris. Then, again through Freeman, she met Rachmaninoff.

"Freeman had known Rachmaninoff very well," she continued. "He and Rachmaninoff often played two-piano recitals. As Rachmaninoff was concertizing widely at this time, I traveled for almost three years throughout Europe, whenever I knew he had to be in a certain place, had a concert, or something like that. And he was kind enough to hear me, to discuss music with me.

"Studying with Rachmaninoff was one of the greatest experiences of my life. One of the biggest experiences was to discuss music with him, to discuss form and interpretation and especially how to produce a beautiful sound. He was really one of the great specialists in tone, in color. For him the sound he was producing was the greatest, most important thing. Technique and so on took a second place. The first place was color, color, color.

"And another thing he was adamant about was that I take great consideration of what the orchestra does when playing a concerto. He was always saying that it was never written in the piano score what the orchestra really does. Except for the two Chopin Concertos, he called concertos 'symphonies with piano.' He wanted the orchestra to be equal in importance to the soloist. And that is why he wanted a soloist to have a perfect knowledge of the orchestration and of every instrument that would collaborate with him, so that in the concert every chord would sound perfectly balanced between the soloist and the orchestra.

"I find that I was extremely lucky to be able to work with three great people of different schools, very often different opinions, but still three very great musicians."

"Did you work on technique with Rachmaninoff?" I asked.

"I will tell you," she answered, "with Rachmaninoff I have not done much technique, and we didn't solve many technical problems, because he himself was such a natural pianist. For him everything came so naturally, it was difficult for him to explain how he did it.

"To give you an example how this man . . . what a wonderful natural pianist he was: One day when I went to play for him he had to hear a young pianist — I think it was a young Brazilian student — who came with a letter from a friend of Rachmaninoff. This young boy, before sitting down to play, turned around to Rachmaninoff and said, 'Please, Master, kindly tell me what is the best way to sit in front of the piano. Is it better to sit low and play high or to sit high and play low?'

"And Rachmaninoff who had never thought about it, said, 'I don't know; I think the best way is to sit comfortably and to play well!' For him, everything came naturally.

"I have many of his pieces in which he has written fingerings for me and even some things he has changed in his Concertos that he was playing in another way after he had edited them. And certainly this can be of great help to students, and I want one day to give all that so that a new edition for certain works comes out. Some of his fingerings and markings are simply wonderful, in his concertos, the Tchaikovsky Concerto, the Brahms Paganini Variations, et cetera."

Hanon Practice

"But one of the basic things Rachmaninoff did was to practice Hanon," Gina Bachauer continued. "Every day before his real practicing, he practiced Hanon and in different ways. This was also what Woldemar Freeman did. Freeman believed in the exercises of Hanon and Brahms so very much. And I have practiced Hanon all my life and still do now when I practice technique."

"How do you practice?" I asked.

"When I practice now I always start with technical exercises. I start with one or two Hanon exercises . . ."

"From the beginning of the book?"

"Yes, I start with one or two Hanon exercises, depending on the time available: Numbers 1, 2, 3, 4, or 5. But I don't play them as written. I always hold the first note — the first finger in the right hand and the fifth finger in the left hand going up, the fifth finger in the right hand and the first finger in the left hand going down — and repeat the last four notes, so that it makes four groups of sixteenth notes in the bar":

"First I play the Hanon all the way through slow, always holding the first note. Then I continue, playing it through all the keys chromatically, always holding the first note, alternating each new key piano and forte, slow and fast. Then gradually . . . faster and faster. And this is before my scales and my octaves. And certainly I practice scales and octaves continuously."

Scale Practice

"How do you practice scales?"

"My scale practice is something that suits very much, you know, to me. Perhaps it will not be of the same help to somebody else. At each practice session, I take one scale, playing first each hand separate, extremely piano and extremely even . . . then hands together, again very soft and very even. And then I go faster, faster, and faster . . . also in thirds, sixths, and tenths, four octaves always, with the same scale.

"And then certainly I play scales in double thirds, major and minor, one scale at each session . . . and then chromatic scales in double thirds. I use my fingerings that suit me for double-third scales; and again I say that for my hand my fingerings are all right, but for another hand perhaps they would not be all right. I find that the Hanon

double-third scale fingerings are extremely good."

Octave Practice

"How do you practice octaves?"

"Octaves I practice in a peculiar way. First I practice them with my wrist, slowly, with up and down wrist movement, the arm still . . . one or two scales, not more. And then I practice them with my wrist up and a sort of glissando octaves, a sort of vibrating wrist-forearm, fast octaves, in one or two scales. And again in thirds, sixths, and tenths."

"You play forearm octaves struck from very high," I remarked.

"No, no," she replied. "I never practice forearm octaves struck from very high. When I play a very loud chord or octave certainly I use my shoulders, and I bring the whole force from my shoulder blade. But when I play soft octaves or when I play very quick octaves, then I use my wrist."

Arpeggio and Chord Practice

"And then certainly you must practice arpeggios and chords. Arpeggios I practice in the same way that I practice my scales, and chords I practice by playing major and minor chords in octave position":

"I've always been amazed at your accuracy in jumps and chord playing," I said. "Any special thing that you've thought of to get such accuracy for coming down like that?"

"I think you get used to that," she said with a laugh. "It is not difficult to strike a chord with accuracy if you have worked very hard for hours on a passage. In the end it comes out . . ."

Concentration and Evenness

"I find that one of the things that is very important is what Gieseking was saying always. And he was a very great master; he was a man for whom I have had an enormous, enormous admiration. And he said that it is not how long you practice your exercises and pieces but how much you concentrate when you practice. He believed in and achieved phenomenal evenness through concentration.

"People and students sometimes practice exercises while reading a book. This is terrible; it doesn't help at all. You must practice your exercises with the same concentration that you will play a few days afterwards. Because only in this way can you acquire the same evenness in all five fingers. You must play with five strong, absolutely even fingers.

"In practicing with great concentration you must hear that every finger sounds the same; you must not have three fingers that sound more and two that sound less. And you can acquire this evenness if you practice very slowly and softly, listening to every note, knowing exactly — and slowly, slowly — that your five fingers are equal in tone.

"And it is very important to concentrate on your scales, arpeggios, and exercises in the same way that you concentrate when you practice something else."

Reger Variations

Next I wanted to ask Gina Bachauer about the performance of big-structured works and phrasing for which she is renowned. "I remember your performance in Town Hall of the Reger *Variations and Fugue on a Theme of Bach,* Op. 81," I said. "You made the big structure of the work so forceful, the phrasing so beautiful."

"You know," she began with a smile, "I would like to record this work, but I don't know if there would be any market for it. The other day I was discussing this work with Serkin. And he said, 'For heaven's sake don't stop playing these Variations because we are the only two who play this beautiful work.' But it is difficult to put on a program because it is not accepted. It is something the public doesn't want to hear; the public finds it long. I don't know . . . I adore this piece, and I find that Reger was a very great musician, a very great composer. His big pieces are his greatest works. His concerto for piano is a very beautiful piece, but only Serkin plays it; otherwise, it's not played at all. I hope with all my heart that Reger's music will come back more and more because it is a pity we hear so little of it."

Phrasing

"You seem to phrase in a big line," I continued. "For example, the second themes of the Beethoven Waldstein Sonata and especially the first movement of the Chopin B Minor Sonata, you didn't phrase in two short phrases, but almost combined the two into one. What are your ideas on big-line phrasing versus smaller phrasing?"

"I believe in big-line phrasing. Absolutely," she answered. "I don't like to feel that a big piece like the first part of a sonata or a concerto is cut in pieces. I want one line from the beginning to the end, and that's why I have difficulties when I record and they stop me in certain places and want me to start over again. I can never start in the middle of a piece; I can never stop after certain phrases. And so when I record I very often play the whole first movement of a concerto four or five times until they have a good take. I can't play small fragments and put them together.

"And I find that the Chopin Sonata, especially the B Minor which you mentioned, is a work that is composed with small phrases. If you look at it, it is not a big line from the beginning to the end, especially the first movement. So it needs to be worked with inner voices and with certain bridges from one phrase to the other so that when you hear it, it appears in one piece from the beginning to the end. As you said, I played the second theme, not as two short phrases, but almost combined as one":

(not ⟍ *pp*)

"Regarding big-line versus smaller-unit phrasing, especially in Chopin," I continued, "how would you phrase the bridge section back to the first theme in the Chopin

F Minor Nocturne, Op. 55, No. 1? . . . four small phrases or one big line?"

"One big line," she replied emphatically. "Yes, definitely, one long phrase."

Melody Playing and Coloring

"How do you approach melody playing?" I asked next. "Do you play a melody as singing from within you, coloring it according to the rise and fall of the phrase, do you color it pianistically, or do you approach a melody according to its structure?"

"I think that the structure of a melody shows you exactly what you have to do with the melody," Gina Bachauer replied. "If you look at your score carefully, if you play your melody, really hearing what you are doing — you must hear every note; you must be your worst critic — the structure of the piece, the structure of the melody and the phrase will tell you what you have to do. And often, too, you must let your instincts speak because this is beautiful. How you play must not always be what you have learned and what your head says, but also what your heart says."

"Regarding the coloring of a melody," I continued, ". . . in the fourth phrase in the first subject of the Chopin G Minor Ballade, the question often comes up whether to play this phrase a little louder or softer":

"I will tell you what it is," Madame Bachauer replied. "I would play it softer because I find that the change of color here, the change of harmony, will be much more of a surprise, if this phrase is played softer than if it's played louder. And surprises are also beautiful things in music.

"I don't know if you noticed in Schumann's *Kinderscenen* which I played yesterday evening . . . in the next to last piece, when the child falls asleep, when at the Recapitulation of the beginning theme, there is one *B* that comes suddenly out that is completely unexpected. If this *B* is played a little louder, it loses completely its *raison d'etre*, its reason to exist. But if you prepare the phrase before with a retard and this *B* suddenly comes out in a very *pianissimo*

and beautiful color, then it is one of the most extraordinary surprises. No one would even think that something like that could be written. So very often the change of a harmony in piano is more of a surprise than if you play it louder."

"You don't go in much for bringing out inner parts the

way some performers do," I said. "Your melodic playing is more straightforward. What do you think of the interpretative device of bringing out inner voices?"

"I like to bring out the second voices but not always," she answered, "because the melodic line must never be cut. And a second voice must always be a second voice; it is not a predominant voice. In some pieces the second voice takes the lead for a little while, but only for a very little while. The line of the melody must never be broken."

Pedaling

"What are your principles regarding pedaling?" I asked. "Do you pedal different composers differently for stylistic reasons? Or, do you pedal principally for structure and tone?"

"No . . . for structure and tone definitely," she replied. "But I try to use very little soft pedal. I find that the results are much better if you use the *poids,* the weight, of your hand to change the color and to play the pianissimo that you want than if you use the soft pedal. I believe that in the greatest pianissimo in the world, the hand must have all the weight that it needs, so that the pianissimo doesn't become something that is on the surface but something that will sound for a very long time and will sing in the same way that a melody will sing if you play it in mezzo forte or even forte."

"You have mentioned tone . . . I was going to ask you what you think of the various tones of Rachmaninoff, Gieseking, Rubinstein, Horowitz, Richter? And what is your ideal of beautiful tone?"

"I think that when you are young and are so much taken with a very great artist, you think no one else can produce a tone like that. I think that nobody else has produced the sound that Rachmaninoff produced. But certainly every great artist — and all these artists you have mentioned are very great — has his own way of producing the sound that he wants. That is why we have this great variation of sounds, interpretations, and artists because each great artist has *his* way and each way is wonderful. When I hear a great master like Horowitz, Rubinstein, or Serkin, at that moment I say: 'This is the most beautiful sound. This is the way it has to be played.'

"At a later time if I hear another great master, then perhaps I say: 'This is the way.' If at the moment a musician plays he convinces you that his is *the* way to do it, then he is a great master. If he cannot convince his public that his is the only way to play at that moment, then he is not great. Therein lies one of the beauties of music."

Great Pianists

Critics are always saying who, in their opinion, are the greatest pianists, but I think great pianists know far better than the critics who their greatest colleagues are. I asked Madame Bachauer who, in her opinion, have been the greatest pianists of this century.

"In the past," she said, "Busoni certainly was a great pianist. I never heard Hofmann in person — I heard him only on records — but I was astounded to hear this man. I think he was a very great man. Rachmaninoff was another one. And I think Gieseking was a very, very great master . . . Backhaus too.

"In the present I would say Rubinstein, Horowitz, Serkin, Richter, and Gilels . . . One cannot compare them one to the other as each is great in his own way, entirely individual in his approach to and interpretation of music."

Hand Rearrangements for Power

"Madame Bachauer," I said, "in the ending of the Chopin Scherzo from the B Minor Sonata, you played the accented notes all with the left hand, as octaves. And in the Beethoven Waldstein Sonata first-movement trill, you played the trill's after-notes with the right hand. Do these hand divisions stem from a tradition, or do you divide the hands for power? What do you think of hand rearrangements versus playing exactly as the composer notated?"

"In the ending of the Chopin Scherzo from the B Minor Sonata," she replied, "I play the accented notes as left-hand octaves because the crescendo in this scherzo must be very, very great, very powerful. It is impossible to achieve the crescendo and power with single notes; the octaves make it sound much bigger. I divide and finger the notes as follows":

"And the trill towards the end of the first movement of the Beethoven Waldstein Sonata, measure 234, where I took the trill's after-notes with the right hand . . . This rearrangement of the hands, suggested by Von Bülow in his edition published by *J. G. Cotta'sche Buchhandlung Nachfolger,* Stuttgart 1899, is extremely effective. Von Bülow's rearrangement is much better than the other way of doing it; it makes a much bigger crescendo."

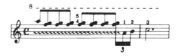

"Von Bülow says: 'He, to whom the difficulty of skipping in the left hand should be insurmountable (a pause, no matter how slight, is not allowable), may execute the complementary notes of the trill with the right hand, whereby the left hand will be liberated sooner.'

"But, my dear friend, regarding playing the notes exactly as Beethoven notated them . . . the other day Serkin and I were looking at the Beethoven manuscript for the Waldstein Sonata, and do you know how many wrong notes are printed?"

"Gieseking told me one," I interjected: "the F in the bass in the left hand, measure 105."*

"Yes," continued Madame Bachauer, "I can't understand why no edition has this F flat. This F flat is so much more logical because two bars after that the same thing

---

*Gieseking was the first one to notice this. In 1948 he marked the flat before the F in my copy after he had been perusing the original manuscript owned by Dr. Hans C. Bodmer in Zürich. And Gieseking later wrote in an essay: " . . . it can no longer be verified where the erroneous version got started. Perhaps a printing error in the original edition was overlooked. Perhaps Czerny, too, had known the incorrect version for he, as Carl Krebs in the notes to the Breitkopf & Härtel Urtext edition points out, had recommended changing the preceding measure, measure 104. Czerny recommended playing F, A flat, D flat, F instead of F, B flat, D flat, F. And Carl Krebs said, 'it is undeniable that the first inversion of the D flat chord here is much better than the second inversion of the B flat minor chord.' I do not believe Czerny would have thought of making this change, if the harmonies of the original manuscript had been correctly printed from the beginning . . . " Walter Gieseking, *So Wurde Ich Pianist,* trans. Dean Elder (Wiesbaden: F.A. Brockhaus, 1962), pp. 127-28.

happens and it is a D flat. Why should it be a minor second the first time and a major second the second? It must be absolutely the same in both places.

"And not only this F flat . . . but also in the first movement — almost near the coda — the jumps in the left hand, measures 268 *et al* . . . all the editions have it printed with the little notes anticipated and coming before. It is not like that in the manuscript of Beethoven. The grace notes are written together with the first sixteenth note of the right hand":

"And in the middle of the Development of the third movement — not actually third movement because the sonata is not in three parts, the middle part is an Intermezzo only — when the theme comes back again in C major in fortissimo, measure 313 . . . And then when it goes back to the dominant, the first G in measures 321 and 325 is written fortissimo by Beethoven. And this doesn't happen anywhere in any edition except the Henle. Other editions have these measures marked piano or pianissimo."

"So when we say that we play exactly as it has been written, as it has been published, it depends what sort of edition we use. It depends on who has edited the piece, what his ideas are, and all that."

I asked Gina Bachauer if she remembered a particularly embarrassing or dramatic moment in her career.

"Embarrassing I can't say but dramatic yes," she answered. "I was in Egypt, where during the Second World War I spent six years as a sort of war refugee. One night I was to be soloist at a charity concert for the Red Cross with the Palestine Orchestra — it was not the Israel Philharmonic at this time. The house was sold out. As I came down from my hotel to go to the concert, I saw the newspaper headlines: 'German Troops Invade Greece.' I thought that

perhaps I would never see any of my family again. Nevertheless, I went to the concert and I played. But suddenly, in the middle of the Beethoven Emperor Concerto, I felt that my fingers were slipping off the keys; I realized that the whole keyboard was wet because I was crying so desperately."

And although she laughed as she recalled one of the most terrifying concerts she had ever played, I could sense compassion in Gina Bachauer's voice. Also . . . as she continued about teaching:

Teaching

"I don't teach because I don't have time, but I adore to teach. During the second World War, apart from playing for the soldiers at this time in Egypt, I gave some lessons to some very gifted students. And I liked teaching very much. But unfortunately now, with all this work I have to do, with all this traveling, it's difficult to teach. But I hope in some years to be able to give some time to young students because I am terribly interested, and if I can help them in any way, I would do it with the greatest pleasure in the world."

Advice to Students

"And if I can give an advice to students, I would say that besides practicing at least six or seven hours every day, they must have an extraordinary perseverance and an extraordinary discipline. If they have decided to become professional musicians, music must always come first. Everything else must take second place. If something else takes first place, then it is absolutely impossible to give what you must give to music.

"Music is an art that is full of beautiful moments, of extraordinary experiences, but it is an art that demands that you give and give. It doesn't take half measures; you must devote all your life.

"The life of an artist is a beautiful life, but it is a very strenuous life. I adore to play the piano and that is why I do it. But I don't like all this traveling and everything that comes with it. But you have to learn to love these things too if you want to do your job properly.

"And certainly with all that I said about perseverance, discipline, and very hard work — Music needs also a little madness." Here she smiled: "If you aren't a little mad, you will never undertake this life!"

BACH TALK

with ROSALYN TURECK

interview August 6, 1977

It is written that Rosalyn Tureck, the "center of an adoring international cult," receives visitors by "dim light, sweeping into the room in exotic Oriental robe and striking a small brass gong to summon maid or secretary." If there is anything disappointing about the "high priestess of Bach," it would be the results she achieves with the gong, for such are her ties with Johann Sebastian that one would expect no less than he to respond to her ring.

Short of delivering Bach bodily, Miss Tureck has done about all a mortal can do to resurrect the composer. She has performed his keyboard music on everything not excepting the Moog synthesizer to standing-room only audiences the world over. Her unprecedented 1937 marathon performance in New York City and her 1953 debut in London were seminal events in bringing Bach to life. Her three-volume An Introduction to the Performance of Bach *is known even in Japanese and her hundreds of articles and lectures have helped establish Miss Tureck as a pre-eminent academic as well as artistic interpretor of Bach.*

If not exactly born to Bach in 1914, Miss Tureck was not long in finding him in Chicago where her parents had escaped the Soviet revolution. After receiving her first lessons from Sophia Brilliant-Liven, who had been a pupil and assistant of Anton Rubinstein, the nine-year-old Miss Tureck made her debut in two solo recitals. At 11 she appeared with the Chicago Symphony and at 13 won first prize among 15,000 youngsters in the Greater Chicago Playing Tournament. By then she belonged to Bach and at 14 began to study with Bach scholar Jan Chiapusso.

Since then, of course, she has been devoted to Bach and, after three marriages, dedicates herself to his — and her — work. However exotic the atmosphere of her apartments in New York and London, it was a down-to-earth gongless though glamorous Rosalyn Tureck who talked informally to me at breakfast the morning after one of her recent magnificent recitals.

Miss Tureck, let's discuss some of the repertoire you were playing before you became a Bach specialist. I remember you played the Beethoven Emperor Concerto with the New York Philharmonic. Was that shortly after you'd been studying with Olga Samaroff?

When I played with the New York Philharmonic, I had already been launched on a career. I made my debut with the Philadelphia Orchestra playing the Brahms B♭ Concerto as the result of winning what was then perhaps the biggest contest in the world, the National Federation of Music Clubs and the Schubert Memorial combined. The Schubert Memorial offered a debut of three concerts with the Philadelphia Orchestra: one at Carnegie Hall and two in Philadelphia. I played the Brahms B♭ for that debut with Ormandy and then for the National Federation of Music Clubs' Award, I played a Town Hall recital: Bach's *Sonata* in D minor, Brahms's *Handel Variations*, six Chopin *Etudes*, the *Ballade* in G minor, *Triana* of Albeniz, a work of Debussy, and one of Ravel. I ended the program with a transcription from the *Firebird* of the

"Dance Kashchei," arranged by Agosti (of which Stravinsky wholly approved, I asked him about it). That was the range of my work.

That's a tremendous program. Was that Guido Agosti?
Yes. We met many years later, in Europe, I think.

Was the Bach Sonata in D minor Bach's transcription of his A minor violin sonata, BG XLII?

Yes, and I still play this work.

Why don't more young pianists perform this piece?
The eight-page fugue probably frightens them, as may the sparse writing of the first, third, and even the fourth movements.

Had you already been a Bach specialist before you made this auspicious Town Hall debut?
Yes, I had been a Bach specialist since the age of 14, when I came to Jan Chiapusso. He discovered my talent for Bach interpretation; and I began to study Bach with him, along with the conventional piano repertoire. I had two courses of study just as in later years I had two careers: one centered on Bach's works and the other on the standard repertoire.

I studied the harpsichord, the organ, the clavichord, and the piano from the age of 14; and I believe knowledge of these instruments is essential to play Bach. These antique instruments entered my blood and bones, my whole psychology and sense of sonorities. When I play Bach on the piano, I don't imitate the clavichord or harpsichord; I play with a separate technique suited to the instrument. I have had to learn the piano more intimately than I ever would have, had I continued with just the standard repertoire.

From what sources did Jan Chiapusso's Bach interpretation stem?
Chiapusso carried on the best Western European tradition, that of Bischoff; and because he was Dutch-Italian, he had the Dutch tradition as well. He studied in Holland and received the profound, very fundamental kind of music education typical of that country. He studied with Leschetizky and Josef Lhevinne, and was a concert artist. He was also a Bach scholar and represented the best of the Dutch school of Bach playing. But his teaching transcended any one school, and he had me study all the early instruments as well as the piano. I began studies in musicology, and researched the transcribers.

I began to play all-Bach concerts when I was 15. I had already played several all-Bach programs besides other kinds of programs when I arrived at Juilliard at age 16. The required pieces for entrance at Juilliard were a work of Bach, a Beethoven sonata, a Chopin work, and a piece of your own choice. I presented 16 preludes and fugues from *The Well-Tempered Clavier*, the Bach-Busoni *Chaconne*, the Beethoven *Sonata op. 2 no. 2*, Chopin's G minor *Ballade*, and *La Campanella* of Liszt. So that again gives the range.

In a class of yours, you made the interesting statement that Bach establishes the tonic at the beginning, Beethoven at the end.

Yes, I think it is not strongly enough noticed that Bach's sense of key emphasizes the tonic in the opening of his works with enormous power. For instance, in the *Toccata* in D major, the whole preamble is an assertion of the tonality using tonic, dominant, and dominant seventh chords, for four or five continuous lines. This strong establishment of tonality at the beginning makes it possible for Bach in the Baroque fashion to go far away from the tonic in his flights of fancy, certainly in all the free improvisational works. Even in the fugues he often moves very far from the tonic, and in the preludes too he establishes a strong tonic before wandering into modulations.

Could you cite an example where Beethoven establishes the tonic strongly at the end?

There are numerous examples all over the place, among them the endings of the "Eroica" Symphony and of the Fifth Symphony, where the tonic and dominant chords are repeated over and over again.

You mentioned that in your teaching you don't insist on your own phrasing or articulation, that instead you develop the student's intuition. Education and custom will change but not intuition. Would you discuss how you work with your students in their Bach playing and specifically their choice of articulation?

I try to open up the form of the work: the form of every motive, the relationship of motive to motive, of rhythmic motive to rhythmic and melodic motive, and so forth, and also the counterpoint. I work tremendously hard on every detail in order to open up the student's perception of what's going on. I also teach different modes of articulation and different designs and patterns — those which fit and those which don't. After the student sees this vast wealth of material and he begins to perceive the suitability of certain articulation to particular motives, then he can start choosing his own. But I can assure you, he does not choose his own right away.

What determines when you use staccato in Bach? I believe you play the opening ascending scale in the last movement of the Italian Concerto, staccato:

I play the whole movement detached. I work according to deep fundamental principles. My choice of touch is not made lightly, but is dictated by the fundamental principles I have developed for Bach interpretation. I am clear about what I'm doing, why and how; I can articulate it and teach it. But nothing is a formula.

For one thing, I don't play the piano pianistically. I mean I don't play in the style typical of the last 75 years or so. I have created a totally new technique of

playing. I play differently from everyone else in the world. I have covered the entire repertoire, and I know the techniques, styles, and sonorities appropriate for the various periods. To satisfy myself that I was playing Bach with authenticity on the piano, I had to develop an entirely new technique of playing. Let me tell you how this came about.

At my first lesson with Samaroff at Juilliard I came in and said, "I have the first 16 preludes and fugues from *The Well-Tempered Clavier*, and I want to finish all 48." She gasped and said, "Well, if you think you can do it." So I went ahead, learning three per week. On Friday afternoon I'd present the three I had learned and memorized that week.

For three months I continued in this way, learning three preludes and fugues per week as well as Beethoven sonatas and other works, and playing the Bach works at Samaroff's musicales on Saturday nights. Then I had a very unusual experience. I had just started the A minor *Fugue* from Book I, which is a very complex one, when suddenly I lost consciousness.

I don't know how long I was unconscious; but when I came to, I had received an insight into the structure of Bach's music which dictated a totally new kind of playing, if it was to be on the piano. I found I had to create a totally new technique — fingers, sounds, phrasing, articulation — everything. And I started from absolute scratch.

After this experience, my practice habits changed drastically. Whereas before I had been learning three preludes and fugues and other works also from Monday to Friday, I now could learn only four lines, the exposition. My whole mental process and physical approach had changed.

When I came to Samaroff for my next lesson, I told her what had happened and what my new ideas were. I played the four lines of music I had learned, incorporating my new approach. She said she thought it was marvelous, if it could be carried through, but she didn't think that was possible. Well, I couldn't rest on my laurels with those four lines; I had entered a new universe; I had gone through that door and could never return. So I went ahead. I had to find every inch of the way myself, and I developed a fundamentally different mental process in terms of how you think music.

Bach's compositional technique represented the peak of several centuries of musical development. Now, over two hundred years later, our habits of thinking music are entirely different. Our habits must be integrated into those of Bach to achieve authenticity, no matter what instrument we use. Authenticity is determined by the mental, psychological, and musical processes and techniques which express the music, not by the instrument used. If you play the harpsichord but have contemporary habits of musical thought, you are not playing with authenticity.

What is one new physical or technical approach which resulted from this experience you had?

It's difficult to single out one element from an entire system. I suppose one fundamental thing is total independence of the fingers — I mean really *total*. In order to achieve this, independence of the brain processes is essential. The performer must be able to think four lines simultaneously, horizontally as well as vertically. That takes an enormous amount of mental training.

Until you can think both horizontally and vertically, your fingers will not obey you. It's hard enough for the fingers to play the notes anyway. The mental process has to intergrate with the physical. But each element of the music must be treated individually. I treat dynamics contrapuntally as well as harmonically, a concept which I know doesn't exist in most pianists' minds.

You suggested sliding out on the keys with weight to achieve control of tone. Do you use this technique in Bach?

Yes, indeed. I utilize every resource of the piano. As I say, I had to learn the possibilities of the piano very deeply, very thoroughly, in the most refined way.

The piano has changed tremendously since it was born. The *Klavier* of Bach's time was different from the pianos of early Beethoven, late Beethoven, Chopin, Liszt, Brahms, Rachmaninoff, Prokofieff, and Stravinsky. It has grown in physical size but size in itself is not the major factor. People talk about the fact that today's piano is loud whereas Bach's instruments were not, but the loudness factor is also secondary. The important factor is the piano's fundamental characteristics: the hammer action, the possibility of a comparatively long-durationed singing tone, the capability of crescendo-diminuendo, and an enormous dynamic range.

The clavichord, although its maximum tone is what we would consider small, also has a large dynamic range if you know how to play it. It's amazing how few people realize that the fundamental, essential clavichord touch is vibrato. The bits of clavichord playing that one hears often are either wholly without or with very little vibrato, and playing the clavichord without vibrato makes it sound like a spinet with a ping to the tone. Ralph Kirkpatrick states on the jacket of his clavichord recording of the "48" that he does not employ vibrato, that vibrato influences the pitch, making it less clean. There I differ with him. I'm at the other end of the pole: the very quality of clavichord tone involves this wavering, this effusion of sound which is not a computer-clean kind of hitting "right between the eyes" in pitch. You need the vibrato for crescendo-diminuendo on one note, and you can make dynamic gradations within lines as well.

The harpsichord with its jack action and drier, more brilliant tone, is entirely different. It has its own marvelous qualities, and I love it. But if you try to approach an authentic Bach style by playing or hearing only the harpsichord, you have only a worm's-eye view of this genius and of the authentic instrumental situation in Bach's time.

Would you comment on the characteristics of sarabande rhythm? A student in your class had the misconception that the emphasis in the following example is on the half note:

The rhythm, after all, of the sarabande is the movement of the comparatively short note to the comparatively long note in the bar, the long duration occurring on the second beat. Just because a note may be of longer duration does not mean that it gets the emphasis that the rhythm demands of the first beat. Music would become terribly lopsided if every time you faced a half note, you gave it the emphasis of the rhythmic first beat. The very essence of the sarabande is the downbeat on the quarter note and the long duration on the half note. That's the essence of the rhythm which you completely distort if you try to do it the other way.

97

Would you discuss some ways of memorizing Bach?

That's a big chapter in itself. I'll try to briefly outline a few techniques for sure memorization — memorization you can depend on when you're playing in public under the most nervous or difficult conditions. Such conditions are the acid test, aren't they?

First, analyze. If the piece is a fugue, analyze the counterpoint and structure in the greatest detail: the subject(s), counter-subjects, and episodes. Then analyze the harmonic structure.

Memorize in sections, the smaller the better, determined by the harmonic modulations and cadences of the piece. If you have a memory lapse, the harmonic structure is not clear enough in your mind. Contrapuntal structure should be noticed and analyzed in non-fugal works as well.

Young artists with originality are too often eliminated in contests. Does this problem of originality affect the pursuit of a career, the pursuit of your Bach career?

Yes, absolutely. You know the power of your own possibilities and if you have courage, guts, you go ahead despite what other people say. As you know, I had a great success as a pianist in all the repertoire; I was engaged with all the major orchestras and I toured the country playing Rachmaninoff, Beethoven, Brahms and so forth. I played varied programs and I could have gone on doing that as the managers wanted me to do. None of the concert managers wanted me to play Bach. Even the musicians were against my giving my first all-Bach series, six concerts in Town Hall which included the 48 *Preludes* and *Fugues*, the *Gold-*berg *Variations*, *Partitas*, *Suites*, and so forth. For that series I won the first Town Hall Award for the most distinguished performance of the year. Three years previously, I had lost the Naumburg Competition. I had presented an all-Bach program and came right up to the finals, but they said they couldn't give me the prize because no one could make a career playing Bach.

At the presentation ceremony for the Town Hall Award Walter Naumburg, the president of Town Hall, apologized for my not having won the Naumburg Competition saying, "We made an error in thinking no one could make a career playing Bach."

You certainly are an example that originality is necessary for a great artist.

Absolutely. Originality is the stamp of the artist. My advice to everyone who wants to make his life in music is: "Pursue what you believe in." Despite the fact that managers kept saying, "Don't play Bach," I kept doggedly on. My Bach concerts never lost money anywhere. For years I played other music as well as the Bach, and gradually after many years my career blossomed in Europe. I had tremendous, hysterical response everywhere I played in Europe. Finally I was brought back to this country and had a very moving, dramatic, beautiful return indeed. I walked out on the Town Hall stage, and the audience rose.

I did what I believed in despite commercial ideas and even other musicians' opinions. Following your own ideas takes enormous courage and guts; but if your conviction is deep enough, it will carry you through.

A Discussion on Bach Ornamentation

Editor's Note: *Certain aspects of ornamentation in Bach playing (especially how to play pralltrillers, or inverted mordents) were the subject of lively discussion during this interview.*

Hermann Keller in his book Die Klavierwerke Bachs *(published by C.F. Peters) says, "...it can't be concluded from Bach's ornament table in his Friedemann's Klavier book that Bach didn't know the short three-note pralltriller or inverted mordent (~) starting on the note," that "...where this sign is on short notes, sixteenth notes for example, it is possible to play only a pralltriller."*

Keller might, therefore, play the pralltrillers in the first Invention *and in the* Fugue *of the* Toccata *from the E minor* Partita *starting on the note. (I even prefer the ornament in the first* Invention *played as a mordent (⅄) perhaps because I first learned it from the Busoni edition but also because I find the mordent more melodic.) I would like to know your feelings as to whether the short pralltriller or praller (inverted mordent) existed in Bach's time and how you play such examples as these.*

Let's take the E minor *Partita* example first because many people consider it difficult to play a four-note pralltriller or praller. I play four notes, starting with the note above the F♯. I manage to employ this embellishment throughout the piece, although there are some very difficult spots.

As written:

Tureck plays:

Many people think playing four notes all the way through is impossible. Things are not impossible when you stop regarding them as such.

I don't go along with Dolmetsch who says never repeat a note because repeating a note in starting an ornament is not melodic. You see, if you play the three-note embellishment in the *Partita* motive, you get a repeated note:

I don't start on the note above to avoid repeating a note, because now and then repeated notes have their point, but because that way is richer harmonically and more dissonant. In this case, starting on the note above is not very dissonant. But sometimes the dissonance is essential, providing another reason to use the upper note.

For me, the three-note praller starting on the note is more incisive and preserves the suspension-resolution characteristic of the Toccata's *motive from which this fugue theme comes:*

Starting on the note is more dissonant and avoids accented non-Bachian-sounding open octaves:

But what is worse, I find that starting the praller on the note above changes the mood of the music, taking the "bite" out of the ornament.

Finding this subject fascinating and still unresolved in our interview, I wrote to Madame Tureck:

"These short prallers have seemed a hornet's-nest problem to me for a long time. The *Inventions* are full of them. Edwin Fischer, Walter Frey, and Gieseking played them fast as three notes, starting on the note for melodic and pianistic as well as historical reasons. They played Bach partially pianistically or organistically, taking fast tempos, kaleidoscoping, making the works highly palatable for audiences.

"Ludwig Landshoff, editor of Peter's urtext editions, in his 'Comments on the Performance of the Inventions' goes further than Keller: 'The ⌇ sign of the first example in Bach's ornament table in Friedemann's Klavierbuechlein often indicates only the simple three-note pralltriller. For example:

rary. Kreb's copy shows in which places the sign ⌇ requires a trill and which places only a praller. In my notes to individual Inventions, if I give no written out execution, the ⌇ is to be executed as a simple praller.'

"So Landshoff would play these examples from the *Inventions* as three-note prallers, starting on the note:

"Bach's table in Friedemann's book seems to prove that he played the longer praller, starting from the note above but does it prove that he played the short praller this way? In his example, he writes out six notes, not indicating what he would do with three or four notes.

As we know, Bach used this sign where he wanted a long trill too. He used the three signs ⌇ , ⌇ , and ⁓ without indicating any difference of execution, measures 2 and 24 in the second *Invention*, for example:

"I know that you have developed your unique style of playing Bach and have had much success. Do you feel there is only one correct way to play these prallers? I know that the school of ornament playing that starts all ornaments, or nearly all, on the note above, never a three-note praller from on the note, is prevalent especially in the U.S. You have made studies in this area, so I would be interested to know something about the research or intuition that brought you to your conclusion concerning the short praller's correct execution. Pianists still need information on this detail."

Tureck wrote the following reply:

"There is no doubt in my mind after long studies and researches and musical experience with both Bach's musical structures and all modern and antique instruments, that beginning the three-note pralltriller on the note is completely wrong. The idea that playing an embellishment from the note above or on any other auxiliary note than the main note disturbs the melodic line is a 19th-century concept which started perhaps over a hundred years even before Dannreuther.

"This idea is pure nonsense. Melodic line must be understood according to the treatment and concept of each era. The ideas of melodic line from the late 18th through the 19th century and, unfortunately, our inheritance in the 20th century, are based on a different kind of music and different sense of melodic and harmonic structures from that on which Bach's musical structures and psychology are built.

"Therefore, the fundamental concept of beginning on the main note not to disturb the melodic line is incorrect. The three-note ornament does exist in 17th- and 18th-century music, but it is the exception rather than the rule. Bach's table in Wilhelm Friedemann's book calls a pralltriller exactly what I do in the E minor *Partita*. The first embellishment which Bach writes out is the pralltriller. He calls it "trillo." Each country and even different sections of a country gave different names to the same symbols. Bach's trillo shows that the embellishment always starts from the note above. The mordent is the symbol with the line through it; there you have a three-note ornament. But it has nothing to do with beginning

on the main note. The important thing about the mordant is that the auxiliary note is the note below rather than the note above. But the fundamental concept of all embellishment of this period is beginning on the beat and on the auxiliary note, not the main note.

"Another erroneous notion about starting on the main note emerges from viewing embellishment decision only melodically. The harmony and rhythm are rarely given consideration. I never decide about any embellishment until I have considered all three elements — the melodic, the harmonic, the rhythmic — and I add a fourth, the contrapuntal. The voice leading is of infinite importance in deciding how to play an embellishment.

"You will notice in the Wilhelm Friedemann table that Bach never suggests that the ornament begin on the main note. Starting on the note above requires a new psychology, a new approach to music, erasing the habits of over two centuries of the past.

Now to return to the interview conversation:

In the *Invention* a very important structural error occurs if you use the three-note ornament. You land on an augmented fourth, the tri-tone:

Tureck plays:

You have F in the bass, B in the treble and that's very bad. True, it's not parallel fourths, but you come straight into this augmented fourth which is bad contrapuntal writing and in itself would be reason for not playing the three-note ornament.

Yes, but the tri-tone, the augmented fourth, is approached by contrary motion. Even if you begin on the note above, you get a hidden tri-tone.

People who start on the note are thinking only of the upper line. They're not thinking of the second line as counterpoint with it or of the harmonic situation. The harmonic and the contrapuntal must always be considered — and the rhythmic — before you can make up your mind about how to play an embellishment.

Now as to the fundamental question, "Is there such a thing as a three-note ornament and do you ever play an ornament beginning on the main note?" I'd say yes, there are moments. There are times when you play a three-note ornament, but they are rare, and before you consider doing the ornament on the main note, you must consider the melodic, contrapuntal, harmonic, and rhythmic situations. And you'll find that 99 times out of 100 you'll be doing the four-note ornament.

Do you think of an example where you would start on the note and play a quick three-note ornament?

By the way, ornaments are never quick in the sense that pianists play quick trills. Embellishment is not conceived in terms of these kinds of jerks. The pianist who plays a quick trill or quick short ornament is thinking in pianistic terms which cover about 70 years of music history. And although everything within that period is valid and legitimate, the error comes in when the rules of these 70 years are turned into another era. The ear and finger habits of these 70 years are to be avoided in earlier music.

Where Was Amy Beach All These Years?

An Interview with Mary Louise Boehm

interview May 1, 1976

Many musical Americans, feeling like toads under the electronic harrow of contemporary composition, have hopped into the fields of this country's past to find them fertile and still surprisingly frontier.

One of our composers from the past who is coming to the fore is Amy Beach. Described by the New York *Sunday News* as "one of the legendary figures of America's musical past," she is on her way to becoming less of a legend and more of our lives. The revival of

Portrait of Amy Beach, now in Choirmaster's Office, St. Bartholomew's Episcopal Church, New York City.

this prolific composer of scores of piano pieces as well as opera, songs, choral, orchestral and chamber works has been largely thanks to American pianist, Mary Louise Boehm, who has recorded the Beach Piano Quintet, a work she compares with the quintets of Brahms and Fauré.

Paul Hume, the *Washington Post* critic, wrote in glowing indignation, "Where has this music been all its life? Why has it never been heard while performances of quintets that are no better are played annually? If the answer is not that the composer was a woman, I would be fascinated to hear it. The performance, with Mary Louise Boehm as pianist, is gorgeous . . ."

I have known Mary Louise Boehm since our student days in the Gieseking Saarbrücken master classes. She had previously studied with Casadesus, and for the past twenty years has pursued an enterprising concert career, playing throughout much of the world.

Despite her busy schedule as a chamber musician and with solo tours as well she has been in the forefront of the resurrecting "next-to-the-greats" craze, recording for Vox chamber and solo works by such diverse composers as Pixis (1788-1874), Moscheles (1794-1870), Hummel (1778-1837) (*Twenty-four Etudes*, op. 125), Kalkbrenner (1788-1849), and Spohr (1784-8159), all friends of Beethoven so-to-speak; the new Englanders, Arthur Foote (1853-1937), and Daniel Gregory Mason (1873-1953); and the contemporary Americans — George Rochberg, Andrew Imbrie, Donald Waxman, David Diamond, Virgil Thomson, and Robert Palmer.

I interviewed Mary Louise Boehm in her Riverside Drive apartment just two days before she was leaving for Europe to record the Beach Piano Concerto.

The encyclopedias, if they mention her at all, say that Mrs. H.H.A. Beach was born Amy Marcy Cheney in Henniker, New Hampshire on September 5, 1867. What other biographical details have you uncovered?

Well, she was a precocious child. She told the story that when four and playing outside on a hot summer day, she composed in her head a "Snowflake Waltz" and played in on the piano for her mother. Percy Goetschius, in his book on the analysis of Mrs. Beach's works (published by Arthur P. Schmidt in 1906) wrote that this piece is "melodious, faultless in form, with uncommonly original modulations, the work of a true genius."

In another source Mrs. Beach recounts "weaving" her first compositions. "I had been visiting my Grandfather's farm in Maine. When I returned home I told my mother I had made three waltzes. She didn't believe me at first, as there was no piano within miles of the farm. I explained that I had written them in my head, and proved it by playing them on the piano."

These little pieces were the first inkling that Amy Beach was an innately gifted musical child. She studied piano with a local teacher and when her family moved to Boston when she was four, she studied there with various teachers. She went to no school, but all her life studied directly the masterwork scores. In teaching herself theory and orchestration, she translated the treatises of Berlioz and Gaevert. "There is no better way to learn how to write a fugue," she wrote, "than to dissect one by Bach." She must have composed every day of her life; her output was prolific.

It's interesting that in composition she was mostly self-taught. From hearing her Piano Concerto, so perfect in form, harmony, and musical grammar, I would have thought she had been thoroughly schooled by the New England traditionalists.

She was clever besides gifted. She did a lot of playing and analyzing. One of her repertoire pieces was the Saint-Saëns g minor Concerto. She liked the French school but she also adored Beethoven and Brahms. She played the American premier of the Brahms Quintet with Kneisel String Quartet. Brahms sent her his autographed picture on the back of which he sketched the oboe theme from the second movement of his B♭ Concerto.

She was well acquainted with the works of Brahms and Franck. She was already a full-fledged composer when Edward MacDowell was studying in Europe. The Boston crowd of the time — Chadwick, Mason, Foote, MacDowell — all had great influence on each other.

She and MacDowell (1861-1908) knew each other very well. The interesting thing is that MacDowell was more influenced than Amy Beach by the French and German compositional schools. I think she kept her individuality to a greater degree by staying in this country. If a man's name had been put on her music, she would long ago have been accepted as an important American composer. But since she was a woman, her music died with her. During her lifetime, however, there were both MacDowell and Beach clubs. She was known as America's greatest woman composer.

Maybe her name worked against her.

You mean Mrs. H.H.A. Beach. They used to call her Mrs. Ha-Ha Beach. At 17, she married an eminent surgeon, who was 24 years older. She was very much in love with him and preferred to drop her own name and use his. Today we call her Amy Beach.

Who were other prominent women in music at the time?

Chaminade, Teresa Carreno. There were other American women too, but Amy Beach was the top; her

Mary Louise Boehm in her apartment

music was performed the most. She wrote a lot of religious music, a Mass in E♭, op. 5, for example, which she began at 19 and finished at 21. She wrote some beautiful anthems and motets. When she came to New York — that was after Dr. Beach had died and she had been concertizing in Europe for four years — she belonged to St. Bartholomew's Episcopal Church on Park Avenue at 50th Street. She knew the organist there very well and she composed music for that particular choir.

She wrote at least 200 songs. In Boston, she belonged to the Browning Society and composed to Browning's poems three of her best-known songs: "The Year's at the Spring," "Ah Love but a Day," and "Pippa Passes." "Ecstasy," a setting of a poem by Victor Hugo, was a favorite of Lillian Nordica.

In concerts, she'd often perform her own Concerto. Her *Gaelic Symphony* would often be on the same program. She wrote a cadenza to the Beethoven c minor Concerto which she played a lot. The reviews and her music indicate she was a fine pianist.

She composed one of her best pieces, the "Festival Jubilate," in 1895 for the Chicago Exposition and the dedication of the Women's Building there.

You recorded her Piano Quintet in f♯ minor, op. 67 for Vox. The more I listen the more this work grows on me. I find it genteel, yet deep, haunting, rather sad, dark-hued, very well orchestrated. How did you discover the Beach Quintet?

I had heard of this piece and moved heaven and earth to get it. I finally found it in a private collection (the manuscript is now at the University of Missouri) and was struck by the work. You could tell from the way she voiced her chords and melodies against the accompaniment, from her use of the piano, the dynamics, how right she was. The color she got from pedal effects and the way she stressed certain notes — all indicated in the score — showed a superb ear. The way she wrote for the strings was beautiful and colorful. Some people at first find other composers with which to compare this quintet: there's some Brahms, Chopin, Franck, D'Indy, Fauré. So what? We're so enamored of the Bach-Beethoven-Brahms bit that we don't take into account there are other worthwhile composers too.

You've played much chamber music. With what masterwork would you compare the Beach work?

103

I'd compare it with the Brahms Quintet as far as length, melodies, treatment. I think it has the stature of the Fauré Quartet in c minor.

Where can you get the music?

You can't. We're trying to persuade publishers to reprint it. It would have to be a major publisher. Small publishers couldn't afford to publish her works.

When did you become interested in her Concerto in c♯ minor, op. 45?

After I had played and recorded the Quintet, I heard about her Piano Concerto. My manager said, "Look, I want you to find a major concerto that no one else plays, and by rights it should be American!" I laughed and said, "Uh, huh." And then I thought, "If her Quintet is so fine, I wonder what her Concerto is like." So I went to the New York Public Library and dug up some reviews. There's a file of clippings about her performances. Every reviewer said it was a great piece.

From 1900, when Mrs. Beach premiered this concerto from manuscript with the Boston Symphony, to 1917 when she again played it in Boston, she had performed it in Chicago, Pittsburgh, St. Louis, San Francisco, Leipzig, Hamburg, Berlin, and many other places. The reviewer of the 1917 Boston concert, a Mr. Parker, said it would be a shame if this work is forgotten because it is one of our best Americn works. And forgotten is what happened; it's been on the shelf ever since.

I tried to find it. There was no copy in the New York Public Library or the Library of Congress, nor in Boston or the MacDowell Colony in New Hampshire where Mrs. Beach had spent many summers. Someone told me I could probably find it in a private collection, and I did.

Finally, I found a copy of the score and the orchestral parts in the Edwin Fleisher Collection in Philadelphia and I thought, "My gosh, this is an important work." Unfortunately, a private person can't take it out from the Fleisher Collection. You have to go there and write out things. Only an organization can take it out. Here's this library sitting on all this fantastic music, and a private person can't even zerox.

I notice the Concerto is 87 pages.

Yes, 87 very difficult pages! Tchaikovsky and Schumann are pushovers in certain respects for someone who has played this work; it's tricky to put together with orchestra.

It's a long piece — approximately 35 minutes — but should not be cut. Amy Beach knew what she was doing. She's clever in making the Concerto a showpiece for both piano and orchestra.

She starts with muted strings, attuning the audience to an interesting pianissimo mood.

After the muted orchestral introduction, the piano comes in with a bravura cadenza. The cadenza has a lot of octaves, Lisztian you can say. She even uses the sostenuto pedal, remarkable in 1900.

When I started studying this thing I thought, "What shall I do? Is this Brahms?" Then I got to the point, "No, there's a little Fauré in this." So I'd play it like a combination of the two. And then I realized that it

makes its own statement.

In the Concerto's big development, she pulls out full orchestra, the piano playing over it. There are octaves similar to those in the first movement of the Tchaikovsky. She has a big, spectacular trill leading again into full orchestra. There are octaves all over the place and double-handed trills — all the Liszt tricks — really pianistic stuff. Why not? The piano's a romantic instrument.

Her recapitulation is like Brahms in that she doesn't make a definite statement of the recapitulation. She just brings it in condensed by the orchestra. She has the second theme blown up a la Rachmaninoff. Her orthography — the way she spells and writes modulating chords — is perfect. Her music is full of augmented sixth chords, for example.

I think her big, full-blown, romantic cadenza is another beautiful thing. As the orchestra fades out and the cellos echo the second theme the piano is in the upper treble playing pianissimo trills. Then she brings in ascending melismata like buzzing bees, leading into the cadenza proper.

The closing is like the Brahms Violin Concerto, where it's very soft. The orchestra just has a pedal point and then builds to a big climax, ending brilliantly which is tough for the orchestra. I remember playing it with one conductor who said, "There are no problems. It's cut and dried. Don't worry about it." That was his first mistake. The double sharps and enharmonic changes are difficult for the orchestra. C♯ minor is a rough key for string players and there are tricky ensemble spots. The conductor has to be on the ball.

That interlocking-chord ending makes me wonder if Rachmaninoff knew this work.

There's a lot of Rachmaninoff in it, isn't there? And his concertos were written after this work. All that stuff was in the wind those days.

I think the second movement, a *perpetuum mobile*, is one of the most unique movements in all piano writing. The piano plays non-stop staccato sixteenth notes which have to come out above the orchestra. It's four and a half minutes, and you live about 40 years during that time.

The third movement Largo is a kind of introduction to the last movement and goes right into the fourth movement. In mood, the theme reminds me of the George Huë song, *"J'ai pleuré en reve."* The last movement is a cross between a 6/8 dance and a bolero rhythm. Naturally, there's another big cadenza.

Now that I've heard this concerto a number of times, I think it could become a repertoire piece along with Tchaikovsky and Rachmaninoff, at least for a change. My first impression was that it is certainly as good as the MacDowell d minor.

I feel it's better than the MacDowell, but it has to be republished before it can be played very much. It was probably published in a limited edition during Beach's lifetime. As far as I know, the score and parts were never published. I suppose she had a score and parts that she took with her. Kalkbrenner did.

Amy Beach's melodies are genteel and at first may seem lacking in strong profile. But once you know them, you realize their subtlety is part of her style. I also found her tempo markings are absolutely right. She's very fond of scales in chromatic thirds.

Pianists of that era must have practiced scales in double thirds.

Yes, and don't forget Amy Beach was brought up on Moscheles. She made her debut at 16, performing the Moscheles E♭ Concerto, which is full of double thirds, with the Boston Symphony.

Let's talk about some of her other piano compositions. I know that Virginia Eskin has recorded 16 of her pieces on Genesis GS 1054 and I see that you have the Prelude and Fugue, op. 81, here on the piano.

It's a big, brilliant, proclamative work, smaller than the Franck *Prelude Chorale and Fugue* in scope. It would be a good program opener for a young pianist instead of the usual Bach or Liszt transcriptions. Again it's full of double thirds. The fugue is very chromatic, like Liszt's organ fugue on BACH. This work was copyrighted by Schirmer in 1918. You can no longer buy it but the Library of Congress has it.

The *Four Sketches*, — "In Autumn," "Phantoms," "Dreaming," and "Fireflies," — are more interesting than similar works of MacDowell. Hofmann used to play the "Fireflies," which is a gem.

Fireflies seemed to have inspired composers of that era: Moszkowski, Liszt, Philipp, and others.

Beach's is an early work. She must have known the Liszt. She wrote a lot of student pieces like "Morning Glories." Some of her teaching pieces are fascinating. The "Scottish Legend" is reprinted in a collection, *American Keyboard Music*, edited by Edward Gold, published by the McAfee Music Corporation. This is the opening theme.

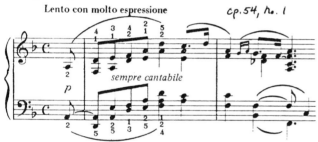

MacDowell also wrote a "Scottish Poem;" Mendelssohn wrote his Scotch Symphony. At the time, people were much interested in the Orient and Scotland.

A very simple, rather charming "Waltz" from the *Children's Album*, op. 36 is in *The American Book for Piano*, edited by Deguire, published by Galaxy.

Her *Summer Dreams*, op. 47 (available from the Library of Congress) is a set of six art duets such as Brahms and Dvorak loved to write. Amy Beach's, though short and written for young students, nevertheless are high-grade teaching pieces.

The *Ballade*, op. 6 has a Fauré-like introductory section followed by a Lisztian-like bigger section. The *Variations on a Balkan Theme* (four hands), op. 60 is one of her best works.

You have to look all over for Amy Beach's compositions. There are surprisingly few in Boston, some in Manchester, New Hampshire. There are none in her birthplace. The MacDowell Colony has only "Morning Glories" and something else unimportant. There are some at the University of Kansas in Kansas City where they have an American Collection. There's not much in the Library of Congress worth doing except her songs. As for chamber music, besides the Piano Quin-

tet, there's a beautiful Piano Trio, a late work, and a Violin and Piano Sonata.

The *Five Improvisations*, op. 148, written in 1938, are available from the Seesaw Music Corporation, 177 East 87th Street, New York City 10028. I love these pieces.

For the first improvisation people might guess Scriabin. I would say it's not typical of her writing.

No, it's one of her last things. She was getting into a more modern idiom, playing with colors. It's like Brahms, reduced to the absolute minimum. To like the late *Improvisations*, you've got to know all the Beach that preceded them. After you've been through all her pyrotechnics, the big sounds, then you realize how she reduced her composition to the least possible sounds.

After having been through so much of Beach, I feel "Here it is in a nutshell," color, beautiful sound, control, and nice melody. There is a certain spirtual qualtiy that comes through. She was very much a sincere person. Every note means something.

What was she like physically?

In her later years she was a tiny, rather plump woman who resembled Queen Victoria. She wrote in very flowery language and apparently spoke that way. She wasn't an unusual or eccentric personality, simply a well-bred New England lady. Towards the end of her life she developed arthritis in her thumbs and feet. She died in New York City on December 27, 1944, at age 77 from complications of high blood pressure and heart trouble.

As a pianist, although she had little hands, she could really move over the keys. Apparently her music has something to say to today's audiences. Wherever I play her music I get the same enthusiastic response: "Where has this music been all these years?"

———

A partial listing of Amy Beach's piano compositions:
Valse Caprice, op. 4
Danse de Fleurs
Ballade, op. 6
Scherzo, From Blackbird Hills
Four Sketches, op. 15
    In Autumn
    Phantoms
    Dreaming
    Fireflies
Trois Morceaux Caracteristiques, op. 28
Children's Album, op. 36
Six Summer Dreams (4-hand), op. 47
    The Brownies
    Robin Redbreast
    Twilight
    Katy-dids
    Elfin Tarantelle
    Good Night
Scottish Legend, op. 54 no. 1
Variations on a Balkan Theme (4-hands), op. 60
Suite (4-hands)
Prelude and Fugue, op. 81
Hermit Thrush at Eve, op. 92 no. 1
Hermit Thrush at Morn, op. 92 no. 2
Nocturne, op. 107
Out of the Depths (Psalm 130), op. 130
Five Improvisations, op. 148

to Alicia de Larrocha

Music Is the Expression of Humanity

interview November 24, 1969

Spain's foremost pianist, Alicia de Larrocha, has been described as a master of refined coloration, rhythmic vivacity, and dazzling technique, "a pianist who can toss off the complex difficulties of the Albeniz *Iberia* and Granados *Goyescas* as if they were basic Czerny."

On stage she is natural and unnervous; off stage, friendly and uncomplicated, a person who smiles and quietly laughs a great deal. As I set up the tape recorder (we spoke in French), I asked why her name is *de* Larrocha and Manuel de Falla's is just Falla — at least according to music criticism a la mode.

"Falla or de Falla — it's about the same," she replied. "Many Spanish families have this *de* in their names, the origin being *marquesado*, aristocratic. I too, am Larrocha or de Larrocha."

Only 4'9" tall and weighing less than a hundred pounds, Alicia de Larrocha (who was born May 23, 1923 in Barcelona) says the amusing moments in her career usually have to do with her size: "Because I am so small, people often don't believe I am the pianist.

"Once I went to a hall to try the piano. A tall, elegant, attractive friend — in fact, *elle est formidable* — went with me. The man in charge said to us, 'Carpenters are working inside; only the pianist can go in.'

" ' *Entrez vous*,' he said to my friend.

" ' But *you*, ' he said, turning to me, 'can't go in.' "

Playing the Piano a Form of Play

Larrocha started piano lessons with her aunt at "two years of age, or something like that.

"Both my mother and my aunt had studied piano with Granados. Marriage ended my mother's career, but my aunt, my mother's sister, taught at home where I used to hear her pupils. Playing the piano was a form of play, meaning more to me than playing with dolls. One day my aunt heard me and decided I should begin lessons.

"After awhile she spoke about me to Frank Marshall, a wonderful pianist and teacher, with whom she had continued her studies after Granados's death. At first, Marshall thought I was too young, but after I had played some small pieces for him — I've been told he tested my ear and so on — he agreed to let me study with him. I was a little over three years old."

"You played a concert when you were five?"

"I played some minuets by Bach and Mozart before an audience, but you couldn't call it a concert. I wasn't a child prodigy. I was a child who had ability for music, in the same way that other children have ability to draw or to do other things — that's all. Beginning very early, nevertheless, was an advantage."

"Do you remember how you learned to read notes?"

"I learned to read notes before I learned to read letters. There were notes in a row on a piece of paper. I played the piano, so I learned to read notes. The process was natural, normal, unconscious."

Marvelous Technician

Alicia de Larrocha apparently gets her extraordinary technique for the massive sonorities and spectacular trills and arpeggios she produces in such works as *Liszt's Sonata in B Minor* and *Schumann's Carnaval* from her fleshy, high arched hands and ample arms and shoulders. She can span a tenth because of an extra long fifth finger, a wide stretch between thumb and first finger, *and* years of stretching exercises.

I told her I found her playing extremely ordered, controlled, and formal — in this respect like the playing of Dinu Lipatti — and orchestral in sonority and melodic approach.

She laughed. "Perhaps what you say is true; I don't know. I have never thought of myself as being equal to or like the others. My playing stems from my schooling, my professor. Each artist must have his *ambiance*, his atmosphere, his 'school,' his temperament. Being completely different is the most important thing."

Ideals and Interpretative Approach

"What are your ideals in piano playing?"

"For me playing the piano is music and it's the music that counts. I try to enter deeply into the music — at least to the extent I believe that's possible — always in my temperament, in my way of seeing things. You must submerge yourself in the music and then work. I recommend that my pupils analyze and work thoroughly *before* being in front of an audience. In front of an audience, you must forget the working or you will lose the spontaneity of the moment."

"What is your approach to the interpretation of various composers?"

"Each composer for me has his own atmosphere and character. Style combines the composer's epoch and his own *humanite*. In Bach, for example — even if he is the culmination of all the polyphony — I find *l'humanite* therein. By *l'humanite* I mean all the meaning of the notes, all that you can feel. I mean all the states of soul that exist in music — horror, tragedy, gaiety, and so on. Music, like all the arts is *l'art de l'humanite, l'expression de l'humanite*."

Great Pianists

"What pianists have you admired most?"

"I would like to commence by saying I admire all pianists, especially today when I see all these young people who play extraordinarily from the pianistic standpoint. But naturally there is always someone special. And for me, Artur Rubinstein has been my idol, my greatest pianistic love. He was a great friend of my professor; they were like brothers. I made Rubinstein's acquaintance when I was five years old, and that is something that lasts all your life.

"But apart from him — and he is completely apart — there are so many extraordinary pianists — Gieseking, Horowitz, Kempff — and I admire each one for different reasons and for their different personalities. Personality is very important. I don't like to hear someone say 'he is very good because he plays like so and so.' To play like someone else is impossible. If a pianist does that, you can do nothing for him."

"Rubinstein and Gieseking," I said, "both had huge hands and photographic memories. They did little repetition practice, Gieseking hardly any at all. On the other hand, other pianists — Richter, Serkin, Bachauer, Darre — admit to practicing much and extremely hard. And I've heard that you practice eight hours a day when preparing for concerts. What are some of the reasons one artist practices much more than another?"

"The amount you have to practice is individual," de Larrocha answered, "and depends, among other things, upon ability to assimilate: one person is far more rapid than another. And then there's the matter of *entrainement*, of being in training. When you have played a long time — Rubinstein all his life, so terribly often — you arrive at the moment where everything has already been worked technically. Preparing is just a question of playing, of redoing the thing. The amount you have to practice is also relative. For example, if you have many different programs to play, you're naturally going to work, the amount depending upon the size of your repertoire and the number of concerts you have to play, as well as upon your ability to assimilate. Sometimes I play all day long and into the night, and other times I don't play at all for several days."

"Do you think it's possible to play different programs nearly every night without much practicing if you don't have a photographic memory?"

"*Si, si.* You can do that. Playing different programs nearly every night without much practicing becomes automatic with time. It's not only photographic memory, but also musical memory — the memory of the form, the construction, and many other things — that count."

Small Hands

"Do you agree that small hands often are fast and can take a great deal of practicing?"

"Yes, that's true. But small hands have the enormous difficulty of playing large stretches. Producing a big sonority is a technical problem, and you can circumvent it to a degree by musical imagination, pedal, phrasing — substituting, arranging."

"Do you believe in stretching exercises for pupils with small hands?"

"Yes, you must give stretching exercises to pupils with closed hands, with hands which haven't much space between the fingers. I do stretching exercises all the time; they're a mania with me.

"I play stretches, for example between the second and fifth fingers, stretching my fingers apart with my other hand and so on — simply opening the hand. I do these exercises *machinalement*, mechanically, on the piano. And then I play chords with the biggest possible stretches, but never until the hand is tired. That's dangerous."

Technical Work

"How do you practice chords?"

"If it's a question of opening up the hand, I practice chords very slowly, staying on the chord to feel the stretch. This kind of practice is exclusively for opening up the hand. Pupils with fairly large hands may have difficulty in achieving solid, even chords but that problem has to do with sonority and is not my problem."

"Do you practice scales?"

"Not *per se,* I don't have time, In general, I practice the technique in the work I'm playing. If I have scales to play, I practice the scales; if I have trills or arpeggios, I practice the trills or arpeggios, and so on. What I practice depends on the difficulty I find in the music."

"What technical work do you give your pupils?"

"I have my pupils do exercises *sur le terrain*, exercises needed at the moment, for the difficulty that they have. Exercises are a kind of medicine which you have to give each pupil according to his needs.

"What I suggest to pupils depends on the sickness, or weakness of the pupil. For example, in Mozart, if the pupil lacks the clarity, or the evenness of the technique and rhythm, I have him work on that. You must show him why he has need of it, explaining the epoch, the style, the phrasing, and so on. You have to look for the path to achieve what the pupil needs: the mechanical means, the evenness, the articulation, the legato — when it is necessary to play legato — the rhythm. You must practice with different rhythms to control the fingers, to secure the security which you have to have to make you free."

"Then you practice in rhythms?"

"Yes, when it is a question of *mecanisme*, a technical problem, I work very much with different rhythms, especially for controlling the fingers and accents."

"Speaking of scales in pieces, how would you have a pupil work on the ending scales of the Chopin Ballade in G Minor, for example?"

"In my opinion, these scales must be absolutely even as well as fast. You must achieve absolute evenness of weight in the fingers. Controlling the weight — the weight which you give each finger — is very, very important."

Memorizing

"What are the principal kinds of memory and how do you memorize?"

"First, there is natural memory. There are passages which you repeat, the difficulties of which you practice very much, that memorize themselves. Without your realizing it one day you know them by heart. But this kind of memory is dangerous.

"Second, there is the kind of memory which for me is almost the most important — musical form memorization. I analyze the work — the phrases, the intervals, the cadences, the form, and so on.

"Third, there is the memory of the fingers, which is also dangerous but which can help.

"Fourth, there is a kind of memory which helps me a lot and which I find interesting: the memory of the accents (so frequent and important in Spanish music) — a phrase where there is an accent, or a phrase where there isn't an accent. This memorization of the rhythmical accent which exists in every musical phrase is *une guide extraordinaire*.

"And fifth, there is a kind of memory which can help and which is also dangerous: the visual memory of the keyboard — what the hands and arms have to do, the distance to be here, to get there. Memory is complex. You must have all these kinds of memory, and of course the musical ear."

Tone and Melody

"What are your ideals in tone, your conception of beautiful tone?"

"I find that the sonority is the portrait of the personality of each pianist or musician. Each artist is like the shape of a face; he has his own sonority, a thing very, very personal. Then each period — the classic, romantic, impressionist — requires a different tone. Therefore it is necessary to have a large palette of tone for this, this, and that. Tone, too, is complex.

"And tone also depends on the climate. The schools of thought about tone in Paris, for instance, are very different from the schools in other cities. And this should be so. Otherwise, music would be boring, if everyone did things the same.

"Tone also depends on the instrument on which you are playing, where you are, the acoustic, and who is listening to you. Your own tone changes all the time, from hall to hall.

"Furthermore, there is the musical conception of artists who view music from an orchestral viewpoint, and of other artists who view music in a smaller or more limited way. What one does with a melody, a phrase, whether one concerns oneself with the palette of the instrument, the polyphony, the diversity of the different voices — these things depend on the artist's musical conception and influence his tone. Absolutely; that is sure. In general, those who think orchestrally, who think big, will have a big, round, large sonority. I don't want to say big in volume, for the quantity is a round thing, a thing of balance."

"Is tone a primary consideration for you?"

"It's very, very important, but there are also other important things. For me, tone is a complement of the whole thing, all things taken together: the form and the tone always go together. For example, rubato is a change in tone as well as tempo. You can't think of the one without thinking of the other."

Melody

"What is your approach to melodic playing?"

"Melody alone rarely exists — sometimes for solo violin, for example. A piano melody depends always on what is beneath or with it. Sometimes one thinks that the melody is more important if one lets it sing alone, very separated from all the rest. But, for me, this is absolutely wrong because there is all the harmony, the entourage that serves this melody; it is there to aid the melody.

"I would even go so far as to say I believe that the melody alone doesn't want to say anything. The melody will be that which all the rest wants it to be. For example, in the Andante Spianato of the big Polonaise of Chopin, all the melody which we have in the right hand depends on the character that you give the left hand. Just the notes in the right hand say nothing by themselves. You can give this melody an intimate, a

dreamy, an agitated, or even a tragic character depending upon what you do with the left hand. The right hand always remains the same; how it sounds depends on the entourage. You can't do anything with just the melody." You have to have other things in order to give it character and atmosphere.

"What is your approach to phrasing?"

"Phrasing depends upon the composer and the work you are playing. Phrasing is the shape of a face, the features of a face. Whether or not you want the visage to have a rude or severe character depends upon how you phrase, how you accent, upon what complement of tone you give and so on. You must search each finality, each thing you want.

"If is for this reason that I say that, in general, technique by itself will do nothing for you. You must see what technique you must apply in the moment and in the piece you are playing, in the style of the composer. Sometimes you must do one thing, sometimes other things."

"Would you say that in Mozart small detailed phrasing is very important, whereas in Chopin the big line is more important?"

"*Si.* Yes, really. But the small details must never disturb the big line because even in Mozart the musical line is always big. The small details must be there without your being aware of them, so natural that you are unaware of them. If a detail stands out, the phrasing is not natural; it is forced."

"Is it more natural to combine two or three phrases into a big line in the romantic composers than in the classic composers?"

"Yes, because in general the phrases in the works of the romantic composers are much longer and larger, the musical form is like *une verre d'esprit*, a glass full of feeling. There is fantasy in romantic works, whereas in the classics, the law of musical form is much more alive."

Spanish Music

"In Spanish music — in Granados and Albeniz, for example — there is much repetition in the phrases. What problems does this repetition of phrasing impose?"

"You take into account the music's folkloric origin. You take the *copies*, the couplets, as the guide to the music. And then, the music of Albeniz and Granados is romantic music — it is written in an absolutely free fashion except in *Iberia* and *Goyescas* which already start to have a form.

"The repetition of phrases does create difficulties in the interpretation: if you don't create variety, the music becomes a routine thing. It is difficult to give variety to all this, but you must look from one side to the other. There is the variation of the rhythm, the color, the state of soul. You must do many things because you have the liberty to do these things."

"What Spanish compositions would you recommend to young pianists as an introduction to Spanish music?"

"I would recommend Albeniz: *Cantos de Espana, Suite Espanola*; Granados: *Danzas Espanolas, Seis piezas sobre cantos populares Espanoles*; and Turina: *Cuentos de la antigua Espana*, and "Sacromonte" and *Zapateado*" from the *Danzas Gitanas, Op. 55.*"

"I like the music of Federico Mompou very much," I said. "I've played and taught almost all of it and pupils like it too." (Madame de Larrocha immediately got up and brought me a color photograph of a

group at luncheon which included herself and Mompou.)

"For him," she said, "the most important thing is tone. In general his melodies are popular. Mompou is an extraordinary pianist. He has a sonority, a personality that you can't imitate; you can't arrive at doing what he can do. The third *Song and Dance,* the one with the Sardana, is dedicated to my teacher, Frank Marshall. Let me see it." (She saw the written initials F.M. on the front of the music which I had brought.)

"Ah, that's the signature of Marshall. How did you get it?"

"No, it's the trademark signature of Federico Mompou."

"But it's Frank Marshall too," she said, laughing gaily. "It's exactly the signature of Frank Marshall."

"It's on most of Mompou's works published by the Union Musical Espanola," I added. "I like the *Songs and Dances* Nos. 5, 6, and 7 very much."

"Yes, they're very beautiful. Number 7 is of popular origin; only Number 5 is original, the themes that is. I'm going to record Numbers 5 and 6 on a disk of contemporary Spanish composers — Mompou, Montsalvatge, Nin-Culmell, Sqrinach, and Ernesto Halffter."

"The *Variations on a Theme of Chopin* could be played in concert," I said.

"*Oui, oui, oui, oui.* That is the most brilliant work pianistically he has composed. I was with him when he composed the eleventh variation. Mompou doesn't like to play very loud or fast; he detests when you play more than mezzo forte or Allegretto. He's worked on a concerto for years, but since it isn't finished, he used the theme in a ballet. Recently he composed an oratory, *Los improperios,* which is perhaps the most important work he has written and which has been recorded. But in general he doesn't like large forms; it is the miniature that he likes. I'll tell him you're writing an article on his music; he'll be pleased."

"I'll tell him . . . he'll be pleased." It was the kind of sweet, sunny, spontaneous remark that seems to characterize Alicia de Larrocha.

Paul Badura-Skoda on

The Schubert Sonatas

interview April 19, 1972

"...Badura-Skoda is a Schubert player with the formidable gifts for the interpretation and technical realization of this music one associates with such giants of the past as Artur Schnabel," wrote Robert C. Marsh in the *Chicago Sun-Times* following Mr. Badura-Skoda's cycle of Schubert's piano music in Chicago two seasons ago.

One of the most prolific recording artists of our era as well as one of the finest pianists of his generation, Mr. Badura-Skoda (born in Vienna in 1927) recently recorded during a two-year span the first recording in existence of the complete set of 20 Schubert sonatas (RCA Victrola) as well as the complete Beethoven sonatas (Musical Heritage) — 24 LPs. In his Schubert sonata recordings, Badura-Skoda has brought to life some of Schubert's long-neglected piano works by reconstructing and completing a number of the unfinished movements.

To lead into our subject, "The Schubert Piano Sonatas," I asked Paul Badura-Skoda — a rather short man of medium build with piercing, black eyes — to tell me his impressions of his teacher, Edwin Fischer (1886-1960), who was himself a great Schubert interpreter:

BADURA-SKODA: Fischer was a creative pianist, in type very close to Artur Schnabel — i.e., he played the same repertoire based on Beethoven, Schubert, and Brahms. But Fischer's approach was slightly different, less intellectual than Schnabel's. When Fischer sat down to play, it was as if the composer himself played and improvised a piece, a sonata, or a fantasy.

As a person, Fischer was very kind, very interested in his students. And one of the great inspirations he gave to me was his credo that an artist must strive for perfection as a human being, combining talent with virtue. Also, an artist ought to have a general knowledge of the arts — poetry, painting, history, and so on.

ELDER: *Fischer as an artist and as a teacher, I believe, often used extra-musical descriptions to invoke inspiration. Do you have memories of his using such descriptions in connection with Schubert?*

BADURA-SKODA: In Schubert, Fischer could draw from his rich knowledge of Schubert's *Lieder* where the same phrases are often linked with poetry. Naturally, if a nearly-identical phrase occurs in a piano work, you will use the underlying text of the given song — I prefer the word *Lied* — to give you an extra-musical inspiration.

For example, the middle section of the Andante sostenuto of the posthumous B flat Sonata has a close resemblance to "*Der Lindenbaum*" (from *Die Winterreise* cycle), where the linden tree is telling the unhappy lover, "Come under my shadow and you will find your rest." This kind of consummation or comfort given by nature, this feeling of becoming one with nature is perhaps one of the most typical expressions of Schubert's music and poetry.

ELDER: *Speaking of nature in Schubert reminds me of something that Gieseking wrote: "Certain composers seem to me so influenced by nature that I feel their music inspired by a specific geography and climate. I identify Schubertian melodies, for example,* with the soft, comforting contours of the Austrian landscape." Do you agree?

BADURA-SKODA: That's very beautifully expressed. I can only affirm that this feeling of the gentle landscape appears again and again in Schubert's music. Schubert is a true composer of Austria. We know from his wonderful account of a journey he took through the valley from Salzburg to Gastein, how vividly he felt the beauty and the richness of the surrounding landscape. He writes to his brother Ferdinand in such a poetic way that for many years this passage in Schubert's letter was used in a reading textbook in Austrian schools:

> Gmunden, 12th September 1825
>
> Dear Brother,
>
> . . . To describe for you the loveliness of the inner Salzburg valley is almost impossible. Think of a garden several miles in extent, with countless castles and estates in it peeping through the trees; think of a river winding through it in manifold twists and turns; think of meadows and fields like so many carpets of the finest colours, then of the many roads tied round them like ribbons; and lastly avenues of enormous trees to walk in for hours, all enclosed by ranges of the highest mountains as far as the eye can reach, as though they were the guardians of this glorious valley; think of all this, and you will have a faint conception of its inexpressible beauty . . . .

Viennese Influence

ELDER: *Going from the Austrian landscape to Vienna, what is Viennese in Schubert's piano music?*

BADURA-SKODA: This is a difficult question to answer. When we come to the nineteenth century, idiomatic expression in music takes on greater importance than it did in the eighteenth century. In the eighteenth century, music had a more international appeal. You don't feel that Mozart, for example, is particularly Salzburgian in his expression, although he is very Austrian. You find in him elements of Italian, German, and French music as well. The music of Bach and Handel is also international. And when you hear Beethoven, you don't think that this is a man who comes from the Rhine country near Bonn, although you find some things specifically German in him.

Probably the greater the artist, the more universal his appeal will be. This is the reason why the music of Bach, Handel, Mozart, or Beethoven has reached the world and has been played well by people of whatever nation.

But with early Schubert, the picture seems to change. Indeed it is helpful to know the Viennese idiom. In some of his dances — particularly in some of his waltzes — and in some of his early piano sonatas, a lot of the specific joy of music which is Viennese — this finesse, this lightness of touch, this sense of delaying or anticipating a note — is inherent. It is necessary to understand this sense of freedom in order to give his music meaning which is true and at the same time alive.

It would be wrong to play Schubert without any tempo change, like a metronome. But of course the same thing can be said of nearly every great piano composition.

And needless to say, the Viennese dance idiom in Schubert has universal appeal. When I played the last movement of the D Major Sonata, Op. 53, D. 850, in a rehearsal in Naples, two cleaning women — people who have little connection with serious music, who are really representative of the populace — left their brooms and danced along with the music. I was delighted. I think their dancing was the greatest compliment to Schubert and to me.

ELDER: *What Schubertian landmarks are there in Vienna?*

BADURA-SKODA: We have Schubert's birthplace, 54 Nussdorferstrasse, which is kept as a museum. It has a wonderful display of important documents, manuscripts, portraits of Schubert and his friends, original letters or reproductions, and perhaps one of the most moving things — his spectacles.

And there are other places in Vienna. But more important to me is the city library which has the largest Schubert collection in the world. I have gone there countless times to find out whether or not a certain printed version is correct.

ELDER: *Would you say something about the influence of Haydn, Beethoven, or Hummel in Schubert?*

BADURA-SKODA: Like every genius, Schubert started out by imitating to a certain degree. You can find that certain passages in his instrumental works remind you of Mozart, Haydn, or Beethoven — much less Hummel. To tell the truth, I haven't found one passage in Schubert that reminds me of Hummel, but some scholars pretend they have found resemblances.

Schubert is perhaps the most sincere, the most open-hearted of all composers. He expects from us, his interpreters, the same sincerity of approach.

I would say rather that Carl Maria von Weber might have had a certain influence. I find certain resemblances, for instance, between Weber's A Flat Sonata — which Schubert might have known, or at least have heard because Weber and Schubert became friends — and a certain way of expression in Schubert's G Major Sonata, Opus 78, D. 894.

But as Schubert grew, he very soon developed his own independent style, fusing elements of other composers into a style of his own — a style so typical that you have to hear but one phrase to know that this is Schubert and no one else.

Regarding Schubert's style, I would particularly mention the enormous wealth of melody you find in any of his works — he was perhaps the world's greatest creator of melody — and his wonderful sense for a long, epic span. This last characteristic resembles a certain trait of Beethoven. But while the epic span is found only occasionally in Beethoven — for example, in his B Flat Trio, the "Archduke," — it becomes the rule in Schubert. Naturally, the resemblances between Schubert and Beethoven are the most numerous because they were contemporaries, living in the same place. It is inevitable that you find resemblances in the work of two giants of this kind, resemblances — this must be emphasized — which are not imitation.

Very often you find a typical Beethoven passage in Schubert written earlier than the respective composition by Beethoven. More often, of course, you find the opposite — a Schubert passage that seems to imitate a work of Beethoven. The laws of music are the same.

Affinity to Mozart

ELDER: *Do you find affinity between Schubert's Sonata in A Minor, Op. 42, D. 845 (composed in 1825) and Mozart's Sonata in A Minor, K. 310 (composed in 1778)?*

BADURA-SKODA: I find some subconscious influence, particularly in the Finale movements. Both of

them are in 2/4 meter, rather rapid. Both of them have an entrancing, dream-like middle section in A major.

And both of them seem to express a certain tragedy together with a defiance, a not giving in to tragedy. All of these similarities might be coincidence.

It is interesting that the same key throughout musical history has produced works in a very similar expression. For example, the key of B minor — which Beethoven called "the black key," the key expressing starkest, hopeless tragedy — is the key not only of Schubert's "Unfinished" Symphony but of Tchaikovsky's Symphony "Pathetique."

Deutsch Numbers

ELDER: *Why did Deutsch re-catalogue Schubert's works?*

BADURA-SKODA: When Schubert died, less than ten percent of his creative output — only three of his piano sonatas, the A Minor, Op. 42, D. 845; the D Major, Op. 53, D. 850; and the G Major, Op. 78, D. 894 — had appeared in print. And in successive years, many of his compositions — early as well as later ones — appeared piecemeal. Each work was given an opus number according to the date it was published. That means a work, let us say, that appeared in 1830 received a lower opus number than a work that appeared in 1840, the opus numbers having nothing to do with the chronology of the works. On the contrary, very often the highest opus numbers were given to works which Schubert wrote in his earliest youth.

To do away with this chronological confusion, musicians prefer now to use the catalogue made by Otto Erich Deutsch which has the same meaning for Schubert as the Koechel catalogue does for Mozart. With few exceptions, a higher Deutsch number indicates a later composition.

Editions

ELDER: *What are the best editions of the sonatas?*

BADURA-SKODA: The Universal (14 sonatas) and particularly the Henle. The Dover reprint of the Breitkopf & Haertel (15 sonatas) has three early sonatas not in the Universal or the Henle.

ELDER: *Have you edited any of Schubert's works?*

BADURA-SKODA: Yes, having been deeply involved with Schubert's music all my life, I prepared an edition of the *Wanderer Fantasy*, the eight *Impromptus*, the six *Moments Musicaux*, and the three posthumous *Klavierstuecke* for Universal Edition, published here by the Presser Company in Pennsylvania. And now I'm publishing a volume of the hitherto unpublished nine sonatas — most of them early — for the German publisher, Henle. Unpublished is perhaps an exaggeration — a few of them have been published, but some of them have never before been published in their original form.

ELDER: *In your integral recording of the 20 Schubert sonatas, you completed a number of the unfinished movements. What led you to do this and what guided you?*

BADURA-SKODA: The study of Schubert's manuscripts. No other great composer left so many unfinished works, thus creating an enigma that cannot be completely solved. Most of the unfinished works were by no means inferior works abandoned because of dissatisfaction. The case of the "Unfinished" Symphony — so complete in itself — proves this. I believe the force of inspiration often prevented Schubert from fin-

with Frank Martin, the Swiss composer who dedicated his Piano Concerto No. 2 to Badura-Skoda

ishing a work. Having barely written down the essential parts of a sonata movement, he immediately started to write the next movement, and so on. Although he had a very quick pen, his mind was far quicker. He may too have been haunted by a premonition of an early death.

Fortunately, Schubert was very systematic in writing down nearly all his unfinished sonata movements up to the recapitulation. As the complete compositions show, most of Schubert's recapitulations are literal or nearly literal transpositions of the exposition. Consequently, completing an unfinished movement remained a somewhat mechanical task, which he left for later moments.

In one instance Schubert carried out this task himself. In the case of the B Major Sonata, Op. 147, D. 575, both the unfinished preliminary and the final versions are extant. So, all I had to do in completing most of the unfinished sonatas — the only exception being the finale of the great C Major Sonata, D. 840, the autograph of which breaks off not *after* but *in* the development — was to follow Schubert's own example.

ELDER: *How do you approach the interpretation of the Schubert piano sonatas?*

BADURA-SKODA: I don't make a different approach for Schubert from any of the other great composers, my first effort being to secure a text which represents the composer's intentions. Regardless of which edition you use, there are bound to be errors of one or the other kind. Every editor, knowingly or unknowingly, interprets the facts. It is nearly impossible to pass on just the facts without interpretation even when it comes to musical text.

So, I have made it a rule to try to see the composer's manuscripts wherever possible. And my travels around the world as a concert artist have enabled me to see many a manuscript, usually inaccessible to the average pianist, in a public library or in a private collection.

After establishing the text, I try to read and to play it without interpreting, simply letting the text speak. I feel today we do too much interpreting. Very often a fine artist spoils his work by "over-interpreting," giving too much meaning to each phrase instead of letting the phrase speak for itself. So, I try to let the music speak its own language. And only after I feel completely in harmony with the music, do I let my own personality enter the composition. In other words, I do not make a point of saying, "this is *my* interpretation."

Schubert Interpreters

ELDER: *Is this, in a way, also the approach of other great Schubert interpreters such as Fischer, Gieseking, Kempff, Lili Kraus, Richter, Schnabel, Serkin, as well as yourself?*

BADURA-SKODA: Thank you. It's very kind of you to call me one of the great Schubert interpreters. I have found particularly with Schubert that similarity of interpretative approach is the case. Schubert as a human being is perhaps the most sincere, the most

open-hearted man of all composers. And therefore, he expects from us, his interpreters, the same sincerity, the same humility of approach. Indeed, if you haven't got the humility to accept this music as a God-given present, as a most wonderful, joyful experience, then you perhaps shouldn't approach Schubert at all. And indeed all the interpreters that you have mentioned seem to have or to have had a similar Schubertian outlook. Edwin Fischer always insisted that we be as simple as possible, letting the music speak in its poetry, searching for the composer's intentions and not our own.

It's the very same I've found out from personal acquaintance with Sviatoslav Richter. Richter is a most devout Schubertian and has done a great deal for Schubert's case, first in Soviet Russia and later throughout the world. Richter told me that when he started to play the Schubert sonatas, he was considered kind of crazy: people would say "Who cares for this music which has no virtuoso effects, which is so easy, which is so long?" And Wilhelm Kempff, a true servant of the great composers, approaches Schubert in much the same way, with humility.

Characteristics

ELDER: *Would you comment on the following characteristics of Schubert's piano sonatas? Characteristic 1: A feature of many of Schubert's slow movements is that the agitated mood of the middle section persists into the repetition of the main section.*

BADURA-SKODA: Very good. This feature is found in quite a few of his slow movements. The middle section need not be really agitated, but usually it has a quicker motion than the opening section, the quicker motion frequently being carried over into the recapitulation. A beautiful example of this is found in the Andante movement of the unfinished C Major Sonata, D. 840, the "Relique" sonata, which I consider one of Schubert's most beautiful works. At the recapitulation of the main theme, the motion of the middle section is carried over as a kind of underlying countermelody. The two motions are united or combined:

ELDER: *Characteristic 2: In Schubert's sonatas, moderate tempos abound, whereas in Beethoven's piano works "moderato" occurs only once — in the Allegro moderato of the Fourth Concerto.*

BADURA-SKODA: Beethoven seems almost afraid that his pieces might be played too slowly, writing "Allegro con fuoco," "Allegro vivace," "Allegro con brio," "Allegro appasionata," and so on. Schubert, on the other hand, seems afraid that his music might be played too fast, tempering down the would-be quick player with "Allegro moderato," "Moderato," or "Allegro non troppo."

As it turns out, very often these indications are carried to the extreme. Many Beethoven movements are played too fast, and many Schubert movements too slow. People overreact. We must not forget that at the time Schubert lived, a rather light, lively approach to music was the habit, with little striking under the surface. People played through a sonata movement

genuine dances in his minuet movements, something Beethoven seldom did.

BADURA-SKODA: It is true that in Beethoven the folk music element appears only occasionally as in the famous minuet from Op. 49, No. 2 which indeed has a folk music flavor:

*Badura-Skoda's articulation derives partly from Beethoven's own in the Septet, Op. 20, where Beethoven uses the same theme.

But in Schubert you find the folk music element much more often, particularly in his scherzo movements which sometimes are nothing but a waltz in disguise.

I find, however, that as Schubert grows — and he grows rapidly because he had so little time to spend on this earth (1797-1828) — the Viennese expression, also in the dance movements, nearly disappears. Schubert becomes universal. And here one fact needs to be noted: Schubert, the only one of the great classical composers born in Vienna, was not of Viennese descent. Both his parents came from north of the Austrian Monarchy, from Silesia, a German part of Moravia. The Silesians were known for a kind of mystical, introverted way of life — nearly the opposite from the gay Viennese.

ELDER: *Characteristic 4: Schubert's frequent passing from minor to major. What emotions does this device convey?*

Those pianists who know how to bring out the upper voice produce the most sensuous, beautiful tone.

---

lightly and elegantly in a rather quick and superficial way. In view of this prevalent approach to music-making, Schubert's warning not to play too fast, but to play with meaning, was very necessary.

Today, however, his indications might lead to a too-heavy interpretation. And Schubert should not be too heavy. You should always bear in mind that he is the greatest of all *Lied* composers. In a *Lied*, the length of a phrase is usually decided by the breath of the singer. Similarly, in a piano phrase, you should feel that you can sing a four-bar phrase as a unit without taking more than one respiration. By so doing, you will not come to these extremely slow tempi which are sometimes performed.

ELDER: *Does this lyric quality carry over into the type of tone that you use?*

BADURA-SKODA: Very much so. Particularly in my recording, I took the greatest pains to try to get a singing tone — a tone which by its sheer tone quality and beauty gives the lyrical feeling of Schubert's music. Nothing is more difficult than making the piano, which is basically a percussion instrument, sing.

ELDER: *When did you record the 20 Schubert sonatas?*

BADURA-SKODA: I did them over a period, starting in 1967 in the RCA studios in Rome, continuing later in Vienna, redoing a few sonatas two and even three times until I found I had approached the sound, the truth.

ELDER: *Characteristic 3: Schubert introduces*

BADURA-SKODA: Repeating a minor phrase in major and vice versa is indeed one of Schubert's favorite compositional devices. He is not, however, the only composer to use it. Mozart used it quite often and even used an expression for it: "chiaroscuro," "*Hell-dunkel*" in German, "light and shade" in English.

These changes from major to minor always reflect a change in mood, major and minor being two opposite poles of expression in classical music — like male and female, or bright and dark. In general, minor is a depression of major.

ELDER: *Characteristic 5: Schubert's passing, with little or no preparation, into the key a major third below his tonic.*

BADURA-SKODA: This characteristic is often the expression of loftiness, as in the Finale of Beethoven's Ninth Symphony:

Schubert uses this device frequently — in the first movement of the posthumous Sonata in B Flat Major and in the first section of the *Wanderer Fantasy*, for example:

The highly original Finale is superb as is the Scherzo which has the only recapitulation on record starting in the supertonic — in this instance, D major!

ELDER: *Characteristic 6: As the content grew more individual, Schubert's sonata form grew more conventional, the opposite from Beethoven.*

BADURA-SKODA: I don't agree. Take the Finale of the C Minor Sonata, D. 958, one of the longest finales in the literature. The first subject group starts in C minor:

The second subject group — very rich in modulations — is in C sharp minor:

I think this erroneous impression that Schubert's sonata form grew more conventional as the content grew more individual stems from the fact that his sonata structures unfold with perfection. Because the compositional effort is not felt and the various elements blend smoothly, one gets the erroneous impression that the structures are conventional.

In Beethoven's last sonatas, on the other hand, the compositional effort is at times indeed felt. The connecting seam is not hidden. In the recapitulation section of the first movement of Op. 110, what an effort — nearly clumsy — Beethoven goes through to get back from E major to the second subject in A flat major!

Schubert couldn't stand "the damnable thumping which pleases neither the ear nor the mind."

The third subject group — "dreamlike" — is in B major:

And the fourth subject group is a huge development, combining material from the third group with motivic fragments from the first two groups, leading to an enormous, powerful climax — one of the longest crescendos in piano literature.

The recapitulation of the first group is in the expected C minor, but the second group starts in B flat minor. Then the coda, in C minor, quotes one part of the first group which had been left out in the recapitulation and omits the C major section of the first theme, ending the movement in stark tragedy.

There is nothing conventional in this structure. The use of tonality — the most important element in classical, formal construction — is so unconventional that Schumann, Chopin, and Brahms never dared do anything like it. Only Bruckner did, much later.

The four-hand Sonata in C Major of 1824, called "Grand Duo," Op. 140, is another unconventional sonata form from every point of view.

ELDER: *Characteristic 7: Schubert's practice of announcing the opening theme of a movement in bare octaves.*

BADURA-SKODA: Schubert does this particularly in works in the minor key with a special poignant, stark effect, as in the Sonata in A Minor, Op. 143, D. 784:

(A foretaste of Bruckner: compare the fortissimo theme in Bruckner's Ninth Symphony.) Such passages are often pregnant with harmony and inspire Schubert to dramatic results in the development sections.

There are numerous other works which Schubert begins with bare octaves. For example:

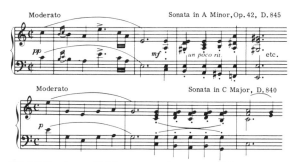

ELDER: *In a 1928 essay, Sir Donald Tovey suggested that the intellectual drive behind the Schubert sonatas need not be sought solely in theme manipulation, or in the Beethoven architectural schemes; it may be found equally in Schubert's patterns of modulation, in the juxtaposition and combination of the tonal colors implied by the key in which he was composing.*

BADURA-SKODA: Indeed, this article by Tovey in which he took the Trio from the Scherzo in the great C Major Symphony as an example of Schubert's ingenuous use of harmony, was and still is a most valuable contribution to the understanding of Schubert. I hope that many musicians will read it.* Such an article should be recommended for study in classes in advanced harmony.

Subduing Accompaniments

ELDER: *Serkin said to me of the Andantino of the posthumous A Major Sonata: "If the lower parts are really accompaniment, I believe in subduing them. But the A Major Sonata slow movement is different.*

*"Tonality in Schubert" from **Music and Letters**, October 1928, is reprinted in **The Main Stream of Music and Other Essays**, by Donald Francis Tovey, Meridian Books, Inc., New York, 1959.

I would compare it to a string trio.

Gieseking, on the other hand, for whom melody could never be singing enough, would not have made the left hand as prominent as the right — even though he, like Serkin, wanted the first left-hand C sharps brought out somewhat. What is your feeling about subduing this kind of accompaniment in Schubert?

BADURA-SKODA: Gieseking was a master in bringing out the leading, singing voice which accounted in part for the unsurpassed beauty of his playing. And in general I find that those pianists who know how to bring out the upper voice produce the most sensuous, beautiful tone. Wilhelm Kempff, or to mention two other very different kinds of artists — Horowitz and Cortot — also know or knew how to bring out the upper voice. On the other hand, I believe that Serkin wants to get away from the purely sensuous appeal that can result from emphasizing the upper voice too much.

Here I would like to quote Schubert who, in a beautiful letter, mentioned that he was proud of having received praise for making the piano sing and that he couldn't stand "the damnable thumping which is peculiar to even the most distinguished pianists and which pleases neither the ear nor the mind."

I believe in subduing particularly the inner voice, not so much the bass line which in Schubert usually is very melodic, a kind of countermelody. I don't see any contradiction between subduing the accompaniment on the piano and chamber music playing: in a good string quartet or string trio, the first violin will stick out a little.

ELDER: *Do you pedal through the staccato in this kind of Schubert bass accompaniment?*

BADURA-SKODA: In this question there is disagreement among pianists. Alfred Brendel, for example, pedals through the measure whereas I prefer the "orchestral" treatment, maintaining the pizzicato effect by making a pedal change or half change after the first note. This is the way Edwin Fischer pedaled these basses.

As other examples of this kind of staccato bass accompaniment, so often found in Schubert, one could quote the second subject of the first movement in the Sonata in E Flat Major, D. 568 and the theme of the Impromptu in B Flat Major, Op. 142, No. 3, D. 935:

with Mrs. Badura-Skoda, in Vienna

I believe to have proved in my recordings that the subtle change of the pedal does not ruin the beauty of the legato, singing right-hand line. The Andante sostenuto of the posthumous Sonata in B Flat Major, D. 960, however, is an exception, Schubert having expressly marked it "with pedal":

Works with which to Begin

ELDER: *What Schubert sonata or movements would you suggest as being the easiest for students? Teachers and students, in general, don't know the Schubert sonatas well, expecially the early inaccessible ones.*

BADURA-SKODA: Unfortunately, this is true. As you know, pianists didn't play Mozart in concert during the nineteenth century. Mozart was as nonexistent as Schubert. But Mozart was at least considered good stuff for children, whereas Schubert most of the time didn't even get this benefit. Schubert's music is not so easy as Mozart's as far as the notes are concerned and does not always gain by being played by children.

ELDER: *What Schubert sonatas would you suggest for high school students or a talented student who has played several Beethoven sonatas?*

BADURA-SKODA: I can easily mention a few. And I hope my recordings and my forthcoming volume for Henle will be helpful. Most of the so-called easier sonatas — the earlier Schubert sonatas not found in most collections, some of which have never before been published — will be in this volume.

The delightful, poetical Sonata in E Minor, D. 566 can be played by students who have played one or two of the easier Beethoven sonatas:

This sonata has survived in four movements, but some people doubt whether the third and fourth movements really belong to it. I believe that they do. Kempff, on the other hand, believes that this sonata is better represented by playing only the first two movements, making a counterpart to Beethoven's Sonata in E Minor, Op. 90.

The Haydnesque Sonata in A Flat Major, D. 557, composed in May 1817, is not difficult:

And the Sonata in F Sharp Minor, D. 571, with its romantic moods, is also one of those works which present no great technical demands, particularly the first movement:

But perhaps as an introduction to the piano sonatas of Schubert, the first movement of the Sonata in E Major, D. 157, Schubert's first sonata, with its vigorous flow and ingratiating, light-hearted second subject, might be the most immediately appealing and accessible of all.

Suggestions for Performance of D. 157

The whole movement needs a strong masculine rhythm, the up and down motion of the theme accompanied by a slight crescendo and decrescendo. The staccato notes in measures 9-14 should be played without pedal and considerably lighter than the ensuing half notes:

The same holds true for the left hand from measure 65 onward:

The most difficult problem in the interpretation lies in the long general pause in measures 43-44 which should not be a dead silence but should be rather like a deep respiration before reaching the dominant key of the second subject. The staccato notes of the second theme should be played delicately and not too short, the two-note appoggiaturas always gracefully and not too fast. And there should be a slight emphasis on the first notes in measures 49, 51, and 53:

The development section — measures 108 et al —
should be vigorous and stormy, the eighth notes non-
legato, martellato throughout:

Speaking through their own beauty and poetry, the
Schubert piano sonatas do not need description. For
me they are the most moving music, the one music
that speaks immediately to the heart of any listener.
They do not require any intellectual training to understand their message, but have the gayest expression,
which can lead from the most earthbound rhythms to
the most enraptured sounds. In Schubert's terms, our
world was incomplete and left much to be desired, but
his music transcends our own world and seems to
come from another.

* * * * * * * * * * * * * * *

Alternate Versions for Use in the Repeats

On February 11, 1815, Schubert wrote a preliminary version — up to the development — of this
movement, an Allegro, D. 154 (which can be found in
the appendix volume 18 of the Dover edition of Schubert's complete works). On the repeat of the exposition, I substitute the following measures from the preliminary draft, D. 154, for measures 65-71 and measures 73-89 respectively of D. 157:

Photos courtesy of Mariedi Anders Artist Management Inc.

WALTER KLIEN:
Intuitive Interpreter

interview

August 11, 1976

If it is true that every human being is "a millionaire in emotions," as Nobel Prizewinner Isaac Bashevis Singer says, too few spend this inheritance as intuitively as Walter Klien. The Austrian pianist is known for his recordings of the complete solo works of Mozart and Brahms and the Schubert sonatas, but he should also be known for just being Walter Klien.

"Nowadays many people think everything must be fixed, that there must be rules," he says. "That's what I try to avoid."

Klien's contempt for rules does not extend to those in the position to make rules, such as master pianists Rudolf Serkin and Arturo Benedetti Michelangeli, both important influences in his career. Five years after his birth in Graz, Austria in 1928 Klien headed for the piano, studying in Austria and Germany. Since 1954 he has toured extensively as a recitalist and symphony soloist and on occasion has played four-hand works with his wife, Beatrice, and pianists Alfred Brendel and Rena Kyriakou.

Klien's approach to piano playing is singing, intuitive, and musicianly, not super-emotional. In a recent program of Mozart, Brahms, and Beethoven, his interpretations displayed individual voice-leadings and tonal balances. His Brahms *Fantasies,* Op. 116 were rock-solid, stylistically correct, spontaneously beautiful.

Nor is he a flamboyant teacher. In his masterclass Klien spoke succinctly, saying no more than the essential without trying to be wordy or colorful. He says "It is harder for me to express myself in words than to play." As in his playing, the ideas he expressed were musicianly. He emphasized singing line and style, pointing out details in melody playing, phrasing, moving voices and harmonies, overall mood, dynamics — ideas dictated by the music's message and flow.

I asked him what he had learned from Michelangeli. "I learned a lot concerning touch and the use of the pedal. It was strange studying with him — he's a complicated person, yes? But if he is interested in someone, then he may spend more time with you. There are no lessons in the usual sense. A lesson would last an afternoon or a whole morning, you know. I didn't work technique with him, just expression, phrasing, breathing. I played for him a long time ago, in 1952, when I was 24."

When you were on the faculty at Marlboro, did you learn anything from Serkin?

Oh yes. When one speaks about Serkin, one doesn't speak only about a pianist. He is a great personality, a man one has to love. He is the man I admire most. I never had lessons with him, but I have his recordings. I would have liked him to criticize more when I played, but he didn't. I learned a lot from his concerts.

What is your interpretative approach to Mozart?

I try to avoid the old historic approach to Mozart or to play his music on the old instruments. It is interesting to know the limits of the instruments Mozart had, but I don't think he was always happy with them. Beethoven, you know, pushed the Stein people to develop new and improved instruments, so I don't think the composers' ideas were always for the instruments they had. I sometimes go to the Hoffberg Museum in Vienna where there are old instruments. It is fascinating to know how they sound and what instruments the composers had in their lives, but when I come to the concert halls, I am happy with a lovely modern concert grand. I think Bach, Mozart, and Beethoven would have preferred it too.

What famous Mozart and Brahms players have you admired?

Oh well, with Mozart of course Gieseking, Fischer, and Schnabel; and with Brahms I admire Kempff. Backhaus' playing I respected more than I liked. With Gieseking one had to admire his approach and all that he wrote about how to play Mozart, which was new in his time. I heard one of his last concerts in Vienna when he played the last Mozart sonata, Debussy, and Ravel.

A young pianist told me that from listening to Schnabel's recordings, he can't understand why Schnabel was so famous.

I don't understand this reaction. Not all of Schnabel's recordings are outstanding, but some of them are out of this world. Maybe some young people don't understand the flurried passages. Artists didn't use to make retakes. There was no tape splicing.

In your class yesterday, were there things you mentioned to students about Haydn and Schubert which could also apply to Mozart and Brahms?

The legato and dynamics are always important. In the Haydn Sonata in A♭, as in Mozart, Brahms or whomever, one shouldn't play one note after the other but should phrase the long line. For instance, the first three measures should be played legato as one melodic line, uninterrupted by the ornaments.

Also in the slow movement, the first four measures should be played in one line, not chopped up. The E♭, D♭, C, D♭ in measures 3-4 should diminuendo with no accent on the E♭. Don't play all the notes at the same volume.

Notes that come after longer notes need to be played softer. In these figures in measure seven, you shouldn't accent the A♭ in the B♭-A♭-G♭-F figure or the next A♭. If you sang this, you would never accent these A♭'s. These are important considerations in performing any composer.

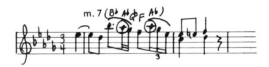

How do you practice the Mozart or Brahms pieces that you often play?

I like to practice slowly, without much pedal, trying to hear the piece, to have it new. I try to avoid routine feeling. When one plays a piece very often, there is the danger that one knows it too well. So, I try to discover new things — inner voices or whatever — to find a new approach to the work.

What do you think about as you perform, for example, the Brahms Op. 116 pieces you are going to perform tonight?

That is an important question. I read about the poets of Brahms' time, or people he admired. In Vienna we have the Brahms library. He gave his books to the *Gesellschaft der Musikfreunde,* and one can see them there. They are full of markings. There are books by Eichendorff, Fontana, E.T. Hoffmann, and a lot of books on German history and politics which one wouldn't expect. All these books Brahms owned are together in one room.

Are there manuscripts in this Brahms library?

Oh yes, the *German Requiem,* for instance. The *Variations on a Theme of Schumann,* Op. 9 is there, too. Of Mozart, there is the Concerto in D Minor. There are Schubert's "Unfinished" and C Major Symphonies, Beethoven sonatas, Haydn quartets — unbelievable what they have.

Do you practice a technical regime, exercises, scales?

No, I don't. I try to find difficulties in the works and transpose them.

For example, are there difficult parts in the Brahms Op. 116 where you would do technical work?

Yes, especially in the last piece, the *Capriccio* in D Minor; and in the *Intermezzo* in E Minor, the fifth piece, the *anschlag* or touch is especially important.

Andante con grazia ed intimissimo sentimento.

What is this Intermezzo *about?*

It is special, unique, the most "inner" piece in all of Brahms. He writes *"intimissimo sentimento."* I think the Op. 116 should be played like improvisations, especially the slow pieces. They should be very free, with not too much rubato, but with an unhurried feeling, with beautiful singing melodies, and again phrased in long lines. They should flow.

When I came into the hall just now you were practicing the ending trills of Beethoven's Sonata, Op. 111 slowly, getting the left hand exactly together with the right, getting the exact tone you wanted.

This ending section is a problem on every piano, getting the right tone on all three parts, making the melody sing.

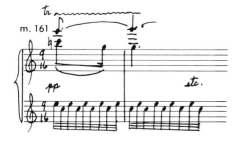

What does the second movement, and especially the ending, of this Sonata mean to you?

I speak too poorly to express this with words. If I could express the meaning with words, then it wouldn't be the music. The first movement is a hard, tragic life; the second movement, the Nirvana.

In *Doktor Faustus,* Thomas Mann has Mr. Kretschmar, a kind of school master, explain Op. 111 to a small audience. As he plays, Kretschmar says the motif of the Arietta theme can be scanned as "heav-en's blue, lov-ers' pain, etc."

He goes on, mingling his singing with shouts, "These chains of trills!" and so on. What Mann writes about the ending is especially fascinating.[1] But I think the music doesn't need extra-musical explanation.

Cortot, Fischer, and Schnabel often tried to express music's content in words. Kempff, too, I am told often thinks in terms of a story or poetic idea. But you don't think music can benefit from extra-musical explanation?

Honestly, for the most part, I don't. For me, music is just music. Of course when Brahms, in the *Intermezzo* in E♭, Op. 117 No. 1, quotes a folksong — "Lie still and sleep gently my child, it grieves me to see you weep" — then one has a certain idea about the piece. One could get the impression of a mother singing to her child or something like that.

The "Edward" *Ballade,* Op. 10 No. 1 is another example. Also in the second movement of the Sonata in C, Op. 1, where Brahms also quotes from a folksong (see example), then one knows what he means. But in most cases, I think music is just music.

Footnote

1. Mann writes: "Much else happens before the end. But when it ends and while it ends, something comes, after so much rage, persistence, obstinacy, extravagance: something entirely unexpected and touching in its mildness and goodness. With the motif passed through many vicissitudes, which takes leave and in so doing becomes itself entirely leave-taking, a parting wave and call, with this D, G, G occurs a slight change, it experiences a small melodic expansion. After an introductory C, it puts a C♯ before the D, so that it no longer scans 'heaven's blue,'...but 'O-thou heaven's blue,'...and this added C♯ is the most moving, consolatory, pathetically reconciling thing in the world.

"It is like having one's hair or cheek stroked, lovingly, understandingly, like a deep and silent farewell look. It blesses the object, the frightfully harried formulation, with overpowering humanity, lies in parting so gently on the hearer's heart in eternal farewell that the eyes run over. 'Now for-get the pain,' it says. 'Great was — God in us.' 'Twas all — but a dream,' 'Friendly — be to me.' Then it breaks off. Quick, hard triplets hasten to a conclusion with which any other piece might have ended."

Some Viennese pianists to whom I've talked have em-phasized intellectual ideas, but you don't. You seem to think or feel in terms of tone, melody — just playing music.

Yes, that is what I try. I think one should know a lot about music but not too much. People sometimes ask me questions about ornaments. Should they start from the note above or from the note? There are few hard and fast rules. How you play them should be a matter of taste, fantasy, improvisation. Nowadays many people think everything must be fixed, that there must be rules.

Yes, like the ornament in the first Bach Two-Part Inven-tion. We have proof that that inverted three-note mor-dent, starting on the note, did exist in Bach's time. Yet some Bach players insist that it didn't. I think it sounds terrible to start that ornament on the note above.

Yes, yes, terrible. Yet many people say it has to be played exactly that way. Why? There are too many books and too many clever people who know everything and tell you how to play everything. I think that is wrong.

None of the great pianists play the ornaments the same in Bach and even in Mozart.

Of course. In the Mozart Sonata in C, K. 279, which I will play tonight, there are many ways of playing the or-naments. For instance, the trill in measure 16. The first time I would play only three notes, then on the repeat perhaps more. Or, the first time you could play more notes than the second.

Ornamentation should be rather improvisational. There should be a wide field for variety or contrast.

My approach to these things is very personal and I'm sure many people wouldn't understand me. Being in-stinctive, sometimes on the spur of the moment I im-provise. I try to make a piece become alive, not to have it sound as if it is played too often. It's difficult to make a piece sound new, as if written today, but I try.

Jörg Demus —

Interview November 6, 1965

"Siciliano tempo is not too slow. It is up to you cellos to give the right tempo. If you don't from the first measure...we are already off... "

Jörg Demus was rehearsing the Bach Concerto in E Major with the New York Chamber Orchestra in Philharmonic Hall, for his performance of four Bach Piano Concerti the next evening. I was in the front of the auditorium waiting to interview him.

I was glad I'd arrived early. I'd heard his concert the week before, but I felt privileged now, listening to the rehearsal of the noted Viennese pianist described by *Paris Presse* as "the most perfect pianist of the younger generation," who is especially known for his Bach interpretations.

At the end of the rehearsal, Demus stood up and nodded to the men. "I am looking forward with great joy to the concert."

I walked up to greet him as he came off stage. Of medium build, with slightly hunched shoulders and a good head of light brown hair, Jorg Dëmus is an affable, tactful man. He spoke with managers, stage-hands, and a photographer; then we

went upstairs to the West Green Room. After he'd changed into a dry shirt, we began our discussion.

Elder: Mr. Demus, last October 24th, on short notice, you substituted for João Carlos Martins who was scheduled to play the first book of Bach's *Well-Tempered Clavier* in Philharmonic Hall.

Demus: Yes, I got a telephone call 13 days before, in Gelsenkirche, Germany. That's not really short notice, but for the *Well-Tempered Clavier* it's rather brief.

Elder: You recorded all of the *Well-Tempered Clavier* for Westminster Records in 1955, over ten years ago.

Demus: Those records! I look back and find some of the tempos unsatisfactory. Sometimes you change: in the fast things you have a greater feeling of vitality, you learn how to bring out more details, so you don't need such a quick tempo to bring them to life. And in the slow things, if you plan them on a larger scale, you don't always need such a slow tempo to give the required feeling of spaciousness. The C Sharp Minor

Fugue, for example, I find too slow on the record because now I plan further ahead and that compensates.

Elder: Bach has always been one of my favorite composers and obviously he has been one of yours too.

Demus: He has been one of my favorites instinctively from childhood. My mother used to be an amateur violinist and as a young woman, she played professionally. When she was 54, she memorized the six violin Partitas to commemorate the 200th anniversary of her violin, a Landolfi, and also to commemorate the second century of Bach's death. Memorizing them didn't give her any trouble at all. As a child I never had Bach forced on me. I liked him just as much as Mozart or Beethoven; he never seemed heavy to me.

Elder: How old were you when you started to learn the *Well-Tempered Clavier?*

Demus: It goes back to my academic days. I looked forward to work on these Preludes and Fugues and finally, when I was 12, my teacher allowed me to start. Since then I have almost constantly worked or reworked one or another of them.

Elder: From what editions did you learn the *Well-Tempered Clavier?*

Demus: I worked with the silly old Czerny edition in the beginning. Czerny claimed in his Forward: "I have heard most of these Preludes and Fugues interpreted by my teacher Beethoven." Czerny's edition has a lot of sforzatos on the weaker beats, the second and fourth beats of 4/4 time for example, as is part of Beethoven's style. And Czerny adds these sforzatos to Bach. After the Czerny edition, I used the Bischoff

An Interview in which the noted concert pianist discusses the *Well-Tempered Clavier*

which is a beautiful edition because it gives so many variations of the text. There are four extant autographs of the *Well-Tempered Clavier*, as everyone knows, as well as the copies of Bach's pupils. Bischoff mentions all the variants contained in these autographs and copies. (See the E Minor Prelude, for example.) Recently I have been using the Tovey edition. His preface for every Prelude and Fugue, in which he gives not a strict interpretation but says this piece is composed of this or that and therefore I think the character should be this and this, is not arbitrary and has enriched my understanding of these Preludes and Fugues greatly. The Kroll Peters edition is rather pure; they call it the Urtext. Being the first Urtext edition, it became famous, but I think we have passed that age of needed purification. Bischoff which offers all the variations is much more recommendable.

Elder: How did you learn all these Preludes and Fugues?

Demus: I found fingering very important. Because I can't have time to go over them every time before I play them, it is important that the hand positions and finger movements be built into my hand, even in the easy pieces. My hand somehow knows where to go automatically. It is hand, head, and heart which have to function.

The expression "playing by heart" is the key to the first resource, the "heart," your subconscious musical feelings and instincts. When you are young, you play almost unconscious of what you are doing, other than expressing what you feel about the music.

But at a later age, and I consider myself very old [37!], this unconscious approach doesn't work any more so we have to support the heart by the "brains" and use much of Gieseking's mental method: analyzing, realizing this entry comes here, this voice does this, here is the first big climax, here is an augmentation, a diminution, a stretto and so on. You have to have a detailed knowledge of what you are playing. Then if your heart fails you, your brain will come to the rescue.

The third resource I use in keeping these Preludes and Fugues memorized is, as I mentioned before, my "hand." The fingerings are so well worked out, the hand and finger movements are so well trained in my hands, that they work almost unconsciously for me. I, myself, do not have any visual memory. As compensation, I am not hampered by a strange edition, whereas people who have visual memory are disturbed by this.

Elder: Wasn't it amazing how Gieseking, with whom we both had the great privilege to study, could play all these things from memory and yet be almost unconscious of what fingerings he used, and would, on the spur of the moment when going after this or that effect, even on the stage, use a spontaneous fingering?

Demus: Gieseking was a motoric genius. The electric circuit from his fingers to his brain worked on such short notice, it was like an automatic electric response. But if you don't have such a motoric response (and few mortals do), then you had better work out your fingerings or you will stumble. Incidentally, we all owe a lot to Walter. I think his recordings are the greatest we have,

a wonderful legacy.

Elder: You have mentioned the use of the heart, brains, and hand in playing from memory. What about the use of the ear?

Demus: You must of course, hear what will come. But relying on ear memory for what comes at the moment is insufficient. When I walk on the street I can play through an entire Prelude and Fugue with my inner ear. The outer ear is more reserved for interpretation, for the sound, how I grade my touch.

Incidentally, Gieseking taught me an important lesson about playing from memory. At one of the Saarbrücken Master Classes I played the Bach Goldberg Variations. At the next month's classes, Mrs. Gieseking was there. Wanting her to hear them, Gieseking asked me to play the Goldberg Variations again. I told him I hadn't even looked at them during the past month. "That shouldn't make any difference," he said. "You can't always rehearse things just before you have to play them. Concentrate sufficiently so that you can play them anyway. You know this music inside yourself; simply listen and concentrate. Your fingers are trained; they will do what you tell them to do. Too many pianists play by automation." This advice has helped me a great deal. It works too.

About getting all these Preludes and Fugues securely memorized, I found it important to forget them and then restudy them. By the time you have done this fifty times, your subconscious has completely swallowed it all. "Playing by heart" should mean that it comes out of you easily, not "Oh my God, I have to play by heart!"

In Variation 28, the trill variation, there is always this broken trill in the middle, just as in the last variation of Beethoven's Sonata, Op. 109. Even instrumentally Bach was very rich.

(See examples of above parallels on page 133)

Bach was the end of a development, whereas Mozart or Haydn stood at the beginning of a development. In this sense Bach is more modern than Haydn. Haydn explored a virgin field—the sonata, the new dynamics, and instrumentation; he worked in a virgin territory and got magnificent results. Bach, on the other hand, had the whole 200 years of German mystic development, and the old Netherlandic counterpoint and mathamatical canon at his disposal; he was the last granitic figure in this sense. He was modern not only for his time, but for all time, because he represents the summing up of a centuries-old period of European music. And he will always be modern, for he was not surpassed; he wasn't even continued. Already his sons turned away from his art in developing the beginning of Viennese Classic.

In the famous painting of blind old Bach by E. G. Haussman, Bach holds in his hand the *Canon triplex à 6 voc.* which he submitted as a work to qualify him for the Mizler Society, a musical society he joined in 1745. At that time—in the 18th century—they didn't write out a canon. The first canon written out was by Mozart. Earlier, it was enough to indicate when the voices would come in. The brain was quite active. In this painting of Bach, only one voice is written out; he had the other voices in his head. Bach's head must have been the first computer.

Returning to the religious aspects in Bach's music, I find that Bach's religion would be above any orthodox limitations. I feel genuine religious response in Japanese listeners, for example, who don't know Christian religions. I would say an overall belief in certain orders and aims and important rules would, of course, be conveyed by Bach's music. But his overall belief isn't limited to the Protestant spirit as is often said. Bach fought half of his life with the Protestant authorities. He confused the community; his cantatas were too mystical, and other things were too hard to perform. You could also classify him as a quarreler, he fought so much of the time. He was a kind of

Elder: The statement I liked best in *The New York Times* review was: "the recital was a matter of musical light and shade, joy and gravity, propulsive energy and lyrical ease." Although you achieved gossamer lightness in the D Major Prelude and sparkling bounce in such works as the E Major, A Minor, and B Flat Major Fugues, I felt you were primarily concerned with projecting Bach's inner warmth, tranquility, and spirituality or religious feeling. How do you feel about this? How do you approach Bach?

Demus: The greatness of a composer shows in the variety of ways he can be approached; he leaves room for many kinds of understanding. Goethe, for example, as a great poet offers many possibilities of being explained: as a scientist, a lyricist, a dramatist, a naturalist, or a romanti-

cist. With Bach, too, a sign of his greatness is that so many approaches are possible if they are done thoroughly, with an open mind. You can approach him from the emotional point of view and do him justice. Or, you can approach him architecturally or instrumentally.

Elder: Students and music lovers often comment on how modern Bach is.

Demus: Yes, there are many things anticipated in Bach's works as well as their being the culmination point in a historical development. In Variation 29 of the Goldberg Variations there are figurations which occur in Schumann's *Kreisleriana* and in the Liszt Transcendental Etude in F Minor: the beginning is like the Liszt F Minor Etude, and the second half is like the middle section of Schumann's *Kreisleriana No. 1*.

revolutionary. He even wrote Catholic music when required. He offers many aspects of life, so I don't limit him to a single branch of Christianity. The broad religious feeling, however, is one of his essentials.

His acceptance of death—you will never find any passage where Bach fights death as Beethoven does. Beethoven fights—he wants life, whereas Bach's goal is a quiet death which would unify him with the universe. "You have nothing to be afraid of," is what he seems to say. I have never found a single text in which he was against death. One of his sweetest movements is where the death bell is ringing: *Schlage doch Gewünschte Stunde* is the most lyrical music written to the accompaniment of a death bell. And the slow movement of the E Major Concerto is out of the cantata with the text *Stirb in mir*.

Elder: Piano students and teachers will be interested in your technical approach to the *Well-Tempered Clavier*. Technically, I noticed you play with high top knuckles; you have a rather heavy hand, square, with strong arch. You played trills with the hand as a unit, keeping fingers in contact with the keys. You used a fluttering finger motion, close to keys with a quiet hand. What about hand position in playing these Preludes and Fugues in juxtaposition to the works of the Romantic era for example?

Demus: Generally speaking in all piano-playing, I consider the natural hand position the best. I used to ask Gieseking about hand position. He considered the most natural position the best. Just as he would put a glass of wine in his hand or pick up a suitcase, he would just put his hand to the keys. The best hand position is where you don't think any more of having any position.

But in Bach you have to play not two parts but three or four parts with just two hands. The middle parts or voices are constantly split. Therefore in playing Bach's polyphonic works, the hand needs to be kept in an open or "spread" position. One hand must be ready to jump in to take over parts of the other hand in a four-part fugue, for example. The hand must be composed, calm, quiet, and *open*.

In piano-playing you have the two techniques: the technique of the closed or contracted hand and the technique of the open or extended hand. In much of Bach you have to use the technique of the open or extended hand. On the other hand, in much of Chopin you should use a closed or contracted hand: the hand extends and contracts, stretches and then immediately closes. A classic example is the Etude in C Major, Op. 10, No. 1. The hand spreads out to the interval of a tenth and then closes to the interval of a third on the E-C where you use the fingering 5-1.

(See example 3, page 133)
Chopin here requires a constant opening and closing. Chopin requires the technique of the small or "closed" hand in the sense that for a run your hand is kept small. For a Chopin run, your thumb goes under your hand because it has so far to go, because it is much easier. On the other hand in Bach (although Bach was the first composer to use the thumb), the thumb practically doesn't count. He hardly ever uses this thumb-under kind of technique in his polyphonic pieces, the B Flat Major Prelude, for example.

Elder: To mention one other technical thing, you took the beginning of the theme entrance of the D Major Fugue with the right hand. It certainly wasn't for lack of left-hand facility, for in the B Flat Major Prelude you took all the left-hand thirty-second notes in measures 13-14 (which are so often divided) all with the left hand. Any reason?

Demus: Yes definitely. That opening entrance of the D Major Fugue is an upbeat and needs to be solid, important. Playing it with the right hand gives it importance. I do this wherever possible. The left hand could play the notes just as well, but it wouldn't have quite the same physical *élan* or *Schwung*. When I have a very important entry, I think the right hand has more authority. This theme is very intricate. It starts on the second beat of the bar. To get its full rhythmic importance as a *dux* (leader), this theme benefits from the authority of the right hand. I like to split *between* hands when a passage is not too rapid and I want to give it a lot of phrasing. But sometimes in Bach you have a run which should be as quick as possible, as in the Chromatic Fantasy. In such cases, I consider one hand preferable.

Elder: What about pedal in Bach?
Demus: In my student days I had to get rid of preconceived ideas about terrace dynamics, no pedal, etc. The first musician who had a pedal was Mozart. When he was 19 he wrote to his father that in Augsburg he had seen the Stein pianos with this new pedal. If something newly invented charmed Mozart, why would Bach have objected to it?

Regarding tempo, pedal, and ornaments in Bach, we have to activate our own taste. Karl Philipp Emanuel Bach and Quantz, in their writings, always end by saying "the taste of the player has to decide."

In the 19th century we had a romantic way of playing Bach. Almost everything was in transcription form. Then we went through the period of *Sachlichkeit* (strictness). Everything had to be played strictly with no rubato, no crescendos or diminuendos; personal taste had no place. Now we have outgrown this approach. Carl Richter's Bach on the organ is more or less based on the same ideas as mine. Scherchen's playing is always full of personal taste and freedom.

Elder: You studied with a number of famous pianists, famous for their Bach. Which one influenced your performance most?

Demus: Yves Nat, in Paris, greatly influenced my Schumann; Gieseking influenced my Debussy, Mozart, and Schumann too; Fischer influenced my Brahms, Beethoven and so on. I probably learned something from all of them. But I didn't get any specific inspiration for my Bach—they were all from a different generation. Edwin Fischer retained aspects of the 19th Century Romantic approach; transcriptions reigned in his youth. Gieseking's wonderful Bach still reflected a little bit the *Sachlichkeit* approach; he didn't allow much rhythmic freedom in his Bach as he did in his Schumann and Mendelssohn, for example. So I learned from my teachers, but I formed my own concept by combining elements of my own generation's approach, discarding aspects of the romantic approach of the 19th century and the too mechanical approach of the first half of the 20th century.

Elder: In recent years several Bach players have made, I feel, a fetish in making the piano imitate the harpsichord. I must say I admire their skill and technical perfection, but I feel they are on the wrong track: they concentrate so much on harpsichord "effects" that the music is not heard for itself. Again to quote *The New York Times*, I think the critic had these interpreters in mind when he wrote that "Mr. Demus is not the kind of Bach specialist who approaches the works of the master as though they were monuments almost too sacred to touch. Nor does he assume the airs of one divinely anointed for his task, possessed of insights available only to him." What is your feeling about this "harpsichord" approach?

Demus: The pretext for the *Well-Tempered Clavier* was that Bach wanted to propagate the invention of tempered tuning which Werkmeister invented in 1699 and which is still in use. For example, they compromised between F Sharp and G Flat so that each tonality could be equally and harmoniously beautiful. Bach wrote this set, the *Well-Tempered Clavier* (*Clavier* means keyboard: *Cla* - key; *vier* - board).

Now did he write for one specific type of keyboard? No. The instruments these Preludes and Fugues can be played on are widely spread as possible: some are best on the clavichord, some the organ, some the harpsichord. They do equally well on the piano.

Our concert halls are the practical reason for playing on the piano. The texture of a five-voice fugue is complicated. On a record, harpsichord is perfect; but in a large hall, I would say with a harpsichord you get a kind of overall noise, but you can't really hear every note. In these Bach concertos which I played with orchestra here in New York, had I been playing a harpsichord, I would have had to get the players always to play softer. With the piano, on the other hand, I animate and say to them, "more life, more sonority," to this or that.

Elder: Throughout the evening people were thinking about the *music*. An elderly man several seats from me was following the score. He excitedly exclaimed to his wife: "Hear how he brought out that inner voice; it was marvelous." And he hummed and sang. Walking up the aisle, a lady was saying, "They're all so great, it's impossible to single out this or that Prelude and Fugue as greater."

Demus: Yes, you can't say one Prelude and Fugue is greater than the others. When I started to study the *Well-Tempered Clavier*, every two or three weeks I would work on a new Prelude and Fugue. I could choose it. My favorite occupation was to browse and pick one out. In my index I made a little *x* for those I especially liked. I started with a few *x*'s and within a year, all the Preludes and Fugues had *x*'s on them. It is hard to browse where everything is supreme.

Elder: Wanda Landowska has written that when the *Well-Tempered Clavier* is performed integrally, each Prelude and Fugue should be interpreted as separate unit.

Demus: Landowska is absolutely right. There was no overall plan that all the Preludes and Fugues should build together. The *Well-Tempered Clavier* is not meant as a whole; it is meant as a collection. You must just get the most out of each individual Prelude and Fugue. It is only fortunate that the last piece of volume one should be spiritually such a climax. In volume two, the last piece is an anti-climax.

As far as playing the first volume in one evening is concerned, it is a big help that the two or three at the end—the B Flat Minor and the B Minor particularly—are among the most beautiful in the whole volume. The B Flat Minor five-voice Fugue is one of the pillars of the whole set. The Prelude is always very striking even to people who are unfamiliar with these works.

And the 24th Fugue is a monument in itself. The theme of the Fugue is the first twelve-tone theme I have found in the entire literature. We all know the whole *Well-Tempered Clavier* deals with the chromatic scale, a Prelude and Fugue in every key, ascending chromatically. And to crown it all Bach used all twelve tones in the subject of the 24th Fugue. (*See example 4 on next page.*)

Elder: I found an evening devoted to 24 Preludes and Fugues a refreshing change from the usual piano recital. Programs of virtuoso music can leave one excited and ecstatic over the performer's interpretation, technique, or personality. But there's already so much that is frenetic today. Your evening, on the other hand, left one peaceful, in a mood of calm. You could feel people become relaxed and tranquil during the evening. Toward the end, particularly, the audience was completely hushed, listening to the inner calm of Bach's music.

Demus: Yes, I felt the same thing sitting on the stage. If the audience had become restless, they would have hampered my concentration. But at the end there was absolutely no rustling or coughing. The great concentration impressed me; I was utterly rewarded.

Elder: How did the audiences in Paris, Rome, and Perugia compare?

Demus: I would say that as far as appreciation was concerned, the New York audience was the best. Perhaps in a small circle where the room had lovely frescoes on the walls, etc., more direct communication would be possible. But in the way that a public sits through 24 Preludes and Fugues and is not deadly tired at the end— that speaks for itself. I was afraid there'd be no one left at the end of such a long program, or that I'd get a reaction like that of one of my colleagues when asked about the performance of another musician: "What do you think of his execution?" Replied the colleague, "I'm all for it."

Examples for Dean Elder's interview with Jörg Demus

Example 1. "The beginning of Bach's 29th Goldberg Variation is like the Liszt F Minor Etude, and the second half is like the middle section of Schumann's Kreisleriana No. 1."

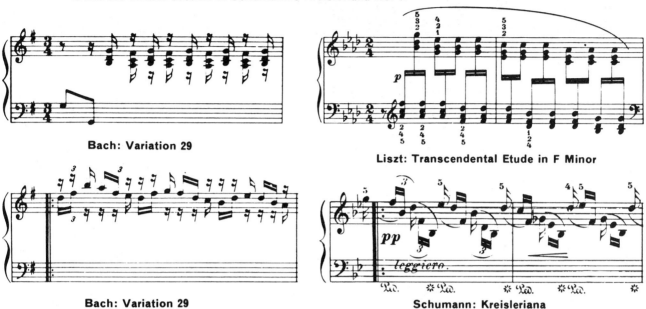

Bach: Variation 29

Liszt: Transcendental Etude in F Minor

Bach: Variation 29

Schumann: Kreisleriana

Example 2. In Variation 28, there is always this broken trill in the middle just as in the last variation of Beethoven's Opus 109. Even instrumentally Bach was very rich.

Bach: Variation 28

Beethoven: Opus 109

Example 3. In Chopin's Etude in C Major, Opus 10, No. 1, "the hand spreads out to the interval of a tenth and then closes to the interval of a third on the E-C where you use the fingering 5-1."

Example 4. Bach's Fugue in B Minor from the **Well-Tempered Clavier,** vol. 1..."the first twelve-note theme in the entire literature." Though it is not a strict twelve-tone row, the theme includes all twelve tones of the chromatic scale.

133

A Virtuoso's Approach to Interpretation

Támas Vásary

interview August 10, 1976

Támas Vásary's success in international competitions, his distinguished recordings, and his extensive repertoire have made him one of the major pianists of our time. Born in Hungary in 1933, he was urged at age nine by Dohnányi to study at the Budapest Franz Liszt Academy. From 1944 to 1953 he studied at the Academy with Lajos Hernádi, József Gát, Zoltan Kodály, and later with Annie Fischer. In 1956 he settled in Switzerland where he played for Clara Haskil. He and his wife currently live in London. In this interview he was extraordinarily animated and articulate as he discussed his emotional approach to interpretation, how he prepares to perform, and his advice for young players.

What advanced training did you seek?

My schooling at the Academy Franz Liszt in Hungary was thorough. Afterwards, to help find my own way I played for different great artists such as Clara Haskil, Backhaus, and Horowitz. I think that if you stay around a great artist too long, his personality will be overwhelming. The sooner you find your own way and recognize your own personality, the better it is.

Would you say that, as a Hungarian pianist, Kodály and Bartók are in your blood?

Yes, but I believe that great music is above nationalism. A non-Hungarian can interpret Hungarian music as well or better than many Hungarians. I remember how a young Chinese entrant in the 1956 Liszt Competition in Budapest played a Liszt Rhapsody, which was by far the best Liszt interpretation of the whole lot.

In earlier times when you crossed the boundary into a different country, the world changed. Nowadays, however, nations have such good communication through recordings and personal contact that it is not of overwhelming significance whether you are a native of the country whose music you are interpreting.

You have said that Hungarians always accent the first syllable of words, so that the first note of such figures as ♪.in Bartók and Kodály parlando phrases should always be accented.

Yes, lots of Bartók and Kodály music has this kind of accentuation. My name is Támas Vásary (TAH-mash VAH-shary), with the accent being on the first syllable of each word. In the first phrase of Kodály's "Transylvanian Dirge" from *Seven Pieces*, op. 11,

Rubato, parlando

Si-rass él-děs a-nyóm, mig e - löt - ted já - rok

Kodály doesn't mark the accentuation; all the notes look equal. But this melody, which is a thousand years old, must have accents based on where the first syllables fall in the text of each verse. Therefore it's no use to write the accents for one phrase because you can't play the other phrases like it. You have to know the text and imply small accents on the first syllables accordingly.

———————

Why do you sit so high at the piano?

Professor Lajos Hernádi, my first teacher at the Liszt Academy, suggested I sit higher than I was sitting. I was eleven. As a good pupil I sat higher and higher until finally I felt unhappy with my position.

Then I studied three years with József Gát who wanted me to sit very low. When I sat lower, I felt that I had a better, more human contact with the instrument. I felt that I got a warmer tone. Finally, I sat even lower than he wanted. I was practically sitting on the floor.

After a while I couldn't play technically. I have long arms and my hands, especially my right one, were strained. I couldn't play works such as the Liszt *Transcendental Etudes*. It was a horrible time for me. I felt that this low position was the only one in which I could produce the sound I wanted. When I tried to sit higher, the sound became harder. I was struggling. I knew Glenn Gould has very long arms and sits low, so why shouldn't I?

Finally, I obeyed my instincts and found the position in which I am most comfortable. It looks very high, but the position of my arms in relation to the instrument is quite normal because I have a very short body and very long arms. When I play four hands with another pianist, our relation to the keyboard will be the same, but my stool will be high and his low.

Everyone must find his own way: Pollini sits very low, Horowitz medium high, Rubinstein and Arrau sit high, Darré and Cherkassky very high. You can't say that someone plays better because he sits high or low. The length of our arms, the length of our thumbs in relation to the other fingers, all these proportions must be taken into consideration.

John Browning once said to me that he plays different works at a different seating height, putting the stool higher for Bach and lower for Beethoven. I notice that often I adjust my stool during a concert according to the piece I'm playing. For instance, when I play lots of *jeu perlé* [a light staccato] as in Chopin Etudes or Preludes, I like to sit higher. For a Beethoven sonata I like to sit a bit lower. The height preference has something to do with the physical feeling of the work.

What is your approach to interpretation?

For me music is like a poem. I must feel an emotional logic in the music like the logic you feel in a dream. Sometimes I can't find the appropriate words for this logic, this emotional content; if I could find the appropriate words and could be sure what a work is saying to me, I would be a poet, you see.

Lieder and opera have beautiful texts or poems to which a composer has written beautiful music. In listening to a composition, then, I feel there is a beautiful poem behind it.

For me this emotional content is the essential quality. If I don't feel something of this kind in the music, then I don't learn the piece. It has no message for me or for me to convey to others.

When I hear a concert by a great interpreter, I feel he is telling me a story. I am guided to a fairyland as in my dreams. Something is happening: now a monster comes, now an angel, now I am unhappy, now I am happy. All these moods and emotions are going through a work, and the artist's difficult role is to sense this imaginative quality and to communicate it.

In the Chopin posthumous Nocturne in C# minor, for example, I could demonstrate note by note exactly what I feel. Every note of this work has a message for me. Starting with the introduction, I immediately picture Chopin sitting before his piano. He plays a few improvisatory chords:

He is sad, nostalgic for his youth, perhaps for his first love. As he improvises, suddenly this beautiful theme comes into his mind:

It is a reminiscence of the theme of the second movement of his *Concerto in F Minor:*

They were written about the same time?

Yes, but even if you didn't know that, you would still have the impression that both works live in the same emotional climate. What is important is to have a conviction in your interpretation. The audience is seeking this conviction, feeling cheated, dissatisfied, perhaps even indisposed towards further concertgoing if they don't receive this conviction.

An audience's silence gives me great pleasure. Clapping can be merely polite, but not silence.

Of course the work has structure, harmony, melody, and rhythm. The interpretation must be clean, the pedaling proper. You must care about these aspects. But what interests me more and more as a listener and as a performer is finding the spiritual message. As a performer I view the work as a sort of spiritual medium through which to give the message of the composer to the public.

During a concert if 2,000 people are sitting in absorbed silence, they sense that something significant is happening. An idea, a message is emerging that is compelling their attention. Their silence acknowledges this moment. For me this silence is the best moment on stage, giving me the greatest pleasure. Clapping can be merely polite, but not silence.

Is your poetic approach similar to what Cortot looked for?

Yes. His titles to the Chopin Preludes are very poetic and apropos. For example, he labeled the first one "Feverish Waiting for the Loved One," the second "Painful Meditation, the Solitary Sea in the Distance," and the third "The Song of the Brook." One shouldn't make a rule of expressing poetic ideas, however, nor force pupils to explain their pieces in such a way.

I am happy when I feel this poetic content in a work. Then I dash to learn the work. But if I don't have this reaction, I either don't learn the work or I just play as much as I feel in it.

The thing is that I wouldn't impose my idea of this content on anybody else, do you see? I try to encourage a pupil not to be shy about showing what he feels. Everything should be sacrificed to get through to this feeling.

For example, there are big declamations, gestures, and big jumps in the Brahms B♭ Concerto. Now if you want to be sure of not hitting a wrong note, you will put your hand safely on the right place: the notes will be right but not the gesture. Or in the opening of the Brahms F minor Sonata, you really need to risk hitting a wrong note. I vote for those artists who, for the sake of the music's character, are willing to take risks. Of course it is easy to sit here and tell you in a big voice that I vote for taking risks. But sometimes when I go on stage I am scared. Not wanting to hit wrong notes, I don't take risks either.

Before you played the Schubert G Major Sonata last night a young pianist competitor told me that for him that sonata is the most beautiful composition on this earth. What do you feel to be the spiritual message of this work?

I think the first movement starts like a spiritual devotion. You hardly touch the keyboard. You put this first chord down and then without resting you feel in your soul you are floating on to the next chord:

Starting with these long chords is like being in church or out in nature, just looking at something, the beauty itself. It is a simple G major chord, yet something is coming out of it.

You can analyze some music, seeing it as a marvelous mathematical devising as in a Bach fugue, a work of Stockhausen or Boulez, or perhaps a Mahler symphony. But here, with this simple G major chord, I become mystical about music. Nothing happened before this chord and after two bars nothing much has happened but this chord. And yet something miraculous is present. I can try to analyze what it is, but my analysis would be only the impression I get from the music and nothing I can prove to be true.

There is a spiritual side of music, for me the most valuable, which is inexplainable. If you can explain something, it becomes more and more a matter of science. But music and art have their right to live because they can offer something extra, something more than science or anything else. Music can be a medium to leave this earth, to reach a state of mind and of spirit in which you are a much more refined person with almost half a leg in heaven. The greatest music is that which is able to help us leave the suffering of this material plane, to find a sublimated world which you can call heaven, an exalted state of mind, or whatever you like. The Schubert G major Sonata is one of those mediums which enable us to communicate with this other world. I agree with your friend about the beauty and value of this work.

When I play I'm always thinking in terms of orchestral instruments or the voice.

You seem to listen very intensely as you play. What are you listening for?

I don't like to hear a piano sound. I always orchestrate. When I play, a work becomes either vocal or orchestral. Therefore I'm not a real pianist inasmuch as I'm always thinking in terms of orchestral instruments or the voice.

I am sort of a frustrated conductor, having wanted to conduct since early childhood. Why didn't I become a conductor? Perhaps I wasn't strong enough to fight all the circumstances of my life. But in the bottom of my heart, I have always been a conductor which sometimes has helped and sometimes interfered with my piano playing.

In big works like Liszt's "Dante" Sonata from *Années de Pèlerinage* I don't want the exactitude of percussive sound, the brilliant brisk piano sound. I prefer a sort of big, blurred orchestral string sound. These chords, for example, seem to me like big chords played by the brass and wind instruments and the octaves are, as in Wagner, filled with the sound of lots of string.

Who are your favorite pianists?

My favorite pianists are quite different. I find Annie Fischer the most artistic in spirit. She is the real artist with whom I am able to forget the instrument. I consider Glenn Gould a genius who is able to see things in a work which I never thought existed. The Bach *Two-and Three-Part Inventions* are really inventions as he plays them. Suddenly he lets you see tremendous vistas inside these works; they become as fabulous as cathedrals. Until I heard him play these beautiful, small works I didn't realize how big and marvelous they are.

Then there is Horowitz, "The King of Pianists," who plays piano as nobody else does. In his playing you hear and enjoy 100 percent the marvels of the instrument. You are keenly aware of the piano all of the

time he is playing. His is the greatest pianistic achievement you can find.

I have tremendous admiration for my young colleague, Radu Lupu and my fellow Hungarian, Peter Frankl. Of the older pianists I have fantastic memories of Richter, Rubinstein, Arrau, and Michelangeli.

Let's talk about your interpretation of Chopin, whose works you have recorded so extensively. I've noticed that you play the Chopin Prelude in E♭ minor rather slowly.

This is a torturous, frustrated piece. It wants to go in a certain direction, starting as if to go forward. Then it falters and falls back. It is a very chromatic work, alternating between minor and major, the tendencies of its chromaticism being always contradicted. At the end you fall on the tonic without a preceding dominant. You are here but no solution. This is the atmosphere I find. Therefore I don't play it quickly because I would lose this torturous, frustrated, faltering, contradictory quality.

Some people think of this Prelude in relation to the last movement of the Sonata in B♭ Minor.

This comparison is valid because in the last movement of the Sonata there is also a tendency toward atonality. The modulations are so daring and constant that you don't find yourself at any moment to be in any key. This uncertainty of key is true of both works. Also in both there is a weirdness and uncanniness. In the Sonata you will find an airy, ghostly thing floating around, whereas in the Prelude a living person is suffering. A ghost has an easier time getting around than a human being.

You play the Prelude in A♭ a little faster than perhaps is customary.

I am often criticized for this. If I were to play the A♭ alone and not in the context of the 24, I would probably play it slower. Each prelude sets the mood of the following one.

I find that the Preludes fall into groups: No. 8-12 (the F# minor through the G# minor) form a big block of movement; No. 13-15 (the F# major through the D major) a block of meditation, so that after the one

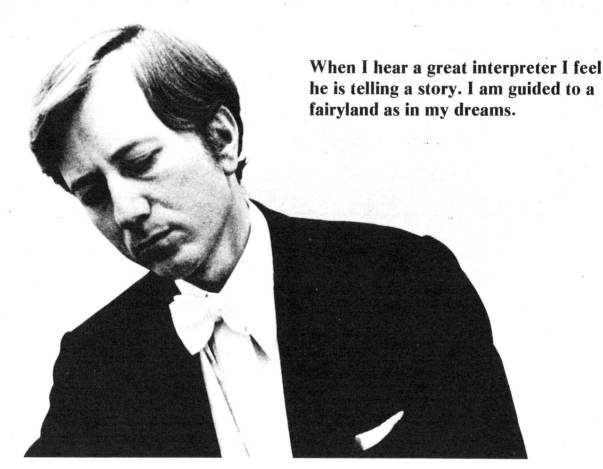

When I hear a great interpreter I feel he is telling a story. I am guided to a fairyland as in my dreams.

short sparkle of No. 16, I can't stop myself. I am still in a passionate mood. Therefore, I play the A♭ quicker and more passionately than I would play it as a solo piece.

You play the famous 11 low A♭'s of the last page with the whole hand sideways.

I played not with the side of the hand but with the fist, the fist giving a firmness without harshness. It's like hitting the timpani or a big gong with a mallet that has a cotton end. The fist produces a full sound without a brisk percussive effect. It has the necessary weight but at the same time is soft.

You played Beethoven's Sonata in A♭, op. 26, as an encore. Do you often play such long encores?

Yes, I like to play long encores. At the end of a concert I am usually in a good mood. When I finish with the feeling that it was a relatively good concert, I am happy to play some more. I don't like going out and in again to play short pieces. I find it embarrassing, somewhat ridiculous.

I can show the public that I appreciate their approbation by staying and playing a long work, at the same time pleasing myself. I have finished what I was paid to play. Now I can play something extra and feel freer, more relaxed. These are good, valuable moments.

You have played the Hammerklavier Sonata and the Goldberg Variations as a program?

Yes, I played this program for my New York recital debut in Carnegie Hall. Then I played it at the Salzburg Festival, in London, and in the Berlin New Philharmonic hall. The *Hammerklavier* is a perfect, if hair-raising, opener, tremendously demanding for the public. But if the public listens to nothing else in the first

half, they aren't tired.

Although the *Goldberg Variations* is a long work, there are short pieces in the middle so if the audience sleeps a little in the middle they can pick up the thread somewhere later. To start with the big, rocky *Hammerklavier* and to finish with the "Air" of the *Goldberg Variations* is heavenly, especially if one plays well. I confess I was fearful about playing this program because it demands great nervous stamina. Also I don't usually like to play Bach in the second half of a program. But this program could work only in this way.

What do you think about as you play?

This is a very good question. I constantly revise what I think about. Nowadays I cut out my concentration on notes. I find that if I concentrate too much on what is coming next, I will spoil the thing. But on the other hand, I need to know the work so well that my fingers can play it without my thinking or my brain can reproduce it without my playing.

When one is playing, the mechanical movements of the hands and the mental work of the memory go hand in hand. Sometimes you don't know which is operating, sometimes both, sometimes only one.

It is dangerous when only either the hands or the brain is operating. So I prefer that both fingers and brain be solidly there. Then if one gets tired, you can reach to the other. Of course, when both fingers and brain get tired, you may have a memory lapse.

When I am in an airplane or a taxi, I try to recall every note. But on stage I try not to think about or to concentrate on the notes. If I remain in a half-dreaming state, I know what is coming very clearly. But if I concentrate too hard on what is coming next, I have a sort of mental cramp.

How do you practice?

I practice differently depending on whether I'm just starting the piece, I'm in the middle, or it is just before a concert.

First I learn a piece until I can play it by heart, knowing it half instinctively and half consciously. I close the music, playing it with ear, hand, visual memory — everything. I repeat it until I'm able to play it for myself or for my wife.

Then comes the "insurance company." I set to work to learn every note away from the piano. When I'm traveling I work on visual memorizing. On an airplane I try to engrave every note into my memory, literally thinking every note. I hate it when they play music on planes because it keeps me from doing this work.

Then I practice starting from various points so that I have at least eight signposts. This kind of practice is vital in preparing a Bach fugue and also less complicated works. After all these processes I practice in detail at slow and medium tempos, repeating things many times. I also like to be able to play the two hands separately from memory.

Two weeks before a concert I play through the whole program every day in full tempo but not with full expression. Three or four days before the concert I play it as I would in concert. Better still is to have two or three engagements before an important concert.

You mentioned that you like to be able to play each hand separately from memory. Is this process essential?

I'm not sure it's absolutely necessary. Playing each hand alone reassures that I really know the music. But it's not good to play hands separately the day before a concert because you will have been concentrating on one hand, which can mix you up in the performance.

Do you have a technical regime?

I used to when I was at the Budapest Academy. Nowadays I like to play difficult technical works which are difficult for both hands, for example, the Rachmaninoff concertos, especially No. 3 which has thousands of notes for both hands. Then I like to practice Chopin Etudes, playing with the left hand the same thing that is written for the right.

Do you use the Godowsky arrangements?

No, I play every note as it is written for the right hand. In the case of the "Chromatic Study," op. 10 no. 2, I do the chromatic part on the bottom of the left hand:

The "Black Key" Etude is also good, as is No. 7. When there is a difficult passage in the right hand I learn it in the left hand too, for example double-note descending chromatic passages as in the Liszt A major Concerto. I play the hands together.

I like to practice octaves for five or ten minutes to keep my biceps in shape. I also play some trills with the left hand with 5-4 fingering while holding the thumb on a note. I do extra exercises with the left hand to balance my hands, the right hand having so much more to do in the literature.

I also do thirds until I feel a certain tiredness in the muscles. Then I slow down and relax. I don't do this very much, 10 or 15 minutes, and only when I have very demanding left-hand passages. Otherwise, I take it easy.

Do you have any career advice for young pianists?

I confess that I am pessimistic about the life of the pianist today. The pianistic profession is tough. I think it realistic to say that out of every 100 pianists who are capable of an international career, only one is succeeding. The other 99 are starving, so to speak. But as a pianist you are hooked by your talent and by your love of the music to invest tremendous energy and work in your profession. It is a question not only of making a living but of not being frustrated. You need to be internationally recognized, and if this doesn't happen, it may be too late to change your line of work.

When I am asked if a young player should become a professional pianist, I say if there is any way out, then for heaven's sake no.

When I am asked if a young player should become a professional pianist, I say if there is any way out, then for heaven's sake no. I see very few who are not frustrated, including myself, my colleagues, and those venerable ones of the older generation. I know only one great old man who is happy, and that is Rubinstein. Why has he decided to be happy? Somewhere in his life he made a psychological switch after which he says he became happy. For this I have great admiration but I think he is unique. Otherwise, he wouldn't be able to play concerts at age 90. I'm sure I won't be able to. I take everything too much to heart. I'm unable to be smiling and happy about everything.

First of all there is my playing. If I play something less well than I should, I eat myself up for weeks remembering a passage which I spoiled. Not to mention recordings which I can't change and which I would like to break into pieces.

On the other hand there is the tremendous pleasure of living with this literature. This pleasure is the crux of the matter. If someone were to ask me, "What is the requirement for becoming a professional pianist?" I would say that the desire to live intimately with this music all your life must outweigh all the difficulties, suffering, and crucifixion, because it is crucifixion, that you will experience. Then and only then should you go ahead. You will have no choice but to pursue this life.

Philippe Entremont

interview August 1, 1977

" Le Pianiſte Atomique "

Philippe Entremont was born on June 7, 1934 in Rheims, big bubble of France's champagne country. He received his first piano lessons from his mother, a first-prize graduate of the Paris Conservatoire and a pupil of Marguérite Long. A child prodigy, Entremont also studied privately in Paris with Mme. Long. Afterwards he studied at the Conservatoire with Jean Doyen, winning first prizes in sight-reading at the age of 12, in chamber music at 14, and in piano at 15, after playing Liszt's Mazeppa. *This work was also on the program at his first public concert at age 16 in Barcelona.*

In Tunis the concert piano was so dirty he had to ask them to clean it. They did, with a hose, leaving the piano unsoiled but drowned. In South America the French Embassy sent him on a concert tour so deep into the interior that there were no pianos to play. In a Johannesburg concert he played the Rachmaninoff Second Concerto until three of the piano's legs collapsed.

Such indignities were inflicted on Philippe Entremont early in his career and now have the sound of a few clinkers written into a score so exuberant that it shouldn't be played without them. Philippe says that "nothing very terrible has happened in the last few years, most everything goes smoothly," which is no small achievement for a man who this year played 125 concerts with 60 more as soloist-conductor of the Vienna Chamber Orchestra.

One of the world's more popular pianists calls his concert schedule "idiotic" ("That's the *foutaise*,"

says he) but laughs about his annual ten-month trots over the globe. "I must like it," he says, of his hectic schedule.

At the University of Maryland International Piano Festival several years ago he magnetized those in attendance at his master class. Later on the same day he spent some time going over his recital program in the cavernous concert hall. The hall was empty except for us, and he took a break to join me in the front row.

I opened our conversation with a comment about his style of teaching. Watching Philippe teach ("Do it this way!" he once snapped at a student, demonstrating the passage in question) reminded me of that untender tradition enforced by teachers like Philippe's own Marguérite Long as well as Cortot and Jeanne-Marie Darré in France; Isabelle Vengerova, Adele Marcus, Gorodnitski, and Genhart in this country; and Heinrich Neuhaus in the Soviet Union. "Like many of the older generation," I said, "you seem to keep a rather strict teacher-pupil relationship, whereas most younger teachers perhaps are less strict."

He seemed surprised. "You find me strict? I don't think I'm very strict. I've learned to be patient. At the Maurice Ravel Academy in France where I teach a month or two each year, one of my students recently commented, 'Really, with you only the very strong survive.'" Phillippe laughs heartily.

"I'm very attached to my students. I love to work with them, and I think they feel this too. At first

© The Instrumentalist Company 1980. All rights reserved.

141

perhaps they're surprised by my manner. Sometimes I yell at them. Sometimes they yell back.

"But it's true you can't teach today the way I was taught. The relation between the teacher and his pupil today in France as well as in other countries is more on an equal basis. That's no doubt. I'm all for it."

An irrepressible and light-hearted person such as this Frenchman cannot go without levity for long. For instance, he had listened to a computerized rendering of Liszt's "Invocation" from *Harmonies poetiques et religieuses* and quipped to the student, "I'm going to ask you to play a little poetic and religious. It's not a Western, heh?"

Later, he said of playing Liszt, "You have to have a wonderful sense of drama. You lose something if you play the octaves with two hands."

Philippe had made an observation about Fauré's Sixth Nocturne — "one of the most beautiful pieces in the French repertoire, very difficult

---

"Sometimes I don't know who is playing on the radio and I like it. I'm surprised to find out it's me."

---

to play well" — that reminded me of something Gieseking said about Fauré being "very beautiful but perhaps too *intime*, inward for concerts. No matter how beautifully I play his works the people sit on their hands." I asked Philippe what he thinks about that statement. "You know, I stopped playing Fauré in concerts almost 20 years ago," he answered. "Fauré is very intimate music, not suitable for large halls. This is music that a musician likes for himself. I don't particularly like to share my pleasure in playing Fauré with other people. What Gieseking said is true. Fauré's music goes over the head of the audience. I don't understand but this is the way it goes.

"It has been the same with the *Valses nobles et sentimentales*, one of the most beautiful pieces written by Ravel, but again a piece that goes over audiences' heads. Perhaps audiences are getting so they like it. Last year I received a burst of bravos after the *Valses nobles*. I was stunned."

In his teaching Philippe emphasized bringing out the top notes, the melody. Yet in his recording of Tchaikowsky's *Chanson Triste*, for example, he plays the harmonic elements almost as loud as the melody, something that Casadesus also did. Has his approach to melody playing changed?

"The line of the melody has to be there instinctively. Students drop the top notes. I don't know why. I recorded *Chanson Triste* in Los Angeles, but I don't remember how I played it. I think the melodic line has to be very well defined but I don't drop the inner voices by any means.

"I'm in love with the shape of a phrase. In that way I've changed very much in recent years. I'm no longer interested in the technical aspect of performance. Technique *per se* bores me to death. I re-

member a great performance for what it brings me musically, not for its technical aspect. Some of the greatest performances I've heard were not the most polished, but they had something extra. If you can mix the two elements, that's great!"

What pianists of the past has Philippe most admired? "I was always fascinated by the recordings of Rachmaninoff, and I've heard concerts of Rubinstein which were stunning. When I was 17 I played Beethoven's Op. 101 for Backhaus. He was very sweet. I think he liked it. He didn't say much but at least he listened. That was great; what a pianist he was. I remember a tremendous performance of the Beethoven Fourth Concerto in Vienna just a few months before his death."

Of course, people have said of Philippe himself, "What a pianist he is!" As a matter of fact, he tells me that "sometimes I don't know who is playing on the radio and I like it. I'm surprised to find out it's me."

As a young pianist Philippe Entremont epitomized the snappy, splashy, tempestuous virtuoso, earning him the label *"Le Pianiste Atomique"* from *Paris France-Soir*. His recordings (which have helped immensely in building his career) have the same characteristics. I asked him about how many records he has made.

"In this country 76, to be precise. It's hard to be at your best on records. It took me a long time to get rid of microphone fear. It's horrible to go into a hall at nine o'clock in the morning and just 'bing!' sit down and play a so-called definitive performance." He laughs again. "It's hard to say if I have favorites. Usually I listen to them once and that's it, you know. Never again."

Together we remembered Jean Doyen, one of Entremont's early teachers at the Conservatoire. "I think Doyen is one of the most incredible pianists I have ever heard," said Entremont. "He has a fantastic technique and a beautiful tone. Maybe you're going to ask why he hasn't made an international career. I think it was his choice not to. He hates to travel, likes to stay at home. We have a good saying in French for that — he's a *pantouflard*. He has never enjoyed this crazy life of a touring artist, a difficult one, you know. You have to adjust to a lot of things."

I asked Philippe about his early training in solfège. Did this training start him off on the right note, so to speak?

"I don't regret my French solfège training," he answers. Solfège training is a fantastic asset. Before starting to play the piano I had two years of solfège. French children don't always have solfège before they start the instrument, but I think they should. Sometimes solfège kills the interest in music; it is a bore at the beginning. But if you survive, it is a tremendous help.

"After spending two years reading notes and rhythms, I progressed very fast afterwards at the piano. Maybe I am gifted for the instrument — I hope so. Playing the piano was very easy for me, knowing so much about the notes from solfège. I think I saved many years."

However, his years with Marguérite Long may have seemed long indeed. Mme. Long (1874-1966) was a demanding teacher, and a distinguished one; among her pupils were Jean Doyen, Jeanne-Marie Darré, Nicole Henriot-Schweitzer, Samson François, and Aldo Ciccolini. "She was very strict," he says. We had fights. It was necessary to play her way; there was no other. Consequently, I try to give my students freedom. I don't like them to copy anything. The frame is large enough to do a lot of things inside that frame. I'd hate to have peo-

"I try to give my students freedom. I don't like them to copy anything."

ple around playing the way I do. That wouldn't be fun, especially for me." He laughs.

"Did she inflict her notorious finger exercises on you?"

Oh, yes. But that was all right. I'm not a complete product of the French School by any means, fortunately. But I don't regret learning what we call the French School."

Philippe also was helped by his father, a conductor.

"I played under him many times at the beginning of my career. We even made a recording, now deleted. I learned from him, but I claim you don't learn conducting; you're born a conductor. You have to develop technique, but if you're a born conductor half the work is done.

"Playing with some of the world's greatest conductors, from an early age, has been the best schooling for me. I've never been the type of pianist to arrive, play my concerto and rush back to my hotel. You've no idea how many hours I've stayed in the hall, watching the conductor work. And I have my own orchestra now, the Vienna Chamber. I'm its permanent conductor."

"Do you follow a technical regime?" I asked.

"I don't eat too much. I'm proud of that! Fortunately, I don't need much time to warm up at the piano. Anyway, in this profession we don't have time to practice much. Traveling the way we do, spending so much time going to and from airports, in airports, waiting for planes, we waste a lot of time. Terrible."

"Before airplanes you would have wasted more. Think of going from New York to San Francisco by train."

"That's true!"

"So you just practice to keep up your repertoire?"

"I add repertoire every year. I don't practice technical exercises. I don't know if it is good... but at least I enjoy what I'm doing.

"Of course you have to practice technique when you are young, and I did. I don't have excellent memories of that. I was the most rebellious of Marguérite Long's pupils, that's for sure! I had a terrific fear of her. She was cruel with me (for a very good reason most of the time). I was a lousy student. She despaired sometimes, seeing the negativeness of my approach. But she was wonderful, had a good heart."

Philippe Entremont is a good example of a major talent who has lost an individual battle of competition but has won the war of building a successful career. In the 1952 Queen Elizabeth Brussels Competition, he came in tenth. (At this time he was only 17 years of age.) Olin Downes, one of the judges, apparently thought he should have placed higher, singling him out in his *New York Times* review as having stunned listeners with his "magnificent playing of the Rachmaninoff Second Concerto." Entremont went on at 18 to win the Marguérite Long Competition in Paris and has had a bigger career than all the pianists classed above him in the 1952 Brussels. The moral seems to be: major talents should never despair if they don't win a specific contest. Lazar Berman placed only fifth in the 1956 Brussels.

"Do you have memories of the contests you entered?" I asked.

"Yeah, bad ones. I never had the right nerves for competitions, I was too young. You have to be in shape and feel well at the exact time of the performance. You don't have a second chance. Sometimes the difference between first and second prize depends on a single wrong note. Or the person who won second should have won first or vice versa.

"I refuse to be on juries any more. Judging is a big responsibility; there are too many competitions. They give so much hope to young musicians and we still have very few openings for a good career.

"The prizes have become too much. There's a fantastic inflation about prizes. If you're a good pianist under 30 you can follow the circuit, like the golf or tennis, enter all the competitions, making a good living out of it. You can't blame the young pianists. They need considerable money for their living expenses during their study, and most talented people are not wealthy."

Stephen Bishop — Kovacevich

"We Don't All Sound Alike!"

interview August 5, 1971

"That makes me angry," said Stephen Bishop, the handsome, 32-year old American pianist (protégé of the late Dame Myra Hess), as we were eating lunch. I had said that several world-famous virtuosos of the older generation had told me they find today's younger pianists tend to sound alike, that "being together and playing for each other so much, they don't develop their own personalities."

"I just don't see it at all," Stephen Bishop continued as he jabbed his fork. "In the first place, a lot of the so-called personality of that generation — and I'm not denying that some of them were and are great — is what many people would consider somewhat frivolous, bordering on eccentricity — not real personality. Secondly, personality is not so frail that it is going to be damaged by proximity to another marvelous musician. Thirdly, we don't all sound alike. That's the final proof.

"Of course the mediocre pianists sound alike. And there are more mediocre pianists today because the level of technique is very high. A lot of people can play the piano brilliantly who don't necessarily have important artistic talent. That wasn't true 20 or 30 years ago. So today we have a lot of artistic mediocrity. But the best people don't sound like each other: Barenboim doesn't sound like Ashkenazy, Ashkenazy doesn't sound like Argerich, and I don't sound like any of them."

ᘒᘒᘒ

Since the original publication of this article, Stephen Bishop has adopted the surname of his father, Kovacevich, and is currently performing under the name of Stephen Bishop Kovacevich.

"All right," I said, "but for the sake of discussion, let's take a group of pianists born in 1895: Gieseking, Iturbi, Kempff, and Novaes. Granted that was a banner year and a bumper crop — but are there younger pianists close in age with comparable individuality?"

"We're talking in 1972," Stephen rebutted, his sheaf of brown hair falling in his face. "You ask me that question in the year 2000, and it might have answered itself. I won't deny that the general level today can be monotonous and similar; but if the person is really good, you will hear individuality. I mean . . . Glenn Gould, one of the most gifted musicians we have, doesn't sound like anyone else.

"George Szell, in an interview, answered this question by saying there's a general trend towards so-called objectivity — a meaningless term — but it does mean that, to a certain extent, we check our sources more today than the older generation did. Personal liberties — playing forte when the music is marked piano, all this kind of thing — we don't do so often. So, not taking personal liberties gives a certain limit to what my generation does, whereas before they really were much freer. Let's not for the moment get into the argument as to whether or not that's any better."

"I want to pursue this generation controversy further," I said. "But before we do, I'd like to start at the beginning: Where were you born? How did

ᘒᘒᘒ

you start to play the piano?"

"I was born in San Pedro, near Los Angeles, in 1940, of a Croatian immigrant father and a first-generation Croatian-American mother. When I was three and four, I sat in front of the gramophone, listening to a lot of music; but I don't remember how I started playing. I do remember — although I had some early lessons — that I didn't start learning much until I was eight. From the age of eight to 18, I studied with Lev Schorr, a very good teacher, in San Francisco where we had moved, and then I started to learn something. Schorr had been a pupil of Annette Essipoff, who had been a pupil of Leschetitzky. I found it difficult to practice during adolescence. I didn't start working well until I was on my own in London, when I was about 18."

Study With Myra Hess

At 11 Stephen Bishop made his solo debut, and at 13 and 14 he played the Schumann and Ravel Concertos with the San Francisco Symphony. In the summer of 1959 he went to England (where he's lived ever since) to study with Myra Hess. Having heard him the previous spring in California, she had agreed to take him as a student:

"Dame Myra helped me develop a technique for getting sound. I remember she once asked, 'How would you hold a postage stamp if you wanted to decide how much it weighed?' Obviously you wouldn't hold it with a vise-like grip. Similarly, when feeling the weight of the key or the keyboard, you shouldn't be rigid. If you are rigid, you won't feel the weight and the resistance; you won't be able to get the varied sounds that you want.

"She taught me that a principal factor in style is getting the sound that's right for the work or the composer you're playing. (She and I once spent 45 minutes getting the right sound for the beginning of Bach's D Major Partita.) She might say, 'It's too heavy a sound, and yet it must be brilliant. You must hear it and then react physically to the sound you have in your head.' And she made me pay more attention to the markings of the composer.

"Then too she got me away from thinking of speed. I had thought it necessary to play most brilliant things as fast as possible. She showed me that more deliberate tempos can be incredibly exciting. I studied Bach, Beethoven sonatas and concertos, Schubert, Schumann, Brahms — in that area of composers we did at least one of the main pieces of each. I studied with her about three years, two years intensively — four years before she died. The last two years of her life, she was too ill to teach. Also I started having concerts, which meant I wasn't there."

Establishing His Career

Playing the Berg Sonata, Bach, and Beethoven's Diabelli Variations, Stephen Bishop won unanimous praise for his London debut in November of 1961. His four subsequent London recitals during the next year and a half, plus tours throughout England and Europe, established his reputation as one of the most

gifted pianists of his generation. During the past two years he has played all of the Mozart concertos with the Geraint Jones orchestra, two concertos an evening, one evening a month. "My approach to Mozart is in the spirit of the operatic style, limiting the extremes of sound so that the fortes are brilliant but not massive, not Beethovenian," he said.

"Do you play contemporary music?" I asked.

"If you mean Bartok and Stravinsky, yes; if you mean Xenakis, Stockhausen, Berio, and Boulez, no. Richard Rodney Bennett wrote a very fine concerto for me several years ago. It uses tone-row technique to a certain extent, but isn't atonal as such. It's not modern in the sense of Stockhausen or Berio."

Practice and Memory

I had been impressed by the imposing list of Stephen Bishop's performances — from solo recitals and concerto appearances, last year alone, in Europe, Japan, Australia, and the United States to a four-hand program with Ashkenazy for the Norwegian Television. "How do you practice — obviously a lot — and how do you memorize?" I asked.

"I practice five or six hours a day. Memory for me is completely unconscious, coming as a result of practice. I wouldn't know how to memorize phrase by phrase. For me, practicing isn't a question of memory; I just need to work.

"Often I start my practice by playing something not too fast, a prelude or slow movement of Bach, for example, to get my fingers going. Then I start working, perhaps on something in which I'm weak. Let's say I might find broken octaves difficult. So, instead of practicing only the broken octaves in a particular piece, I practice broken octaves in general which naturally helps the piece.

"When I have time, I do practice scales. I think scales are important. Practicing them always makes me play better. I have developed a series of technical exercises, and when I have time I do them too. In the Bartok Second Concerto (there are pieces as difficult as this one but not more so) if you practice and practice certain passages, you can get stiff. Or, perhaps you've practiced the passage until you can't take it any more, and it still doesn't come. Then I devise exercises to strengthen whatever weaknesses there were in that passage. I practice these exercises to get away from the concerto, and this helps to play the concerto itself.

"When I know a piece very well — besides sometimes playing it all the way through without stopping — I practice it in sections. If it is a sonata, I may practice the Exposition, the Development, or the Recapitulation. I practice until I get the feeling that the shape — the actual construction of the work — is alive in me. Then I feel I can relax more and be freer to emphasize this or that. If the structure is ingrained, the piece doesn't fall apart, no matter what I do."

Ideal of Tone

Stephen Bishop's recordings for Philips have been highly praised. Commenting on his Beethoven, *The New York Times* said his playing is "brilliant but remarkably refined. There is a quicksilver, darting quality to his pianism. and a controlled, unruffled elegance." Thinking of his "brilliant but remarkably refined" tone, I asked him about his ideal of tone.

"I would say my ideal is to have an appropriate sound for every composer," he answered, "and more than that an appropriate sound for different periods in a composer's life. I recognize a certain sound in my playing, but I don't try to get my own sound: my own sound happens as a result of what I'm trying to do."

"What pianist's tone have you most admired?"

"That depends. For Chopin, Horowitz's tone is perfect."

"What pianists have you most admired?"

". . . in the older generation, Rachmaninoff, Horowitz, Richter, and Schnabel . . . in the younger generation, Ashkenazy and Martha Argerich."

The Generation Gap

I steered the conversation back to the older generation's criticism of the younger. Knowing he had recorded the Beethoven Diabelli Variations, I asked Stephen Bishop if he agreed with Claudio Arrau that "many young pianists, making their debuts with Opus 106 and the Diabelli Variations, seem to want to take short cuts, to skip and start with the big things — that you can't understand the late sonatas or the Diabelli Variations without first knowing the whole line of Beethoven in all its aspects."

"Well, I obviously disagree," Stephen Bishop answered. "There are young pianists who play 106 or the Diabelli very well, who by no means know Beethoven's entire output. In the first place, anyone who plays late Beethoven as a young man is going to play it differently, more richly as he gets older. But if anyone has such a love of a piece that he wants to do it — that's enough reason to do it then.

"We're very grateful to the greatness of these older people. But a different climate or approach is no reason to pontificate that one shouldn't play the *Hammerklavier* until one has played everything else. You'll probably play the *Hammerklavier* better having played it all your life as part of your bones. On the other hand, not playing it until you've played all the other sonatas assumes that there's a time when you're ready for the *Hammerklavier*. When do you wake up and say, 'I'm ready for the *Hammerklavier* . . . I'm ready for the last Schubert Sonata?'"

Communication the Important Test

"You mentioned," I said, "that today the level of technique is higher than formerly. But is the level of communication consistently as high?"

"I will admit that there is a tendency for my generation to play safe," Stephen answered. "It's the normal human thing when we know the audience knows the music through records. The older generation didn't have to worry about the audience and the critics being used to the artificial sound of a perfect recording. Knowing this makes us pay more attention than we should to getting the right notes.

"If today's artists get nervous at concerts, it's often because they're afraid they can't play so well as they did on their recordings. And there's of course truth in that. But when you are in shape, when for some reason things are going well, you do forget about the technical side and you do just think about the music — as good people have always done and presumably always will.

"I think the generation gap, though real, is a little bit of a waste of time. When you hear a young person play a good concert, you hear the same things that were supposed to be the exclusive province of the old-timers: you hear communication; you hear excitement. And these are the things for which one strives.

"I don't go along with the idea that 'if another Rubinstein or Horowitz would appear we'd have no trouble filling the halls,' nor do I believe that classical music is dying. I think there are whole worlds yet unexplored in Beethoven, in Schubert. There is a lot to be said that hasn't been said. I can imagine a future generation's getting closer to what I think is the real spirit of the music than we've done and that even people in the past have done, as great as they were. So, in terms of interpretation, there is a lot of room to go, which is a marvelous thing. It means that music is limitless and we are getting closer and closer.

"In terms of composition, I really don't know. I have no crystal ball; I have only my intuition. I don't know what electronic music will come to, if it's a valid way in which people are going to compose. This I can't say, but in my own concern, I strongly feel there's great room for artistic development.

"I don't think we're replacing the older generation; I think we're an extension. Don't forget that just as they were influenced by their time, we can't help but be influenced by ours. Which of us has not been influenced by Horowitz, Gieseking, Serkin, Schnabel, Furtwangler, Toscanini? We're influenced and we're a continuation. So, I see the development of artists as a continuous thing — we're not talking about whether we're as good or as bad. But I don't think that we're a different species, that one is the musician and the other the automaton. I don't believe that.

"Let's also wait until my generation comes into maturity, until we're 50. I know there are early recordings of the older generation which already show their individual imprint. But I could present to you recordings of the younger generation I've mentioned which are just magnificent. And I can't believe that anybody would feel starved by them. We can select from the hundreds of recordings we've made. We can select certain pieces, wonderfully played, and go from there and see what happens."

As I left, Stephen Bishop, the suave, amiable man and artist that he is, said he felt he'd been slightly belligerent. (After all I had baited him.) But when I greeted him after his recital — Bach, Schubert, and Beethoven superbly played — he was all smiles: "I missed some notes. So I *do* sound like the older generation after all!" he said.

The Mercurial MARTHA ARGERICH: an interview

interview February 5, 1978

Making her entrance, she is a flag, gracefully unfurling, saluted by every eye. In the yellow light her tresses are ebony, streaming down to her red and black gown. She faces the audience and bows very deeply, quickly. Shoulders straighten and spines tingle, for Martha Argerich is about to play and prove that not all of Paradise has been lost.

An evening with the Argentinian "La Argerich" is an evening with one of the world's most gifted pianists. She is considered by *cognoscenti* and public to be in the front rank of her generation. Few pianists are viewed with such awed admiration by their colleagues. Few pianists receive such frenzied ovations.

The thrill of her entrance has not yet ebbed as she quickly sits at the piano. She is almost fragile looking, about 5'4", and her marvelously developed hands are delicate in her lap during the orchestra's *tutti*.

The performance of Mozart's great *Concerto* in C, K. 503 is exciting and note-perfect. She plays Mozart with a beautiful, silvery, limpid tone. She points hand and fingers, often taking the end of a phrase or a staccato note with all of her fingers held together and pointed.

The New York Philharmonic conducted by Raphael Kubelik plays superbly. It is lovely Mozart, like a bird song, fresh and unpredictable. Argerich plays freely, effortlessly. Broken octaves ripple, turns are tossed off. The vehemence of her octaves and the brilliance of her passage work are as striking as her immense rhythmic vitality and feeling for tonal values. This concerto with its multitudinous melodies has never seemed more spontaneous. Never before have I heard the contrapuntal entrances made so clear. The last movement is taken at a good clip, and Mozart's F major theme (see example below), one of his simplest and most personal, in the development of the sonata rondo is played so refreshingly that one finds himself singing the tune even as shouts of "Bravo! Bravo!" rise at the end.

Martha Argerich has been rewarded with raves since she was 16 and the winner in two of the most renowned international music competitions: the Busoni and Geneva Competitions, just three weeks apart. Eight years later, in 1965, she won first prize at the great Chopin Competition in Warsaw, showing superiority over 85 young pianists from all over the world. One never would have known that she had been idle three years while she watched television in New York and considered becoming a secretary.

Since 1965 she, along with Bishop-Kovacevich, Freire, Slobodyanik, Pollini, Watts, and other greats in their 30s have signaled that the time has come to dry the eyes over the passing of the Rachmaninoffs and Giesekings, the Guiomar Novaeses and Gina Bachauers — no matter how much we miss them.

However, an Argerich concert is all too rare an event, and often one must settle instead for listening to a *Deutsche Grammophon* recording. "I love very much to play the piano," she says, "but I don't like to be a pianist." Audiences are spellbound by her fiery and fast-flowing pianism, and Herbert Barrett, her New York manager says, "We could book her 365 days a year if only she would play that many concerts." But being a cult figure has not made Argerich any less of a free spirit, and while she has played fairly frequently in this country and especially abroad, she still has not performed as often as might be expected of one of her stature.

If a concert hereabouts by Argerich is all too rare, to obtain an interview with her it helps to know Nelson Freire. The two have been good friends since their 1958 student days, and mention of the Brazilian pianist slows the flight of this gingerale-sipping, quick-talking scarlet tanager as she darts from admirer to admirer in the Avery Fisher Green Room.

An interview with Martha Argerich is an exploration of a woman who loves to laugh and who yearns for the verdant and azure spaces of a more natural life.

149

Our interview began after Argerich had been practicing for a Washington, D.C. performance, learning some new pieces of Ginastera in less than an hour. She had several things on her mind. Besides personal matters, she was somewhat startled and upset by a Harold Schonberg review in *The New York Times* calling her Mozart performance "rather superficial." I began by asking her about Mozart.

Did you choose to play Mozart to show another facet of your artistry?

Oh, no, no. I was supposed to play the Dvorak Concerto, but there was some strange confusion about that. Then I was to play Schumann, but Firkusny was playing Schumann, and then the only thing I could do was Mozart, I was told. It is interesting for me to play Mozart anyway because some important things have happened to me in relationship with playing Mozart. And it is important for me to know where I stand in that way. That's why this review upsets me very much: it was painful because it was Mozart. This time particularly.

Gieseking believed in his way of playing Mozart, which audiences loved, and he continued to play it regardless of what a few critics wrote. Your performance was really very moving.

But Schonberg said it was very shy or something. Kubelik told me, on the contrary, that he was happy because it was so singing, and that was exactly the opposite of what Schonberg said.

Just keeping playing. He'll come around.

Okay (little laugh of amusement).

At 16, in 1957, you won the Busoni and the Geneva Competitions within three weeks. Do you have memories of the repertoire you prepared, the atmosphere, the judges, how you played?

Well, yes, a lot of memories. I didn't expect to get through the preliminaries. I was expecting to be eliminated so I never worked from one round to the next, you know. I didn't want to practice if I wasn't going to get through, so when my name was announced I would go on and practice for the next round. I was always thinking *no*.

At the Busoni, in Bolzano, the first eliminatory round was quite private in front of only three or four judges. Because I had never made any other competiton, I had to play in the eliminatory round. I went and I played. They said to me, "That's enough. You can leave." And I was very eager and curious to know if I was going to get into the next round so I said, *"Arriverderci* or is it *Addio?"* I wanted to know if it was "goodbye" or *"Auf Wiedersehen."* I don't know how you say it in English, but I wanted to know if they were going to see me again or not. (Laughing)

What did they say?

They said, "Yes, *arriverderci."* And that was where I met Ivan Davis. He came to see who was playing behind the door and said he was so very impressed with the practicing. (I was practicing the Prokofieff *Toccata.*) He opened the door, saying, "What's this?" and saw me there smoking. Ivan always remembers that. He was a very good colleague in that competition.

I think the 1957 Busoni Competition was the highest level that I have ever been in a competition. There was Ivan Davis, Jerry Lewenthal, and Ludwig Hoffman, an excellent German pianist. And they could play very well, you know, really!

You must have prepared a lot of repertoire to enter both the Busoni and the Geneva Competitions within three weeks of each other.

No, the Geneva repertoire was very short and not very interesting. When I won the Busoni, the officials didn't want me to enter the Geneva only 10 days after. The President of the Jury in Bolzano, Cesare Inordio, was absolutely furious when he knew that I was. He said, "Now you are going to Geneva and you are not going to get the first prize, and then what happens with our competition?" But then when I got the first prize in Geneva, he was very happy. He sent me a telegram.

The Geneva repertoire was short. I remember I had to play Beethoven's *Sonata* op. 10 no. 3, a Bach *Prelude and Fugue,* Ravel's *Toccata,* one or two Chopin *Etudes,* the Schumann *Concerto,* and the Liszt *Sixth Hungarian Rhapsody.* That's where I played the Liszt the first time. I hadn't played it before, not even for myself. At that time I was very superstitious so I wouldn't play a piece all the way through even for myself. I was afraid that something...so I just waited until I passed to the next round to learn the next pieces.

You must have a photographic memory.

Memory was not the problem. It was the playing. I was afraid that I couldn't, so I didn't want to play, you see.

What is the ancestry of the name Argerich?

It is complicated. The name has been in Argentina for about 200 years, but some say it is from Catalonia, that it was there in the 12th century already. Four or five Argerichs come to see me when I play in Barcelona. It is a strange name, no? And sometimes they say as well it is from Yugoslavia because there is a village named like this too, a Croatian thing.

You pronounce it "Ahr-ge-ritch?"

That depends where. In Argentina they pronounce it the Spanish way which is not right because it is not a Spanish name. So they say, "Ahr'-he-reech." But in Barcelona they say, "Ahr'-szhe-reek." They think this is the right way. I don't know. I say, "Ahr-ge-reech." Whatever comes it doesn't matter.

Tell me how your interest in music began.

I was very young. I was at the kindergarten in a competitive program when I was two years and eight months. I was much younger than the rest of the children. I had a little friend who was always teasing me; he was five and was always telling me, "You can't do this, you can't do that." And I would always do whatever he said I couldn't.

Once he got the idea of telling me I couldn't play the piano. (Laughter) That's how it started. I still remember it. I immediately got up, went to the piano, and started playing a tune that the teacher was playing all the time. I played the tune by ear and perfectly. The teacher immediately called my mother, and they started making a fuss. And it was all because of this boy who said, "You can't play the piano."

At the same time my mother wanted to start learning piano or singing. There was a piano at home, but after this incident I didn't let her go to the piano. I was very jealous and I would take her away; I wanted to play myself. Our conflicts began at that time.

When did you begin lessons?

Well, almost immediately with a lady who was a specialist in this type of thing, but only until I was five. She used to teach children without music, you see. She had about 15 or 20 pupils who could play by ear.

Were you forced to practice?

Later, yes I was and I hated it. I didn't want to be a pianist in the first place. I still don't really want to be, but it is the only thing that I can do more or less. (Laughter) I wanted to be a doctor!

Do you think you would love to do it more if you hadn't been forced to practice?

I don't know. It is a mixture of things. I love very much to play the piano, but I don't like to be a pianist. I don't like the profession. And when one plays, of course, it is important to practice. But the profession itself — the traveling and the way of life — all this has nothing to do with playing or with music, absolutely nothing! This is what I do not enjoy about being a concert pianist. You never know when you are very young, when you are studying, what this profession is about. No one tells you, and the people outside the profession don't have a clue. They think it is marvelous.

Do you think it's harder for a woman than for a man?

I suppose, but it is complicated for me because I had the type of teacher and parents who used to tell me when I was a little girl that my fiancé was the piano. I didn't have much freedom as a child.

I've read that Myra Hess used to say her fiancé was the piano.

And isn't that terrible! (Laughter) My teacher used to tell me this to hypnotize me I suppose — I don't know what. I hate this type of reasoning, this idea of being high priestess or something. I don't like this attitude in life, generally. I would never do that with a child of mind.

Tell me about the concert you played with orchestra at the age of eight.

How do you know about this? I played the Mozart *D minor Concerto* (isn't that funny, all the *Wunderkinder* play that and it is one of the most difficult in certain respects) and the first Beethoven *Concerto* and the Bach G major *French Suite* in between.

The Gigue's not so easy.

I don't remember. I don't play it now. But I heard a tape the other day of a concert of mine, of the Schumann *Concerto* when I was 11 and of that Mozart *Concerto* when I was nine. It's a very distorted tape, but I was touched because, my God, pianistically, it is absolutely amazing. I mean, I don't understand how I did those things. I just brought this tape back to my mother. It had been in a deposit box in Switzerland for ten years.

You have told me about playing for Gieseking when you were eight, and that he told your parents to leave you in peace. Did it seem to him that they were forcing you to play?

I played the last movement of Beethoven's *Sonata* in E♭ op. 31 no. 3, and probably he could notice that I was not enjoying the situation very much. I was glad he told them because that was what I wanted.

But they didn't take his advice.

It was very difficult I suppose for them to understand. I used to do horrible things to myself in order not to play. I was told if you soaked blotter paper in water and put it in your shoes, you would get fever, so I would hide in the bathroom and put water in my shoes. And I used to hide under the table at *soirées* instead of meeting people. Daniel Barenboim was at those musical evenings too, but he enjoyed playing for those people very much; I hated it. We used to meet under the table when I was hiding there.

Argerich (on crutches) with cellist Mstislav Rostropovich

That's interesting because you have a magnetism when you walk out on stage that goes out to people.

You think so?

Yes, and an artist either has it or doesn't. Gieseking, with whom I studied, loved playing the piano more than life itself so to speak. He couldn't stay away from the piano. He seemingly couldn't talk about anything else but for a short time, and then he had to be back playing the piano.

Really? Well, some people do. Nelson likes to play the piano quite a lot, more than I do. I have long periods without touching the piano, and I don't miss it. And then I can get possessed by the piano for a while as well. But I enjoy completely different things like going for walks, talking with people, non-musicians, and being in a completely different atmosphere.

When you have been all your life put into a frame of being a pianist, of being a musician in spite of yourself, it is unfair for the rest of your personality. You have something else you want to express. It looks theoretical in my case, but I try. I don't know if I succeed, but I hope to be able to express myself otherwise too.

I've read that Arrau, Solomon, Szigeti, Francescatti, and Von Beinem heard you play.

Szigeti was very touching. I played for him when I was 12, and he wrote me a letter from the plane. Then I met him again when I was 17 in Genoa and I played some sonatas with him. It was about the first time I had any chamber music experience. I was terrified because I had to sight-read. I didn't know the music. And I was so touched because he went into another room to warm up for 20 or 30 minutes before starting to play with me. I was a 17-year-old with no experience. I mean who was I? I was just nothing, you know. It was incredible!

Shall we mention Vincenzo Scaramuzza?

He was an extraordinary teacher I suppose, but I didn't do many of the things he told me. I was hearing other people tell me how to practice. He would tell me what to do, and I would do what the other people told me. I studied with him from age five to ten in Argentina.

You played Friedrich Gulda's cadenza to the Mozart Concerto in C, K. 503.

Gulda was my first teacher outside Argentina. He is fantastic. I love him. I believe he is one of the most talented people I have ever met. For me, playing for him was a fantastic experience.

Do you remember anything that you especially learned from him?

Oh, all kinds of things. A lot of Debussy and Ravel. Isn't that funny? And Bach quite a lot too. I was with him one year and a half. He used to record the lesson. And after, he wanted me to listen with him, to criticize my own things, you see? This was very interesting because it was very democratic. He liked to know what I had to say, what I thought. It was not this thing that usually happens between pupil and teacher. It was fantastic. I learned a lot with him.

Sometimes he would challenge me because I would be lazy. I wouldn't work and learn fast enough. I was going through a sort of mystic crisis about God, whether I believed in God and the immortal soul. It was complicated. I used to arrive late at every lesson and start talking about this with him. I was so worried and he had to answer, and at the same time he knew I was doing this because I hadn't prepared.

Once I was about a month with a Schubert sonata. And he said, "I don't know Martha what is the matter with you. Maybe I was wrong. I thought you were very talented, but now I don't know what is the problem with you." So he said, "For your next lesson, five days from now, you have to bring me all of Ravel's *Gaspard de la nuit* and Schumann's *Abegg Variations.*"

All right, so I brought them all learned; it was not difficult because I didn't know that it was supposed to be. When one doesn't know that a piece is very difficult, one learns it easily. If you know already from everybody that this piece is difficult, then you don't learn it fast. I didn't know this, so I learned these pieces fast, and he was very happy about it.

I spoke to Nikita Magaloff at the 1977 Cliburn Competition in Ft. Worth and asked him what he taught you.

What did he say?

"Oh, she could already play everything. But I worry when she cancels concerts."

He always says that to me.

What about your study with Michelangeli?

Well, I was one year and a half with him, and I had four lessons. It's not much. Once he said to David Ruben from Steinway, "Oh, I've done a lot for that girl." And David said, "But *Maestro* I know that you gave her only four lessons." And he said, "Yes, but I taught her the music of silence." It's all very mysterious. (Laughter)

Obviously you don't have to practice much, and you learn phenomenally fast. You are a natural pianist. Tell me that anecdote about how you learned the Proko-fieff Third Concerto.

Well, I was rooming with a girl who used to practice it while I was asleep in the mornings. We had only this one room. Somehow this music came subconsciously into my mind, even with the wrong notes she was playing. I noticed I knew it when I started to play it.

And you learned the wrong notes that she played?

Yes, I did. (Laughter) She was practicing the difficult parts and had these problems . . .

Both you and Nelson Freire learn phenomenally fast.

Nelson has the greatest facility I have ever seen. He can sight-read like I've never seen in my life except for Gulda. Nelson is always looking for new things to play or to read. He is one who enjoys playing the piano as you were saying, like Gieseking, not like me. I have a conflict.

I hope you will be able to make both things work. Tell me about your first recording you made when you were 20.

I went with Nelson on a train to Hanover. We were young, and we arrived in a state. I had no idea how to make a record so I said, "I want to play everything three times, and that's it." I would never listen, nothing. I had told Nelson that if there was something they wanted I couldn't play, he could play instead. No one would see.

It was very funny. Nelson was in another room practicing the same things that I was. This recording engineer understood very much about piano playing, and he was flabbergasted: "What's this?" Nelson was in the next room practicing and giving me lessons because I didn't really play the Brahms *Rhapsodies* op. 79. He was giving me all his advice.

I read that Horowitz expressed his admiration of your Prokofieff Toccata recording. Horowitz and Rachmaninoff have been your pianistic idols?

I love them, but not only them. I love Gieseking and Cortot too. I like Schnabel, Glenn Gould — a lot of people. Of the older people, Cortot is quite important for me. Even Backhaus had some things I used to love. His recording of the Beethoven *Third Concerto* with Boehm is fantastic. When I was a little girl in Argentina, I was very much attracted to the classical pianists. Backhaus and Gulda impressed me the most. Isn't that interesting? I was not impressed by other things and did the opposite finally.

In January 1978 you and Nelson flew to New York to hear Vladimir Horowitz's first appearance with an orchestra in 25 years. What did you think of his Rachmaninoff Third *Performance?*

It was the first time I heard him in the flesh, you know. It was an incredible shock for me because it was more Horowitz than what I thought Horowitz was. Nelson and I were sitting there holding hands, tense. The strength of his expression, the sound, and this incredible violence he has inside which is so strange, weird, and frightening. That he can express it. He's like possessed. I've read about this, but this was the first time that I saw on stage someone who has *that*!

Speaking of Horowitz makes me think of the Liszt Sonata *in B minor, one of his greatest interpretations and one of yours. I think your recording has tremendous architectural sweep from the first note to the last, fantastic emotional and technical drive, with contrasting affecting lyricism. When did you record it?*

I don't remember when I did this record...about seven years ago I think.

What are your ideas about this work? Is it a favorite of yours?

I don't like to listen to it, not played by me, not played by anybody. Isn't that funny? I get very impatient. There is something that bothers me about it, not because I've heard it too much. On the other hand, I am very interested in what Cortot says about "the dispute of conscience which fills Faust's tormented soul in his search for truth," in reference to the passages of Goethe's *Faust* that inspired Liszt's *Sonata*. Some people hate what Cortot wrote in his edition, but I think it opens up a lot of horizons like his playing did too. I don't believe that it works for everything. But for me, yes, for some things it does and well. What Cortot wrote seems very important.

In that Scarlatti Sonata *in D minor, the one with repeated change-of-finger right-hand notes against rolled left-hand notes, that you played as an encore in Avery Fisher Hall, your fingers were wiggling even before you began to play. The incredible speed of your repeated notes brought down the house.*

I play it always as an encore. I learned it when I was a very little girl; and I've never seen the music since, you know.

You should make a recording of Scarlatti sonatas.

Well, no, I can't. I have a horror of all those little trills. You see little trills are my horrible obsession, and most of Scarlatti is full of them. Long, fast trills go all right, but the little ones — they are for me the horror — you know, sometimes I get stuck. I don't lift my fingers enough. It's like stuttering if I'm not in shape. Let's say I'm sight-reading something, and there are some little trills. Then they go. But the moment I know in advance that I have to do them, then ugh! — It's terrible.

I forgot to show you these programs of Stefan Askenase whom I heard in Zürich.

My God! I studied with him, you know, and his wife helped me so much. If it hadn't been for her, I wouldn't be playing now. I had stopped playing and a lot of people tried to help me start playing again. This was just before the 1965 Chopin Competition. I had a child when I was 22, and I went to the competition in Brussels in 1964. My mother wanted me to enter — this was one month after the birth of my first child, ridiculous, no? I couldn't; I wasn't prepared. I had been away from the piano for about three years, really away from it, coming from Michelangeli to the States where I did practically nothing. I was one year here in New York, and all I did was watch television. Some people were trying to help me to go back, like Fou T'Song. But I couldn't. It just didn't work.

And then I went to Brussels to see Stefan Askenase, whom I had known when I was very little. Because I couldn't enter this competition, I thought, "I am going to become a secretary." The night before the competition I said to myself, "Well, now, Martha, it is over for you. You have been a pianist but now you are not. You cannot play, so what kind of a pianist are you? You know some languages; you must start to earn your livelihood as a secretary." I remember this very well. And then I went to see the Askenases in the morning. My mother said, "Go and see," and she phoned. I met this woman, Stefan's wife, who was extraordinary. Little by little, I started. I went there every day. I was absolutely fascinated by this woman. She had something very special, like a sun. She gave me strength and security. I started to believe again that I could, and little by little I started to play — very bad, wrong notes all over the place, and I couldn't stand it. I was thinking, "What is the matter with me?" I went on and on like this. Because of her I started to play again, and almost immediately I went to the Chopin Competition. It was because of her. Otherwise, I couldn't have done it.

What would you say is your interpretive goal?

I think interpretation is trying to liberate what one is unconscious about. When one can let go some things one doesn't know are there — the unexpected things and the surprises in the performance — that's when it's worthwhile. This is also what I appreciate in other performers. When they are masters of their means of expression, this does not exactly interest me. That interests me in a teacher, but in a performer I am interested in what happens behind or in spite of the things the performer consciously wants to do. Maybe I am a little bit of a *voyeur*, you know, that way. But this is what I love.

Slobodyanik

interview fall, 1973

SLOBODYANIK (Slō-bōd-yah'-nik)! It's a tongue twister at first, but once you know it you won't forget it. And once you've seen and heard him play — "exceedingly handsome, he could become a concert idol on looks alone . . . perhaps the finest pianist to come from Soviet Russia since Gilels and Richter" say the critics — you won't forget his playing.

Aleksander Slobodyanik began playing in the United States in the fall of 1968 and, receiving rave reviews from coast to coast, has returned every season since. I first heard him on the radio, playing Chopin. The poetic drive, the singing tone, the effortless, big technique, and the distinct personality made me want to hear more. So I attended his standing-room-only recital in Philharmonic Hall's Great Performer Series in November 1972. An unnervous performer, with a fast-flowing music-making mechanism, he literally threw himself into the program of Shostakovich (see music on pages 25-32), Schumann, Chopin, Liszt, and Stravinsky.

This season at his Hunter College afternoon recital, he walked calmly to the piano. "I had got off the plane late the night before and was still somewhat sleepy," he explained to me later. Of his stage deportment on another occasion, one critic wrote that "the lithe

Slobodyanik saunters on and off stage like a graceful wolfhound. And as he brushes back his long, sandy hair to take a bow, one almost senses romantic ladies on the verge of swooning."

Offstage, I found him warm, gracious, serious, without pretense or exaggeration. His sense of humor, not the snappy-rejoinder type, is genuine, as is his broad smile. You wouldn't have to know him long, I felt, before you called him Alek.

We were sitting in an office of Columbia Artists Management, across from Carnegie Hall. Maxim Gershunoff, the Columbia Artists manager, sat in to interpret. From time to time, Slobodyanik, who six years ago knew no English, asked him for a word or two. At other times the two of them lapsed into a volley of Russian.

I asked Slobodyanik first about Kiev, Russia's third

155

largest city (population 1,175,000), where he was born during the War, in 1942.

"As you know," he answered pensively, "Kiev was long time ago the capital of Russia and is now the capital of the Ukrainian Republic. Kiev is a beautiful city, a little bit like San Francisco, with many hills and trees, beautiful countryside around. And now it's very interesting also for its cultural life, its many halls and orchestras. I was born in Kiev, but in 1945 my family moved to Lvov, where my father still lives, in the west of the Ukraine, about 40 miles from Poland. Lvov was in Poland before the War. Having influences from both Poland and Austria, it has a completely different style of architecture and many things from Kiev."

"Did you hear any great pianists as a child?" I asked.

"In Lvov when I was a boy I remember Sviatoslav Richter and Heinrich Neuhaus. When I listened to them, I decided to move to Moscow to study with one of them. And in 1956 my dream was fulfilled. I started studying with Professor Heinrich Neuhaus in Central Music School in Moscow."

Like most virtuoso pianists, Slobodyanik began playing the piano when he was very small. "The atmosphere in my family was musical. My mother played piano, my father violin. My father was not a professional musician. After the conservatory he studied medicine. Now he is a doctor. My first lessons were with my mother when I was five years old. She taught me for many years. I was advanced when I went to Neuhaus."

"Do you remember what you first played for Neuhaus?"

"The Third Concerto by Beethoven, the Third Ballade by Chopin, some Chopin Etudes, and some Bach Preludes and Fugues."

Heinrich Neuhaus (1888-1964), one of this century's great teachers, had studied with Barth in Berlin at the same time as Arthur Rubinstein, and later with Godowsky. Rubinstein, concertizing in Moscow, had visited Neuhaus in the hospital the morning of the day he died.

"What made Neuhaus a great teacher?" I asked.

"It is difficult to speak about Neuhaus in a few words," Alek replied. "He was one of the greatest cultured persons in the century. He was a fantastic teacher beacuse he knew very well literature, history, all kinds of art. He had studied in Berlin and had lived in Italy. He had a fantastic education. His uncle, Felix Blumenfeld, was the teacher of Horowitz. From 1919 to 1932 Neuhaus taught in Kiev. Horowitz, Neuhaus, Blumenfeld — many great artists worked in Kiev.

"After 1932, maybe I'm wrong a few years, Neuhaus moved to Moscow. The poet Boris Pasternak, was his best friend."

"Neuhaus had many fine pupils," I said.

"Yakov Zak was one of them. Gilels studied with him a couple of years. Richter many years. Those are the three . . ."

"Neuhaus described you as 'endowed with enormous innate talent.' Tell me of your study with him."

"Oh, I began studying with him when I was 15, and often to play to him was difficult. He worked

you very hard and if you weren't prepared, if you didn't practice very hard, he would scold you. He was very severe sometimes. There were some funny and some touching moments. He could curse like hell. He could break a lamp, anything. He went wild. I tried very hard but I can't say that I was one of his most gifted students. I don't think I was totally prepared for what he expected of me sometimes."

"Does his book, *The Art of Piano Playing* (Praeger, 1973), give a good idea of his teaching?"

"The book is not the best of him because his personality was everything. His presence was the factor that made you work and learn."

"I've heard that gifted children in Russia are singled out at age four and given special training," I said.

"Since four?" Slobodyanik exclaimed. "Four is too early, but from six or seven, they go to special Central Music Schools not only in Moscow but in Kiev, Kharkov, Lvov, the biggest cities. They go to school free, having not only music education but all kinds of subjects."

"Your press material," I continued, "says that at 16 you decided to compete in the Warsaw Competition, that bitterly discouraged and disappointed from winning only seventh place, you refused to practice even for Professor Neuhaus and were expelled for a time from the Conservatory."

"I was 18," Alek immediately corrected.

"And your consequent bitter disappointment?"

(Laugh). "That's why I told this sometimes. Yes, I had only about three months to prepare."

"What did you prepare in three months?"

"It was a Chopin competition. A concerto, some ballades. Some works I knew before, but many things I prepared just for the competition. Maurizio Pollini won first place. Many prize-winners you never hear from again, but Pollini's gotten better."

"Did you really think you would give up the piano?"

"*Netakda kontsa*, not totally. Not winning was one of my first big disappointments, not only with music in general, but with life. I realized that there are circumstances in life that don't have to do totally with you. There are other elements involved. When things happen to you that are not very pleasant, you get a certain reaction. I was very disturbed at the time."

"With whom did you study when you re-entered the Moscow Conservatory, and when did you begin your career?"

"After one year I continued with Neuhaus. I studied about six or seven years with him altogether, and then after he died I studied with Professor Vera Gornostayeva, a young, very talented professor in Moscow Conservatory, who also had studied with Professor Neuhaus. I prepared my Tschaikowsky Competition program with her. After the 1966 Tschaikowsky Competition I began my concert career."

"Do you remember any anecdotes about the 1966 Tschaikowsky Competition?"

"The most exciting part was the announcing — who is winner, who is first, second, third — at two o'clock in the morning. The enthusiasm and reaction of the public — there was booing. Some people were even ready to hit the jurists. I won fourth prize."

"Who won first?"

"Grigori Sokolof."

How He Practices

Slobodyanik's method of practice depends upon his schedule. If he has concerts with new programs very soon, he practices six or six and a half hours a day. But when on tour, "when I have no chance to practice enough," he thinks the best way to keep in form is "to play three intense weeks of concerts and then to prepare new programs for three weeks."

His hands are large — even from the stage you notice the immense stretch between the fourth and fifth fingers. Up close you see his hands are finely proportioned, with widely-spaced fingers, not spidery like Cliburn's nor spatulate like Rubinstein's, but rather fleshy.

A "natural" pianist, Slobodyanik has no special regimen for technique. "In my practicing I mostly play the whole piece through," he says. "If there is something wrong I repeat some places."

"Then you belong to the category of artist who doesn't practice details, who practices mostly the 'big' line," I said. "Like Rubinstein who says he doesn't know how he does anything, that what he does is mostly instinct?"

Alek laughed. "I understand."

"That's the way you feel?"

"Sometimes."

"But when you sat down to play the Brahms F Minor Sonata you knew what you were going to do," I pressed. "Possibly because you haven't taught you don't put your thinking into words. You keep what you think in your subconscious and it comes out as you play."

"When I play, yes, it is for the moment; but basi-cally I know exactly what I'm doing," he answered. I finally got it out!

Slobodyanik's integral recording of the Chopin Etudes (Angel-Melodiya SR-4024 and 4025), recorded at an actual concert in the Big Hall of the Moscow Conservatory, has been praised by critics as one of the finest sets of piano disks of recent years. There is effortless technique of course, but always and foremost, there is naturalness, singing line, and heart.

When I told Slobodyanik that I find his recording of the Chopin Etudes in many ways the best that there is, even better than Pollini's studio-made disks which won a first prize in the HIGH FIDELITY Montreux International Awards, he grabbed my arm.

"Thank you," he said.

"Had you prepared especially for this performance?"

"I had played the 24 Etudes out of town, in some provinces, before the Moscow recital. When I got out on the stage, I saw the microphone. I had no idea the recital was to be recorded. 'Why?' I asked. 'Well,' they said, 'We'll see what happens out of it.' In the first part of the program I played the Schumann Symphonic Etudes, in the second part the 24 Chopin Etudes."

"How had you prepared for playing the 24 Etudes as a cycle?"

"I knew most of them before and special for this idea I prepared maybe eight more. And then when I knew all 24, one year later I played them in cycle."

"Surely in this case you must have done special technical work on each one."

"No, I never did. They are very plastic, comfortable works. You can work each etude, you can always improve on each one, you can always do things with them if you want. Regretfully, maybe I'm missing certain things but I think of them as an overall cycle. I want the overall concept in my mind rather than separate details, everything exact. I never think of technical work by itself. When you want to make music, the technique goes along by itself. If you're thinking of the music, the technique has to do it."

Approach To Interpretation

"What is your approach to interpretation?" I asked.

"Interpretation of what?"

"Music." A terse, instinctive person, Slobodyanik was puzzled by my question. Then he lapsed into Russian, translated:

"Interpretation is always a mystery. But you do have to know the history of the piece, who wrote it and when. That's the first thing. Secondly, music should be very emotional. Even works of the Classical period, which should be very rational, still should be focused through the heart. In concerts I feel something is missing if the playing is mathematical, even if the playing is of high quality.

"People come to a concert to see something of theater, of an actor's temperament. They're waiting either for the blood of the artist or for something very pleasant. They want bad and good."

"Some pianists of your generation, Martha Argerich, for example, play fast tempos, comparatively speaking, even for slow movements," I said. "You, on the contrary, often take slower tempos than we're accustomed to, say the beginning of the Chopin F

Minor Fantasy. Is your rather slow tempo something you just feel, or does it stem from a tradition?"

"The beginning of the F Minor Fantasy, maybe it's my own opinion or feeling, I don't know. I remember very well that Neuhaus always slowed a little bit the right tempo. Richter tempos sometimes are absolutely different from what we imagine. In the B Flat Posthumous Sonata by Schubert, Richter's tempo is extremely slow. Backstage after one concert Yakov Zak said to Richter, 'Good, good, but I think your tempo is a little bit slow. It seems the form maybe is destroyed.' 'No,' Richter answered, 'It's my fault. The tempo should be still slower.'

"So how slow a tempo you play depends upon how successfully you do it. Any idea, within a border of tradition, is possible to bring on the stage if the public follows."

"I have the feeling that you concentrate very much on beautiful tone. What is your ideal of tone?"

"Someone asked Neuhaus, 'Where does the quality of sound come from?' Neuhaus thought and then he said, 'From here, from the heart, well and from the brain, and from the hand too.' Also the leg comes into it a little bit, also intuition. Nobody knows just how. There are so many kinds of touch, qualities of sound, because each pianist has his own heart.

"For Chopin, Brahms, for Romantic music, sound is very important. In other literature perhaps you have foremost in your task other things except sound. But foremost in Romantic music, you must have beautiful sound because the melodic line is so important.

"Color in Mozart or Debussy is quite different from that in Chopin or Schumann. Each composer needs a change of imagination, whether to be sharp or to be relaxed, or a little bit mysterious as in Scriabin or Debussy. For Beethoven sonatas you need clear fingers; you must practice Cramer Etudes. Each composer is absolutely a different task and thought. So

first of all you need to know in what epoch the composer wrote.

"But tone is a very difficult question. For example, now there is a big discussion over how to play Mozart or composers who wrote before Mozart — to do it in modern style or to emulate as it was before. When I was in Salzburg I heard the piano of Mozart. And I was so surprised that although the sound of Mozart's piano was soft, there was a romantic element in its tone. Its tone was nothing like that of the harpsichord, without overtones. Mozart's piano had overtones, so he wrote his pieces imagining romantic music. Modern young pianists sometimes try to make a beautiful piano sound like a harpsichord — they try to play Mozart too much with sharp staccato precision, with a quality so *secco,* too dry. Why? Mozart has so big heart. He likes many things in life."

"Have you made new recordings?" I asked.

"The Liszt Sonata. I'll do now the first and second Chopin Concertos with Yuri Temarkanov and the Leningrad Symphony."

Max Gershunoff asked whether I was familiar with Termarkanov. "He made a big sensation here this year with the Philadelphia Orchestra," Max said. "Age 34, a fabulous conductor, he's been re-engaged for the next two years with the Philadelphia Orchestra. So you have the combination in these new recordings of Slobodyanik and Temarkanov, two of the stars of the younger set."

"You're leaving Sunday for Moscow?" I said.

"Aha!" Alek threw up his arms, extended full-length, wide in gesture, his face lighting up in a tremendous beam. "Oh Moscow," he said, with raised, light-hearted voice. "I'm going home."

"Moscow, Idaho?" I kidded.

He caught on quickly. "I *was* in Odessa, Texas," he answered.

Nelson Freire

interview August 7, 1975

In 1969, when Nelson Freire (pronounced Frayruh) burst forth on the American recording horizon with a two-record album — Tschaikowsky, Schumann, Grieg, and Liszt Totentanz *Concertos — James Goodfriend of* Stereo Review *called him "a cockeyed sensation;" Irving Kolodin of* Saturday Review, *"a hurricane of pianistic power."*

At this past summer's University of Maryland Piano Festival, I heard the man Guimar Novaes had called her "greatly gifted compatriot" triumph in solo recital. Everything in his playing is astonishingly easy — spontaneous, not super-practiced: compositions kaleidoscope, original voicings and timbres scintillate, and tempos often take your breath away. During intermission, Irwin Freundlich, Professor at the Juilliard School, exclaimed, "He's one of the greats!"

The next day Nelson Freire and I chatted over lunch. He was dressed in a bright red polo shirt and white denim trousers. An athletically-built, handsome man of medium height, with curly brown hair and a charismatic, wide boyish smile, he answered my questions — while chain-smoking — with disarming, Latin suavity.

Rio de Janeiro has always fascinated me. Do you live right in Rio?

Rio is in the shape of a big semi-circle. There's one beach, then a mountain, then another beach. One of the first beaches is Flamingo, then comes Botafogo, then Copacabana, then a big set of mountains, then Ipanema. I have a home in Ipanema. You know the song, "The Girl from Ipanema?" I'm the boy from Ipanema.

Let's get your vital statistics. And incidentally, how did you get the name, Nelson?

I was born October 18, 1944 in Boa Esperanza, a very small town, in the central eastern state of Minas Gerias, north of Rio. Nelson is very common in Brazil as a first name. We have many English first names. Freire is Portuguese.

Do you come from a large family?

I was the fifth child in the family. I have two older sisters and two older brothers. My father was a pharmacist, my mother a school teacher.

Like all genuine prodigies, you must have been full of music before you heard it. How did you start to play?

My mother had an upright piano — Zimmermann, I remember. She wanted very much for one of her girls to play. When I was 2 or 3, my greatest joy was to be at my eldest sister's side when she was playing. She is 14 years older than me. I would interrupt anything I was doing and run to listen to the music.

I played by ear what she played, but this wasn't enough. I wanted to read the music. I learned the G clef, but again I wasn't happy. I wanted to read the F clef too. My mother told me I had to skip one note from the G clef note to get the F clef note. And so in half an hour I could read!

Who was your first teacher?

My parents, noticing I had this gift for reading music instantly, took me to Varginha, the nearest city. There was a piano teacher there named Fernandez, from Uruguay. I found his accent very eccentric. In Uruguay the language is Spanish.

My mother and I traveled the four hours from Boa Esperanza to Varginha in a very old, bumpy bus. Roads didn't have asphalt at that time. As my lessons were at 10 in the morning, I had to wake up at 5 a.m.

After 12 lessons, this teacher talked seriously to my father. "Listen," he said, "we could make a fortune with this kid" — I was 5 — "making him play concerts all over Brazil. But I know what usually happens with prodigies. I advise you to move to Rio and search for a musical education from a good teacher."

Whether or not to move to Rio was a terribly important decision for my parents to make. Should they leave their jobs, family, friends, and venture to Rio, so I could try to develop my musical gifts? It didn't take them long to reach their decision. We moved to Rio.

How did you react to the big city?

I was amazed seeing for the first time the skyline buildings, and especially the sea. I couldn't believe all that water could be salty. I remember tasting it.

I was very sad living in an apartment. In Minas, we had an enormous house with lots of ground, all kinds of trees, and plenty of fruits and animals. In contrast, living in an apartment in Rio seemed like being in jail.

What happened to you musically?

I couldn't escape being a child prodigy. My photos were on the front pages of the main newspapers. I was terrible-looking then, very slim, with an enormous head — almost the same size as today. And I was a very ill child, allergic to many foods. I remember playing for the Russian pianist, Nikolai Orloff, when I was 6 and he said, "This boy has golden hands." When I was 10, I had a street named after me in Boa Esperanza, my birthplace. And so on.

But it seemed impossible to find the right teacher. I had my way of playing — arrangements of Liszt's Hungarian Rhapsody No. 2, improvisations, etc. I didn't want to grind away on scales and exercises. I was rebellious. I got into a physical fight with a famous 70-year-old teacher.

When everyone was at the point of giving up on my pursuing a musical career, my mother took a last chance. She heard of a lady named Lucia Branco who had studied in Europe with a pupil of Liszt. Branco heard me, talked to me, and said to my father, "The child is a phenomenon, but he is completely 'nuts.' However, I know someone else who is completely 'nuts.' If she gets interested in the kid, study could work out."

Branco was thinking of Nise Obino, a 32-year-old former pupil of Dona Lucia. I met Nise, and it was love at first sight. I was 7. When she wanted to talk seriously with me she'd say, "Nelson, let's talk man to man." She was very pretty, divorced, and she smoked. All that for a kid from Boa Esperanza was like being with Greta Garbo, you know!

How did this "love at first sight" work out?

Everything worked out! After three months of daily lessons with Nise, I also began studying with Lucia Branco. And until I went to Europe at 14, I stayed with them.

Did you perform publicly?

When I was 5, I had performed Mozart's *Turkish March* Sonata, Rachmaninoff's c♯ minor Prelude, and my own improvisations on popular Brazilian songs. I gave recitals each year. As a result of winning concerto competitions, I played Mozart's Concerto K. 271 when I was 11 and Beethoven's Emperor Concerto when I was 12. Then came a great musical event — the first International Piano Competition of Rio de Janeiro. I was 12 and the competition committee invited me to participate. Dona Lucia, with whom I was also studying, told me it would be interesting to see what an international competition would be like. "Of course

you will have no chance of winning, competing with more than 80 pianists, much older than you, from all over the world." So I only prepared the first round: Chopin's c♯ minor Nocturne, op. 27 no. 1; the Etude in F op. 10 no. 8; and the Polonaise in A♭. Lili Kraus, Marguerite Long, and Guiomar Novaes were on the jury.

I made it to the semi-finals and thought, "Don't expect to be in the finals." I played a Chopin Mazurka, another Etude, and the Ballade No. 4. I was placed among the 12 finalists and played the Emperor Concerto.

And you won! What happened next?

The President of Brazil, Juscelino Kubitschek, the one who founded Brasilia, the new capitol, gave me a scholarship to study abroad. I chose Vienna, where I went by myself at 14, and studied for two years with Bruno Seidlhofer, who had taught Friedrich Gulda. I had heard Gulda play all the Beethoven sonatas in Brazil when he was 24. (He had played them first when he was 16.) I was 10.

Then, in Vienna, I met Martha Argerich who became my best friend and has remained so ever since. She's the greatest pianist of her generation.

In 1964 you won the Dinu Lipatti Medal in London. How did that happen?

Winning it was a big surprise. At that time I'd never played in London and I couldn't imagine why they gave me that medal. I received it by mail.

And didn't you win the Vianna da Motta contest in Lisbon the same year?

Yes, I decided to enter it two days before it started. It was amusing, I arrived in Portugal not knowing the required piece. It was a sonata or toccata — I don't remember which, it sounded like a toccata — in g by Carlos Seixas. Everybody laughed when I asked for the music. I thought I would have time to learn it while the other contestants played. I thought I would be the last one to play. But at the drawing of lots I drew number one!

I said to myself I'd better work fast, or it will be a disaster. I played it from beginning to the end. No disaster.

You got the piece two days before the contest, worked on it, and then played it in the contest? How did you learn it so fast?

It was about four pages long and quite difficult technically, toccata-like. But I was 20 then. I went to a piano and rattled through it.

Have you and Martha Argerich played two-pianos publicly?

In 1968 we played at two pianos in the Queen Elizabeth Hall in London. We were together in Europe. We decided to go to Brazil — it was July, the concert was to be in August — to rehearse the pieces, no? The program was Rachmaninoff Suite No. 2, Debussy *En blanc et noir*, and Bartok Sonata for Two Pianos and Percussion. But when we arrived in Brazil, we didn't know the pieces, so we couldn't rehearse. Neither of us practiced. There were other things to do — visiting friends, swimming, sightseeing, etc. Martha was there for the first time.

Martha left for Argentina to practice. Then she had to play in Czechoslovakia. I remember she lost all her luggage there. So, we met in London the day before the concert. We were very nervous.

Stephen Bishop turned the pages for Martha. We all lived in the London Musical Club, the most incredibly messy, crazy, funny place you can imagine. It's for musicians. You have a piano in your room and can play until two o'clock in the morning. Everyone lived there — Stephen, Martha, me. Rafael Orozco also.

All our friends knew about the concert and were terribly nervous about us. We trembled to the stage. As Stephen turned one of the pages, Martha said to him, "I can hear the beatings of your heart!"

That must have been a mad occasion! Why did you use the music?

The music? Even *with* the music we lost each other! The percussion players for the Bartok were from the London Symphony. They were the tops. I was supposed to conduct them from the piano. They knew the piece much better than we did.

Did you get reviews?

Funny ones. One said, "For sheer animal excitement it was all right." The other said that *"En blanc et noir"* was *"En gris et rose."* I think they broadcast that recital.

I have played four hands very much with Martha. We like to play operettas and things like that. She has a very nice house near Geneva.

Why don't you and Martha spice the New York season's fare with a two-piano recital?

Ah, two pianos? Me and Martha? It's very difficult, no?

Today famous pianists don't play two-piano recitals. The older generation sometimes did. Have you heard the Gabrilowitsch-Harold Bauer recording of the Arensky Waltz?

Oh, it's fantastic:

(humming)

Who are the great pianists of the past you have most admired?

I have a great admiration for the old generation. Rachmaninoff, Novaes, Hofmann, Gieseking.

How long have you known Novaes?

I have known and loved her since I was a kid. I find your interview with her very good. It's just the way she is.

She always comes to my concerts. I have all of her records and many tapes of fantastic live performances. It was a struggle with her to make records. She's spontaneous; she does many things just once. One time she was recording, the red light was on and her daughter was turning pages. Suddenly Guiomar turned to her daughter, whose arms were covered with bracelets, and asked in her tiny, high voice, "Why so many jewels?" They had to start the recording over again.

Guiomar has inspired me a lot. She's a very special woman and artist. It wasn't what she said — she said almost nothing — but it was the way she said it. It's hard to explain.

In the Chopin Fantasy, she showed me a way to divide the hands. In m. 85, I take the B$\flat$ and the C$\flat$ with the left hand. In the next measure, the C$\natural$ and the D$\flat$ — always when this comes.

In ms. 88 and 92, she suggested taking the second three eighths with the left hand. I think all this Fantasy is basically based on a march rhythm. It's a wonderful piece.

And I played the Chopin Preludes for her. We spent

a whole afternoon with them — I would play and then she would play each one after me. I also played the *Fledermaus* paraphrase which she used to play. She was very interested to hear it again.

It was very special when I played the Schumann Symphonic Etudes for her. I played the theme and she said, "Oh it's very good, but it could be more beautiful. Why don't you put more harmonies, no? You are singing a little too much on the top notes." She pressed her hand on top of mine on the opening chords:

In Var. IV, ms. 11-12, she wanted the sforzati to be very surprising.

In Var. VI, she told me to keep the hands close to the keys.

And she suggested keeping the last note of Var. VII sounding right to the following variation.

How do you practice?

Practice? I don't have any special way. It depends upon what I'm practicing or what for.

Did you bone up for last night's recital?

I had to, I was so scared about the Chopin E major Scherzo.

Why were you scared of it?

I learned it only a month ago. Last night was the first time I had played it in public. I had wanted to play it in Brazil two weeks ago before I came here. It was on the program; but as I didn't feel ready, I substituted the b minor Scherzo at the last minute.

Do you have a photographic memory?

I think I have all kinds of memory.

You don't have to repeat very much?

Repeat? You think it's never enough when you have not played it before, no? You never know what can happen.

So, how did you practice yesterday?

I went to the auditorium and practiced the Scherzo. I suddenly realized I had never played it from the beginning to the end without the score. So I tried it once like that — no matter what happened — just to see. It went much worse than it did in the concert.

And then I played everything I was going to play except the encores. Ever since I was very young I have been superstitious about practicing encores. I think, "If I practice them, no one will ask for one." Sometimes it's terrible. I arrive at the piano and don't know what to play.

What are some of your favorite encores?

I often play the *Polichinello* of Villa-Lobos, but that was on the program last night. And the Godowsky arrangement of Albeniz's Tango. I would like to make a record of encores, mostly pieces that aren't played as encores nowadays — some transcriptions, some Moszkowski pieces like *La Jongleuse*, the Spanish Capriccio; the Strauss-Godowsky *Fledermaus* paraphrase. Gluck has some nice things that Guiomar plays. Wagner-Liszt *La Fileuse*, some Rachmaninoff things, the *Polka by V.R.*

Last night, in the Finale of the Schumann Symphonic Etudes, you scared me. I thought for a moment you had forgotten. Which edition did you play?

Aha! I played the first edition variants. There is a little change — some repeated notes — in the first variation, in the bass of measure 12. In the Finale, the theme comes three times the same, no? Changing a little the second time, makes something different. It's not a big change.

How do you feel about today's grueling concert schedules?

I think it's important not to play too much. I don't ever want, like some colleagues, to play over 100 concerts a year. Everything nowadays is so rushed, you don't have time for living, also for the music. I think 50 concerts a year, not more, would be ideal.

wınneɾ ın waɾsaw

Conversation with Garrick Ohlsson

interview May 28, 1974

In 1970, Garrick Ohlsson, then 21 years old, became the first American winner of the prestigious Chopin International Piano Competition in Warsaw. Launched on his career as a result, he now performs over 65 concerts a year, touring in Europe, the United States, New Zealand, Australia, and Japan.

He has made several recordings and his performances of the Chopin Polonaises, the Scherzos, and the F Minor Fantasy, as well as a Liszt album, are currently available. Just two days before our interview, Garrick had recorded the 24 Chopin Preludes in London. I asked him if he had had a beautiful piano.

"Yes, I did," he replied. "I used the same German Steinway that Alicia de Larrocha had used for record-

ing the Preludes the previous week for London Records. Isn't that insane? Same pieces — same piano!"

Garrick Ohlsson was born in White Plains, New York, the son of a Swedish father and an Italian mother. Six feet four and weighing almost 200 pounds, he looks perhaps more like a football player than the once-upon-a-time stereotype wan and fragile concert pianist. He wears a beard and moustache and dresses casually when he isn't performing. In fact, he was barefoot when we talked in his upper West Side Manhattan apartment.

Since he has won three major international piano contests in four years — the 1967 Busoni, the 1968 Montreal, and the 1970 Warsaw — I had planned to ask him about these contests. First I asked:

Garrick, what prompted you to enter the Busoni?

I was 18 and working with Sascha Gorodnitzky at Juilliard. My parents and I were planning a summer trip to Europe, since we've all kinds of ancestors and relatives there. Gorodnitzky suggested it might be good to enter the Busoni to see what an international competition is like. In other words, to get my feet wet. I was eventually going to have to enter and hopefully win one of the big ones. I hadn't expected to place or to do well. As a matter of fact, Gorodnitzky had two other pupils entering on whom he was counting much more heavily than on me. The International Institute of Education was behind them and lots of other people. I got the impression from everybody else, "Why are you bothering?" And I didn't know why I was bothering. I certainly wasn't overly nervous about it. So I entered rather haphazardly, and I won. In retrospect, winning was an immense thing when it happened in my non-existent career.

What is Bolzano like?

It's a beautiful little town — half Italian, half Austrian — up in the Dolomites, in northern Italy. At the time of the competition, in September, the people were terribly worried that hailstones would knock the grapes off the vines. So, occasionally people would shoot big flare rockets into the clouds to heat the atmosphere. Sometimes during the competition you'd hear a bomb go off in the sky.

Did the rockets do some good?

The wine's certainly all right, but I don't know if the rockets helped the morale of the poor competitors trying to play. Compared to some competitions, the Busoni is relaxed. Being in Italy, it's more haphazardly run. You never know quite what or when you're supposed to play.

Who was on the jury?

Friedrich Wuehrer, Nikita Magaloff . . . all kinds of people you may never have heard of: Panacek from Bulgaria, Frantisek Rauch from Czechoslovakia, Robert Zeller from the United States, and various, sundry Italians. Michelangeli was supposed to have come. Just as he does in concerts, he cancelled.

What repertoire do they require?

You have to play a Beethoven sonata, a Haydn or a Mozart sonata, a major Romantic work, a smaller Romantic work, a Bach piece, a concerto, and some Busoni piece.

I notice you've been on the Busoni Competition jury.

Right. That was a real switch. After I won the Warsaw Chopin Competition in 1970, the Busoni people invited me back as a juror. I thought it was a bit pompous of me to accept. But I decided for once to take myself out of the competitor's circle. And what a nightmare being on a jury is! Just to sit and listen to piano playing for eight or nine hours a day in that hot, stuffy Bolzano Conservatory in the summer is really something.

Montreal Contest

Tell me about the Montreal.

I entered that one gung ho for the first prize. You're much more nervous when you know you've a chance of winning. The jury was rather distinguished I thought — Leon Fleischer, Alicia de Larrocha, Friedrich Wuehrer again, Louis Kentner. Novaes was supposed to come but she was sick.

The Montreal was exciting because the whole thing is more keyed up. It's a big competition — held in the Salle Claude Champagne in the Conservatoire Vincent d'Indy — whereas the Busoni still smacks of a local competition even though it's international. The Montreal is super organized. The public is there cheering you on; the reporters are covering it. It's a momentous event.

Would you rate the Montreal above the Busoni?

I would rate the Montreal way above the Busoni in terms of difficulty, the level of playing, the pressure, and the prizes which are much higher. I won ten thousand dollars.

And the resulting engagements?

That's an item one must talk about carefully because, as we all know, the real reason for entering a competition is to get engagements. The follow-up PR at Montreal wasn't as effective as I thought it should have been. Winning did result, however, in American management for me, the best thing that could have happened. As soon as I won the Montreal I was approached by four people in New York, including Hurok, Columbia, and Judson.

And you chose Harold Shaw?

Right. He was with Hurok at that point. I liked Mr. Shaw best of the people I met. He promised the least which was good for me at that time. I wasn't yet ready to embark upon what I'm doing now. I don't even think I'm ready now. Frightening thought!

Warsaw Contest

Next came the big one. Tell me how you decided to enter the Warsaw.

A lot of people say piano competitions give diminishing returns. For instance, I'm in the field and I don't know who won Rio in 1969, so how do you expect the man on the street even to know there is a competition in Rio? The basic line is that you have to win one of the very biggest ones to create a really international PR and follow-up. And then strike and really forge ahead.

Part of the problem at Montreal was that I was still hesitant to give the big financial push career-wise — to get the PR machines going, brochures printed, and my name plastered on every symphony desk in the world, to say "Here's Garrick Ohlsson. You can't do without him." I didn't feel ready for all that and in retrospect I'm glad I didn't.

But in 1970, although I was accumulating dates here and there — an occasional date in Winnipeg, in Florida, or a few dates in Italy still hanging over from the Busoni — I felt I wanted to do more. And in 1970, both the Warsaw and the Tschaikowsky were coming up. Everybody told me to enter the Tschaikowsky, that no American could ever win the Warsaw Chopin prize. Rosina Lhevinne, with whom I was studying, was dead set against my going to Warsaw. She's had pupils have great success in Moscow and, being Russian, she felt the Poles would not accept an American playing Chopin.

Anyway, I stuck to my guns. First, I knew that winning the Warsaw would be just about as unusual as winning the Tschaikowsky. The resultant PR would be very good. Secondly, I wanted to concentrate on Chopin repertoire, something I felt the need to do musically.

The one piece of advice I'd like to give young artists is to try to make entering a competition a positive event. Don't go into a competition just to win, because if you don't win, your morale will be knocked way down.

When I decided to enter the Warsaw Chopin Competition, I learned practically all the repertoire from scratch. Even had I not won, I would have learned all this beautiful music. For example, you've got to learn the E Minor Concerto sometime. It's a beautiful work and learning it is a nice benefit. On the other hand, I didn't feel like working on everything you have to learn for the Tschaikowsky — a Shostakovitch Prelude and Fugue, a Glinka Rondo, a Balakirev Fantasy on Saudi-Arabian themes, or whatever. There's a lot of repertoire you learn for the Tschaikowsky that you will only play there and never play again. Whereas all the Chopin is great stuff. Furthermore, something in my blood told me that Warsaw was a better idea than Moscow. That indetermined element, that little voice inside me said, "Go to Warsaw." I listened and I'm very happy that I did.

So you left for Warsaw. Did the contest pay your expenses while you were there? Do contests usually?

In the Busoni they don't pay your expenses because they don't have much money. If you are one of the first two applicants from any country, however, you get free living. In Montreal they house you in private homes at the competition's expense. In Warsaw they house you at the expense of the Chopin Society which sponsors the Competition. Both for Warsaw and Montreal I got travel grants from the International Institute of Education, so I didn't have to pay for my plane tickets.

Who were the judges at Warsaw?

There were 19 judges, but no Americans. Fleisher was supposed to be the American judge but was ill and did not arrive. So we didn't have anyone pulling for our side. There were six judges from Poland including Malcuzynski, Jan Hofmann, Ekier, Regina Smendzienka, Wojtowicz. And there were six from other Socialist countries including Nicolai Ivoff from the Soviet Union, Panacek again from Bulgaria, and Hug Stefan from Czechoslovakia.

From the western world there were Monique Haas and Enrico Agosti. The jury at Warsaw was not as prestigious as the one in Montreal. But having 19 judges was good in that it eliminates, to a certain extent, crank opinions.

What was the atmosphere like at the Competition?

Tense. There were 90 contestants from 30 countries. The Warsaw is a big event. The international press is there.

Did you play in a big hall?

Yes. The Competition is held in the Philharmonic Hall, a beautiful, elegant hall which was totally re-constructed after the War as was the whole city. It's a big, square hall — a much more beautiful version of Symphony Hall in Boston — with gorgeous acoustics, a fabulous chandelier — the whole thing.

Every stage of the Competition — about eight hours a day of music — is public. And every seat for every hour of that music was sold out three months in advance! It was a scalper's market to get in to hear the Competition. Everybody's talking about it. It's in all the headlines. When you take the tram, people run up to talk to you. It's an incredible national event, almost a Brazilian soccer fervor.

What did you play in the first stage?

The Chopin Competition is distinguished in not being an endurance test as are Moscow and other places. In Moscow you have to prepare lots of music by lots of people, and you know that the jury can't hear all the pieces you prepare. So in Moscow, Montreal, or Brussels you have that nagging suspicion that "Well, I don't really play that piece very well. With luck, they won't hear it."

But that kind of preparation is dangerous!

It is dangerous, but you'd be surprised how many competitors have that thought in mind. In the Busoni, thank God the jury didn't hear my Prokofiev *"Suggestion Diabolique"* or else they would not have thought so highly of me. Consistency is important in competitions. You may have someone who does marvelously and then royally messes up some piece, has a memory slip or something. Then what can the jury do? Even if the jury is rooting for you, they can't overlook the fact that you couldn't play one of your numbers.

In Warsaw you play about one recital's worth of Chopin solo music and one concerto. In the first round — about half an hour — you play one of the three great Polonaises — either the Fantasy Polonaise, the F Sharp Minor, or the great A Flat; one Nocturne out of the six biggest that they choose; three Etudes; and either a Ballade, the F Minor Fantasy, or the Barcarolle.

In the second round — about 45 minutes — you play a Scherzo, three Mazurkas from one opus, and either the B Flat Minor or the B Minor Sonata. And then in the last round, you play either the E Minor or the F Minor Concerto. So the test is not how much music you can swallow and regurgitate. It's sort of how well you can play each piece. It's not just a general idea of Chopin but "Can he play Mazurkas, can he play Nocturnes, and so on?"

And the audience started yelling for you to have first prize?

Well...almost! The audience was very enthusiastic. But there were other people who made great shows. Jeffrey Swann, the American pianist, played extraordinarily well in certain of his pieces. And the audience took him to heart. Luckily, I was also one of their favorites.

In Warsaw they give a whole slew of prizes besides first, second, third...down to twelfth. There's a prize for the best Concerto performance, best Polonaise, best Mazurkas, and something else. I got both the Mazurka and the Concerto prizes. The Mazurka prize was the killer inasmuch as it traditionally goes to a Pole, and if not to a Pole at least to a Slav of some kind. I never could figure that one out. Nor could Madame Lhevinne when I got back!

Perhaps she had listened too much to Rubinstein's propaganda that only a Pole can play the Mazurkas.

Could be. The Poles all tell you that themselves. I'm a bit of an anomaly — not even part Polish. But I try.

So your career really took off after you won the Warsaw?

Immediately I got stories in *Time* and *Newsweek*. My winning was plastered over the international news. Every major newspaper carried some kind of story. And then Ormandy, who was guest-conducting in Cleveland, read about me in *The New York Times* and called his manager: "Let's get Ohlsson back here." Less than two weeks after winning — I was touring around Poland — I got a cable: "Come back immediately for the Philadelphia Orchestra." Naturally, I dropped everything and ran home. First I played in New York with Ormandy. I was still on European time, exhausted, a mess. And then I played in Philadelphia. These opportunities created a terrific momentum of public relations. A month later I got an invitation from the New York Philharmonic. Someone had fallen sick.

Was it at this time that you took on a PR manager?

Right at this point, yes, on the advice of Harold Shaw. When I returned from Warsaw, everything was bubbling. That's what I mean by striking while the iron's hot.

Winning the Warsaw put you in the same league, so-to-speak, as Van Cliburn, Bobby Fisher, and Mark Spitz.

Well, aren't you kind! Those are really famous people!

And the first season you played 95 concerts?

Yes, but I've cut down to about 65, a much more human load. The first season when I played 95, I was going a little crazy. I went from being a green-behind-the-ears-kid into a cynical professional. I had to get a large repertoire ready which was exhausting. I pride myself, for instance, when I submit a list of concer-

tos — it's not the biggest list anybody's ever seen, as of now it's 15 — that if an orchestra asks for one, I can really play it, as opposed to some professionals who play just two concertos per season.

Teachers

I'd like to ask you about your teachers. Tell me first about Gorodnitzky.

It is difficult to talk about one's teachers objectively. Probably one shouldn't even try. I've been fortunate with all my teachers. I went to Gorodnitzky when I was 13 and studied with him until I was 20. At the Westchester Conservatory, I had been the big fish in a small pond. I thought I was Mr. Terrific. And then I came to New York and suddenly was in a rather high-standard environment. I was crushed at first. Gorodnitzky was extremely severe with me — an absolute taskmaster — not in the sense that he rapped my knuckles, telling me to practice a passage 50 times with my left hand alone. But he'd imply, "I'll show you how, and I'm not going to show you twice. Wash your dirty linens at home."

He made me aware of the standards that have to be met if you are going to be taken seriously. His attitude was not, "My boy, you are the greatest in the world. I'm the only one who can teach you." It was, "Let's get you playing as well as you can. Become a real professional, not a talented kid who gets away on exuberance." I learned sheer professionalism from him and became aware that one has to deliver consistently.

Gorodnitzky was so thoroughly schooled by the Lhevinnes, I should think his teaching would have a carry-over from their approach.

There was a concentration on the two fabulous T's — Tone and Technique. Those were the two big things he taught in conjunction with the Romantic keyboard literature — from Beethoven through Rachmaninoff. I learned to be conscious of tone and a technical sort of Russian discipline — everything in the right place.

Often in the life of a young artist, however, there's a point where he becomes too close to a teacher, rejects him — the way he rejects his parents — and then later comes back and sees that he or they were

right. I feel the same way with Gorodnitzky. When I got away from him, I was glad at first. I thought he was limiting me. But I see in retrospect that a lot of what I consider my basic nature in playing, I got from him. I'm very grateful.

Do you feel that he was your greatest influence?

No, I don't. One of Mr. Gorodnitzky's non-favorite areas is the French Impressionists. He is not very interested in Debussy and Ravel, which, when 18, I began to want to play. And if you've never had any preparation in this area, you may not know what to do. You are swimming a new current, learning a new language. I wanted to learn *Gaspard de la Nuit* and was having difficulty.

So about this time I began to study with Olga Barabini, a woman, about 70, who lives in Rye, in Westchester, who became my greatest influence. She had studied with two very individual great pianists — Hofmann, at Curtis, and later with Arrau — a mixed bag of schooling, dare one say, and rather individual and strong-minded on both ends. I had known Olga Barabini for some time. People spoke of her with great respect as a musician, as a pianist. She had never had a career as she had married a wealthy man and had terrible nerves.

Her great passion, however, was the French Impressionists. So, when she heard I was playing *Gaspard*, she asked me to play it for her. "I can't possibly," I said. "I don't know it." And she said, "Why not? I have a few fingerings that might help you through the maze." When I played for her, she gave me an incredible three-hour lesson on "Scarbo," a real eye-opener for me.

I had never before met a teacher who worked in the way that she did. She draws out of the individual what he has rather than dictating what he must do. Much teaching is "Do it this way. Play it this way.

This is the tradition. Use this fingering." Barabini's teaching is more to ask "What's going wrong? Why is your wrist stiff? Why can't you do this?" — a sort of laser-beam focus on you and your relationship with the music and how you understand and grow.

I was excited and a little frightened because this new kind of teaching opened all kinds of intellectual and emotional doors for me. My learning became a matter of "What do I feel? What do I want to do? Here Beethoven writes crescendo. Here Ravel writes triple pianissimo. What does that mean to me?" Barabini was opening a Pandora's box for me. I had a few lessons with her over the next year or so and developed a real rapport both musically and personally. I wanted to study with her. She was not associated with the Juilliard School, however, and I had to be in a school to stay out of the Army. Studying simultaneously with two teachers — moonlighting as it's called at Juilliard — is not the most moral aspect of our profession. I didn't know what to do.

So I had a talk with Rosina Lhevinne and resolved my problem by studying with her. Madame Lhevinne was unique among the Juilliard teachers in having what I call an open mind. Even at age 90 and with her prestige, she would sit with the score open on her lap and say, "What about this?" not "Do this." If you played a phrase musically, she would exclaim, "Oh, by the way, that's beautiful!" Sometimes she would even admit, "That's different. I never thought of that. That's very nice!" She was encouraging, having that element of the Russian personality that is generous and responsive. I worked with her at the Juilliard about every other week.

In the meantime I worked toward the Chopin Competition, doing the major bulk of this work with Olga Barabini over the summer. The Juilliard year was over in May; the Competition was in October. During those intervening five months I must have seen Olga every third day. That was when she made her absolutely biggest impression on me.

One of the most important things she did for me was to loosen me up physically. Once when I was 18 and playing a whole bunch of Scriabin in a masterclass of Gorodnitzky's, I pulled something in my left forearm and wrist. I had to be taken to a hospital emergency room to be given a shot to relax the nerve and be bandaged up. We all realized that something terribly wrong was going on there. That shouldn't have happened.

If you had seen me play at 18, I don't think you would have recognized me — elbows in tight, a sort of pigeon-toed, neurotic, big kid. I played like a bat out of hell in those days. People used to sit hoping I could get through a thing. Horowitz was one of my gods. I think every young pianist goes through that brilliance, that incredible electric energy stage these days.

I was trying to achieve super-brilliance but at great cost to tone and to my body. I was becoming locked up. So Madame Barabini worked with me very intensively, using Arrau's rather Yogaesque way of using weight to advantage — i.e., working with the piano and the body, not against them.

I was having terrible control problems; I was very stiff-wristed. So she worked with me on relaxation, distribution of weight, flexibility, and different kinds of tone coloring — which also result from the way you play the piano. She was incredibly scientific. She didn't tell me what she was doing, but she worked to remove tension and not all at once as some teachers try to do. First she got rid of my finger tension — making me realize it doesn't take much effort to push a key down. She got me to put the tension in larger muscle groups where it is easier to handle — the wrists, the arms, and the shoulders. Of course it is important to know how to control all those areas. She kept pushing the tension I had been developing into major muscle areas. Until finally the worst that would happen was that I would get tense shoulders. And now I've even got away from that.

Many teachers who are very good with this sort of thing will try to change your whole technique: "Oh no, you are doing this all wrong. You must start all over." You know how piano theories are. Olga Barabini didn't do that with me. She just bit by bit constructively worked to break down what she considered bad pianistic habits, without sacrificing anything I could do at the moment. There was no stoppage. She said things would be better five per cent at a time, there being no such thing as a hundred per cent changeover. She said, "You are already a very good pianist. If I can help you five per cent, you'll be just that much better."

How do you practice finger technique?

Well, thank God, I almost don't anymore. Back in the old days it was very Russian, very fingery, high fingers — lots of slow and very firm practice. Whereas now I do whatever the passage requires. For instance, if I have to play a rather intricate running passage, I will work it firmly at first. I will work not only from the fingers but will use whatever muscle groups are necessary to articulate.

I don't follow any technical regime anymore. I play the repertoire, doing whatever technical work the repertoire requires. I am basically much more relaxed now and not inclined to be finger-oriented. I've got quite a lot of close-to-the-key coordination.

The Chopin Polonaise, Op. 44

In your recording of the Chopin Polonaises, Garrick, I was impressed with the two arpeggio outbursts in the F Sharp Minor Polonaise, Op. 44.

Aha! House specialty, eh?

In a recent international competition, I heard a fine young pianist stumble on these runs. Why don't we print the music and you tell people how to learn them?

Terrific! First the fingering. I use what you call a quick fingering, the simplest fingering in the book: the right hand all 1, 2, 3, ending on the thumb; the left hand just the reverse. Start with the thumb, then all 3, 2, 1, ending on the thumb. Most people play these runs fingered in groups of four, requiring more frequent change of hand position.

Second, I play these runs with rotation — very much the way Amy Fay described Liszt's teaching of

the E Major scale: "Pretend you have a ball inside your hand and roll it up." You apply more and more weight as you need it. The thumb functions as a different joint from the rest of the hand. It's important to know which direction the fingers want to move naturally. If you twiddle your thumbs — I think it was Busoni or some great pianist who said — you twiddle them forward and not backward. Part of the problem of playing brilliantly comes from having been taught to pass the thumbs under which often imposes a strain. Whereas, when you are going very brilliantly, it's almost as easy to pass the thumbs over in the right hand as you run up. So play the first note with a downward stroke of the wrist, then roll up — sort of northeastwards — carrying your thumb along with you. What you do is a series of very small rotations.

Sounds like something Arrau would do.

I think he would. As I said, Olga studied with Arrau for a long time. A lot of technical work she did with him was based on his principles. Of course you have to be concerned with the quality of tone so that when you pass over you don't hear breaks. When you finger every three notes rather than four, and the rhythm is in four, instead of getting six impulses, you get a constantly shifting accent that fools the ear slightly and sounds more even. Concentrate much more on the left hand. In brilliant unison passages it is a cardinal principle for me that the lower voice vibrates much more — you almost don't need the right hand. In order to add strength, just add a push from the whole arm to the basic hand movements. It's almost as if you were pushing the piano away from you. Push into the piano with a sort of vibrating motion.

What do these arpeggios mean to you? What is their meaning in the music?

Cannon shots or something. They are one of Chopin's most violent affairs. Obviously they are a return to the opening after the tranquility of the mazurka section. They are incredible shocks. They're the world, the anger, the essence of all that passion and that anger that was so controlled in the other section (bar 9 et al), bursting forth here in a small form.

Also in playing an outburst like this, it is very important to take a nice deep breath before. And don't hold the breath as you are playing — almost phhhht! Almost as if you are going to shout. It's a real shout or a scream.

A man once said to me, "I could pay Horowitz a thousand dollars to teach me how to play his octaves, but the point is what does Horowitz feel when he plays those octaves?" It doesn't matter so much what you are doing physically as what you are feeling emotionally. If you think these two measures are a shout or a scream — a terrific outburst — you have to feel that, plus being, hopefully, perfectly prepared technically. Then you put all these things together and the run will sound like dynamite.

Winner of the 1971
National Guild of Piano Teachers
Recording Competition
and
University of Maryland International Piano Competition

Mark Westcott

interview August 8, 1971

Mark Westcott, at the University of Maryland International Piano Festival in the large Tawes Theater auditorium, was playing in the final competition session. In the midst of a stunning performance of Ravel's *Gaspard de la Nuit*, having just finished *Le Gibet*, he paused, took off his jacket, laid it on the floor, and then plunged into *Scarbo*. After his performance there were shouts of "Bravo." And the first thing he did when he came on stage to accept the $2,500 first prize was to kiss second prize winner, Diane Walsh, of New York. For Mark Westcott is a sparkling stage personality as well as a superbly-equipped pianist (As I found out later, he is also an articulate, modest though confident, disarmingly frank young man with a terrific sense of humor and so much *joie de vivre* that he's fun just to be around).

The first annual International Piano Festival and Competition held last year from August 1-7 at the University of Maryland and covered daily and enthusiastically in the Washington D.C. press, had been a feast of high-caliber piano playing. Starting at 8:30 every morning and running through an evening concert, there had been among the events, concerts, and master classes by some of the world's greatest artists, including Gina Bachauer, Stephen Bishop, and Alicia de Larrocha, as well as stimulating lectures by Juilliard's Adele Marcus, Scriabin-specialist Faubion Bowers, and the brilliant avant-garde specialist Marie-Françoise Bucquet.

Each afternoon three of the Piano Competition's 15 semi-finalists — who had been chosen from hundreds of entrants from the United States, Canada, and Europe — played a 45 minute program, the *niveau* of the playing being exceedingly high. Besides the winners, Emanuel Ax (who won the Baldwin prize for the finest program by one of the nonfinalists), Zola Shaulis, Edward Newman, Patrick Mullins, and Roger von Hanwehr had all shown outstanding qualities.

But from the first notes of the slow movement of Beethoven's *Hammerklavier* Sonata with which Mark Westcott (Portland, Oregon, 23 years old, winner of numerous awards including third prize in the 1969 Van Cliburn International Piano Competition) began the second portion of his semi-final program, it was apparent he was the probable winner. A real artist, individual without being eccentric, he has that rare quality of truly listening, of seeming to be transfixed by the music he plays.

The morning after his triumph in the finals, Mark Westcott and I met over coffee. "Mark," I said, *You're a young pianist who doesn't sound like all the others. Your playing kept me on the edge of my seat. What is your approach to piano playing?*

I've always believed in taking a chance. If I'm prepared, I'd just as soon — as far as my temperament goes — throw caution to the wind and play as I hear at the moment. But at the same time, I've always beeen suspicious of "effect." I think, unfortunately, that many talented young musicians try to develop peculiarities in their playing. They become deliberately technical-conscious, or they develop certain outstanding traits to get your attention right away, but which won't support a major work. For instance, if

you're playing the *Hammerklavier* Sonata, who cares if you have gleaming Horowitzian octaves? They're not going to help you, because maybe there are two good octave passages, and then for the rest of the work you're really swimming.

Specifically, I try to walk the line between taking a chance and staying under control. I accept the nervousness before and even while I'm playing. A few years ago, when I was growing technically and trying to learn really how to perform — of course one is always learning that — every time I was the least bit careful, I think my playing suffered.

I've always been very involved with the playing of what you might call the "old" masters. Even when I was in high school and had not been exposed to a great deal of piano playing, Schnabel, on many occasions, had a tremendous impact on me, as did people like Lipatti and Edwin Fischer. The first time I heard some of Fischer's recordings, I flipped. And I thought — even then I said — "No matter what I hear around me that I like so much but can't really identify with, this is the kind of playing I want. This is the tradition to which I feel I might belong some day." And my learning was a process then — well, I guess it's always a process — of building up musical vocabulary and really trying to understand how to achieve the kind of "inner" playing which is my goal.

Mark the Dramatist

When did you begin studying the piano?

I had been champing at the bit for years. Finally at nine, my parents found a teacher whom they thought they could trust, and I began studying with Aurora Underwood in Portland, Oregon. But even when I was a little kid — before I started to study the piano — I was quite a dramatist. I had thunder and lightning going. I would tell sagas at the piano, screaming, yelling, and jumping up and down. The piano was my tool to glorify my own stories. That was sort of how I got involved.

My sister, who is three and one-half years older than I am, was a very good pianist as a little girl. I learned a lot about playing the piano just by listening to her practice. And my mother was a fine singer when she was young. Music in our house was a part of everyday life. My sister, Mom, and I used to sit at the piano for simple entertainment.in the evening. We'd sing, laugh — just make music, you know.

We didn't have a phonograph; we didn't hear a great deal of music. In grade school, I could count on one hand the number of concerts to which I went. And yet musical experience was something so intensely important to me as a part of daily, psychic activity, that it was a very natural outgrowth to try to develop this thing as best I can.

Good, Solid Background

Tell me about your early training.

I've had a mixture of different kinds of emphases. I was raised by a woman who was a pupil of an old Leschetitzkian. I received a good solid technical background, a good solid musicianship. She was intent on letting me express myself, sometimes even going overboard and sinking when I got into trouble,

really crashing completely. But she believed in that — in going all out.

Did you do exercises, Czerny, scales?

She was very good at saving time. I never did much Hanon or Czerny. Of course you have to do all the scales, *et cetera* — you have to be able to do this stuff inside out as part of your workshop. But she was a genius at writing out tiny, highly-concentrated exercises for me — something that I believe in, maybe because it was a part of my training, but more importantly because I think that exercises if done too much are damaging to the ear. They're sort of a false emphasis. If you can get a kid the equipment quickly, do it.

I think the interpretative demand always has to come from the ear first and then the technical equipment built up to meet that demand. I'm very suspicious of having lots of undirected facility. I think undirected facility produces a pianistic approach to making music with sort of a slapped-on musical scheme that one sort of tries to fit the pianism into in a meaningful way.

Children should be taught to be a conductor from the word "go." "Now, we know what we want here, or we have an idea. So how are we going to do it?" This is where special exercises come in. Often before I started a big piece, Aurora would give me exercises. It was always like a big surprise when I was going to play a new piece. "Here's the music. Whoopee!" I would open the music and here would be this beautiful, beautiful black score. And I would love it — sort of scared and thrilled at the same time.

About a month before she gave me the Grieg Concerto — she didn't tell me I was going to play it — she started giving me exercises, for example for the descending double thirds in the first movement. I was 12 years old; I had never had anything like these double-third runs before. I did the exercises and had the runs whipped by the time I got into the piece. Then she gave me exercises for a few octave passages and a few tricky finger passages in the last movement. These techniques were all built into my abilities before I got the piece. So that when I was confronted with this gaping work, I had technical landmarks that let me relax enough to try to conceive such a big score at that age. And it worked. It was good teaching.

Tell me about your later training.

After high school I went to the Oberlin Conservatory and studied with John Perry who had done the greater part of his training with two of my later teachers, Cecile Genhart and Frank Mannheimer. Perry was just right for me. He has total understanding of how to play the instrument and can convey it. He can communicate the fine points of playing the piano. Instead of saying, "Try it; do it;" he can tell you how. And when you get to the stage between having facility and trying to develop a really beautiful technique, you need someone like this.

Perry is a consumate musician. He is another person who approaches everything from the conductor's standpoint: part of being in his class is knowing the symphonic literature and all of music. He is at heart a *"Wiener."* There is always this cameraderie in his studio — a mutual love of music and the highest standards.

Is Perry really Viennese?

No, he was born in Minnesota, but he did a lot of his study in Europe. He is one of this country's outstanding pianists, a great Beethoven player. I studied with him four years at Oberlin, and then in the summers I studied with Frank Mannheimer, a pupil of Tobias Matthay in London. Studying with Mannheimer was, among many things, a time for developing coloristic aspects. He's an expert at developing tonal differences, color, and the quiet and intimate sides of piano playing — a marvelous teacher of Schumann and Mozart, difficult composers to teach.

After Oberlin, I did a year of master study at Eastman with Cecile Genhart. That was a year of taking all this information, sometimes playing like a student and sometimes playing more like an artist. It was a matter of taking this ability and training and subjecting it to a person who hears everything. She is a woman who can hear "intent" as well as the product you are getting out, and she knows how to bring all this out. She is an expert teacher at all levels — detail and overall.

Studying with her was a revelation because suddenly I was with a person who had lived music with people like Busoni — she knew Busoni. She had known Edwin Fischer — had toured with him for five years. After my quasi-fantasies in high school, studying with Mrs. Genhart was like becoming a member of a wonderful tradition that I had always really liked. And I don't think this tradition is necessarily nineteenth-centuryism — I don't think it's vulgar at all — I think it's very misunderstood. The recordings we have of these people are so inaccurate.

So, my study at Eastman was like making a big circle, with a lot of knowledge added to my instincts when I returned.

And now Mrs. Genhart is returning to Zürich?

Yes, she just finished her last year at Eastman.

Practice: Natural, Good Coordination

Did you practice a lot as a child?

No, not an awful lot at first. With me piano was purely recreational.

Do you belong to the breed of "natural" pianists as opposed to those who practice like fiends?

I think there is such a thing as a natural pianist up to a point, but I think that everyone who has wanted to aim for the highest level, suddenly feels he isn't a natural anymore even if he might have been. In my own case, I've always had natural, good coordination. My father is a great athlete.

Nevertheless, when I got to my junior year in high school, I had to start really working on technique because I wanted to do big pieces. For example, at 16 I played the Beethoven C Minor Concerto — that's a tough work by anybody's standards — and I had to develop the equipment to play it. In my senior year in high school I won the Young Musicians Foundation competition. I brought pieces like Beethoven's Sonata in D Major, Op. 10, No. 3 and Liszt's *La Campanella*. I think I really won the competition with my performance of the Schumann Toccata. It was a part of my training to play virtuoso works too.

How do you practice now?

Fiendishly. I have to practice. I don't feel good inside if I miss much practice. Even going on a vacation is hard for me. I'm not a masochist about it or anything, but I love to practice. Practicing excites me. I do about seven hours a day on the average. When I was at Oberlin, my first two and a half years or so, I did eight hours a day by the clock. It was sort of sick.

Day in and day out?

I rarely missed a day.

"Real" pianists seem to have muscles that will take this kind of practice or playing.

It's a part of building them up too — endurance.

But some people's muscles won't ever build up to that; sometimes conservatory students get pains in their arms and have to stop.

You may be right. Frankly, between you and me, if I could have accomplished what I thought I should and done less practice, my God, I would have done less. That's a lot of practicing to be doing and going to classes and still trying to be a human being. You have to have some friends and play around....

It's fantastic that you got through all the other college courses.

Well, on occasion, I barely did. But I had very understanding profs.

Memorizing the First Thing

How do you memorize?

Usually I have no problems with memory. I'm a believer in analysis when learning a score. I don't mean classroom analysis; I mean total analysis which is something theory teachers don't seem to teach, or any theory teacher I've come across, if you know what I mean. Also, I like to memorize a piece right off cold. I do that first, and then usually I'm a little saturated with it.

Do you memorize at the piano, phrase by phrase, or the entire work at once?

I memorize at the piano, usually phrase by phrase, the first thing. For me, a piece never starts to mature, to develop subconsciously, until it's memorized. As far as I'm concerned, if you spend a month or even a couple of weeks working on a piece — and I can't afford a day at this stage — and it's not memorized, it's only water passing under the bridge. So it may take a few days, a week, maybe two weeks — with something like Op. 106, the *Hammerklavier*, you get down on your knees practically and just memorize.

How long does it take to memorize the Hammerklavier?

It took me about....well, there was that fugue.... It took me a couple of weeks, and then I had it in my fingers. I could play through the piece slowly.

You found the last movement more difficult to memorize than the slow movement?

Yes, the slow movement of the *Hammerklavier* was a funny work for me. Have you ever had the feeling that you just seemed to know a piece? You got involved and it seemed to be a part of you right from the beginning? It was something you felt very deeply for?

Have you heard it a lot?

Not a lot, but I had heard it, and I played it because I love it so intensely. It's my favorite of all the late Beethoven sonatas. I know some people might think I play it because it's so darned big, but that's not the reason. I really like it the best.

Learning Big Works

A surprising number of young pianists seem to start with Op. 106 and the Diabelli Variations. Do you think they should play all the other sonatas first?

Michael Tilson Thomas and I were talking about mastering big, mature works, He said something to me that was really smart — and he's a guy who's conducting all over — and I agree with him although I've never put it so well: "I don't think it's a matter of studying everything else until you get up to this or that work. If you've got a brain, the enthusiasm, and the ability for involving yourself, mastering a big work is a matter of spending the time."

Mrs. Genhart, although happy, was suspicious of my doing Opus 106. "Have you mastered *all* the other late Beethoven sonatas?" she asked. "No," I said. "You're doing Opus 106?" "Yes." "Well, bring it in." As far as I was concerned 106 was the synthesis of all the late Beethoven sonatas. It's like a catalogue of "sonata" in big capital letters: this is what a sonata can be. So I said to myself, "Why not tackle it and understand all these sides of Beethoven? And then move back into 101, 109, 110, and 111." I think this is a perfectly valid thing to do. Now I'll play those pieces much better having studied 106.

One of the hardest things is to develop your mind

to span the biggest works in one fell swoop. The goal, right from the beginning, should always be to get the over-all picture, as well as the infinitesimal details, because, in the last analysis, it's total knowledge that sets you free. You know you can rely on your instincts then because you really know what's going on. And you can get great ideas under pressure, just great ideas.

Competitions and Awards

In 1969 you placed third in the Van Cliburn International Competition, the highest ranking American. How did the Cliburn and the Maryland competitions compare?

Both competitions were beautifully run. The Cliburn had a ridiculous amount of required repertoire, whereas this competition had a more reasonable amount, but included a big tape audition.

What did you submit for the tape audition?

They wanted a classic work — I did a Mozart sonata; a romantic work — I did the Schumann Symphonic Etudes; a modern work — I did the Bartok Sonata; two Chopin Etudes, and a Bach Prelude and Fugue. This has been a tremendously well-run competition. The idea of having a Bach Prelude and Fugue on the audition tape is important. That's your meat and potatoes; you have to be able to play Bach Preludes and Fugues. The Cliburn competition is a little flashier — there's a concerto finals — but the quality of playing at this Washington competition was extremely high, every bit as high as the Cliburn competition in which I competed.

I understand that as the winner of another contest you performed under Michael Tilson Thomas. When and where was this?

I was 18 and had won the Young Musicians Debut auditions in Los Angeles the previous spring. The prize was a debut in the Los Angeles Music Pavillion, Michael Tilson Thomas conducting. I played the Mendelssohn Concerto in G Minor which was not the piece I really wanted to play; but at that stage I was thankful to be able to play at all.

And just this spring you won the National Guild of Piano Teachers International Piano Recording Competition. What works did you submit and with what work did you win?

I won the $1,000 Grand Prize with my recording of the Bartok Sonata. I had also submitted Ravel's *Gaspard de la Nuit* and Beethoven's Fourth Concerto. I found out later that I was competing against my own tapes in the finals. Contests are funny sometimes: although the Beethoven Concerto is the most difficult of the three works I submitted, my recording of it really was better than my other two. However, my execution of one melodic turn in the first movement so infuriated the judge that he dismissed any important qualities my playing may have had.

Exciting Chopin

I admired the spontaneity, color, and emotional gamut in your Chopin Ballade in F Minor. In the first theme — after the eight-measure introduction — I felt your instincts and sense of color guided you more than did predetermined phrasing or structuring. What is your approach to the phrasing and coloring of this

melody?

First of all I feel this is a very difficult two pages of music. I've rarely heard it played to my satisfaction. Despite the intense emotion in the harmonies and the melancholy, tragic aspect of that line — it has to be terribly simple and yet dignified. It's like the memory of a loved one or some person with whom one was very involved and suddenly taken away from. It's not big and yet it's not *dolce*. It's just songlike — an idea, a thought, a memory, little pauses, little moments of not being quite sure how to say the next sentence, and then taking the chance and saying it. "No, that wasn't quite what I meant either," and it leads you that way naturally into the spot where the sixteenth notes start.

Then it's primarily your poetic instincts that lead you rather than specifically musical ideas on proportioning, coloring, or phrasing?

Actually I always work those things out, but hopefully to guide my instincts in a more meaningful way and to make sure that I won't repeat myself.

Do you know Cortot's Chopin playing?

Yes, wonderful. A recording that had a big influence on me in the F Minor Ballade was Josef Hofmann's. That's a marvelous performance — one sweep, beautifully subjective and tender. It's a very tender piece. It's not a giant piece, not until you get to the coda, and even the coda is a melodic invention of what has happened before. The coda is not just violence at the keyboard as I've heard it played many times.

Communicative Melodic Tone

Many pianists, when playing soft, play with a contemplative, far-away melodic tone which doesn't carry. I was pleased to hear you're not afraid to play with a big, communicative, melodic tone.

Well, I'm the son of a singer. And she had a voice that could fill a barn. However, I do get a little tired of pianists who are told to "project." People often confuse projection in terms of volume instead of mood intensity. I think they're wrong. I've made the mistake; I think everybody has.

I think that exactly what these pianists don't do is "project" when they play soft. Even Richter's soft melodic playing, on occasion, has left me cold. On the other hand, for Gieseking, melody was everything: melody always sang out of him.

Yes, and another thing about Gieseking's playing that has always thrilled me is his complete mastery of color, harmonic, and rhythmic color, just everything. Solomon is another of my favorite pianists.

Pedal in Bach

Bach playing seems to run in cycles; some pianists are using more pedal again. Your Bach E Minor Partita had individuality and definitive stylistic qualities, despite quite a lot of pedal.

I believe in pedaling every note instead of pedaling over a lot of notes in Bach. Let's put it that way. I use pedal, but change often. I hope it doesn't sound like a lot of pedal, for Bach has to be very clear.

Strong Hands

How would you describe your hands?

They're a mess. I haven't got big, big hands; I have a ninth in each hand. They look bigger because the fingers are rather thin. The hand is good and strong, but the fingers are skinny.

I didn't notice your having to roll chords in Le Gibet.

Those are only ninths, but I tell you I'm leaned way over when I'm playing some of them. On two occasions, did you see me drop my shoulder to get that hand down there, when there are descending chords and the bells in the middle still, in the middle section. There are a couple of chords I can barely get; but I get 'em. I strain a gut!

As a matter of fact I've been doing some stretching and a few things to try to get another note, because believe it or not, at 23, I'm still growing. My octave size keeps changing, which is very frustrating.

Extraordinary Ravel

The Washington Post *quoted one of the judges as saying that your Ravel* Gaspard de la Nuit *was "the finest performance of the entire evening." An individual touch I liked in your "Ondine" was your holding the pedal through the entire "Très lent" pianissimo recitative before the brilliant ending cascades.*

The first-place winner congratulates second-place winner, Diane Walsh, at the University of Maryland 1971 Piano Competition.

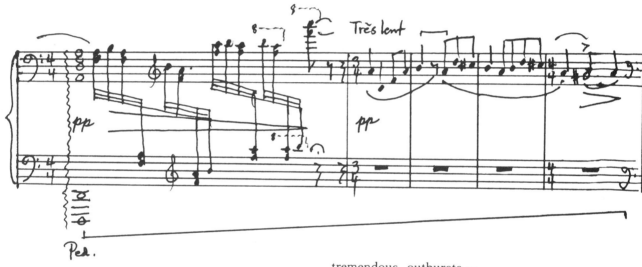

First off, I'd say that after all that beautiful color and fullness, I think one single-line melody would sound rather dry, if the harmony were not held through. Also, Ondine, who lives in a watery world, at this moment has just been denied her love of a mortal and quietly weeps. With the pedal down, the feeling is more tender. It is the same kind of longing as in the first-movement recitatives in Beethoven's *Tempest Sonata*, where Beethoven wrote to hold the pedal down.

Your Scarbo *too was individual, an exciting, impressionistic performance; you didn't play it à la Czerny or Prokofiev as it is, unfortunately, often played.*

Scarbo is an incredibly difficult piece musically. Everybody knows it's hard to play; if it's well played, every pianist in the hall wants to go out and commit suicide. But the thing about *Scarbo* is that everything — with the exception of those three outbursts, just

tremendous outbursts —

is piano, pianissimo, and triple pianissimo. Scarbo's unseen. You know he's there; he just appears in a flash. The excitement is in this nervous, frightened, gasping quality, that little devilish motive that comes and then you can't see it; you don't hear it. All these things happen. And then all of a sudden:

the motive is there again. This piece should not be ground out like the Prokofiev Toccata. I'm sick of hearing *Scarbo* beat to death. And it's to one's benefit not to do so because then when you get to that last climax in B Major, with those tremendous chord runs that go all the way up the piano, over and over, with that great motive, when he's grown to the size of the steeple —

Emanuel Ax (winner of Baldwin Prize at University of Maryland Festival) with Diane Walsh and Mark Westcott

Oh, it's just overwhelming! — you can make a wonderful thing out of this climax because you have been saving for it, and its·power then is so tremendous in comparison.

You have a wonderful interpretative imagination, Mark, which certainly comes through in your playing.

Actually I'm a real disciplinarian when it comes to strict musical intelligence and using my mind. And then I go to the other extreme and express myself freely, from the nineteenth century viewpoint with spirits, demons, and lost loves . . . .

The Plight of Performer and Composer

You played a sonata by Keats. Who is he?

Donald Keats is a fine composer, in his thirties, who teaches at Antioch College. This sonata is being published by Boosey & Hawkes next year. He's also written a couple of symphonies and a violin sonata. I hope he'll do a piano concerto soon. His string quartets were the first to be published by Boosey & Hawkes since Bartok's.

Composers today seem to compose just a few works in each idiom.

They're plagued — as are the rest of musicians, unless they're really on top of the barrel — by simply not having enough time. We live in a society which is insensitive to the needs of performers and composers. There's no such thing as free time for a musician. We expect too much commitment to humdrum daily life. Artists need to apply their energies to their art.

You cannot be creative or recreative, if you're a performer· and have to teach 20 hours or 20 students a week. The conservatories and big music schools want you to be a great performer; they want you to come and be great and to teach. But they want you to teach too much. They're not willing to say, "Now look, you're

drawing a tremendous amount of fine students and attention to our school. We'll give you six, eight, or at the most ten students. Now play. Be great. Represent us." And this is what performers and composers need.

A pianist is not a commodity who can teach a lesson, grab a cup of coffee, do two hours of practicing, teach another lesson, then go here and there. That's murder; you just can't do that! Even if you can fill the schedule, I don't think your energies can take it. A performer needs a situation totally sympathetic to his needs as a person who needs to build up repertoire, to practice, and to dream.

Pianistic Ambitions

Bravo! What are your pianistic ambitions now? Do you intend to enter the European contests?

Contests are not my ambition, but playing is. I would like this to be one of the last, or perhaps *the* last competition I enter, and I'll tell you why. Competitions are hard on me — I've been in a lot of them and have had good experience from playing in them — but now, even though it was a joy winning this one, I would like to concentrate on playing. I would like to establish a reputation slowly, carefully, as a performer, not as a contest winner who "gets" to perform.

I've been fortunate in having enough playing in small towns, universities, and colleges — but now I think I'm at the stage where progress in a career rests with the reputation I can build in the larger cities with good orchestras. If you get the opportunity to play a concerto, then you can be hired the next year as a recitalist; and if they like you, you'll be brought back and back. I expect my career to take awhile; I don't want it to happen overnight. I don't think anyone who wants a long, solid career does. I don't know exactly what this takes. But I do know it takes time and total commitment.

MASTER LESSONS

A Music Lesson on a Soler Sonata

with Alicia de Larrocha's Interpretive Remarks

interview November 24, 1969

Music printed on pages 184 – 187

"Three hundred sonatas?" I said in disbelief. "But not just by Soler."

"Si, si," she replied. "And there are many others not yet printed."

"But on the jacket notes of your recording — Alicia de Larrocha plays Antonio Soler 8 Piano Sonatas (Epic Record BC 1389) — it says there are 75."

"Yes, but after that was written, many more have been discovered and printed. For the moment, there are six books of them and there will be many more. Padre Soler had a big, big production . . ."

I had chosen a Soler Sonata in D Major as a work to ask Alicia de Larrocha, world-famous interpreter of Spanish music, for lesson suggestions because it is a sonata which young students, as well as intermediate and advanced, can play and enjoy. In no way an esoteric museum piece, of interest mostly to specialists, it is a piece immediately appealing and pedagogically rewarding.

Born in northeastern Spain, Antonio Soler (1729-1783), *el padre*, entered the school of sacred music run by monks in the abbey of Montserrat when six years old. There he received a thorough musical education. When 22, he became organist in the Spanish Court at *El Escorial*, studying with Jose de Nebra and from time to time with Domenico Scarlatti.

Soler played Scarlatti's sonatas, studying his style, his way of combining Spanish folk elements with classical form. I asked Madame de Larrocha how Soler is like Scarlatti and how he is different.

Soler, in general, takes the dances which are absolutely Spanish. There are, for example, several sonatas which have the rhythm of the Zapadeados, popular dances. This is the difference: even if Scarlatti took on some of the essence of

Spain, he is not purely Spanish as is Soler. Soler naturally shows the influence of Scarlatti, of the epoch, of the instruments, the kind of writing and the character of that time.

For 31 years, until his death, Soler was a part of the Spanish court and composed a vast quantity of chamber music, songs, incidental music to plays, keyboard pieces, masses, motets, and concertos, many of which are either still in manuscript or have been lost. It was only in the twentieth century that he was rediscovered.

"What edition do you use?"

I use the UMA, the Union Musical Espanola, edition of Padre Samuel Rubio. It offers the greatest possible guarantees of authenticity and presents the text without any expression signs, with the exception of the rare ones which Soler himself put in the manuscripts. But concerning ornaments and interpretation, my version is completely my own.

"What about interpretation?"

The interpretation of Soler is something difficult to talk about because you know the door to the clavicinists, the door to the 17th and 18th centuries has such a great liberty in the manner of playing, the method of the ornaments, and so on. And it is necessary to see the performance of these works like this. It is not possible to play pieces of this era in any one way.

You must understand the era, the style, and then naturally see the elements which you must have — the rhythm, the clarity, the nuance — and then each person must do what he believes he must do.

"How should students work on the Sonata in D Major?"

First of all, I would tell students to study and understand the

form. They should analyze the form, study the era, and know the sonority they want on their instrument. They must perfect the bass which is the rhythm; their playing must have the necessary clarity and evenness. Then afterwards they should try for color together with the accents, the attack, and do something which makes the piece gay and colorful.

Following are measure by measure comments, based on Alicia de Larrocha's recording of the Sonata in D Major, together with her applicable comments:

Allegro. Gay, colorful, bright ($\downarrow$-circa 80), in general with small accents on "one" of each measure.

M. 1. The first phrase forte, the left-hand upbeat triplet fast. The right-hand sixteenth notes should be well articulated and even, the left-hand eighth notes sharp staccato.

M. 5. The second phrase piano, and this time for color and clarity the right-hand sixteenth notes poco staccato.

M. 8. A fast trill, beginning on the note above.

M. 9. The right-hand sixteenth notes poco staccato, corresponding to the touch of the repeated notes in measure 12, the left-hand eighth-note octaves staccato.

Notice that the phrases are of different lengths — sometimes 1, 2, 3, or 4 measures, sometimes elliptic: measures 9-12, a three-measure group; measures 12-14, a two-measure group; measure 14, one measure; measures 15-17, a two-measure phrase as is its sequence in the next two measures.

Mm. 19-25. Larrocha accents the third-beat left hand notes, phrasing them over to the first beats, not accenting the changes of harmony; whereas the right hand sixteenth notes are accented on the first beats. Notice the descending bass line, the ascending soprano. Measure 19 is again a one-measure group, corresponding to measure 14.

Mm. 27-31. This four-measure melodic fragment, in A major, like a second theme, can be played forte with measures 36-40 piano as echo, or as Larrocha does on her recording: two measures forte, then two piano. I asked her if she preferred echo effects in bigger or smaller phrases:

I don't like to make nuances of very short duration, because it is difficult to hear quick changes from forte to piano, to make the change quickly. Even on the clavecin, it is difficult. But even more so on the piano because the possibility is less to change the sonority suddenly. So in a small part like this, the ear can't capture the change.

"You play forte for two measures, then piano for two measures on your recording," I said.

Is it like that on the recording? Then, I play it differently each time. You can't give a guide for things which you do on the spur of the moment. Fortunately, we change; life changes every moment. Pupils should practice it both ways and then decide.

Staccato

Mm. 31-33. Both hands staccato. Practice it with various touches.

Mm. 33-35. The right-hand sixteenth notes poco staccato with accents on "one," the left hand with accents on "two."

The kind of staccato I play depends on the color which I want to give. If I want to give a very rhythmic character, I play the staccatos dry; if I want a more elegant character, I play less dry. For these reasons I take a little pedal, or use no pedal. The attack is shorter or longer. All the color comes from the way you play the legatos, the staccatos, the accents.

In these measures, sometimes I play staccato for clarity, as on the record, sometimes not. If I play in a hall that has much resonance, which is not very clear, I would play staccato to have more clarity. If I play in a hall that is extremely dry, I wouldn't play it staccato because I would obtain too hard a sound. You have to adapt yourself to each moment.

For recordings you have to play more clearly than in a big hall and you have to know what sonority the technician is giving you. If you listen a little before you make the recording, you will hear what you have to do. And the recording is never successful because you do one thing at the moment, and when you listen afterwards you have absolutely different ears. You don't hear at all the way you heard before. And then when you listen to the recording a year or so later, you feel and hear still differently.

M. 35. Played:

Ornaments

I add ornaments but not octaves. I play according to my ideas. The ornaments are mine; they aren't always written. Sometimes I play more ornaments than written, depending on the sonata. Also playing on the piano is not the same as playing on the harpsichord or clavichord.

The ornaments a pupil plays will, of course, depend upon his facility. If he plays the ornaments poorly, not clearly, and can't give them the necessary sound, I would suggest that he omit them, which is much better than playing them poorly.

On the last page, measure 91, I make a slight variation which is not written:

These things are the liberty which the interpreter had during this epoch. Each person and editor will do different things.

Pedal

On her recording, Alicia de Larrocha takes touches of pedal on wide intervals when forte — measures 27, 28, 36, 37, 51, 52, 53, for example. "What about pedal?" I asked.

In general, without pedal, of course. But pedal, too, depends on the hall and the instrument. If the sound is too dry, I take small pedals from time to time to obtain the sonority or color which I want, but never pedal to connect the notes.

Repeats

"And you believe it desirable to play all the repeats?"

The repeats are the form, and if you don't take the repeats, the form is unbalanced. But from time to time when, for example, I play an encore and the sonata would be too long with the repeats, I cut. But that's not good!

Mm. 55-59. Four measures forte. This second half of the sonata which begins in the parallel minor, D minor, instead of being a reprise of the beginning, develops from measure 55 to measure 79 the idea first stated in measures 12 et al.

Mm. 59-63. Four measures, as echo, in piano.

From m. 65. The right hand is in two-measure melodic sequences, whereas the bass is moving harmonically, in V7-I sequences overlapping the sequential movement of the right hand.

M. 70. The last measure of the sequence is elliptic, becoming the first measure of the ascending right-hand figures. Poco a poco crescendo in these measures to measure 76, corresponding to measures 20-25 of the exposition. Some editions have the last note of measure 73, an ascending A. Larrocha plays it as E flat, keeping the last two notes a descending third as in the other measures of the sequence.

This:

Not this:

"What final advice would you give?" I asked.

You have to give a guide to young pupils. While they are learning the notes, acquiring the necessary evenness, have them practice with various touches. After they have been given a guide and have perfected the notes, they may do other things. That's natural. Years pass, your musical culture and understanding grow; your ideas change. But in the beginning, the pupil has to start step by step, thoroughly and carefully. When you start to ride a bicycle, you can't start by riding without your hands, by just letting the bicycle fly!

Sonata

Edited by Dean Elder
as recorded by Alicia de Larrocha

PADRE ANTONIO SOLER

Lili Kraus --

On Mastering Mozart

The noted Hungarian pianist discusses the problems of style, expression, and technique with her unique skill, charm, and wit as a teacher.

interview August 9, 1969

Ardent applause greeted Lili Kraus, world-famous Mozart interpreter, as she came out on the recital hall stage of the University of Maryland's Fine Arts Building to begin her master classes as part of the twelfth annual American Matthay Festival.

"Thank you so much for your warm welcome," she said, "and let me tell you of my joy in being here. I hope that our joint undertaking will be blessed with valid, fruitful, and illuminating information, to and fro, from listener to player, from student to teacher, and above all from spirit to spirit."

The Matthay Festival had consisted of interesting, informative lecture demonstrations and nightly piano recitals. And Lili Kraus had come to climax the festival with two master classes and two piano recitals in the large concert hall.

She showed herself at the master classes to be an energetic, compelling, inspiring teacher. Possessing a rich speaking voice — her diction having tinges of Hungarian, Viennese, and French vowel timbres — she expressed herself with the conviction of a lifetime of study and performance.

At each session she worked with three students on a first movement from a Mozart sonata. "It is odd," spe said, "that I don't find a single second movement. Everybody plays the first movement, no second or third movements. I wonder why."

As each student played the movement through without interruption, she listened intently, pacing around the stage and the hall. To relax the student she would say: "Are you nervous? Terribly nervous? If you could, would you like to play it once more?" Or, adding a touch of levity, "Who is the next victim?" During the lessons, which lasted 30 to 50 minutes each, the audience, raptly attentive, frequently laughed and applauded.

First Class

1. Sonata in F Major, K. 332 (Allegro)

After the performance, Madame Kraus suggested that the music rack be put down. "When the music rack is up, you cut off your sound." And then she spoke of style:

"Now when we speak of style, what do we really mean? We mean the mode of speech or expression of the particular composer, writer, dancer, painter, through whatever medium he communicates his creative experiences. And it was Mozart's way to speak — through whatever instrument: piano, violin, voice, or orchestra — to use his voice in a restrained manner. He had so much to say and what he had to say came from such depth, that not only was it unnecessary for him to underline, let alone to put on, but all he could do to temper his passion was to limit the dynamic frame, in contrast to the speech of say Schumann, Liszt, or Chopin, to name but a few of the so-called Romantics."

Mozart's Piano

"Furthermore, Mozart's piano didn't allow for a wide dynamic range. I possess such a piano and consequently, I speak from experience: if you play it too loudly, the hammers will break; if you play it too softly, it simply won't speak. Therefore, it is up to you to express all the burning, truthful cosmic experience that Mozart's music reveals, within a narrow dynamic and agogic framework. This is the essential difficulty in interpreting Mozart.

"The performer needs all the imagination, love, and insight he can bring to Mozart's music, first to grasp and then to project the entirety of its meaning. What does this music express? Is the opening dramatic, lyric, sad?"

"Serenely happy?"

"Yes, and then what happens? At which point does it turn into the minor? Where does it become more dramatic? And so on. You must ask yourself these questions." Lili Kraus laughed as she said, "it is healthy to investigate the score *before* you perform."

Her hands raised expressively in the air, she continued: "Music never stands still. It goes, arrives, or it comes back and sets out again for its next goal. If you make an accent on the G of measure three, you stop the flow of the singing line. Do you generally emphasize your last syllable? Then don't emphasize this G. The note at the end of a slur should be lighter. The emphasis is on the six-four chord, and the end of the phrase should not be chopped."

Pre-play What you Play

"The left hand must be beautiful, soft, and even both in concept and in sound. You must have the feeling that you pre-play what you play. The whole chord of the measure must be prepared in the hand. The position must be prepared both as to timing and to volume. You must know in advance what finger comes next, as the foot 'pre-feels' the spot on the ground it will tread on.

"If you want to play the left hand very soft, the slower you travel from the surface to the bottom of the key, the firmer the finger has to be. The slow traveling makes it imperative that the finger be firm and not break, the wrist flexible and not too high. Your wrist is as stiff as a broomstick," she said with a laugh.

What the Music is Doing

"The first four measures were the question posed; measure five begins the answer:"

Ms. 11-12. "This time the phrase clinches forte instead of piano, ending the big phrase. But why so abrupt? The forte must still sound in proportion to the general tone picture."

Ms. 13. "Here comes the transition — serene, light, carefree, enchanting. After the lyric tenderness of the beginning part, you then want to be graceful, unpremeditative, airborne, like a child."

"Don't emphasize the left-hand melody. The melody is in the right hand. You need the bass, but it shouldn't eclipse the right hand."

Ms. 16-17. "What was wrong? It wasn't precise, together. Think the right hand slow and the left hand fast. Make the left hand dominate. You get hung up on the sixteenth note."

"Did you ever investigate why? Why aren't you free enough? Why is your wrist rigid?"

Play from the Top Knuckle

"Every time the finger is not firm enough, the wrist becomes rigid. What does firm enough mean? The first two joints of the finger are not the strongest ones. The strong point is the top knuckle. If you want to have a really firm finger — one that is firm enough — play from the top knuckle or joint."

Expressing the Feeling in Words

Ms. 19-23. "The two little phrases here seem to say, 'That's all; that's all.' The forte — 'Or is it?' — is like a menace it should come to you as a shocking surprise, casting you into the shadow of the minor key.

"That's all, that's all, for is it?"

We must be made to believe that you invent the music as you go along."

M. 41. "The second subject should be dolce, all sweetness, enchantment, seduction. Suddenly he begins to dance:"

M. 56. "For the first time this panting sort of music appears; the rests are the essence."

M. 60. "Not so loud a forte. Your forte eats up the piano. The intensity of the right hand remains, although sempre piano, because the contents don't change within this thought.:"

M. 67. "He hovers over the minor."

M. 71. "Once more the sun is shining. This is so beautiful. Not staccato; it must sing. You know, the contrasts that occur in the music create the different moods, just as in life. Mozart's genius communicates these changes through imperceptible subtlety. The changes occur with lightning speed, brought about with masterly economy of the means employed."

2. Sonata in B Flat Major, K. 333 (Allegro)

The second performer played with nice tone, admirable fluency, clarity, and style. "Bravo," said Lili Kraus. "Your performance is excellent, musical. Your phrasing is good; your conception is absolutley right. There is nothing wrong, except that you, too, don't quite project the happenings in the piece.

The Soul of the Music

"Schopenhauer said, 'music is the world de-materialized, the world without its encumbrances.' It is not enough to say 'here is soul.' You must *be* the soul, the joy of creation. You must be the very essence of this music. Otherwise, I can't feel what the music wants to convey, what moved the composer when he wrote the piece."

M. 71. "For instance, you played the F minor part of the Development with essentially the right dy-

namics. But it didn't turn tragic in you, so how can it turn tragic in me? Dynamically, the phrase should get louder and move forward to the top F of measure 73, diminishing on down the phrase to measure 75."

Technical Approach

"Now as to technical approach. There are many kinds of methods that say no other way of playing is possible. Such a view is too limited. There are though a few essential and indispensable principles. For instance, it makes all the difference to your technique whether you do or do not play from the base of your finger — that is, from the knuckle — thereby using the entire finger as a long lever instead of breaking it up at the joints. You should view and feel the fingertip as the furthermost point of the entire arm: the maximum extension.

"Another essential technical principle is the complicated and opposite simultaneous functioning of wrist and finger: the finger always firm, the wrist always flexible. The one presupposes the other: in order to have a flexible wrist, you must have a firm finger foundation."

Investigate the Harmonic Structure

M. 1. "Do you know how this first theme is put together? When you say a sentence, what do you want to emphasize? If you want me to understand your meaning, you might emphasize something other than the usual word. It is up to you. But you must know what is to be said, that is, what the composer wanted to say.

"Investigate the left hand which is always your guidance. Show me what is happening in the harmony in the left hand. It takes a lifetime — and this doesn't hold true only for pianists — to learn to simplify. To find the essence of what is happening in classic music, you have to investigate the harmonic structure of the work.

"The harmonic life of this music is its very lifeblood. The harmonic life is what makes it go, drive, blossom, and flourish. Then there is the rhythmic aspect. You can say the rhythm is classical music's heartbeat; the form its skeleton, its bone structure; and the melody its face which has to beautify and identify the whole work.

"Unless the bass is completely embodied in you, what you do in the right hand is a fringe benefit, instead of organic essence, so to speak. So let's see what is happening in the left hand. Play the left hand blocked in chords:"

Pedals on the Mozart Piano

"Another thing in playing this kind of bass. The Mozart piano did not have the sort of pedals we have. It had two pedals moved by the knees which could be used simultaneously as well as separately. However, the pedals didn't hold over the middle part of the keyboard. The left knee pedal held up to the E above middle C, allowing the left-hand harmonies to be held while the right-hand melodies remained clear. The left knee pedal could give continuity resonance to the harmonies. But now we don't have this kind of pedal. So we must play as if our fingers were the pedal, holding down the notes of the left hand with the fingers. The left hand must be a perfect legato, or legatissimo, and not dry. And the right hand should go on living and blossoming because of the harmony, so to speak."

Harmonic Function

M. 1 et al. "Where are the emphases in the right hand? In each of the two-note phrases at the beginning of each measure, the second notes must be softer than the first, the C in the first short phrase having just the knowledge of emphasis. Furthermore, in the

first big phrase, which is composed of four small phrases, the third and fourth small phrases should be played lighter than the beginning: the dominant seventh is always softer than the preceding six-four harmony, unless otherwise stated. Once you know this, the phrase becomes intelligible. Awareness of harmonic function is one of the main sources from which my knowledge derives; it is there for your information as well. These details must only be intimated; they must not be rubbed into us."

Strict Adherence to the Text

M. 5. "What happens here? This is a transition leading to the next measure. Again please emphasize sufficiently. How essential and all-revealing it is to notice where Mozart placed the slurs. In Mozart's

scores the indications are so few, that those written are of the utmost importance. So, because of the slurs, the emphasis is on the D's. Emphasizing the C's is what he wanted to avoid."

M. 6. "The sixteenth notes are slurred, but they should not be Czerny-like. Bring out the first B flat slightly. This measure just leads on; follow the harmony."

Superfluous Movements

M. 10. "Please, don't make superfluous movements, either with your fingers or your hands. I used to climb high mountains. The guide would not lift

his foot one inch higher than he had to, to save his strength. Not only for looks but for essence, it is important that nothing happens that is not to the point. The left hand should be soft, the last note being a quarter, without an accent."

M. 12, 13. "Dominant of the dominant harmony . . . sweet like your sweetest sweetheart."

M. 23. (The second subject). "You must pretend in Mozart to play forte through vigor, intensity, rhythm, but not volume — not an earth-bound forte, not too loud a forte. There is no such thing in Mozart."

M. 39. "The forte-piano is nothing but a mischievous accent, like an opera buffa."

M. 57. "Triumphant, not loud."

3. Sonata in C Major, K. 330 (Allegro moderato)
"Wonderful, most lovable playing, very musical," said Lili Kraus after the third performer had played. "But several rhythmical and phrasing details were not right."

M. 19. "What do you see here? One C sharp is a grace note; the other is not. There must have been a reason why Mozart wrote a grace note the first time

and an eighth note the second time, and not twice exactly the same thing. So why do you hide this information from us?"

M. 34. "Mozart wrote sforzato on the D and piano on the G. Please play as written."

M. 36. "The slur ends on the C natural, and there is a rest after it; so, don't accent the C. Playing such a detail correctly makes all the difference in the world. Please, please, adhere to the written text. You are not giving enough emphasis on the D, the point

reached; Mozart would not have written staccato on the notes before, if he hadn't wanted you to go to the D. I don't believe in making markings on the music. It is too crude if you mark an accent; the accent is more an espressivo on this D than anything else. But another accent, in another context, could demand different execution."

M. 37. "If you have to slow down to play five notes in the trill, then start on the note above, or just play E-F #-E.

If you play five notes, starting on the E, the trill must be fast, light like a feather. The taste of the performer has to decide whether to start on the note or on the note above."

Cadence-Conditioned

M. 38. "Do you know what a six-four chord is? The six-four chord, from the bass up, is D, G, B. It is

called six-four because you have the intervals of a sixth and a fourth above the bass note. You have driven to this six-four chord, which you resolve and which clinches your tonality. Classical music is full of these small six-four cadences; it is cadence-conditioned. The six-four chord is the point of emphasis.

You know it and Mozart knew it. But *we* must only sense it and not know it. That means finesse, discretion, judgment, and know-how."

Ms. 39-40. "Use the same arm movement on all the staccato eighth notes."

M. 42. "Like a bird, unpremeditated, innocent, not pressed, not hurried." *M. 43.* "Playing the second G louder than the first was your most severe transgression. The perfection of such a detail is not for

the uninitiated, but it is for the Lord, for the composer for you, and for me."

M. 44-45. "Why isn't it perfect? I want you to find it. Well? The left hand is not there. The harmonic basis must be there too. You need a little emphasis on the left-hand C's."

M. 47. "The six-four chord should be clear; and the dominant seventh chord should be light, in spite of the trill which, however, should start with a tiny accent and then diminish."

Ms. 54-55. "The forte — gay, assured young, slim, radiant, not heavy; then the piano — playful and right on time."

Ms. 59-64. "You emphasized all the high notes in each measure of the right hand. Mozart didn't want that; otherwise he wouldn't have written sforzatos on the top E's, as a surprise, in measures 62 and 63. You don't know when and where to arrive."

"Where is the reached point in each measure? The harmonic movement in the left hand will help you decide. Play the left hand in chords: g-B, F-Ab, E-G, et cetera, and don't leave out the essential chord, the F-Ab.

"In the first measure the left hand has the extraordinary turn, the F-Ab; bring this out a little. Then in the next measure the right hand confirms this harmonic movement with the E-G sharp which you should emphasize lightly. Then in the fourth and fifth measures, the right-hand sforzato E's must be the surprise. And not sforzato so much in quantity as in quality, as an espressivo; these are floating accents. It would be jarring to say '*I love you.*' The G-E-F sharp is 'I *love* you.' These sforzato notes are sixteenth notes, not quarters or eighths. And play the left hand completely legato.

"You must not play sforzatos in measures 59 and 60. To understand, first find out why. Then all you have to do is listen. If you are off the truth, you should discover it and react; you should feel dissatisfied, ill at ease, even angry with yourself. I want to awaken your senses to what is true and thereby, beautiful."

Perfecting Details

M. 59-60. "You are now not really identified with the piece you are playing. The piece wants to be eloquent, still emphasizing the plea: 'Ah come to*mor*row.' It is not '*to*morrow.' Why do you whisper the D? The D is the point to which you must go. Like everything else that goes wrong — in this case the G popping out instead of the D — this error too has a technical reason.

"Ah, come to-mor-row"

Something has to happen so you get the emphasis on the D and not on the G. Put more weight on the D, using a firm finger, not your arm. Give more weight on the finger that plays the D, so the D is really speaking. You play the resolution, the C, too soon and it is soundless.

"Do I pester you beyond endurance?" asked Madame Kraus. "But, you know, the perfection of details, such as two-note phrasings, is one of the things that bring Mozart to life."

M. 64. "In playing this scale," she continued, "the thumb should be as flexible as a rubber spring. When you play the second note — the A — the thumb should already be prepared on the C. Your thumb shouldn't go to the C at the last moment. Really prepare the hand after the thumb plays; take the hand to its next position. Finger the scale in groups: 1-2-3; 1-2-3-4; 1-4-5-2, 3-1-4-1, "arranging" the intervals at the earliest possible moment."

M. 65. "Play the six-four harmony louder than the dominant-seventh harmony, in the left hand too, not only in the right hand."

G I$^6_4$ V$_7$

Ms. 66-71. "In a two-note slur, the first note is the note which is emphasized. This is the most elementary thing. The degree of the crescendo in the notes before will depend on the content of the piece, the crescendo to the E being the reason for the emphasis on the first note of the two-note slur."

"The first time you are in major; all is well. The second time, the F natural is an indication that all is not well. And the third time what indicates we are going to A minor? The G sharp, of course. Alas, it seems you don't know the harmonic turn of events, the knowledge of which is indispensable at any given moment."

Happenings in Great Music are Fast

M. 69. "There is no use trying to express the tension or anguish in the right hand alone when it is the left hand that tells us there is the tension. Like life itself, happenings in great music are fast. You must be alert and flexible. All these infinitely quick and subtle changes are the life of the piece and want to be perfected — first felt, then done, and then understood by you and, last but not least, the listener. A nonmusician has no idea of major or minor, but he feels the essential changes through your tension."

M. 83. "Here you should be uncertain, as if feeling your way; there isn't even a bass. This is not my fancy; it is written this way."

"Measure 85 is the progressing one; measure 87 is the slowing down, the retard which Mozart composes. Your retard was too much. And measure 88, at the reprise of the principal theme, seems to say: 'Here I am again. Love me.' "

Reprise

Dynamics

"Never will dynamics. Dynamics are consequences of the way you have to speak, exactly as when you speak. An actor wouldn't say, 'Here I will speak loudly; here I will speak softly, and so on. If he knows what he has to convey, he will have an infinite palette of colors as a result of the clarity of his thought, his creative strength, and will, depending on what he wants you to understand. In other words, he does not decide to speak one word loudly and another softly. He thinks of the meaning and the louds and softs take care of themselves.

"Mozart wrote this music because he had this infinite magic and charm, this God-given love for music which has to be adored. As Schnabel said about Mozart: 'Mozart is too easy for kids and too hard for artists.' "

Making Mozart Live

interview August 11, 1969

"I am so happy we are foregathered once more," said Lili Kraus as she stepped out on the stage to begin the second session of master classes on Mozart's sonatas. "Where is our first student?"

4. Sonata in B-Flat Major, K. 498a
(Allegro moderato)

"We don't know for sure if this sonata is by Mozart," she said after the performance. "Although it is printed in such editions as the Schirmer (Epstein), Augener, Kalmus (Bartok), and Presser (Lebert), it is not printed in the Urtext editions. Certainly it has no original second or last movements: the second movement given here is an excerpt from the slow movement of the Concerto in B-flat, K. 450, and the last movement is compiled from material in that and other concertos.

"But never mind. It is a beautiful piece, and you play it very beautifully. Let's assume it is by Mozart. In that case, even though it is more contrapuntal and complicated than the general text of the Mozart sonatas, it should nevertheless be played more simply than you played it.

"One reason, among many, which makes Mozart's music so lovable is that it seems so simple. His writing is really the unpremeditated speech of a young child. The stylistic secret is to find this music's almost childlike, deceptive innocence--deceptive, because there is, of course, a world of knowledge behind it."
M. 1. "So, play simply, sweetly. Sing; enjoy it. It is unusual to have the harmonic happening of the piece—the V7 - I harmony in the left hand—at the outset. The important note, the A-flat, is cancelled out if you sing too extrovertedly in the right hand.

"It is perfectly all right to play the right and left-hand B-flats with full tone. But immediately become softer in the left-hand part. Let me give you a little secret: if you play the first left-hand B-flat too soft, you have no interval between the B-flat and the A-flat. Playing the B-flat with sufficient tone makes the interval. You must measure your weight distribution carefully, like a pharmacist, to the tiniest fraction. Of course, the left hand should not be louder than the right, and the A-flat should be discreetly balanced and unaccented."

Prepare Hand Positions

"Whenever you have any kind of interval, instead of playing one note, then the next, and then the next, prepare the interval or chord positions firmly in the hand:

"Preparing the hand positions in advance perhaps doesn't allow so much outlet for your feeling as you might like to have, but it is much truer to the text. And in time, you will find you will be able to say all you want, in spite of a certain restriction. But may I hasten to add, what a blessing it is that you have a surplus of feeling—which can't be taught. You can always keep feeling 'back,' but woe betide if you try to 'put it on.'"

Mozart Slurs

M. 2-3. "If this is really Mozart, it is unlikely that the upbeat would be slurred to the next bar. And if the slur were marked correctly, you wouldn't rush into the next bar. These notes are tail-end and overlapping upbeat at the same time. There is no interdynamic in such a figure. If anything, diminuendo; don't make a crescendo and don't rush. You have finished your say here, before going on with the two-note slur groups."

not this:

M. 3. "Articulate the two note phrasings, just feeling the articulations, playing the second notes shorter, not accentuating. The first beat of measure four is the point to which you are driving."

Ms. 5-6 "And now the left hand has the theme, the right hand the harmonic happening, and both elements must be recognizable. So, play the right hand

dolce and without hurrying. And don't cancel out the importance of the theme in the left hand by accenting the upbeat sixteenth notes and playing the B-flat quarter note too soft."

The Technique of Alberti Basses

M. 8 et al. "Do you want to play this left-hand part soft, bringing out the bottom notes? May I show you why you don't succeed? Play less thumb and play more lower-moving voice, working on the passage

slowly, playing the bottom notes staccato and accented. The staccato note is a fast motion, an immediate and quick contact of the finger with the key; the thumb a slow motion as it travels from the surface to the actual striking point of the key. And when playing the hands together, you don't have to bring out the bottom notes of the left hand so much.

"Your thumb is a little heavy, and it's not in position. And your fingers are not firm. The fingers will be firm only if the distance—the interval between each two notes—is prepared in the hand in advance.

"Extending or contracting the hand is the fastest movement you have. For the first note or position, the hand is completely open; then it contracts as the intervals become smaller. But you can't play with just the hand; you must use the fingers too. And the fingers must have courage: they will have courage only when they have self-confidence: they must be audacious. And don't worry if I hear some wrong notes from this piano before we have parted.

"Don't move a fraction farther than you have to. You have to move to the striking distance—the finger is already on the spot, so-to-speak; the finger doesn't risk anything by moving that far. In fact, this lightning-fast preparation ensures the cleanest playing.

"In stretching for the octave, too much of your thumb is hanging over the key. All this overstretch is so much distance wasted. Only use as much of the thumb as you have to. Open the thumb whatever distance you need, moving from its root, having the feeling that you never let go. In other words, the thumb must get its strength from its root, but must play the key with only its tip.

"You are not getting the sound that you should because your thumb is dead. Your thumb moves like a beetle which has six legs, five working beautifully,

the sixth dragging along. Your thumb should be just as active, as sensitive and agile, as all the other fingers."

At this point Madame Kraus addressed the listeners: "Before we go on, may I beg you not to mind that we are going into such detail. May I tell you a little story which will console you.

"I once taught a master class at the University of Wellington, New Zealand. The dean of the piano department was one of my pupils, and another teacher told him—this I heard afterwards—she would like to play the Mozart C Minor Concerto for me, but that she didn't know it well enough.

" 'What don't you know well enough?' asked the dean.

" 'I can't play the last movement,' she replied.

" 'Last movement? Can you play the first eight bars?'

" 'What do you mean? Of course I can play the first eight bars.'

" 'Then fine. You don't need any more, for you will never get past those first eight bars.' "

"Does that console you?" asked Madame Kraus as she turned back to the player. "That's why I told it to you. I spend so much time on this Alberti bass technique because, as you know, it occurs throughout classic music. And it is really worthwhile to find out how to play it with the utmost perfection."

M. 10. "In this next left-hand figure, when you end the second four sixteenth notes with the thumb, the thumb must be as flexible as possible with no waste movement and should not give an accent. Start farther in on the keys, not making any inward movement when playing the thumb. Only the fourth finger should go to the E-flat. No, you have three fingers over the E-flat. Don't encumber the fourth finger; it should be alone."

Ms. 8-15. "As you play it, this passage has no life. The right hand leads and must not start too loud, because it has a long stretch to continue the golden spiral on, on, and on. And the left hand should be every bit as beautiful, seductive, colorful, and cared-for as the right hand."

Ms. 15-16. "This is Mozart, not Beethoven, which means the forte should be radiant, firm, and vital, but not thundering."

Ms. 17-22. "For this small-intervaled Alberti bass, the fingers must be curved and completely controlled, for it isn't possible to control a hand where the field of action is far removed from the contact that the finger makes with the key."

"Unless we have the harmonic movement in the bass, the music is incomprehensible. Understand the suspensions in the harmony. In measure 18, don't forget that the C has already been introduced; in measure 19, don't

forget the suspended G must be heard and resolve to the F-sharp. Furthermore, as you played it, the left-hand part was too dry; there was too much thumb."
M. 23. "To my understanding, Mozart would have phrased this way , and not all connected together."

M. 33. (Second theme). "For the second theme, Mozart uses a fragment of the first theme - the upbeat, and the reached point. You feel it, but you don't let us hear the transfiguration.

"If anything, the second theme wants to be much more mellow than the first theme was before. *Espressivo* can be as manifold as music itself. The second theme in a sonata can be extrovert, introvert, or it can be the narrator who speaks of life. Here the second theme is an *intime* communication, whereas the first theme was the introduction foretelling what is going to happen. And now with the second theme you turn inward in character and expression, but without change of tempo. You should remain dead on time.

"Before I release you, my friend, let me tell you a story about playing in time. Schnabel once played for a ladies' club. After the concert a lady came up to thank him for the divine concert.

"May I ask you a question?' she asked. 'What school of thought do you belong to, the one which says you must play in time, or the one which says you may play as you feel?'

" 'Madam,' Schnabel replied, 'Do you really think it is beyond every hope to feel in time?'

"And so this second theme, although intimate and personal in character, should continue 'to feel on time!' "

5. Sonata in B-Flat Major, K. 570

(Allegro)

"Mozart wrote in a letter," said Madame Kraus, "that the best interpreter of his music he ever heard was a man who played in a way that made him forget he had composed it. He had the feeling the man improvised as he went along. Further, Mozart adds that 'the man had such a magnificent technique that I never noticed he had any.'

"Spontaneity is the very essence of a performance," she continued. "You should not let on that you know what the next note or bar is or that you have worked on the piece to the point of being sick and tired of it. I want to hear your one-time experience: you have never before seen this music, never known it; you invent it now, as you go along. Now how will you do this? By trying to imagine the ineffable beauty of the piece, by trying to imagine everything that happens in it, by being utterly identified with it — body, soul, and spirit.

"Doesn't it start *unisono*, still and sweet, with a question and then an answer? Then after skipping along, comes the beautiful second subject, quickening into the minor for an instant, and so on. All this happens; make it happen. Don't hurry; nobody is chasing you. it is not easier to play fast; it is much truer if you give

every note its sense, its appointed fate."

'Ah, the sun is bright and high'

M. 1. "Try to live the music for the first time: 'Ah, the sun is bright and high. Let's go out and have a lovely time.' You wouldn't say deadpan, singsong, 'the sun is bright and high let's go out and have a lovely time.' In measure four, the F is not slurred to the following B-flat. There is a separation, so let's have it."

Ms. 12-13. "You are having trouble with these sixteenth note figures because, when you play the G—or respectively the F—you are playing your fifth finger too loud.

The emphasis is on the upbeat, not on the 'one'. And these figures should be full of charm; accenting the quarter notes makes them earth-bound and heavy-footed. Mozart tried very conscientiously to inform you. He writes the slur over the sixteenth notes to show that they are the important thing. And don't play the staccato sixteenth note as an eighth note. Count in subdivisions, playing right in time."

Ms. 19-20. "As when ending a sentence, drop your voice at the end of this phrase. You must not only play the last note softer, but you must feel that it is a quarter, a full syllable."

Ms. 21-22. "These chords are a terrific shock—but not a brutal one. Mozart's speech is always tempered. It should be full, dramatic, incisive, but not coarse, hard, never really blunt. The second beats are single notes—he didn't write two chords—so, he evidently wanted the accent on the first beat:

$$\overset{>}{1}\ 2\ \wr\ \text{and not}\ 1\ \overset{>}{2}\ \wr$$

"And don't play the chords too soon. You must pretend, even to yourself, not to know what is going to happen. You were happy as a lark just before. And suddenly these chords are a threat, only to turn into the sweetness, the assurance of the second theme."

M. 23 (Second theme) "The change from the G minor to the E-flat major didn't happen in you. You played it; but you didn't really experience it. Without any preparation or warning after the chords of the preceding two measures, the music becomes gentle, *dolce*, relieved. Harmonic changes are the highest tensions, the miracles of music.

"In playing the right-hand melody, imagine you are

accompanying a singer who wants to tarry on the first E-flat. Then you will lean on it, nobody being the wiser. Not much tarrying is needed, but that little is necessary. And the bottom notes of the left-hand harmony must sound too."

"I can't hear the last sixteenth note in the group of four (also in measure 12). Take your time between the measures—the slur doesn't go over the bar line—to insure that the last sixteenth is clear and precise."

Even, Accurate Sixteenth Notes

M. 35. et al. "Don't scramble; don't hurry. Instead of lifting and moving the hand and fingers, stay close to the keys.

"Leschetizky was a great teacher. Once when somebody dropped a sixteenth note, he said 'You are a thief.' Why do you steal a sixteenth note? In the first beat, I hear only the two C's:

You may have heard the B natural inside yourself, but it didn't actually sound. Your ear must be so trained that you can't tolerate anything not in accordance with the text. You must listen like a hawk—if hawks listen; I think they look—but you must listen."

M. 39-40. "Do you know why you have trouble starting here? You wobble all over and don't prepare the chord positions. First, work on this measure, blocked in chords:

"Then work on it slowly, as written: when you play the G, C, G, E, C, as soon as your thumb arrives on the last C, your fifth finger should go immediately to the next G; and when you play this G, your hand should immediately prepare the entire next chord, the G, E, C, G.

"Similarly, when you play the G, E, C, G, as soon as your thumb arrives on the last G, your fifth finger should go immediately to the next C; and when you play this C, your hand should immediately prepare the entire next chord, the C, G, E, C. The movements should be tiny, precise, fast, and smooth, with no side movement. In measure 40, the accent is again on 'one':

M. 41. "And now, the left hand is the woodwind, the right hand the flute-*dolce*, unearthly, dematerialized, no flesh, all soul. I am happy you heard that you played the first F too loud and started again. Start the F slowly with your thumb, the finger on the key; then you won't come down too hard."

Fast Trill or Shake

M. 45. "So that's what you try to play, four notes in the trill or shake. I wouldn't have guessed it. No embellishment can be done satisfactorily if you lift your fingers high. The fingers, which should be firm and move from their roots, should play as near the keys as possible, with no unnecessary movements.

"If you want to play four notes, the second finger must not leave its place and, of course, should not stop on the second F; go straight away to the E. When you arrive on the E, the wrist should be flexible.

"But in such a case as this, I don't think it is necessary to play so many notes; an inverted mordent, three notes, is sufficient. Whichever way you play it—either way is all right if you are convincing—never accent the E. Accent the principal note."

Mozart Editions

"The preface to the Henle Urtext edition explains the execution of ornaments very well. The best editions of the Mozart sonatas are the Breitkopf and Hartel Urtext (reprinted here by Kalmus and Schirmer), which has no fingerings; and the Henle Urtext, which has the best fingerings you could possibly dream of. The Broder edition is reputedly the holiest of the holy, very antiseptic, but I don't know it."

M. 49. "Do you want to emphasize the beginning or the end of the slurred figures? The beginning of course. Be persuasive; they must be full of meaning. The last note under the slur should have less tone than the beginning notes."

Ms. 54-57. "Give yourself time on the important D7 harmony. You forgot that the next two bars are the cadence; don't rush. The reached point in measure 56, the chord that clinches your coming home, is the second-beat six-four chord going to the dominant. You are too hasty in the right-hand six-four chord and too loud on the dominant."

M. 57. "Play this kind of passage work very light and close to the keys, the wrist not high. The left hand now has the pattern from above which should be brought out."

M. 67. "This six-four is the climax of the whole thing."

M. 69. "This kind of coda or closing theme, sometimes called the Mozartean signature, is an adorable trick of Mozart's."

M. 77. "And now this says to me, 'It's all over. Let's go; lively, right to the end.'"

Before going on to the next lesson, Lili Kraus relaxed for a moment. Her belief in identifying completely — body, soul, and spirit — with the music brought to mind one of her most cherished memories:

"In the days when I used to smoke," she related, "at the request of my beloved and worried husband, who was dead against my smoking, I used to travel with a vast amount of boxes, each containing 100 nicotine-free cigarettes, available only in Germany.

"During a Scandinavian tour, when playing in Stockholm, I left one of the boxes in the artist's dressing room handy for between numbers. This particular box happened to be almost completely full. Thus I had moved on to another city before I arrived at the last layer of cigarettes. There I found a note: 'Among all the pianists of the world, there are but two real artists — Artur Rubinstein and Lili Kraus.' Signed: 'The backstage hand.' I was deeply moved, needless to say.

"Upon my return appearance, a year later, I found the dear man and thanked him warmly. 'Good, good,' he said smiling. 'So you found my note.'

"What brought you to this conclusion?" I asked. "Why did your choice fall on Rubinstein and me?"

'Because both you and he told in your music, through your piano, of sadness and happiness, of hope and fear,' he said. 'Both of you made me believe that you were speaking to me, personally. So I felt ever so grateful.'"

6. Sonata in A Minor, K. 310

(Allegro maestoso)

Lili Kraus began by asking the student if he knew when, how, and why Mozart had composed this "terrific piece". "I am not stipulating that you have to know the background to play it well," she said. "But, in this case, the background is interesting to know.

"Although he usually traveled with his father, in 1778 Mozart traveled to Paris with his mother. A few weeks after their arrival, his mother became ill and died, leaving him, at 22, alone, and without real friends.

"Besides having to bear his grief, he had the terrible obligation of breaking the news to his family. In some inexplicable way he was able to express his grief in this sonata. The Allegro Maestoso is like an epitaph, full of sorrow, dignified and ennobled by the strict form. The second movement is perhaps the memory of the peace and happiness his mother had given him — except in the middle section where his relentless pain returns. And the last movement somehow is his acceptance of life — childlike, innocent, yet haunted — the only change of mood being the middle A major section where, in a clearing in the clouds, he can see and hear the angels playing a little musette to his mother.

"This is all my fancy. But Mozart did compose only two sonatas in minor: this one and the C minor. And when he sent his report to his family, it was almost matter of fact. He had put his grief and loss into this sonata."

Tempo

"Because of the circumstances surrounding its composition and the Allegro maestoso indication — a marking which Mozart uses only this one time in the sonatas — the tempo shouldn't be really fast. If the tempo is too fast, the piece loses its true character — and it is the character that is *au point* — the rhythm being ▬ ▬ ▬ ▬

♪♪♪♪ ♪♪♪♪ and not ♪♪♪♪ ♪♪♪♪

Tempo is an elusive thing: the impression it gives results not only from how fast you play metronomically, but also from the image you have, or what you feel."

Economy of Means

"The tempo is one important thing to consider; the compositional economy of means is another. Lesser composers have to use a much bigger palette than does Mozart, who composed with unbelievable economy and sparsity.

"For example, in the second statement of the first theme, there is that added F in the bass chord, whereas in the first statement there is just the E. And this F, a very simple device to intensify, marks a heightened happening. Such a detail is for us and the Lord to know. You don't have to shout it out, but you know it. Saint-Saëns and others, in their editions of this sonata, have omitted this F both here and in the reprise, apparently finding the F too jarring, or shocking!"

M. 1. "It is for you to decide whether to play the opening grace note fast or slow (the grace note in measure two *is* written out with two eighth notes in measure 10.). Contrary to general belief, Mozart was meticulous in writing his indications. However, whether you play a short or a long grace note, in no case should you play the first two notes together. There must be two distinct notes. And one impulse of the hand will not produce two sounds; you have to make two movements, best twice down.

"The whole thing lives and dies according to the way you play the left hand. Don't just play the chord but illuminate the bottom A. To do this, keep the hand firm, in contact with the keys, using the arm from the shoulder."

M. 2. "Which do you want to emphasize, the A or the G-sharp? The A, of course. Nevertheless, the G-sharps should not be too soft."

Ms. 3-4 "Keep the opening four measures all in forte. Any decrescendo you might make should still remain in the domain of the forte. There should be no relaxation in tone between measures three and four. Mozart begins the sonata *appassionata;* the second phrase is the same sentence, the running sixteenth notes in measure three taking care of the difference between the phrases."

What the Music Does for You

"If you are a real musician, you have no reason to be afraid that the music will be boring. If you want to change the thing you said, you might emphasize more expression, or if you are afraid of what you said, you might be quieter. But without qualms, you can also say it the same way twice and even three times.

"But, if you have to plan, it is too late. If, when repeating the exposition for example, you do something differently on the spur of the moment, all right. But don't will changes. Try to understand what the music does for you, not what you do for the music."

"If you give music its due, it does everything. You must investigate, check, and really try to penetrate to the core the matter. And then whether or not you vary the repetition of a phrase becomes secondary. It is possible to do something different but unnecessary. In fact, doing something different is almost detrimental. What you do depends upon your imagination, your insight, your dexterity, your inspiration, your instrument—and first and last, upon the musical context of the work."

M. 5. "The second note of the first two right-hand notes should not be heavy. To make the legato, release the bottom C of the first double third earlier than you do the top note.

"The left-hand phrase, staccato in contrast to the right-hand legato, ends the whole sentence. Play it with conviction—not too heavy and not too light—with no accent on the final A. The difference between a "forte" and a "piano" on a Mozart piano is not great, the forte meaning not piano, the piano meaning not forte, as well as the million shades in between."

Ms. 6-7. "In the right hand, make exactly the same movement for each note. You have time to use the arm, or you could use the wrist. One is as good as the other. But above all, use a firm finger and always the same movement to ensure absolute regularity of rhythm."

"The left-hand third-beat resolutions must be soft, the notes held exactly as written. This is terribly important."

M. 8. "Just finish the sentence. For expressive reasons, here the second-beat chord should have the weight. That is why Mozart starts the slur on this chord—a rare case and not my fancy. You must never take anything for granted. Double check; then you will discover these surprises."

M. 12. "I play soft here, not because I want to play it beautifully but because it went to the major, making peace, mellowing into consolation—for the time being at least."

M. 20. "The forte, which I pretend, sounds loud but isn't. In the left hand I play,

not the obvious

Don't play the octave G too soon; be rhythmical."

M. 22. "Don't end too loud—Mozart was young; he was slim."

M. 23. "And now comes a different group of instruments."

Ms. 28-29. "The left hand is contrapuntal, beautiful and sensitive, but it is not the melody. The right hand must run along like clear water—crystalline, bodyless. Leaving out the garlands, it has the same notes as the left hand."

Know the Whole Piece

"It is impossible to get the message of the whole work, if you know only one movement. Can you imagine that you know a Shakespeare drama, knowing only the first act? A sonata is one organic whole. For instance, it would have been impossible for you to conclude this first movement, playing the last three chords slowly, almost diminuendo, if you had had the whole sonata in your head. If you had had the whole sonata in your head, you would have played:

"I can't understand performers who finish such a movement as this and remove their handkerchief from their pocket to wipe their brow before going on. I can't move, because my whole being is filled by the modulation from this A minor to the F major of the next movement: the magic transition from tragic minor to redeemed major.

"Mozart's genius was such that not only had he one work completely composed in his head, but he had another one ready to tumble out too. He made the statement that he had every note of an opera composed simultaneously in his mind. Consequently, when writing out the opera's parts, he had to ask his wife to read him fairy tales, because his next opera—already in his head, waiting to be committed to paper—disturbed him in writing down the opera at hand.

"If Mozart had in his head not only the opera he was composing, from first to last note, but also another opera wanting to come out, the least you can do when you study a sonata is to know the whole work.

"You American music majors, having to carry a full curriculum besides your music courses, have such limited time, I find it a miracle that you can perform as you do. Nevertheless, I would have been happy to have heard at least one slow movement. First and last movements are, so to speak, the strong wings of a bird, carrying the glowing heart of the sonata, the second movement. The second movement is the core and great test of a composer and—boy!—does it ever show up what kind of a performer you are."

The six lessons were over. Amidst the long, loud applause, the last pupil shook hands with *Maestra* Lili Kraus. Raised to a pitch of enthusiasm and excitement, the whole auditorium of teachers and students from the United States and Canada had learned enough to think about for a very long time. For Lili Kraus inspires you to make Mozart live.

സസസ്ര

MASTER CLASS

Lili Kraus offers a lesson on Mozart's Sonata in C minor, K. 457, first movement (printed on pages 204 and 205).

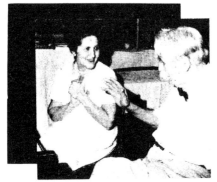

Kraus and Schweitzer: mutual admiration

I can't conceive of playing this Sonata without the preceding Fantasy. What is the mood of the Molto Allegro movement? What do you imagine when you start out with the first theme? It's a tragic piece, isn't it? This Sonata, the preceding Fantasy, and Beethoven's Pathetique Sonata are in the same C minor world. So much so, that there are literal quotations, either conscious or unconscious, in these works. The opening of the Sonata, the Fantasy, and the Beethoven Pathetique are similar in notes and mood:

The second phrase of the Fantasy and the ending notes of the Pathetique's first phrase are similar:

Now what is the meaning of these phrases? To my mind, it is someone bearing the will of life, succumbing to and then surmounting it.

As you play the opening of the Sonata, you must be filled with the experience that must have compelled Mozart to write it down. Try to imagine a high, stark, tragic tension, not overdone, not *fortissimo*. The Sonata's opening mood comes from the complete resignation of the preceding two eighth-notes and the passionate outburst of the Fantasy's final run:

The first measure of the Sonata continues from the ending run of the Fantasy, and the first octave is the reason for the resulting continuation.

Bars 1-2. Play the opening octave firmly and *forte* with guts from above the key. It's a tragic dead-decided theme, and the first note has to have guts. Play every quarter note an equal *forte* with no *dimenuendo*, the last note prolonged, accentuated, or pedaled. The trill figure introduces something new.

Bars 3-4. Don't crescendo the C's; the C harmony resolves to the following diminshed harmony.

Bars 5-6. On a Mozart piano there is not a big difference between *forte* and *piano*. Don't waste all your attention on the trill, but aim for the F in bar 7 which resolves on the G of bar 8. In playing the trill keep the wrist relaxed and stay into the key on the final D of the afternotes. The wrist is down for the trill and afternotes, rebounding for the new sound of the F.

Bars 7-8. Don't change fingers on the repeated B's. If you play F B B B with 4 2 1 1, the stretch and finger-change is an unnecessary difficulty. Always use the most natural fingering possible. If you use 4 on the F, take the easiest and most natural finger that falls on the B, the thumb.

How do you memorize? You figure out what the harmonies are doing and know the sequences. Here you have to know the resolving sequences of

bars 3-4 and 7-8. You have to know them consciously but forget them when you play.

Bars 9-11. Bring out both the alto and soprano lines *piano* and *diminuendo*.

Bar 13. The diminished chord on the fourth beat should be *forte*, resolving to the C Minor chord in bar 14. Here is the harmonic movement of these measures:

Do you or do you not use pedal? What do you mean, "Use it every now and then to connect?" Look what happens when I lift the dampers, playing the notes with cluster technique. The strings sound on and on into each other. The damper pedal was invented to separate the sound. With the two unconnected pedals on Mozart's piano the harmonies in the left hand didn't interfere with the right-hand melody. Because we don't have this pedal arrangement today, you must overlap the notes of say an Alberti bass in slow movement by using finger pedal.

Bars 18-19. Breathe before the return of the first theme. This is indicated in the score by the left-hand G resolving in the treble, not the bass. Use full tone every time the opening theme is repeated.

Bar 23. What is music's outstanding, essential glory? Is it not that as in life the moods or events change with lightning speed? This new E♭ theme is something completely new. Stick to the old rule that the left hand must be in time like a metronome, but within that beat you have freedom. No one can detect if you prolong the bass B♭ long enough for the right-hand thirty-second notes to be unhurried.

Bars 30-34. The repeated three-note motive is like a question and answer of affirmation. By repeating the notes Mozart is reinforcing this answer.

Bar 36. Sing sweetly. For the first time the music is definitely major.

Bar 57. When it mellows into major, such a chord is the turning point.

Bars 59-60. The slur starts on the E♭, indicating the first note not the second gets a slight emphasis.

Bar 63. Every book about trills, whether it's by Leopold Mozart, Emanuel Bach, or whomever, ends by saying: "All these rules are subject to the taste and judgment of the performer." So start the trills on the note.

Bar 66. One word about cadences such as this one: classical music is cadence-conditioned. Nearly every phrase ends with a cadence.

SONATE

Therese von Trattnern gewidmet

Komponiert in Wien wahrscheinlich 1784

Köchel-Verz. 457

Allegro molto*)

*) Nach der Erstausgabe; in der Abschrift (siehe Vorwort) nur *Allegro.*

**) Takte 1–6: Staccato-Zeichen nach A.; späterhin in den Vorlagen unregelmäßig.

***) Der Bogen von *as²–as²* in T. 13/14, 15/16, 112/113, 114/115 nur in Erstausg., nicht in A.

*) According to the first edition; in the copy (see Preface) only *Allegro.*

**) Bars 1–6: staccato marks according to C.; irregular later on in the sources.

***) The slur from *ab²* to *ab²* in bars 13/14, 15/16, 112/113, 114/115 found only in 1st ed.; not in C.

*) D'après la première édition; dans la copie (voir Préface) seulement *Allegro.*

**) Mesures 1–6: signes de staccato d'après C.; plus tard dans les pièces documentaires irréguliers.

***) L'arc de *lab²* à *lab²* dans mes. 13/14, 15/16, 112/113, 114/115, seulement dans la 1re édition, pas dans C.

*) Nach A.; in Erstausg. hier: T. 68:   *) Acc. to C.: in 1st ed. here   B. 68:   *) D'apr. C.; dans 1re éd. ici: Mes. 68:

MASTER CLASS

with WALTER KLIEN

interview August 9, 1976

Walter Klien offers a lesson here on Schubert's posthumous Sonata in B♭, D. 960, first movement

The main problem in this movement is to find one basic tempo with which to express all the things that are written. Fluctuations in tempo should be intuitive and dictated by the music's message and logical flow. You mustn't break between sections and themes, nor should different themes or sections sound like a new tempo. Some of the cantabile of the opening should permeate the entire movement.

Bar 1. Take time before you begin. It comes from another world. You sit down and begin to improvise in one long line. Try to play the opening with wonder, a real *pianissimo, molto moderato.*

Never play two notes the same. The upbeat should not be louder than the second B♭. If you sing it, you will emphasize the second B♭.

Bars 2-3. Don't emphasize the two eighth notes. Take your time; integrate them into the long phrase.

Bars 3-4. Play the alto quarter notes in bar 4 softly. For me, the line is C, C, C, B♭, A/B♭ sustained; the alto notes are subsidiary.

Bars 4-5. Crescendo from the B♭ to the soprano E .

Bars 8-9. Play the trill like a question and then wait a long time.

Bars 10-18. In this second statement of the first phrase, you can move the phrase more. It must be a little louder. (In the Reprise, you will probably color and voice it a little differently than you do here.)

Bars 14-15. Crescendo in the two eighth notes to the following Eb and take your time on the two soprano eighth notes. Sing all the voices. Bring out the soprano line C, B, Eb, D, C and then the bass line G, Gb, F. The bass line mustn't be louder than the soprano, but don't forget it's there.

Bars 16-18. Play this phrase softer than the preceding two-measure phrase. This time don't crescendo on the eighth notes. It's monotonous if you do it twice the same way. Here this phrase can be a little slower, like an improvisation. Diminuendo and take time on the final resolution in bar 18, playing the Bb *pianissimo.*

Bars 19-20. Play the bass trill *pianissimo, mysterioso.* The harmony of bar 20 is a surprise, the change a major third down, from Bb to Gb.

Bar 27. Don't start new here; it's a continuation of the preceding. Keep the same legato, the left hand *ppp.*

Bar 29. The right-hand sixteenth notes should not be mechanical. Try to sing them; they're a variation of two measures before. Keep them *sempre pp.*

Bar 34. Don't start the crescendo before it is marked.

Bars 36-45. You mustn't finish. It is always continuing. *Unendlich,* we say in German. This time the phrase in measures 42-45 gets louder to the whole-note chord of bar 44 which resolves softly to bar 45. You must show this sudden change of harmony. Hesitate.

Bars 46-47. Although this crescendo is rather harsh, don't start it before it is marked.

Bar 48. Play the right-hand thirds clingingly soft, with pedal, but not fast or mechanically.

Bars 49-53. Phrase the viola-like tenor melody with crescendo and diminuendo in one long line. That is, continue in bar 51 through bar 52, bringing out the tenor melody above the other parts. Resolve the D in bar 53 softly to the C#. In the next five measures, the repetition of this phrase, you can bring out some of the soprano, too.

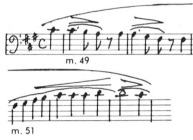

Bar 59. Keep the cantabile mood. Don't get too excited too quickly.

Bars 66-67. Keep the crescendo to the end of the bar. Then play *subito piano* in bar 67.

Bar 68. Play the right-hand grace notes and sixteenth notes clearly, without pedal. Use overlapping finger legato in the left hand as in Mozart where one needs it so often. Bring out the bass line a little.

Bar 73. Use the same overlapping finger legato, etching the descending bass line. You don't need pedal at all.

Bar 80. Again, don't start a new piece here at the second theme. It's a continuation of the triplets in the preceding measure which come out of the half-note chord. It's a cantabile mood from the beginning. It doesn't go *prestissimo*.

Bars 93-97. Often in the last works of Schubert, the music stops suddenly. You should slow down in these measures. You have the feeling the heart has stopped in these rests.

Bar 101. I would use pedal through the portato chords. I wouldn't play them short without pedal.

Bar 102. Take your time. The eighth notes should be played like a sung phrase, not etude-like.

Bars 106-109. Phrase in one long line. Pedal through the eighth rests.

Bar 117 et al (first ending). Accent the first of the two notes, not the second, playing each two-note slur short. Take your time on the *fortissimo* in the seventh measure.

Bar 118 (not counting the first ending). Play this as simply as possible, without any rubato. Play the upbeat E softer than the second E. Overlap the left hand, *legatissimo*.

Bar 120. Take your time for this phrase. It's very sad.

Bar 131 et al. Again this section should come out of the preceding; it should not sound like a new tempo. If you play it too fast, it has no relationship to what preceded and to the rest of the movement. Even in the first two slurred right-hand eighth notes, there should be some cantabile and not much pedal. I would point out the left-hand melody in measures 131 and 132 (in bar 151 it comes in the right hand) and the right-hand melody in measures 133 and 134 (with crescendo and diminuendo).

Bars 148-149. Continue the bass line, bringing it out to the *fortissimo.* Take your time for the decrescendo.

Bar 151. Don't observe much rest in the right-hand eighth rests.

Bar 153. Bring out the upper left-hand voice, the E♭, A♭, B♭♭/A♭.

Bars 157-158. Take your time for this important modulation. The top left-hand voice — F♯, B, C/B — is important.

Bar 173. Don't start a new tempo at this D minor section, but continue the tempo from the preceding *fortissimo.*

Bars 178-179. Show the change of harmony on the last beat of bar 178 with *poco ritardando* and *a tempo* in bar 179.

Bars 180-184. Observe the eighth rests a little, as a string quartet would, throughout this half-note-two-eighth-notes-with-rests theme. Use just a little pedal.

Bars 186-187. Continue the right-hand repeated chords into the left hand, so you don't hear any change.

Bars 188, 194, 200. The first time this phrase is *pp,* the second time *ppp,* the third time *piano.* Make these distinctions.

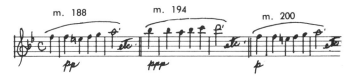

Bar 198. Here, the third time you have the left-hand trill, there is a crescendo.

Bars 202-208. At the *fp,* you begin an important modulation back to B♭ which should be shown. Continue the line of the left-hand chords from the F⁷ chord to the diminished chord of bar 206, resolving to the F⁷ chord in bar 208.

Bars 210-211. Play the run coming down before the Reprise with ritard, not as fast triplets.

Bar 215. Wait a long time at the fermata before the Reprise.

Bars 216 et al. In the second eight-measure phrase of the Reprise of the opening theme, you can add vibrations to the bottom of the right hand as color, but not so the listener thinks the soprano is overpowered by the alto.

Bars 239-240. It's different here from the Exposition. The modulation to F♯ minor must come out, it's violence. Again bring out the ascending right hand A, G♯, A, B/C♯ and then the bass voice F♯, G♯, A.

Bar 254. Show strongly the modulation from the A⁷ to the B♭ chords.

Bars 246-253. Remain *sempre pp* until the last two measures before the *forte* statement of the theme.

Adele Marcus — Workshop Virtuosa

interview 1973, 1974

Former prize-winning pupils of Adele Marcus, distinguished member of the Juilliard faculty, have included Agustin Anievas, Horacio Gutierrez, Byron Janis, Robert Chumbly, Tedd Joselson, Norman Krieger, Panayis Lyras, Ken Noda, Peter Orth, Pamela Paul, Santiago Rodriguez, and Jeffrey Swann.

"Peter says he's so thirsty he can't even spit!"

Adele Marcus, that prodigal producer of contest winners and eminent young artists, is giving a masterclass. Peter Orth, one of her gifted Juilliard students, has excitingly ripped through the Barber Sonata's fourth-movement *Fuga*. Another master teacher might have torn such a high-tensioned, hell-bent-for-leather performance to shreds. But not Adele Marcus.

"You had a good time and that's important," she says. "When you feel in the mood to break the piano in pieces and you are convincing, then the effect is good. I love to see someone so involved that he wants to snap all the ivories off the keys.

Yes, Adele Marcus tries not to inhibit her students. On the contrary, she tries to realize the great importance and effectiveness of positive criticism, taking enormous pains to praise the honest reactions of her pupils to the music they play. She acknowledges the validity of much of what they do, encouraging them to experiment, tactfully guiding them to reactions and conclusions which no doubt they would come to themselves one day.

No two master teachers emphasize exactly the same things. I would say she stresses personality, projection, individuality, long line, tone, and general mood. Hers is a Romantic virtuoso approach — "I like to see virtuoso blood in my pupils' veins," she says, stemming in part from her warm qualities as a person and performer, as well as from her Russian ancestry, her training with Josef Lhevinne, and her friendship with such musicians as Vladimir Horowitz.

She tries to get her students to take flight, often beginning with remarks such as "I liked your feeling. I liked your spontaneity." She is motherly, an extrovert. One pupil, who feels she has a real friend in

211

With her student Agustin Anievas, Spring 1962.

Miss Marcus, told me "If I have a problem I can telephone her even in the middle of the night." To be sure, such talented people as this Juilliard brood need and deserve careful shepherding and encouraging pats on the back. But Adele Marcus, far more than usual, freely bestows approving hugs, compliments, and urgings on.

In workshop sessions, she is a virtuosa. Stepping onstage before a large audience, she skillfully creates vitality and excitement as she expresses cogent ideas about the music to be played.

What are her ideas? How does she teach? In interview form I am condensing some of her lectures and masterclasses.

WORKSHOP LECTURES

Miss Marcus, what is the benefit of masterclasses for students?

I consider masterclasses the halfway mark between the studio and the concert stage. In the studio lesson, the student is accustomed to his teacher and plays in a more or less relaxed atmosphere. In the masterclass, he has an opportunity to play under a certain amount of the tension that an audience affords. At the same time, there isn't the demand for the supreme accuracy of the concert stage.

In the masterclass, furthermore, there is the advantage of an objective and hopefully friendly pair of ears hearing the student for the first time. There is also the possible benefit of a few constructive comments.

Students will remember things told them in a masterclass, which their own teachers have been trying to tell them for years. And as far as being unnerved at playing for a masterclass — that's the least problem. Incidentally, being unnerved reminds me of the story of Godowsky and Hofmann at a famous colleague's London recital. As the colleague was having memory trouble, Hofmann turned to Godowsky and exclaimed, "My God, isn't it terrible what he forgot!" "No," replied Godowsky. "It's much worse what he remembered!" So, never worry about what you forgot.

What do you include in your teaching of musicianship?

Musicianship for me, in the main, means reasoning. We have to reason everything from the cover on the music to everything on the printed sheet.

The Talmud says, "If you want to understand the invisible, study carefully the visible." The invisible things are the infinite varieties of emotions and feelings elicited by musical sounds. The visible things are the symbols and special words used in writing music. If we are to convey a composer's intentions, we must study carefully what he has written down.

Anything indicated in the music can be learned more or less, if we are intelligent and willing to think. But in my view, study must go deeper. Behind the thinking there must be that element of the invisible which is feeling or else the result is dry dust. There must be an emotional response to these musical symbols to bring them to life.

What do you mean by an "emotional response"?

Sometimes a pupil will come to a lesson and painfully illustrate his lack of emotional response. I may have awakened that morning with a splitting headache but suddenly I'm alert. "Please," I will say, "bring me two pages of music. I don't care what you read into them, but don't bring me just notes." Syllables must create a word. Words must relate to a sentence. A sentence must relate to an idea, and the idea must permeate the piece you are playing. Innate emotional response is a vital element of creative musicianship.

How can teachers stimulate an emotional response?

You can't say "Feel something!" anymore than you can say, "Love me!" But you can say, for example, "Dance a gavotte!" You can open the way imaginatively to what you, the teacher, feel about the music. Consequently, it is advantageous to study with someone alive rather than to depend on recordings. If someone says, "This artist does it this way on his recording, this one does it that say," I say it is cheaper to study with RCA Victor, Columbia, or Deutsche Grammophon.

Cicero said, "You have to tell someone in three different ways how to do something." I found you have to tell children — whom I taught exclusively for ten years — in 133 different ways. I would say something to a student, and the next week he would show there had been no response. Then, because during those years I had infinite patience, I'd try something else.

Because I feel all music must either sing or speak, I usually ask someone to sing a slow piece of music. I ask him to sing inside, letting it come out somehow or other. If a student says, "I never sing when I play," I'm wary of that student. I cannot imagine not wanting to sing when you have a marvelous theme such as a recitative in a Bach Toccata or a Haydn slow movement. It is important to feel that you are related to the music from the inside out.

We teachers walk around with our Geiger counters, trying to bring out the bits of uranium we see or feel here and there. But we can't guarantee total transformation. Emotional response requires living. Maybe the piano stands in front of the student like eighty-eight big black-and-white teeth ready to gobble him up the minute he sits down. The student shouldn't be afraid of his instrument. He should feel it is his friend.

212

What else does musicianship include?

Musicianship also includes knowledge and understanding of the various styles. As musicians we have to understand something about the periods in which Galuppi, Scarlatti, Mozart, Beethoven, or Brahms lived. We know that in the time of Mozart, the student didn't greet the teacher with "Hi!" He would curtsy or bow. There was respect for the older person. People wore powdered wigs, satins, and ruffles. It was an age of decorum and elegance. The characteristics, the style, of the age are revealed in the music. When Mozart writes

there is a phrase feeling — like an elegant, refined curtsy. If I can't get someone to do a two-note slur properly I say, "Get up and curtsy. Do 'tee-dum' like that!"

Do you use musicological sources to aid the understanding of style?

If we want to substantiate what we think and feel about the music, it is good to go to musicological sources. But musicological sources do not tell us how to react to the score. If we are lacking in innate stylistic responses, musicology won't help. Music is an aural language. It is our "hearing" that summons in us the answer to the composer's intentions.

Do you consider musicianship the basis of interpretation?

Yes, and musicianship includes the realization that interpretation is the end goal of performance. We sometimes get so hung-up that we try to isolate technique from interpretation.

When I was nineteen and played for Walter Gieseking, he said, "There is no difference between technique and interpretation." It took me twenty years to understand that he meant that technique, in the larger sense, is inseparably related to interpretation and to musicianship. Technique is the "how" of everything we do — how we draw sound out of the instrument, how we draw sound out of the instrument, how we work through a piece with conviction and authority.

But many students — and even performing artists —arrive at an interpretation according to their technical limitations.

I don't believe in that. I believe that — no matter what age you are or what stage you are at — if you envisage in your mind's eye, your heart, your psyche, or your whole being something about a piece of music, you will have to find the way to realize what you want to do. Interpretation is what we feel about the music, what we choose to reveal.

If Rubinstein, Horowitz, Gilels, Serkin, or Richter all play the same Beethoven sonata, they will all sound different because of their individual metabolism, hearing, tactile approach, and mechanics. Their projection of themselves through the music will be different. Another interesting thing you will find among these great pianists is that they play most the music which reveals them felicitously. They play the music in which they have the most authenticity and conviction.

My own teacher, Josef Lhevinne, for instance, was a fantastic pianist whose imagination lay primiarily in the hues he could achieve in "pianistic" things. And there's nothing wrong in that. I'm sure he admired tremendously much music that he did not play publicly. But he knew that he could reveal himself as a great artist in the music he did play. "Knowing thyself" is very important.

Do you put your students through a thorough technical training?

Yes, I do. But when someone comes in for an audition and says, "I don't have enough technique," not having enough technique is not the problem. The problem is not having enough insight, not only insight concerning the score but insight concerning the human being. If we don't have a musically logical reasoning behind everything we do, our interpretations usually become a series of isolated fragments rather than a structure with root feeling.

Does practicing scales have anything to do with an interpretative concept?

I believe in practicing scales in every conceivable form for strengthening the fingers just as the dancer gets up to the stretching bar and stretches even though he has danced miraculously the night before. A technical regimen is part of continuously building the resilience of the muscles.

On the other hand, working endlessly at scales has little to do with music unless you are simultaneously developing listening power for evenness of touch, tempo, pulse, et cetera. If the student sits there, preoccupied with what he is going to have for lunch or whatever, then a daily technical regime will be almost useless.

You have to know what you want to achieve from working on scales. It took me years to understand that you shouldn't keep repeating without comprehension. Thoughtless repetition stifles your imagination, your whole creative output. Keep asking yourself, "Why?...What do I want out of this?...I want to play it more evenly...I want to play a faster tempo and be able to control both hands." Then when you come to a unison scale passage in a Beethoven sonata, you have already had that feeling. Your previous technical work has had an interpretative end.

Many people say that you only have to practice pieces. When I use this technique-in-pieces approach, I find that students isolate passages, making exercises out of them, to the extent that when they get to these passages in the pieces, they play them like exercises. I say: don't use music as an exercise.

I've had students come to me who couldn't play eight notes evenly and say, "I think I should work on the Chopin Etudes to develop my technique." Such an approach is preposterous. One should lead up to the study of the Chopin Etudes. Much of the required endurance should already have been developed before you play the "Winter Winds" Etude, for example. The Chopin Etudes are monuments in the piano literature not only for showing how fast and clean you can play, but also for showing what each etude generates insofar as its mood and character are concerned. To be able to play the "Double Thirds" Etude with the lightness, grace, and clarity of a Josef Lhevinne takes many years.

It takes tremendous judgment on our parts as teachers to know when to say no. Today many students at age sixteen play Opus 111. When I was young, we were told we couldn't play Opus 111 because we didn't have sufficient background and maturity, even though our instincts may have been good. One of the difficulties today is that young people are in an awful hurry. But so is everyone and everything; we are living in a fast age. The art of getting out of the instrument what you want to say and how and why you want to say it, is gradually becoming a lost one.

Much of the music we hear today does not require that art. But, on the other hand, when an artist comes along and plays that very music with exceptional craft, we ask "Why does it sound so fantastic?"

So there is value in thorough scale practice when related to musical upbringing and training. How much technical training you want depends upon the standard you set for yourself. If you feel your playing is good enough for now, you have a sense of security. People who are never satisfied can develop insecurities. But often the great artist develops from mastering his insecurities, from aiming for the highest result.

First and foremost, one has to feel that there is the possibility for high achievement. I have a fantastic group of youngsters studying with me, and I believe in most of them with my whole heart. But I often wonder how long they will sustain their desire for a really high standard without wanting to cash in on the immediate result. And in a way I don't blame them, knowing the age in which we live.

What about the changes in a student's interpretation a different stages of his development?

Often, when we restudy a work we have played a long time, we say there must be a fresh response. Not necessarily. You can't recapture an exact mood. Change in interpretation is comparable to your changing reactions in walking around a mountain. You study a work. You start here, you have an impression of it and feel you want to perform it in a certain way. Then you walk a little farther and you have two impressions. As you go around the mountain, you gather different impressions just as you do in life. Then when you arrive at the summit, you look back at these different views that have permeated your thinking and feeling about an interpretation. And as you get older, you may want to go back to your initial impression.

When we are young, we are simple. As we go through the gamut of emotions and gather experiences, ideas, and philosophy, we have possibly true simplicity. We understand the simplicity of Mozart, for example, which has every emotion in it. Yet there is a simplicity of style that is appealing to the young as well as to the old. This is real simplicity. And often we can't recapture that simple, unknowing kind of interpretative response that we had when we were young.

When we are older, the ingredients that make up our interpretation are more complicated than they were before. We don't change our responses, our responses are spontaneous, but we may change the evaluation and the projection of our responses. And

it is because of this continuous change that great music has lived.

What do you mean by your expression "sound in tempo"?

Something loud or excited tends to sound faster than something soft. Therefore, we can play a loud passage slower. And, unless our sound has an unusual carrying quality, we can play a soft passage or a slow movement faster. The singer with a small voice — because of the lack of carrying quality — can sing faster, whereas the singer with a big voice — because of the carrying quality — can sing slower.

Sometimes a student will play a new piece for me with insufficient body of sound and I will say "That's too slow. There is no life in it." Then at the next lesson he will play it much louder and I will say "That's too fast." And, looking at me as if to say I don't know what I'm talking about, he will protest that last week I said it was too slow. We change; we don't always hear the same way. Pianos and acoustics change what we hear.

When a piece is new, you may love it so much you "lolligag" over every note. You've just got to get this emotion out of your system or you are going to die. You think your way of the moment is the way it has to go. Later you may arrive at that point again but with a different quality and feeling, with different nuances.

To illustrate another aspect of "sound in tempo" let's take the finale of the Schumann *Symphonic Etudes*. We have a simple pattern, all in chords. The chords are *forte* and can be approached keyboardwise in a specific way. In order to create the necessary effect without hardness, you emphasize the upper voice, keeping the inner parts of the chords lighter. Played this way, the chords move and sound more transparent. Now as you want to become more intense, you bring in all the harmonies. You will not be playing very much louder, but the effect will be much more sonorous. You will not beat the tar out of the piano nor will you make it sound like wood.

What do you think of continual metronome use?

I think it's deadly, although the metronome is valuable to help set and to maintain a tempo.

It takes imagination to use the metronome creatively. Instead of using a metronome for Mozart practice, I would recommend listening for evenness, for example. I would encourage the pupil to conduct the tempo. Tying a metronome around your neck is not going to give you rhythm and control, which should come from the inside, not the outside.

How do you work with students to establish a tempo, besides having them conduct?

Students have difficulty not only in establishing a

Adele Marcus at her debut recital — a Friday morning musical club appearance — when she was eleven years old and had been studying just under four years.

tempo as indicated in a good edition, but also in maintaining and sustaining this tempo. I try to make students aware that a Mozart Allegro, for instance, written mostly in eighths, will feel slower than an Allegro written in sixteenths. Mozart, by writing in eighths, tells us the tempo is not the fastest Allegro tempo. Furthermore, tempo has to come from a certain pulse. Tempo can't be just a matter of too fast or too slow.

Looking at the thematic material is another way to establish the tempo. If a piece is marked 4/4, do you feel it in two beats even if it isn't marked *alla breve* because of the nature of the melodic material? The opening of Beethoven's Opus 81a is marked *Adagio*, in quarters. But any conductor would conduct it in eighths, not quarters. Then when you get to the next section marked *Allegro*, you can still feel the tempo in eighths. The Allegro won't come like a blast to the nearest subway exit!

It is good for students to work through the seven Toccatas of Bach, correlating the tempos of the various parts — the freedom of form that includes contrapuntal writing, small overtures, ariosos, recitatives and so on.

Then, too, there are acoustic considerations to take into account in setting a tempo. But in short, the right mood will make the right tempo, providing there is a phrase, not a note-to-note or measure-to-measure feeling.

How can we get students to listen to themselves?

The secret of it all! The piano doesn't lend itself to self-listening. When the pianist strikes a key, the sound emanates about three feet away. Therefore, many students feel that once they have struck the note, it's finished. They are not listening.

Listening first entails wanting something out of and giving something to the music. Concentrating on the projection of feeling is as important as all the memorizing and the learning of the notes.

Students are listening to their feelings more than they used to. But they listen to what they feel, not what they hear. They say, "I feel it, I'm dying, I'm torn, I'm this, and I'm that." I say, "Why don't you make *me* feel it? I want to feel it, too."

To make the listener feel what you want to project requires listening. You have to feel strongly enough so you can mold and shape. Sound is as malleable as paint or clay; and if you can't mold sound, you are not going to get the other person to feel what you feel. In addition, you have to feel thirty times more than the other person is going to fell.

Have your pupil sing the phrase. Even if his singing is not on pitch, singing will help get something from the inside out, to get the shape of the phrase. Start with simple things in developing listening ability — scales, a simple melodic line, the posthumous E Minor Nocturne of Chopin, and so on. After simple things, if you are much more advanced, a good tape recroder will help you listen to many aspects of your performance — proportions, tempos, whether there's too much of this or that.

Being aware of inner voices also helps develop listening ability. Some artist once said "When you are young you play like a virtuoso, when you are middle-aged you play like a musician, and when you are older you begin to look for the inner voice."

Would you discuss projection, which is closely connected to listening?

The first thing to realize after you have played a note is that the sound has already left into some kind of outer space. That outer space may be a 12 x 10 studio, a studio such as I have at the Juilliard, which can easily seat 100 or 140 people, or it can be an auditorium. But wherever you are playing, you have to project something real, something which has had to go on in your metabolism, thinking, hearing, feeling, and doing. In other words, what you feel sincerely must somehow or other project itself, so that it reaches out. You send forth from yourself through an instrument.

Another invaluable kind of projection results from drawing your audience to you. I've always been fascinated not only with books but with people who read books. I once walked into a library where there was an unusually hushed feeling. Everyone walked on tiptoes and spoke in whispers. I saw everyone immersed in a book. I liked the atmosphere. What happened? I was drawn to each and every person in that room. Why? Because of their total absorption.

These people attracted me to them, not because they were reaching out to me but because they were deeply involved in what they were doing.

So it is with performing. There are people who appear on the stage who are not in the mood to reach out, but they are in the mood of the work at hand. Their sincerity reaches you as a direct current. When there is sincere absorption, without the *sturm und drang* which you sometimes send forth, you draw your public to you. Both kinds of projection are necessary.

How can we help students to project?

I believe in telling a story about the music when students are old enough to understand. I try to have students conjure in their minds what they are trying to express. When something goes on in the imagination of a student, which reaches an inner emotional feeling, then he begins to project something comparable to music. Music is a replica of the whole gamut of emotions inside.

When I taught children who could hardly form the hand to fit the chord, or play five even notes, I tried to reach their imaginations. I would say, "What is a minuet?" If they didn't know, I danced a minuet with them so they would get the feeling of the dance. If it was a gigue, I did the best I could. Whatever it was, I didn't want them to be tied exclusively to notes.

It is no time to think about projection when you are on the stage. The development of projection must happen long before. As a student, you cannot sit at your piano and say, "Today I am going to project." You have to be motivated toward communication. You have to feel you are drawing sound out of the piano, not pushing sound into it. The sound is in the piano; the music is in you. Projection is not only a question of loudness; it is also the meaningfulness of what you feel and how sincere you are.

If a student says to me, "I have to play an audition," I think first, "How will he project his personality the most felicitously?" If he plays Bach with conviction, understanding, and personal identification, I may say, "Why don't you play the G Minor *English Suite* or the *Aria and Variations in the Italian Manner* of Bach." And he may say, "You want me to start with that?" I will say, "I want you to start with what you feel will present yourself the most convincingly." Every personality presents itself in a more complimentary light in certain areas of the vast piano literature.

Do you have ideas for developing young people's taste for great music?

We cannot expect all young people to grasp great music. But we can give them the best of our experience. Some teachers don't agree. They say, "In time this student will mature and develop on his own." In that case, why not study alone? I think it is important for a teacher to be as much of an inspiration as possible. Even if a student can only drink a little water out of a little glass, fill it to the top.

It is illuminating to watch Adele Marcus teach a class. First she tries to make each student comfortable. Once I heard her preface her lesson remarks with, "You are gifted, and you have a lot of music in you." Then she added with a laugh, "Good things first."

To give the flavor of her remarks, as well as some valuable performance advice, we have printed here the Scherzo from Schubert's Sonata in A Major and highlights of her master lesson on this piece.

See performance hints page 219.

Scherzo from Sonata D. 959

Franz Schubert

Trio
Un poco più lento

Scherzo D.C.

Performance Hints on a Schubert Sonata

by Adele Marcus   interview August 12, 1974

Throughout the lesson, Miss Marcus emphasized playing by phrases, not measure by measure. Notwithstanding that it is practical to label her comments according to the measure involved, the musical thought should not be divided into measures.

M. 1. The accented rolled first-beat chords should be played gracefully, with *Gemütlichkeit*, not with gaiety or vivaciousness. Remember that accents in Schubert, with the exception of big *sforzandi*, mean more a singing quality than sharpness. Touch the pedal a bit on the first chords, like a little violin vibrato, to give color. In other words, hold the first chord slightly, like an agogic accent, so it isn't sharp or crisp.

M. 2. Don't accent the down beat, but carry the phrase over to m. 3 where you have the same figure and feeling as in m. 1. Feel the phrase as rather round, the upbeats of m. 2 leading in feeling to the downbeat of m. 3.

Mm. 5-6. Be aware of the harmonic line in the left-hand chords. Carry the phrase on through m. 10.

Mm. 7-8. Don't poke out the B of m. 8. If you touch me lightly, I can feel it; you don't have to jab me. And play the left hand legato, not sharp. This music should be happy, graceful in Schubert's way. It's not a 'ha-ha-ha' smile. Schubert loved to sit in *Kaffee* houses. He was a homebody. There was simplicity and songfulness in the man. Remember he wrote over 600 songs. I don't mean his music is weak, precious, or sweet; but it has a certain kind of airiness.

Mm. 17-21. Again don't accent every downbeat.

Feel the first two measures in one, going on and on. It lifts up to the accents, but not sharply.

Mm. 23-34. Don't accent the G pedal points. You can play everything — the slurs, the phrasings — but the direction of the music is all of a piece.

M. 34. Be careful your *ff* chords are not Prokofieff-like. They can be strong of course.

Mm. 38-49. Don't play the left-hand chords too short, or they will be frivolous in feeling.

M. 49. This measure doesn't stop but leads on, up and over the downbeat of m. 50.

M. 80. It says *Un poco piu lento,* but it doesn't suddenly become a Chopin nocturne. Always relate a new section to what has been happening. Very singing in the inner melody, but don't be afraid of the basses. And sing the crossed-over D's so that the upper-most line has continuity with the bass. Otherwise, one hears little, unrelated happenings.

In speaking of the same Schubert Sonata's Rondo, Adele Marcus again emphasized phrasing in long lines.

Mm. 1-2. Don't let the slurs of mm. 2 and 6 chop up the longer phrase line. The very first note is almost like an upbeat. The bass half notes should sing. Schubert means to finger-pedal.

Mm. 9-12. The eighth-note pick-ups should lead to the half-note F sharp, going on in one phrase with not much separation in the phrasing in m. 10. The accents are agogic, like a little vibrato to enrich the sound, and must not be sharp or isolated from the line of the big phrase.

Rondo
Allegretto

Master Lesson--

Bach and Schumann

interview August 6, 1971

with Stephen Bishop-Kovacevich

Bach — *English Suite in A Minor*

Prelude. This kind of music must be played absolutely in time. Whatever tempo you take, stick to

it. People won't realize that the piece begins with

an upbeat if you accent the first note. Make sure the left-hand imitation in the second measure sounds clearly.

There are various ways to approach Bach: you can imitate the harpsichord, or you can forget the harpsichord, using the piano's resources, and so on. I think you should try to make the passagework slightly staccato. If, for example, the right hand is separated a bit in the third measure, the left-hand legato will show up more.

M.10: There is a temptation to play the right-hand sixteenth notes with no phrasing — it feels marvelous. But this is a kind of violin bowing. Phrase in short groups, pretending it's your bow arm. Don't

make the phrasing too short, but phrase just enough

so that it doesn't sound all run together. The violins would have to do it that way.

M.14: It should not bludgeon, but the left hand must make a clear entry.

M.36: It's in this kind of passage — after you've done something rather difficult well, and you come to something easier — that one tends to hurry. Don't run, but get a really beautiful fascination from the oscillation in the left hand. If you come down with

too much energy, you get an ugly sound. To get an attack without getting a heavy sound, some pianists — it's an ugly term — "scratch" the notes. You can dissipate the energy by sliding the finger lightly away, resulting in a very sharp sound. You'll find it won't be heavy, but it will be bright. In this kind of descending sequential passage (mm. 36-42) and later where it ascends (mm. 43-46), you have to decide if you are going to make crescendos and diminuendos or terrace dynamics.

M.55 et al: Make a little piu-meno, piu-meno in these four measures. Otherwise it sounds too much the same.

Allemande. Take your time, starting with a relaxed sixteenth-note upbeat. The tempo should not be fast, but singing. Repeat the first section, but not the second. Take a little time at the cadence that ends the first section, and certainly at the end.

It was a practice, especially in these dances, to vary the dynamics and ornamentation on the repeat. Alter the emphasis given to the voices, so that the repeat is not just an exact repetition. For example, in the Goldberg Variations, the performer should add to the composer's variations by varying the repeats. Some of the repeats of the time were quite elaborate. Provided you know what kind of ornaments were used in the period, you can choose among them.

Mm.4-5: One of the difficulties on the piano is to keep a contrapuntal line like this:

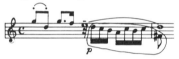

from sounding like one line:

The sixteenths should be softer, the whole-note E sustained and going to the D. There must be no confusion. At the beginning, measure one is not:

And measure two is not:

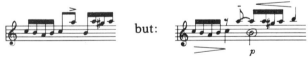

So be sure to clarify the voices.

Courante. This is a brilliant piece, so it needs a bright sound. Begin as if you own the world, head high. One of the features of a courante — and sometimes Bach's courantes are very complicated pieces — is the alternation between the part that counts in "three," and the part that counts in "two." In the first four bars, establish a good, healthy "three":

You can't surprise anybody with a "two" if you haven't established a definite three. So start with as much

rhythmic precision as you are capable of.

Knock the audience off its feet by changing to a "two" in measures five and six:

Then in measure seven, it goes back to three:

And the last measure, which again is a clash, is in two:

This clash of rhythm is what the whole dance is about. On the repeat you can do wild ornaments. It's a dance of great brio and swagger.

Sarabande. Here Bach has written out the ornaments for the repeats. This is exactly what you want; this is a model. The sarabande is very slow, the rhythm very dignified.

Schumann — *Davidsbündlertänze, Op. 6*

No.1. Lively. The first four measures are a fanfare. Even if you don't feel like it, you must throw yourself into it. Play the second little phrase louder, not softer; each little phrase gets louder. The second note of the slur isn't so important; it's the first note that is the stressed one:

M.6: When you have a figure like this, you must not use so much rubato that the ear hears a free figure and not eighth notes. The rubato should not obscure the basic rhythm.

M.42: Bring out the right hand chords when they occur with the left-hand eighth-note figure:

No.2. Heartfelt (Innig). Play the melody with an innocent, tender, intimate, singing tone, the accompaniment notes are very soft. The melody is:

M.10: Here you have a choice: some people feel that it opens up, and you therefore open up your sound; other people feel that it is enough that the major harmony replaces the minor.

An analogy can be drawn to the Beethoven G Major Concerto. I was playing it with Sir Adrian Boult conducting. When we came to the sudden F natural at the Development, I waited. He pointed out that you don't need to wait because the F natural is already so shocking at that tempo. Waiting is doing too many things, and one should just let the F sound:

Mm.17-18: I think the whole point of this Schumann piece is its coming back to the minor here. So wait a bit before the *a Tempo* after the second ending. Otherwise, you take away from the poignancy of the minor harmony.

No.3. With Humor. If you play the eighth notes too fast, there's no contrast left for the sixteenth. So, unless you can play the sixteenths like a riveting machine to make a contrast, don't anticipate that sixteenth. Play the sixteenth brilliantly and very close to the following quarter.

M.10 et al: Don't worry only about the left hand, but be sure to play the right hand as a line. Don't wait between the F sharp and D because of the left-hand jump.

M.47 et al: Don't make phrasings just for the convenience of the hand. Play one long line.

No.4. Impatient. This isn't a succession of fast, even, alternating eighth notes like something by Prokofieff. However, you don't want so much rubato that you obscure the alternating hands effect. Nor do you want the alternating hand to sound like a grace note. This is a wild, impassioned piece. Get to the sforzatos with real gusto.

M.25: Don't get a louder sound here (where the melody is in single notes and mezzo forte) than you did at the beginning, where you had octaves and forte. Maintain the tension until you get here, and then produce a contrasting mezzo forte sound.

No.11. Simply. If you are going to play something different on the repeat, such as bringing out the tenor voice, you must not make us aware that that is what you are planning to do.

M.13 et al. Although there are parts of Schumann that must sing blazingly, certain innocent and tender parts are effective only if you restrict the full sonority. People don't pay enough attention to those parts that are more inside, the really introspective side of Schumann. There is a great difference between the singing tone of Schumann and the singing tone of Brahms. Schumann requires a much more innocent sound, while Brahams needs a full sonority.

The first phrase goes down, diminuendoes, and

takes a breath; the second phrase crescendoes as

it goes up, and diminuendoes in the last measure (in the beginning too). When you hear the first four bars, remember you are going to play the next four as an answer. Don't allow any technical difficulty to cause a break in the phrase before the D.

No.18. Not fast. In the second measure, diminuendo the left-hand notes. Here again, from measure 3,

avoid a Brahmsian tone, but produce a soft, singing whisper. (Don't play the left hand staccato.) Horowitz is a pianist who understands this world of pianissimo very much. Play the next-to-last low C triple piano, and then the last low C pianissimo.

The Performer's Corner

Advice from Master Lessons

of Walter Gieseking

The Opening of Ravel's "Ondine"

Although the teachers at the Paris Conservatory taught technique almost exclusively, whereas Gieseking in his Saarbrücken master classes seldom mentioned it, I felt I learned more technique from Gieseking than I did at the Paris Conservatory. Gieseking could show in one simple movement what was incorrect, or what had to be done in the most advanced stages of technical mastery. He could show you "secrets" which produce more artistic results immediately than do more conventional physical approaches after slaving for hours.

For example, at one class a pupil who already had an excellent technique said, "I want to learn Ravel's *Ondine*. Can you give me some pointers before I start?"

"Go ahead," said Gieseking. "Start."

The pupil put his hand on the keys. "No, no," Gieseking exclaimed. "That isn't right. Don't just put your hand there. Place your hand so that the three fingers which will play the chord are on the keys in one even, horizontal line. Then look at your hand, and it will start playing."

At another class Gieseking gave further advice: "You are moving your fingers too much. Keep your fingers touching the keys, with as little movement as possible. The keys push the hand up, and the hand pushes the keys down again...." And then he began playing *Ondine* with high, articulated fingers. "Paris Conservatory," he said, laughing.

When a pupil asked how he achieved his gossamer, minute-motioned, watery atmosphere in this opening (and make no mistake, it is far more difficult to play these figures an impressionistic pianissimo, than it is to play them a Czerny-like mezzoforte), he said: "Oh, I don't know. I am just relaxed. Practice it until your fingers get so loose and relaxed you can play it...well, *it's almost a triplet figure.*" *Voilà le secret*!

Later he elucidated: "Play the first three thirty-second notes with a pendulum-like movement or arc, not articulating each of the three notes but only articulating, or touching as it were, the fourth thirty-second note again. Technically, these figures are like two triplets and a duplet, but not in accentuation....You must *think* precisely the sound and the tempo you want to hear. And you must hear all the notes, but not too clearly. It is water!"

Sometimes Gieseking recommended avoiding the use of the fourth finger when power is needed. For measures 199 and 211 of the first movement of the Beethoven Concerto in C Major, Op. 15, he said, "This chromatic motive must be very rhythmic. Finger the left hand 121235 and the right hand 532121. Don't use the fourth fingers, as they would give a weaker sound. Accent only the sforzato notes, playing the other notes softer:"

m.199
This: ①②①②③⑤
Not this: 1 2 1 3 4 5

m.211
This: ⑤③②①②①
Not this: 5 4 4 3 2 1

For measure 544 (at the *sempre con fuoco*) of the Chopin Scherzo in B Flat Minor, Op. 31, he said, "Finger the right-hand figure 215321."

This: ②①⑤③②   ①
Not this: 1 2 4 3 2   1

And for measures 240-241 of the last movement of the Schumann Concerto in A Minor, Op. 54, he said, "Finger the left hand 53211, using the strong fingers for power, always accenting and separating the last thumb note from the preceding eighth notes." (Some artists use the fingering 53131, but Gieseking's fingering is even stronger.)

m.239
This: ⑤   ③②①   ①
Not this: 5   4 3 2   1

In other cases Gieseking recommended avoiding the fourth finger, not because power is needed, but to keep the hand together as a unit to achieve extreme evenness and clarity. For example, in the Debussy Prelude, *"La Vent dans la Plaine,"* from Book I, Gieseking said, "Finger the right hand 13531, playing completely without finger movement, the fingers close to the keys. (Play the left-hand B flats all with the third finger for equal weight on each note.) It is important to practice this sextuplet figure slowly so that the sixteenth notes are well regulated and controlled in sonority, absolutely equal in timing. Hold the hand slanting inward."

Animé
♩ = 126
①③⑤①   ①③⑤③①   ①③⑤③①
pp   *senza pedal*   etc.
③   ③   ③
aussi legèrement que possible

The Ending of Debussy's "Clair de Lune"

At the Saarbrücken master classes, I remember a student's saying, "You take your life in your hands to play 'Clair de Lune' for Gieseking. Every note has to be perfect, every tone controlled. And on top of it all you're supposed to communicate in some magical way!" Gieseking himself, who seldom re-recorded, told me that he played *Clair de Lune* 17 times in London for his Angel recording before he was satisfied "that every note was approximately as beautiful" as he wanted.

His way of pedaling and fingering the last three measures is an example of the extraordinary pains he took to color tone: "Use the *una corda* as well as the damper pedal.

Hold the damper pedal through the last two measures — the accompaniment all quiet, nearly like a metronome. Then release the *una corda* pedal for the last rolled

chord. And roll this chord from the bottom to the top, as much as possible without delay. Otherwise, it sounds dull and flat."

Sforzato Chord Pedalings in Schumann's "Carnaval, Op. 9"

In Schumann's pieces students seldom know how to play sforzato chords followed by a silently-depressed soft chord. Gieseking's various suggestions for such chords — the final *ppp* chord in "Paganini" from Schumann's *Carnaval*, for example — not only spur you to listen and think for yourself but illustrate how Gieseking continuously listened, searching for the right tonal effect according to room and to instrument.

"Don't strike the *ppp* E flat seventh chord which arises out of the preceding sforzato F minor chords, '*les coups d'applaudissements*,' 'the applause,'" he said. "But depress this *ppp* chord silently, put down the soft pedal and take plenty of time before going on, so that your audience can hear what goes on."

Another time he said: "Possibly play the four sforzato chords without pedal, sounding the right-hand *ppp* chord a little, silently depressing the left hand."

And still another time: "On former pianos you could depress this chord silently and it would sound. But today, on many pianos, you have to play the chord somewhat. Depress this chord silently except for the top 'G.'"

For the similar kind of chord in measure 46 of "*Pierrot*," from *Carnaval*, Gieseking recommended taking a straight pedal on the sforzato chord. "Then immediately change to a quick half pedal and hold this pedal through the first eighth-note count of the following piano chord. While holding this chord,

take another pedal and hold to the final resolution chord on which you change again. This

pedaling in measure 47 gives the effect of the piano chord's emerging from the vibrations of the sforzato chord. Accent only the right hand in the sforzato chord." Another time Gieseking held the upper B flat in the left hand.

An Upbeat Pedaling for Chopin's "Prelude in E Minor"

Gieseking's recommended pedaling for the opening of Chopin's *Prelude in E Minor*, Op. 28, No. 4 exemplifies his instinctual desire to have the melody clear, sustained, and singing. Unusual, it is a kind of pedaling that can be applied in numerous cases throughout the literature.

"The right-hand upbeat is very important," he said. "Make it meaningful. Pedal first on the second note and hold the same pedal into the first measure."

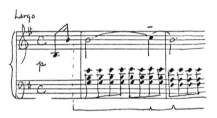

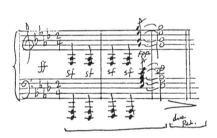

Debussy's "Des pas sur la neige"

Gieseking's phenomenal evenness, both tonal and rhythmic, was one facet of his magical impressionistic style. To achieve rhythmical evenness, he sometimes recommended subdividing the counting. In "*Des pas sur la neige*," — which he once called "the most difficult of the preludes because it has so few notes" — he counted the left-hand ostinato "six" to each half note throughout the entire piece. "Counting this way," he said, "makes it sound more like steps in the snow and transmits the imitated monotony of the snow-covered plain:

"The left hand has a completely separate rhythm from the right hand. To play the left hand pianissimo, keep the wrist very low, using the fingering 5-1, 25-1. (In close-voiced voice-leading, use fingers as far separated as

possible.) Begin *una corda*. Pedal only for connection in this piece — always after the second note of the ostinato; otherwise, use hardly any pedal at all. Nothing should become hazy, merged, dissolved, or melted."

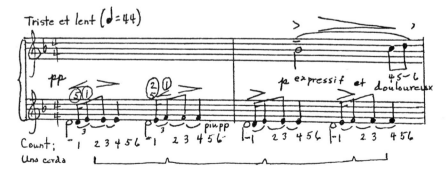

Pedaling

Brahms' Intermezzos

In the Intermezzos of Brahms, I immediately think of three endings that Gieseking's pedalings and fingerings make especially subtle and beautiful. For the last three measures of the Intermezzo in E Major, Op. 116, No. 6, he said: "Pedal as follows and make the following fingering and hand changes in order to resolve lightly the tenor A to G sharp and to bring out clearly and beautifully the principal resolution, the soprano F sharp to E:"

And for the endings of the Intermezzo in B Flat Minor, Op. 117, No. 2 and the one in E Flat Minor, Op. 118, No. 6, he wanted the following pedaling:

The Ending of Debussy's "Reflêts dans l'eau"

Recently I heard a world-famous pianist play the ending of *Reflêts dans l'eau* with inexact rhythm and a rubato that was stylistically out of place. Like so many other pianists, he didn't achieve to a magical degree the "harmonious and faraway sonority" which Debussy prescribed.

To achieve utter calm and beauty, Gieseking wanted these last 14 measures, the *Lent* section, counted six beats to each measure, the octaves arpeggiated evenly from the bottom to the top. "This ending section should be played in absolutely strict time," he said, "not one little pebble disturbing the fading, concentric reflections...."

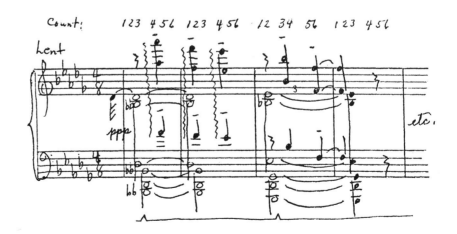

Cortot

Sketch of Cortot drawn by Carolyn Elder during one of the Interpretation Classes.

on

interview March 1951,
written 1964

Alfred Cortot, the eminent French pianist who died in 1962 at the age of eighty-four, was generally recognized as one of the century's greatest Schumann interpreters. Gina Bachauer once said of him: "I think Cortot's Schumann was the most beautiful I have ever heard in my life."

There are few great interpreters of Schumann in the world at any one time. Even some distinguished artists fail to do this composer full justice: their melodic tone does not live, is not compelling. At the other extreme are performers who tend to a hard tone and excessive speed. It was the genius of Cortot to understand the nuances of mood, tone and tempo so essential if Schumann playing is to find its fullest expression.

As an outstanding teacher and musical personality, Cortot was revered throughout Europe and America, and nowhere more so than at the *Ecole Normale de Musique*, the school he founded in Paris in 1920. His presence stimulated the students to an extraordinary degree. Some of my most vivid recollections are of incidents that occurred while I was a student there.

I remember the high-pressure day when the examinations in counterpoint, fugue and composition were given. No practicing was allowed in the school that day; each student was closeted in his room with a piano that was taped and locked. After working all day on counterpoint and

Schumann

a fugue (we had each brought a lunch with us so that we could work straight through), I tried to find the concierge in order to turn in my Opus, but his door was locked. Determined to find someone responsible I went next to the Secretariat and knocked several times. When the door finally opened I found myself looking into the deeply-lined face and black-socketed eyes of *Le Maitre* himself, whom I had obviously disturbed at his work.

It was a contretemps but no doubt he was used to interruptions; they did not keep him from doing an impressive amount of writing, in addition to concertizing throughout his life and teaching. His three major publications, *Editions de travail,* *Principes rationnels de la technique pianistique,* and *Aspects de Chopin* testify to the scope of his interests and his intelligence. "I am a man," he said, "who has always believed that life is not made of what one finds in it, but of what one brings to it."

Although he was a great musician-virtuoso, Cortot was first and foremost a poet. His forte as interpreter was his ability to communicate the poetic or inner content of the music he played. In an essay on Schumann he wrote: "The interpreter's art — at least for the man who does not intend to restrict it to the barren successes of instrumental virtuosity — has as its essential aim the transmission of the feelings or impressions which a

musical idea reflects."

In the spring of 1951 Cortot conducted Interpretation Classes at the *Ecole Normale* on most of the piano works of Schumann. The classes were held in the school's concert hall which consists of a stage and steeply-staggered semi-circular rows of seats rising from orchestra to balcony. It is an intimate hall with excellent acoustics and an unimpeded view of the stage from any seat.

The classes were held in the evening. At every session the hall was filled with music-lovers, including distinguished musicians and students.

The performers were seated on the stage behind two Pleyel concert grands. Each performer was required to submit an essay on Schumann which Cortot himself read. After a girl of twelve had played the *Arabesque, Op. 18* with technical polish and artistic sensitivity, Cortot asked if she had written her essay herself. "Oui, Maitre, but I had a little help."

"What does morbid mean?" asked Cortot. There was a long silence. "Oh, that's the word they helped you with."

"Yes, yes," the girl agreed with a sigh of relief.

In connection with another performer, Cortot discussed the relationship between physique and tone and the predisposition of pianists to those composers whose physical characteristics resemble their own. Edwin

Fischer has advanced a similar theory in his *Beethoven's Pianoforte Sonatas:* "Thick-set players with thick fleshy hands are predestined for the interpretation of works by composers of similar frame, while tall, long-fingered sinewy players are likewise the best interpreters of the works of similarly constituted composers.... Thus the Beethoven and Brahms players Rubinstein and d'Albert were thick-set types whereas Liszt and Cortot were Chopin and Liszt players *par excellence.*"

Cortot's sense of humor frequently enlivened his criticisms. To a performer playing the *Carnaval* he pointed out that *Chiarina* represented the ardent side of Clara Wieck and should be *ravissante.* "Your Chiarina is forty years too old!" After a rather stolid performance of "Important Event" from the *Kinderscenen,* he asked, "In your childhood didn't you ever tell jokes?"

But on the whole Cortot was of serious mien. In his opening lecture he observed: "By studying the life of the composer, and especially by inquiring into his private affairs...the interpreter tries to discover the man in his work and identify the generating motive by visualizing the human moment which preceded the artistic creation." Throughout the course he supplied the background of each piece through reference to Schumann's letters; there was discussion of father Wieck and Ernestine von Fricken, of Schumann's courtship of Clara, their marriage, and the deaths of several of their children. Cortot spoke of the musical games Schumann loved to play as a boy—how he made up character sketches at the piano and had his comrades guess what people they represented.

Cortot emphasized the strong literary influences apparent in Schumann's compositions. He pointed out that whereas in Beethoven the contrast is between the masculine and feminine, in Schumann the contrast is between moods represented by the fictitious Florestan and Eusebius (the pseudonyms the composer used to symbolize the two contradictory aspects of his nature: dream and exaltation). Each piece of the *Davidsbuendlertaenze*, for example, bears one or the other of these pseudonyms (the first edition did not mention Schumann at all), and in the *Carnaval* there are individual pieces named Eusebius and Florestan. Themes and sections representing these two contrasting moods abound in Schumann's works.

Another theme represents the composer's wife, Clara: as in the beginning of the *Third Sonata, Op. 14* (Ex. 1); the *Sonata in G Minor, Op. 22* (Ex. 2); and the opening theme of the *Concerto in A Minor, Op. 54* (Ex. 3). The notes C, B, A (in German, C, H, A) and their various transpositions stand for *Chiarina*, the Italian diminutive of *Clara*.

Ex. 1

Ex. 2

Ex. 3

Very little was said in the Interpretation Classes about technique. Occasionally Cortot would suggest a rearrangement of hands:

> *Sonata in F-Sharp Minor*, last movement, bars 102, 103: "Rearrange the hands." (Ex. 4)

Ex. 4

Sometimes, for power and bigness, he added octaves:

Faschingsschwank aus Wien, ending: "Play a low octave in the bass and the right hand an octave higher." (Ex. 5)

Ex. 5

At the end of the *F-Sharp Minor Sonata* he added a low octave (Ex. 6), and in the ending section of *Carnaval* he added low octaves in the tradition of late-nineteenth, early-twentieth century romantic pianists.

Ex. 6

As all the performers played well technically, Cortot could concentrate on interpretation. Opposed to empty virtuosity, he cautioned against excessively fast Schumann agitato tempos. "Not *too* fast," he would say or, "Don't rush." Here are selections from his comments on steady tempo, melodic playing and tone, taken down in shorthand during the *Ecole Normale* classes and translated from the French:

Steady Tempo

Fantasy in C Major, second movement:

Bar 38 — "Don't rush."
Bar 51 — "It's a march in cut time, it shouldn't budge, keep a steady tempo."
Bar 89 — "Don't rush! Fast tempos are more effective when not rushed."
Bar 113 — (etwas langsamer), "It is the same picture, softened, but the mood and rhythm continue."
Bar 220 — "The rhythm stays the same throughout the piece; the timbres change but not the rhythm."

Melodic Playing and Tone

In Schumann melodic playing, Cortot's discussion of phrase-rubato pointed out two main types:

1. "In general the phrases of Schumann are not broadened (*retenu*) at the beginning but at the end of the phrase, whereas the Chopin rubato is in the middle of a phrase, in a harmony, or at a delicate harmony." (Ex's. 7 and 8).

Ex. 7, Novelette, Op. 21, No. 1, bar 24

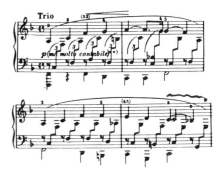

Ex. 8, Carnaval, "Chopin," bars 3-4

2. "Broaden the beginning of the phrase. Afterwards move forward to the end." (Ex's. 9 and 10)

Ex. 9, *Arabesque*, "Plus tranquille (Ruhiger) section:" "Here a change of sonority, a speaking sonority; use a full *mf* tone in the melody to begin. Don't use just the fingers for this; also use the wrist. Move forward in bar 2, then ritard in bar 4. In the second phrase: full tone to start, then move forward, etc. The final F-sharp of the third phrase *ppp*. The fourth phrase like asking a question." (Cortot's comments here are given in full, as students seldom have any idea of how to play this section).

Ex. 9, Bar 89

Ex. 10, *Humoresque*, "Zum Beschluss section:" "Use two hands for the opening octaves. Hesitate a little on the first three notes, then move forward to the end of the phrase. In mood it's like the regret of being a man like the others but with regrets that the others don't have."

Ex. 10

A beautiful melodic tone was one of the most important characteristics of Cortot's school of playing. "Even when soft, the tone should still be alive—never a dead sonority," he said of the "Chopin" section of the *Carnaval*. "Living, elegant, not elegiac or sentimental but played with enthusiasm," he said of the second theme of the first movement, bar 94, of the *F-Sharp Minor Sonata*. Over and over he would describe in words the mood and sonority: "Schumann's melody needs to be really pianistic, rather large, not like a Chopin Nocturne, a beautiful sonority, full, warm... there are always harmonies. A Schumann melody should be sung as a voice."

Balance of tone between hands as well as variety of color were stressed. He often wanted the left-hand melody to help the right hand when in unison, particularly in higher registers:

Arabesque, bar 81: "Only the right hand produces a sharp sonority. Use the left hand too to obtain a full *ff* sonority." (Ex. 11)

Ex. 11

On repeats he sometimes advocated bringing out the bass or another voice for special tonal effect or variety:

Papillons, No. 10, bar 25: "The first time the right hand as real melody; the second time (the repeat), bring out the bass." (Ex. 12)

Ex. 12

Kinderscenen, "Of Foreign Lands bar 9: "On the repeat bring out the left-hand melody." (Ex. 13)

Ex. 13

Cortot had a gift for expressing in a striking and concise manner the character of a theme or movement:

"The loves of a poet," (*Davidsbuendlertaenze*).

"A fluttering of wings," (*Toccata*, bar 151).

"A veritable domestic squabble!" (*Carnaval*, "Pantalon et Colombine").

"A roar of laughter," (*Sonata in F-Sharp Minor*, "Intermezzo," bar 16).

"A notebook of wild and savage things," (*Kreisleriana*, No. 5).

"Pansies, not orchids," (*Waldscenen*, "Solitary Flowers").

Often he would single out a motive as giving the characteristic of the mood, the content of a mood in a figure (the impact of this on a whole piece is far-reaching!):

Fantasiestuecke, Op. 12, No. 2 "Soaring," bar 1: "All the elan rests on these two chords, the last two eighth notes." (Ex. 14)

Ex. 14

Ex. 18

Kinderscenen, Op. 15, No. 5 "Perfect Happiness," bars 2-3: "This gives the sentiment." (Ex. 15)

Ex. 15

It was always the *just* nuance Cortot sought. He counseled against exaggerating the mood of a composition. The following suggestions, although given to a specific performer, have an almost universal application:

Fantasiestuecke, Op. 12, No. 8 "The Song's End:" "It is the end of a song not the end of an opera." (Ex. 16)

Sonata in G Minor, Op. 22, Rondo: "Effervescent, not fiery." (Ex. 17)

Fantasy in C Major, Op. 17, third movement, bar 60: "A metaphysical reverie, not a concerto for piano." (Ex. 18)

Ex. 16

Ex. 17

To discover and reveal the beauty, poetry and true meaning of each work were the high ambitions Cortot communicated to his students; they constituted the remarkable appeal of his own thrilling interpretations of Schumann.

Claudio Arrau

Master Lesson

on Seven Pieces from Schumann's Carnaval

interview 1961

Claudio Arrau holds his master classes in the music room of his home. His white, two-story frame house on Long Island overlooks the western side of the Douglaston Peninsula Sound. In front of the house, a walk, rather crowded with overhanging bushes, leads up to the front steps.

Inside, the view from the foyer is one of book-lined rooms, oriental scatter rugs over the carpeting. At the left, steps go down to the music room—an inviting room, about 15 by 30 feet, decorated in rich greens and dark colors.

When I arrived to attend a lesson, about sixteen pupils, eager and nervous, were milling around the music room. They were American, British, Chilean, Cuban, German, Mexican and Viennese.

The pupils stood as Mr. Arrau entered and took his chair near the bench before the keyboard. Raphael de Silva, his genial assistant, sat in a chair beside Arrau. I sat on a chair in the wing of the piano, and put my music on the long coffee table in front of me.

The first pupil, a young woman, was to play seven pieces from Schumann's *Carnaval*, continuing from where she had left off at a previous lesson. Mr. Arrau, who had brought the original edition with him, began the lesson.

"Even in Clara Schumann's edition, published in this country by Kalmus," Mr. Arrau said, "some changes have been made. For example, the first repeat of "Valse noble" has been cut. In "Promenade" measure 18, the bottom note of the left-hand, third-beat chord should be D, not C. The rest are small details that are different.

"There are no metronome markings in the original edition," Mr. Arrau continued. "They are all from Madame Schumann."

Mr. Arrau turned his music to "Sphynx," the mysterious cryptic notes inserted between the eighth and ninth numbers of *Carnaval*, in which Schumann reveals that the music is a set of variations on three of the possible musical translations of ASCH* (S being Es, German for E flat; H, German for B Natural).

During the summer of 1834, at the age of 24, Schumann had fallen madly in love with Ernestine von Fricken and had begun the composition of *Carnaval*. As is well known, *Carnaval* is a musical diary of his life at this time. ASCH was the name of the town where Ernestine was born and also contained the musical letters in Schumann's own surname — SCHA.

"Don't play 'Sphynx'" said Mr. Arrau.

Someone in the class mentioned that Cortot, Rachmaninoff, and Gieseking play it in their recordings. But Mr. Arrau did not pursue the point. Instead he asked me if I knew Cortot's arrangement of the notes. (See below.)

And then the young woman proceeded to play the next seven pieces, numbers 9 through 15, of *Carnaval*. Mr. Arrau made comments after each piece.

Papillions

Bar 1. "We have to bring out A, S, C, and H (the first four right-hand notes—A, E flat, C, C flat); then after that play very lightly. Use a lot of finger action for those four notes every time.

"Pedal the first beat, taking the pedal with the left-hand bass grace note, and then off at the second beat. Really bring out the grace note and sforzato first chord in the left hand: that is, the first two left-hand chords different from the rest."

Bar 9. "Bring out the right-hand lower voice and the left-hand lower voice."

Bar 10. "Bring out the right-hand upper voice and the left-hand lower voice. In measures 9 and 10, the left-hand lower voice legato. Then cut after these two bars of piano before the forte of measure 11."

Bar 11. "Here is the left-hand fingering for the first four sixteenth notes: 5-2-1-2. Articulate these notes, the ASCH theme, clearly, loudly."

Bar 17 et al. (Middle Trio section.) " 'Flying, *volante*,' Busoni always said. I would even rush a little bit here, give the feeling of rushing."

Bar 20. "In the last bar of this phrase, bring out particularly the left hand." (Mr. Arrau took for granted the pupil would connect the right-hand notes with the fingers, as written.)

Bars 25, 26. " . . . the right hand mainly almost cantabile; pedal for every two left-hand notes."

Bars 27, 28. " . . . with very light crescendo."

"So we have this kind of mixture of purposeful bringing out the original motive and the rest very light, dancing, very light in character.

"The beginning should not sound rushed; it should be controlled. In the Trio (bar 17 et al) on purpose going forward a little, but not in the beginning.

A.S.C.H. — S.C.H.A.
(Lettres dansantes)

"It is too heavy, darling. You are playing a little too much in the keys... light staccati with your arms hanging loosely over the keys...very light, relaxed, hanging wrist. Your upper arms higher, darling. Have the feeling you hardly touch the keys except for the little accents...very little weight on the keys. Stay high except when you come down on the sforzati. The accent on the third beat is very small. Forget about it; it comes by itself."

(The above is an example of an artist teacher's coaching on the finest details. Only when the student has perfected the finger, hand, and arm movements, can play with the necessary clarity, and is slurring and phrasing correctly, will he be able to fulfill Mr. Arrau's advice and achieve the necessary gossamer quality: "the letters will dance.")

Bar 1. "Right-hand fingering: 2-4, 1-2, 2-5, a fingering assuring better evenness with less changing of hand position than is found in many editions."

Bar 12. " . . . next section, fourth and eighth bars, the left-hand octave resolution C flat to the third-beat

Cortot's Arrangement of Sphynx

B flat, *legato*, as if written:

"Then, please, the differences in dynamics: the first time, from bar 9, piano; when it comes back, from bar 17, pianissimo; the transition to the Da Capo, from bar 25, pianissimo with a little crescendo.

"In the third and fourth bars of this transition, bars 27 and 28, the right-hand ♩ .♩ 's cantabile;"

in the fifth and sixth bars, bars 29 and 30, we have the right hand light-heavy, the left hand heavy-light."

Bars 31-32. "Ritardando means getting slower and slower, not just slower.

"Throughout, really get the little grace notes clear, articulated, distinct."

Chiarina

"As you played it, it is heavy and pedestrian; it doesn't have any freedom of expression. Chiarina (Clara Wieck) was 15 years old, a wild little girl at the moment. This piece has to have arrogance, and on the other hand, a tremendous passion at the climaxes; it should be free and capricious and driven and arrogant.

"To make the difference between the opening forte phrase and the fortissimo second phrase starting in bar 8, don't become too loud in the first eight bars. Then when you come to the B flat, the climax of the phrase—bars 5 and 13—go into it and linger, or linger before. Or, you can do both: the first time go into it; the second time hesitate."

Use of the thumb on black keys for accuracy and power. "In the middle section—bars 17 and 18—we have

the problem of the stretch. If you can't stretch it, you have to rely on the pedal. But be very precise; be very careful with the pedal. Just hold it until the next sustained voice. Then you can use the thumbs on the upper A flats, and then you have very strong A flats and you can't miss."

Bars 16-17. ". . . exaggerated mf, a little less than mf, et cetera."

Bars 21-24. "Spread out the crescendo over the last four bars, not forte right away. Really go after the forte A flats. You could, of course, hold back for the last A flats."

Transitions Between Pieces

". . . Now the transitions, how long we wait between one and the next piece. Play the last bar of "Papillons" and the first bar of "Lettres dansantes." You waited just right; you waited just a moment.

"Now play the last bar of "Lettres dansantes" and the first bar of "Chiarina". . . No, that was too soon. We have to get this very light picture out of our minds, and we are not ready yet for the passionate Chiarina. I know you would do it right in performance but I wanted to remind you.

You can spoil things by coming too soon or too late.

"Now play the last bar of 'Chiarina' and the first bar of 'Chopin.' According to the passionate, violent character of 'Chiarina,' you can't finish by holding the last note. You have to tear, end it with emphasis, with breath going up—the end was too dry. You lifted the pedal too early."

Chopin

"Why this shyness? After all this is almost an exaggerated picture, almost a caricature of Chopin, this fashionable figure in Paris appearing with all the legend around him: the fainting, the swooning, the elegance.

"In phrasing in romantic music, we have to avoid dynamic evenness in tone. In a real melody there shouldn't be two notes exactly equally loud.

". . . We have a terrific thing going on in the left hand. Pedal whole bars as Schumann marked in the first edition, except in measures 6, 9, and 13 where you should pedal twice to the bar. The sign for taking off the pedal is at the very end of the bar. He wants waves of sound."

Bars 1-2. "Play the first phrase

Cover of original edition, in possession of Mr. Arrau. →

with the first two E flats softer; go towards the third E flat."

"The pianissimo repeat is from Clara Schumann. In bars 7 and 8 of the repeat — 20 and 21 when written out — crescendo to the sf. But not too much crescendo, rather accelerando."

Bar 10 (23). "The notes written in small notes should start pianissimo like little drops, and toward the end of the bar you can become a little louder again. Curve your fifth finger like a little nail into the key at the top of those little notes. If you find an action that doesn't respond, you are sunk. Why don't you linger more on the right-hand E flat?"

Bars 11-12 (24-25). "Start the phrase soft and crescendo to the long note. When I play this piece myself, I have always the feeling Chopin is walking away from people here.

" . . . the second time, on the repeat — bars 14 and so forth — use the soft pedal, the tone a little bit like Debussy. No crescendo at the end the second time; the crescendo is for the repeat. I, myself, change the pedal quickly between the A flat and G in the next to last measure.

"Remember always, even when you play the pianissimo repeat, that it says agitato."

Estrella

"You played it much too fast; it lacks the arrogance this girl, Ernestine von Fricken, probably had. This piece should be arrogant, broad, proud; the rhythm in the 3/4 bar at the same time feminine, coquettish.

"Again, don't play all these octaves equally loud; shade the melody. In measures 7 and 8, in the original, the G, G, and G sharp octaves in the right hand are all staccato, the next A natural octave being marked with an accent."

From bar 13 (Piu presto). "What comes now is tender and passionate at the same time. Before, she was contemptuous; now she has a tiny little love duet for 8 bars (2x8). Use much more pedal; Clara Schumann has a very big pedaling from the first of the bar . . . a little bit *he* leading, *she* yielding. Go forward toward the high C and then slow down again, the 6th (18th) and 8th (20th) bars held back.

"Don't play the last two bars too fast. Throughout the piece, in the rhythm ♪ ♩ , don't play the eighth note too short; play it exactly right."

Reconnaissance

"The sixteenth notes should have this trembling of emotion; you see someone again." (Mr. Arrau illustrated, singing.) "I must learn how to sing. You should almost stay on the keys for the staccato.

"In the second section — bars 9 to 17 — you have two two-bar phrases and then a period of four bars. Start each phrase soft so you can crescendo.

Pedale. From bar 17. "In the Trio Schumann writes *pedale*. When he writes *pedale* he wants quite a lot of pedal, with quick changes.

"In the Trio the tone should be more sensuous. You must be actually in ecstasy. The French word *reconnaissance* means recognition; it also means gratefulness. Thus: enchanted gratefulness . . .

"The danger with syncopated double rhythms is that students tend to play them metronomically. These rhythms express trembling of emotion; play them freely and with rubato."

Bar 22 (from bar 6 of the Trio). "When you have phrases in sequence, you make the same kind of rubato again and again. Measures 7, 8, 9

you did exactly. Towards the D sharp of bar 10, I would already prepare the slowing down in the C sharp, C double sharp. Let your imagination take wing, flight."

Bar 23 (7). "I never hear the left-hand first-beat B. Is it because of the repeated B?"

From bar 29. "The problem of the descending sequences after the F sharp major . . . I think it should get softer, more tender, and more relaxed."

Bar 39. "Six measures from the end of the middle section . . . bring out the left hand here where it is one octave apart."

Pantalon et Columbine

"This is not a couple of lovers but father and daughter, * and not incestuous either. They are really fighting. In the middle section, they try to make up.

"Use a bouncing, shaking-out-of-your-body staccato."

Bar 5. "Take pedal for every four sixteenths, Schumann's pedaling . . ."

Bar 16. "Show me the double sixths. Good . . ."

At this point the lesson ended. A thorough and painstaking teacher, Mr. Arrau believes in isolating and perfecting the various pieces of a large work such as Schumann's *Carnaval.* The rest of the work he would hear at another lesson.

After a brief intermission, other pupils were to play the Chopin E Minor and the Mendelssohn G Minor Concertos. Unfortunately, I had to leave. But not before Mr. Arrau, a gracious as well as stimulating host, had asked me to return.

* **Colombine** was the daughter of **Pantalon** and the sweetheart of **Harlequin**, stock characters in early Italian comedy and in pantomime.

Jorge Bolet

interview August 16, 1973

If you've never heard Liszt's transcription of Wagner's Overture to "Tannhäuser" played by Jorge Bolet, you've missed something really special. The audience at the 1973 University of Maryland International Piano Festival stood en masse at Mr. Bolet's recital roaring its approval, as it did for his Rachmaninoff encores.

Later in the week, Jorge Bolet expounded dynamically in his masterclass, immediately setting a mood of seriousness and authority coupled with hilarity. As the preceding classes had taken a sort of "bird's-eye view of the works being played," he thought it would be more interesting to limit his teaching to "one or two sections of each composition."

"Before we hear any music," he began, with understated humor, "I would like to tell you I'm a very quiet person, having a rather forbidding exterior — or so I've been told. And although my students are terrified of me, I think they hold me in high regard and have a certain affection for my austerity.

"When I teach, I believe a great deal must be done to instill in the student: first of all, how bad he is; second, how much better he could be; and third, how far he can go. I believe in opening doors, letting him see into the far horizons so he will eventually get on what I call 'the right track.'

"Then I think you have to instill in him a love of what he's doing. I believe in being enthusiastic about music. That means that, because of my Spanish blood, whenever I get enthusiastic I start screaming. I don't want you to get the idea — this applies especially to our performers — that when I scream, I am angry. As a matter of fact when I really get angry, I am most calm and speak in my lowest voice. With those preliminaries, let's hear the Bartok *Improvisations on 8 Hungarian Peasant Songs*, Op. 20." The mood had been set.

Bartok Improvisations, Op. 20, Nos. 1, 2, and 5
Music for No. 1 is printed on page 243.

After the Bartok had been played, Mr. Bolet, a big man with a big voice almost as dark as his mustache, complimented the student. "When a student does something really beautifully, I believe in letting him know. Encouragement is a basic element in teaching," he said.

And then he started hammering a grossly-neglected principle (which should be intuitive!) — namely, the bringing out of the melody.

No. I. Molto moderato
"In all the long history of public performances," he quipped, "no one has ever paid admission to hear

Jorge Bolet was born in Havana, Cuba. A child prodigy, he studied first with his sister and later with David Saperton at the Curtis Institute. At 16, when he appeared as soloist in Carnegie Hall, Fritz Reiner conducting, his audience included Rachmaninoff, Milstein, Elman, Alma Gluck, Marcella Sembrich, Zimbalist, Horowitz, Hofmann, and Godowsky! After serving as an officer in the United States Army during World War II, Bolet resumed his career, recording the sound track of "Song Without End," a film biography of Liszt, among other things. He has recently completed a series of Rachmaninoff and Liszt releases — including the Transcendental Etudes — for RCA. And when not on tour, he teaches at the University of Indiana.

an Alberti bass. Therefore, I believe in screaming at the top of my voice, 'I don't hear the tune' Basically, these are Hungarian peasant songs with very elaborate, fancy, and, for the most part, sorrowful dress. And the tune, the melody, is what we are interested in. The public doesn't want to hear the nonessentials."

M. 1. "In the first place, don't bang out the E flat under which Bartok wrote a little line. Just put your finger on the key and push the note down a little farther than you did on the note before."

M. 2. "Beware of accenting passing notes. If anything, play the *A* lighter than the other notes."

At the end of M. 4. "Go on, go on. Don't go out for coffee."

Ms. 5-8. "Play the grace-note figures very softly, even though you hold them down with the fingers and use pedal. We want the tune brought out, supporting lines in the background. Practice the melody alone. Then add the grace-note figures, keeping them very soft."

M. 5. "It bothers me to hear the two last quarter notes in the same pedal — what I call 'melodic mud.' Hold the grace-note figure with the fingers and then change pedal for the C. Similarly in the next two measures and the first two beats in the fourth measure: take a pedal on each one of those quarter notes."

M. 12. "In order to change the pedal and not lose all of the bass chord, go back and recatch some of the chord. Don't be lazy, you've got big paws."

No. II. Molto capriccioso

Again Jorge Bolet expounded on the importance of bringing out the melody: "It's very hard for melodic lines to compete with this kind of dissonance. Practice the melody alone loud, then the dissonant accompaniment notes extremely softly, and finally the two together."

Ms. 24-26. "I wouldn't hold back these two measures. It's more effective to push right into the *Meno mosso.*"

M. 30. "Here it says 'a tempo tranquillo!' The secret in playing calmly is to play absolutely evenly in tempo."

Ms. 37-43. Vivace-Lento-Vivace. "Correlating tempos is often a problem. For example, in the International Piano Competition here, the 15 semi-finalists have all had to play the *Sonata Brevis* by Donald Lybbert. There is one place in this piece where the composer indicates a chord to be held for 17 measures. Nothing else is happening. Then he writes 8 bars rest and then one solitary pianissimo chord at the very top end of the keyboard, where there is very little sound anyway. And this chord is to be held for seven measures! At the release of this chord, there is a little plink. Then you rest for another six bars and so on.

"I have the highest respect for composers; otherwise I wouldn't even bother with them. But if a composer writes something so completely against all laws of performance common sense and psychological reaction between performer and audience, then I say 'to hell with the composer.' The greatest pianist in the world couldn't hold an audience enthralled through one of those interminable waits where nothing happens.

"Now you see this is what I mean: don't play the Vivace too fast and then the Lento so slow that the piece dies. On top of the Lento, Bartok writes ritardando, so take the Lento with a grain of salt. Then you can make a ritardando without the piece's coming to a halt."

M. 50 to end. "Don't accelerate the last three measures. If you play the *Piu Presto* strictly in tempo, it has bite."

M. 53. "Don't play the last two eighth-note chords *fff*. The loudest stress should be on the first-beat chord. Think loud-down, soft-up."

No. V. Allegro molto

Ms. 1-21. "Nobody gives a damn about those half-step seconds in the right hand or the left-hand fifths and sevenths in measures 27 *et al.* Play such things as rhythmic tension but not as anything important. In the introduction, you can bring out the half-step seconds because there's nothing else, but when the tune comes in — 'psst,' play them soft.

"I think the rhythm should be strongly syncopated, accenting the quarter notes, not the eighth notes as marked in the score."

M. 25 et al. "In the left hand, keep the accent on the syncopated quarters and play them *tenuto*, long, not *staccato*. Stick to the keys; put chewing gum on your fingers."

M. 26-27. "The left-hand phrase with the legato sign is beautiful if you play legato. Detached it's not the same thing."

M. 43. "*Poco ritardando*, not stop."

M. 48. "The left-hand chords are not the tune. Play them piano. I want to hear the soprano."

M. 57 et al. "In the last two lines, Bartok writes *forzandi* in the left hand, then the right, then the left et cetera. Don't play accents in both hands simultaneously."

M. 68. "The last two chords should be big, wild — the top *G* the loudest note.

"These *Improvisations* are fascinating pieces full of marvelous coloristic possibilities. You have to play this music with a lot of color and rhythmic bite. I don't want anybody to think after this brief session that I have said everything about anything. I could go on for hours, days, and years. The wealth of detail, of nuance, of pianistic and musical wisdom in a great composition is endless."

Schumann Kreisleriana, Op. 16

Next Jorge Bolet commented in considerable detail on the first two pieces of *Kreisleriana*. I am including Mr. Bolet's valuable remarks on the first piece for it is a complete, brilliant piece in itself and can be played by pianists not ready for the entire set. I hope the reader will play the musical

The charming monument to Clara and Robert Schumann at their grave outside Bonn, Germany. Photo by Dean Elder.

examples as he reads and will avail himself of a copy of *Kreisleriana* in order to appreciate fully Mr. Bolet's suggestions.

No. I. Ausserst bewegt

M. 1 et al. "Agitatissimo. Subdue the left hand. Give the right hand real prominence, really crescendoing in each figure, ever more as the line ascends, so the piece gives a sensation of rushing forward by these tremendous gushes. But don't rush in tempo."

M. 9. "I find a lack of breathing in many performers. Here is an example: after the left-hand three eighth-note phrases, breathe. You have to release the pedal.

"You have a *forzando* on the second note. If you play the first and third notes almost as loud as the *forzando* note, the effect of the *forzando* is obliterated."

M. 25 (middle section). "Don't connect the last left-hand note of each figure into the next with the pedal. Release the pedal, taking a new pedal exactly on the first and second beats. The sixteenth notes have to be absolutely even. Don't rush the left-hand notes.

"Now we have a real tune in the upper right-hand notes. We want to hear the tune, the other notes extremely quiet. The other notes are elaboration, just so much froth, frilly lace.

"Don't sectionalize by sort of stopping and then starting again, at the end of the first part of this middle section, for example. Think more of the music's

just flowing. Do your sectionalizing with nuance, with dynamics, but not with tempo.

"For variety, at the return of the first section of this middle section (*A tempo*), you might play the second note of the right-hand two-note slurred notes, a bit staccato."

No. II. Sehr innig und nicht zu rasch

"Works like *Kreisleriana* must sing. I remember what Josef Krips once told me, and every time I have played with him or met him he has told me the same thing: 'All music is singing and what is not singing is not music.' Sing! Sing! You have to project things to the last row of the top balcony. Whispering can be terribly effective, but whisper something briefly. Long-winded whispering is the most boring thing."

M. 1. "Don't slide into the tempo. Before you start, sing the first phrase to yourself. Schumann marked this piece '*nicht zu rasch*, not too fast.' It isn't even *schnell. Rasch* has the connotation of not necessarily as fast but with an impetuosity. Basically this is a very quiet piece. Just play the first phrase poetically, lyrically, with calm crescendo-diminuendo — without drama. You'd be surprised how much more slowly you can play this piece, or any piece like it, if you will play in tempo. Try it ♩ = circa 76.

"We could spend three hours shaping these first two phrases, one with the other. I'm glad that you see we must not play these identical phrases alike. This rule applies to most music, but in romantic music it's a must. You do something once and the audience is fascinated; do it the second time the same way and the audience is bored. If you get the point that I am looking at music from an audience's point-of-view, you're right. Music only becomes a living thing when we play, when we hear it. We must consider the listener because he is the one who is hearing it."

M. 5, the third phrase. "Now sing the top. The inner voices must not be muddy from overpedaling; they must be clear."

M. 10. "The left-hand sixteenths must be clean; you cannot use pedal for those four notes."

Ms. 17-20. "Clean! Clean! Don't muddy it up. When you have a melodic line ascending as long as this, from *G* up an octave to *A*, you must carry it up to the top. You must start pianissimo. Then the thing really rises. The crescendo must be very gradual and always in good proportion, melodic line paramount, supporting lines softer in tone. Don't feel that when you get to the top of the line, you have to stay there. In other words, try to do everything you can by means

of dynamic control, color, attack, textures. Use rhythmic liberties as a last resort. Try to get up to the top and back down without any rhythmic fluctuation at all — even, quiet."

Ms. 23-24. "The bass B♭-D-F-G-B♭-A-A♭-G is very important; it's the first time he uses it."

Ms. 26-27. "All right, have that logical end-of-phrase in the middle of measure 26, and then the new phrase tenses. But don't retard the end of the phrase and don't rush the new phrase. You're trying to carry the melodic line up to the top in measure 27; you're building a kind of tension. So in doing that, the most normal, human thing is to rush.

People want to build a climax, so they play faster. And nothing kills a climax like speed. When you want to build a climax, play slower, hold back."

Ms. 31, 33. "Most romantic ornamentation is basically melodic. It's not the same thing as baroque ornamentation. Play the grace notes before the beat and clearly."

Ms. 36, 37 (Adagio). "I don't know why so many composers love to play with crossed hands. Sometimes things don't sound the same way, but I play it with uncrossed hands and make it sound crossed. The top G flat-F of the sixths are the important notes, not the bottom notes.

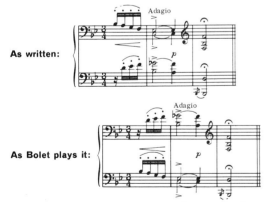

"There are certain points of arrival where you can stay as long as you want, certain places with tension and expectancy. Places that are not the end of anything, but just before the end. Once you resolve, however, you must resolve. In other words, in the Adagio, you can stay on the G flat half note as long as you want, but after you have resolved to the F, don't linger before playing the final chord in the next measure."

Intermède I, Sehr lebhaft. "Don't overemphasize loud-soft, loud-soft in the soprano. Try not to make a big difference between the first and second notes of the right-hand slurred notes. The left-hand staccato sixteenths should be very precise, even."

M. 9 et al. "This is a completely different kettle of fish. Now we have a legato, melodic line with marvelous harmonic modulations."

Ms. 12-13. "Yup-ee, yup-ee, yup-ee. These right-hand sixteenths, the slurred broken octaves, leading back to the first theme are marvelous. They're an entirely different element. Both notes of the broken octave have to be brought out. But don't accent the thumb; if anything accent the top. It's the space between the top and bottom notes, the space between the slurs, that's going to give the right effect."

Intermède II, Etwas bewegter. "It's not much of a tune, but bring it out; the arpeggio sixteenths keep soft.

Then we also want to hear the left hand countermelody. You have to think of both the right and left hands."

M. 9. "Forget about the thumb and second finger sixteenth notes. Let them play by themselves, pianissimo. Concentrate on the upper melodic line."

"The last two chords: loud-and-short! long!"

Langsamer, Tempo I. Ms. 1-4. "This is a long, long phrase, that he repeats again. Then we have another long phrase and you feel he somehow wants to get back to where he started and doesn't know just how he is going to do it. Try playing this very expressively and simply because it's very contrapuntal. And try playing it in tempo. Don't deviate from the tempo unless it is absolutely necessary."

Ms. 5-8. "Here where you cross the hands, I think the top voice, the double counterpoint, should be brought out. He's had it in the bass in the preceding phrase and now he has it in the soprano."

Ms. 9-12. "In the third phrase, where we start this

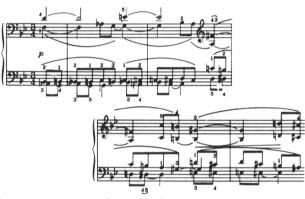

long progression, the ascending top right-hand notes are not the significant part. This is the important part:

Ms. 13-14, 14-15. "A favorite trick of Schumann was to repeat a figure, notating one melodic tone first as a measured note and later as a grace note.

In measure 13-14, he has

and in measure 15-16:

When he used a grace note, I think he really wanted it fast, but of course without any aggressiveness. It

must be played very tenderly."

Ms. 16-17 et al. "This is the first time this theme comes in the six-four position which is not exactly the restful position. Then he takes the bass up a minor second — chromatic — so this doesn't have the peaceful, lyric idea of the beginning. This is getting worked up, the climax being the left-hand sixteenths accelerating to the Adagio of measures 22-23."

2 ms. before the final Adagio. "This sudden harmonic resolution, inserted only this once in the entire piece, should come as a shock. The one chord has to all of a sudden develop into the next one. Don't wait too long on the first chord. The longer you wait, the more difficult it is to make the pianissimo resolution. The top E flat of the bass third must be strong enough so you can resolve to the next chord pianissimo.

"The top G flat of the sixth must be the loudest note, the B flat softer. You can support this sixth a little bit with the third, E flat-E. And then in the resolution of the third, the E natural must be almost nothing, but more than the C sharp. You see what a problem it is to play just two notes!"

Adagio. "Disease number 436: always starting melodic lines on the second note of the melody, not the first. Where does the second note come from?

"How many times have you heard the second theme of the first movement of the Brahms D Minor Concerto begun like this?

You think I'm kidding? Pick up recordings of this concerto and you'll hear what I mean. That's a classic example. This *Kreisleriana* Adagio is another one.

"Sing! The first G must sing — press it, don't hit it. Keep the thumb soft. And you must not hear three slow quarter notes, 'plunnkk, pluunnkk, pluuunnnkkk.' You have to play horizontally, not up and down and up and down. The question of how fast and how slow to play things is a very involved procedure. But one guide line as to the maximum degree of slowness any piece or phrase can have, is, that if every note in the melodic line becomes a stopping point, if you do not feel movement from one note to the next, then the tempo is too slow. There is no piano with a sufficiently singing tone to play those quarter notes without horizontal movement."

Unfortunately, the time was up. The audience, greatly stimulated and entertained by Jorge Bolet's dynamic teaching, stood vigorously applauding. "It's been a great pleasure. I'm glad some of the things have brought a smile to your face," he said.

IMPROVISATIONS

sur des chansons paysannes hongroises

I.

Béla Bartók, Op. 20.

243

Sarabande from *Pour le piano*

CLAUDE DEBUSSY

"...have to hear beautiful sounds come from my piano."

Study with Gieseking

Posthumous Lesson
on Debussy's "Sarabande"
from *Pour le piano*

IN HIS CLASSES AT Saarbruecken, Gieseking took great pains with the works of Debussy; he was proud and happy that his name was so often associated with this marvelous music that seemed to him "so perfectly natural and naturally perfect" as well as "so absolutely sincere and beautiful." Gieseking considered the compositions of Debussy to be among the most interesting in piano literature. "Debussy is not great because he is an impressionist, but because he paints in perfect musical form; for example, *Reflets dans l'eau* is a rondo in three parts. Therefore, one cannot take too many liberties with Debussy. It is better to play Debussy like Mozart than like Liszt. Debussy always remains the musician. He composed objective music."

The date for the composition of *Pour le piano* is 1901, and while the Sarabande is said to have existed in earlier versions, we are concerned with it as the middle movement of the 1901 suite. In this composition, as in all his works, Debussy integrated tonal color with musical structure and promoted timbre to the rank of architectural function, giving it the same importance as the harmony or the rhythm.

245

In the Sarabande Gieseking's demands all find specific application: to make the upper melody sing beautifully, to color sonorous blocks of inner harmonies, to bring out consonant notes while keeping dissonant notes subdued, and to pay attention to low notes which must come out with the necessary clarity. Gieseking wanted the Sarabande played in time and not too slowly (about ♩ = 52): "It is a dance! Always keep in mind the dance rhythm of the sarabande."

The following comments made by Gieseking were noted down during several lessons on the Sarabande:

Singing melody. "Bring out the melody right from the beginning. Play the melody *mf*, all the other notes *pp*, the harmonies of the chord accompaniment very soft so that the fifths don't sound too much. The right hand must be very legato. Gieseking once recommended a fingering for measure 1, which requires a large, supple hand (see score).

Pedaling to sustain low bass harmonies. In bar 2: "Connect the second eighth note to the following half note with one pedal;" in bar 8; "One pedal for the two chords; otherwise, change pedal according to the value

of the notes." In bar 5: "Emphasize the first two eighth notes a little" (naturally, piano).

Crescendo and diminuendo signs. In Debussy's piano music, there are numerous printing errors. Some crescendo and diminuendo signs are omitted or misplaced; others do not make for communicative, pianistic phrasing. In bar 7: "Not crescendo, but diminuendo to measure 8" (see also bars 11 and 30).

Clear pedaling. Bar 9: "Don't pedal on the two sixteenths. Pedal after the *c* sharp, after the second chord, and after the third chord. Don't change pedal for the last eighth note; stress this note somewhat, the third-beat chord soft.

Important left-hand harmony. Bars 11 and 12: "In these measures the left-hand harmony is important too. Bring out the bottom notes of these left-hand chords. Move the crescendo over to the beginning of the measure. Crescendo to the dotted quarter *e*, then diminuendo." Bar 19: "Play the right hand with the top note of the left-hand arpeggiated chords; pedal each full beat."

Pedaling and clear sonorities. Bar 23: "No pedal on

the sixteenth notes, so that the chromatic half-steps are clear." Bar 24: "Hold pedal for all the measure, though the sonorities should always be clear even in the low parts." Bar 30: "Crescendo and diminuendo in this measure instead of just crescendo; diminuendo in the end of the measure;" bars 31-32: "poco ritardando;" bar 31: "Connect the end of the measure (*b, a* sharp, *g* sharp) directly to the following dotted half-note chord."

Sonorous basses: Bar 33: "Bring out the basses here; the basses should be *klingend* (sonorous). Bar 34: "the last eighth diminuendo."

Communicative phrasing: Bar 35: "In this section much pedal, also in the beginning, so that one doesn't hear the fifths so much. The melody singing! Bring out the right-hand fifth fingers, the melody, only the top notes." Bars 35, 37: "The third beat diminuendo, but not too much." Bars 36, 38: "Poco crescendo; the last eighth (of bar 38) accented as in the following measure, the descending line poco diminuendo."

Instrumental color. Bar 42: "Bring out the *f* sharp and the following melody notes like a French horn; use the third finger." Bars 42, 44: "Pedal for the complete measure" (the *g* sharp of bar 44 naturally less strong than the *f* sharp and *a*). Bar 46: "*pp*, very soft, only the top notes singing." Bar 52: "Hold one pedal through the measure; because of the crescendo, the melody on the last eighth will be clear."

Levels of tone: "Never make the harmony thick." In bar 54, for example: "Three levels of dynamics: the melody loudest, then the bass, and all the rest on a third, softer level." In bar 56 Gieseking advised a diminuendo on the *b, a* sharp, and *g* sharp. "The *g* sharp quarter note singing!" Bar 59: "All five notes of the left-hand chord arpeggiated." Bar 62: "diminuendo;" bar 67 to end: "Bring out the top notes of the right-hand chords." Bars 67, 68: "Pedal each two beats;" bars 69, 70: "One pedal; separate a little before the last chord (bar 71), and retard the final left-hand *c* sharps."

Gieseking composed the *dosage de sonorités* and distributed the touches within a chord with a polyphony of sonorities and with a complex structure in movement of which each element, each level, was individualized to the extreme. He, himself, would have thought such a statement too complicated. He simply said, "I have to hear beautiful sounds come from my piano."

According to Gieseking

A Master Lesson on "La Vallee des Cloches"

Gieseking loved the works of Ravel to an imcomparable degree and throughout his career probably played the solo works more, and with greater success, than any other pianist.*

"My affinity for the Impressionists," he once said, "probably originated in my mixture of musical and scientific interests, a kind of after-effect of my youthful butterfly-collecting excursions with my father in the mountains."

Certainly, Gieseking had a marvelous ability to pictorialize nature. When Gieseking played Ravel's *Miroirs,* you could almost see "fireflies" or hear "sad birds" or "bells in the valley."

Although he was terse in his comments and such an incredibly "natural" pianist (his sightreading prowess and memory feats are legendary) that it often seemed he didn't know how he did these things — nevertheless, if you pinned him down, he could always give you a valid, tonal reason for everything he did.

Evenness of touch. Gieseking said that "translating the nuances"

---

*Gieseking played a number of all-Ravel programs, the last — the complete solo works — on October 18, 1954 in the Salle Pleyel in Paris:

Le Tombeau de Couperin
Valses Nobles et Sentimentales
Miroirs

Sonatine
Jeux d'Eau
Gaspard de la Nuit
Encores: Menuet sur le nom
    d'Haydn, Pavane, etc., etc.

Alfred Cortot sent a telegram backstage calling the recital "une soirée historique."

of the music of Ravel "presupposes a perfect touch technique acquired by an absolutely even, precise kind of playing." (This evenness lay on the solid ground-work of perfectly mastered rhythms and a vital attention to the minutest details of the written page.) He attached an incredible importance to evenness — an evenness and lightness of supreme delicacy, always controlled by the ear, that could translate the soft glitterings and sparklings of the *"Noctuelles"* breathtakingly . . . or gather up oceans of sound, presenting them to the delighted eye and ear of the imagination as in *"Une Barque sur l'Ocean."*

Beauty of Tone. Although every truly great pianist has his own tone resulting from his total interpretation, Gieseking perhaps had the most readily recognizable and the longest sustaining tone of all. His was a pure, transparent, nonpercussive tone of great dynamic range resulting from his phenomenal ear for prolonging vibrations, his masterful pedaling and his panlike, melodic outpouring. Music flowed from him effortlessly and enthusiastically, always colored by his innate sense of the exquisite. Yet for him, tone was uncomplicated: "I have to hear beautiful sounds from my piano."

That final sentence is a never-to-be-forgotten credo I learned from him: a pianist, especially when playing Ravel or Debussy, should not think foremost of harmonies, finger movements, form, or what have you. On the contrary, he should spontaneously think foremost of beautiful tone.

Melody. Melody for Gieseking

was inextricably connected with tone. His grunting and heavy breathing made you "give, give, give": "the melody, the melody, the melody" — not colored, structured in a formal, detached manner — but sung from within. Figurations, broken chords, and so on were almost always impressionistic colorings or atmosphere.

Tonal balance. "The satisfying tonal balance in the Impressionists is obtained when the consonant notes are brought out and the dissonant notes are subdued in order of their connection with the principal note or melody." he said. For example, in measures 24-27 of *"La Vallée des Cloches,"* etch the top notes of the right-hand octaves — make them really sing — give secondary importance to the bass notes, and keep the inner triplet bell tones extremely soft.

Or, to cite another example, at measure 140 of the *Animé* movement of the *Sonatine,* he said, "In Ravel, bring out a little the notes that underline the *'féerique,'* character of the melody. The soprano melody notes are very important. Also underline the left-hand thumb notes. Then just touch the rest, especially the sixteenth notes, only a slight trembling of the hand.

248

You must know how to find these important notes in the harmonies of Ravel or Debussy."

Other Gieseking dictums for playing Ravel and Debussy: Changes in tempo (ritardandi, retenuti) and rubatos must not take place except where marked.

"The indications *'cedez'* and *'serrez'* must be played with great discretion. They signify no more change than the moderate rubato of the romantic German style.

"Low notes must come out with the necessary clarity and most often must be held with the pedal. It is only by their relation with the bass that many fluctuating harmonies become clear.

"The damper pedal must be used frequently and can on many occasions be held a long time. All the tones which are thus agglomerated must be differentiated in degree of tone. You have to obtain a delicate mélange of sonorities and not an obscure, thick pulp of notes.

"The playing of a succession of descending melody notes or chords with the pedal down requires very careful shading. Each new note must be louder than, or drown out, the preceding notes. This effect is obtained by a very careful, unnoticeable crescendo.* When holding the pedal through an ascending melodic line, the shading of the notes naturally is much simpler."

"La Vallée des Cloches"
I have chosen *"La Vallée des Cloches,"* the fifth piece of *Miroirs*, for a Gieseking masterlesson because it is accessible to intermediate students — i.e., as far as the number and speed of the notes are concerned. Otherwise, as Gieseking said, "...the slow pieces which do not make so continuous and formidable demands on the virtuosity of the performer are never easy to play. Such a piece as *"La Vallée des Cloches* requires the most minute respect of the most subtle nuances of touch."

Ravel composed *Miroirs* in 1905 (*"La Vallée des Cloches,"* the most Debussyesque of the set, was probably composed earlier), dedicating each of the five pieces to his best-loved fellow Apaches: *"Noctuelles"* to Leon-Paul Fargue, the poet; *"Oiseaux tristes"* to Ricardo Vines, the pianist; *"Une Barque sur l'Ocean"* to Paul Sordes, the painter; *"Alborada del gracioso"* to Calvocoressi, the critic; and *"La Vallée des Cloches"* to Maurice Delage, his composer-pupil and intimate friend.

As Alfred Cortot, ever the poet, says, *"La Vallée des Cloches"* is filled with the silver tones of cattle bells, the rustling of faraway carillons, the crepuscular voice of steeple bells, the confused noise softly muted by slow sonorities of which the waves fade away in the serenity of the contemplative evening. The central lyrical episode is the only fragment of *Miroirs* in which Ravel seems to abandon the expression of subjective sentiment, to the confidence of a personal emotion..."

The following detailed suggestions by Gieseking on *"La Vallée des Cloches"* were notated during several lessons I heard him give to several pianists, including my wife. The student who follows them and also listens to Gieseking's recording in the Angel album 3541-55 or the 78 rpm Columbia LFX 895 (issued in France), should arrive at a stylistically correct, beautiful performance of this work.

Ms. 1, 2. "Play the opening octaves absolutely pianissimo and clear, bell-like, as if heard from a distance."

Ms. 3-11. "Keep the G-sharp octaves pianissimo and clear throughout. All the broken-chord work should be background, pianissimo, atmosphere. These accompaniment figures must be perfect both technically and rhythmically. Practice and listen for absolute evenness and pianissimo, the double notes precisely together. Then the hands exactly together, absolutely in time."

Ms. 4, 5, 6. "Be sure to play the left hand *'un peu marqé*, bringing out the top notes — E, C-sharp."

Ms. 6, 8, 10. "These E-sharps should be bell-like but mezzo forte, very sustained, vibrating, each one a little softer than the preceding."

Ms. 1-6. "Hold one long pedal from measure one through to the second half of the second beat of measure six. Be sure to play the low G with a slight accent as indicated, catching it clearly in a new pedal. You want resonance and clarity."

Ms. 6-11. "The pedal taken in measure six continues without change through measure 11."

Ms. 12, 13. "Pedal by the measure. Play the hands precisely together on the chords, outlining the top of the right hand for a silvery quality. Play the chords and double notes as legato as possible. Keep the bass octaves clear, even through the pedal of the fourth beat."

M. 14. "Change pedal on the first and the fifth beats."

Ms. 15-16. "Observe the crescendo on the second and the third beats of measure 15 into the first beat of measure 16."

Pedal. Ms. 16-19. "Pedal from measure 16 to and including the first beat of measure 20. Exquisitely downgrade the dynamics from mezzo forte, to piano, to pianissimo in measures 16, 17, and 18."

M. 20. "Catch a new pedal on the second beat, holding it through the entire measure and including the first beat of measure 21. Hold the low B-flat — F with the left hand. On the second beat, take the lower D-flat of the melody (in octaves in the middle score) with the thumb of the left hand. Also divide the melody of beats 4½-5 between the hands. Do the same thing in measure 21."

(This subtle arrangement of hands and pedaling in this *'largement chanté'* melodic section is a master stroke!)

Ms. 18-19. "Crescendo from the low C, to the bass C, to the middle C. Imagine the sustained crescendo of a woodwind or a stringed instrument."

Ms. 19 1/2-23. "Play this beautiful, singing melody with a full, mellow tone."

Ms. 23-24. "Take time to catch full-toned basses — the grace notes G-flat, D-flat — in the pedal."

Ms. 24, 25. "Don't hurry this section. Pedal once for these two measures. Sensitively diminuendo the third and fourth beats, the C and B-flat."

---

*For example: measures 12 or 44 of *"La Vallée des Cloches."* In Debussy, see measures 11-12 of *"Danseuses de Delphes;"* the middle chorale section of *"La Cathédrale engloutie;"* or measures 67, 68 et al, the Tempo I (*avec plus d'abandon*), of *"Soirée dans Grenade."*—D.E.

Ms. 24-27. "Play the left hand soft, legato, and perfect rhythmically, the right hand expressive and as legato as possible, bringing out the top notes. Pedal on the first beats of measures 26 and 27. The left hand quarter notes of measure 27 should be soft."

M. 28. "Bring out the top notes, the melody; play the right-hand alto notes mezzo piano, the middle-score thirds pianissimo."

Ms. 28, 29, 30. "Hold one pedal for these measures."

M. 31. "Take care to get a full, even chord on the first beat. Play the right-hand thirds pianissimo."

Ms. 32, 33. "Play the right hand as legato as possible, with singing top notes. The octave melody must sing out above the chords, the eighth notes steady. Pedal once for these two measures."

Ms. 34, 35. "Shade the E-flat octave bells as before — diminuendo. Change pedal on the first and second beats of measure 34. Then hold the pedal through measures 35 and 36, or possibly change on beat 2½ of measure 36."

Ms. 40, 41. "It's good to play the top F of the first-beat octave with the right hand."

M. 44. "Play the right-hand chords piano, the left-hand middle score chords pianissimo."

Ms. 45, 46, 47. "Take care to achieve mezzo forte, piano, and pianissimo as indicated, playing the final eighth-note G-sharp — C-sharp triple piano. Hold one pedal for measures 46 to 49."

M. 47. "It is very difficult [but] bring out the bottom B to G-sharp of the right-hand double notes legato, pianissimo."

Ms. 48, 49. "Make a beautiful legato from the low G-sharp to the low C-sharp octave."

M. 50. "Diminuendo the last right-hand sixteenth notes to triple piano."

M. 52 to end. "Remain in tempo."

La Vallée des cloches

Edited by Dean Elder
with Gieseking's pedalings and markings

MIROIRS

№ V

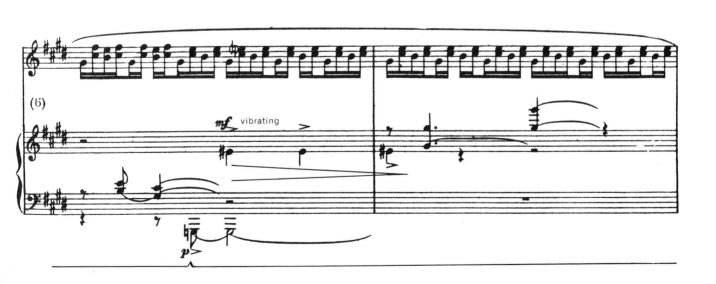

253

254

255

The Piano Music of Octavio Pinto

Octavio Pinto

A Music Lesson
by
Guiomar Novaes

interview December 23, 1970

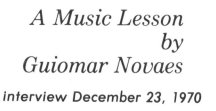

"**M**y husband, Octavio Pinto, had a very great talent for anything he would do," reminisced Madame Novaes. "Once in Chicago, Leopold Godowsky asked him to try his piano. 'You are a concert pianist,' said Godowsky. 'No,' my husband said, 'I cannot be a concert pianist because when I go on the stage I don't feel my feet anymore; I can't find the pedals.'

"But his not being a concert pianist was contrary to my wishes. Besides composing piano pieces and songs, he even wrote an operetta. He was so modest he wrote it anonymously. That operetta was performed daily for over one and one-half years in Sao Paulo. And I only knew that after we were married. He never told me. Someone said, 'You must show your wife your beautiful operetta.' And he said, 'I don't think I even have a copy of it now.'

"He was too modest, too bad — because he was so full of everything, a sympathetic nature. He was educated by the Jesuits with whom he lived for nine years. He spoke six languages; he was interested in everything. Too bad God took him so early . . . ."

Octavio Ribeiro Pinto (1890-1950), like his wife, Guiomar Novaes, had come from Sao Paulo and had studied piano with Chiafarelli. He was 19 when he first met Guiomar, then age 13, at the farewell concert she gave in Brazil on the eve of her departure for Paris. He followed his future wife's career with interest and admiration. After their marriage on December 8, 1922, he often accompanied her on her American and European tours.

Although an architectural engineer by profession and one of Sao Paulo's most important city planners, Pinto was also a composer of some highly successful piano pieces. An especially popular one is "Run, Run!" from his suite *Memories of Childhood*. Novaes told how this suite came to be written:

"While our two small children were running around the garden, my husband, who liked to improvise, improvised these pieces. I liked these *Memories of Childhood* pieces very much and asked him, 'Why don't you write them down and get them published?' And he said, 'because no one will play them.' 'If you write them down,' I said, 'I promise to play them this year in New York.'

"So he wrote them down. I played three recitals in New York that season and put them in my first program. When I played them, the public applauded very much. And the following day one of the owners of Schirmer telephoned to my hotel, asking who Octavio Pinto was.

"'My husband,' I said. 'Is he here?' he asked. 'I am asking because the telephone is ringing — people are asking where they can get this music and we don't know it.'

"My husband came to the telephone. 'Are you going to publish them?' the man from Schirmer's asked. 'No, I don't think I will' my husband replied. 'Why not? We have so many calls here. Would you like Schirmer to publish them? I'll come to talk to you about it.' My husband very simply said, 'I will think it over.'

"In the meantime he asked Sigismond Stojowski — we were very good friends and often asked each other's advice. Mr. Stojowski said, 'My heartiest congratulations, Mr. Pinto. I have a batch of music at Schirmer's and don't know when, if ever, they will publish it. And here they *came* to you to *offer* to publish your work!'

"But my husband said, 'I am an architect; I am not a composer.' 'Don't say that,' cried Stojowski. 'You don't know the talent that you have. Tell Schirmer they can be your publisher.' So it was born, the *Memories of Childhood*. If all this hadn't happened, my husband would never have published this suite. You see, he was that way.

"Rudolf Ganz asked my husband to orchestrate this suite. So he did. And Ganz conducted it in Carnegie Hall in one of his Saturday morning youth concerts — you remember he had a series. He conducted it several times in New York and in Chicago also. Luboshutz and Nemenoff play the two-piano version with great success. (*The two-piano version is not an adaptation but a complete two-piano work in itself and fun to play. D.E.*)

"Schirmer also published some of my husband's songs. He wrote lovely songs, and Bidu Sayao sang them a great deal on her recitals."

CHILDREN'S FESTIVAL

I asked if there was another easy piano work by her husband, perhaps less well known than the *Memories of Childhood*, interesting for young students, which *Clavier* could publish.

"Yes, there is," she said. "The man from Schirmer asked my husband if he had another suite. 'Yes, I have a less complicated one,' my husband answered, 'a *Children's Festival* suite.'

The pieces are very short, mostly one page each. They are very effective. Number five, 'Playing Marbles' is lovely. She went "puhpuhpuhpuhpuhpuh" to indicate the tempo (♩ =M.M.92), and sang the glissando at the end: "rrrrrrrrrringgg. Make sure to play the crescendo in measure six."

"Number one, 'Prelude,' is lovely also. The staccato should be played exactly as it is written in the music. The first three right-hand notes staccato and the fourth and fifth legato. In the second complete measure, the first note should be played staccato and all the other ones legato. In measure four, the staccato comes again from the second note on . . . .

"Number three, the 'Little March,' is also very interesting: 'Um, tum-ta, pa pa pa pa, pa' MM ♩ =circa 138." (She sang quietly with crescendo and diminuendo.)

"Number four, 'Serenade,' is more serene, slower.

If I were to choose two for a student, I would choose 'Serenade' and the last one, 'Playing Marbles,' as lively. My grandchild likes to play number two, the 'Minuet': MM ♩ =168."

VÁSARY
TEACHES
BARTÓK

interview August 10, 1976

Támas Vásary offers a lesson here on Bartók's Suite, *op. 14 He began by discussing the last piece, No. 4 which is reprinted on pages 261-262, and worked backwards through the other pieces. He did not have enough time to comment on the first piece.*

You've got to approach a work like Bartók's *Suite* with boxing gloves, being willing to give the "drop of blood" that Rubinstein speaks about. When you go on stage you just plunge in, not caring about wrong notes or anything. And then this drop of blood comes out.

No. 4 Sostenuto
Bartók was a tortured, suffering person, and his suffering comes out in this piece. The preceding piece is a sort of volcano, a desperation. After this, Bartók doesn't go to heaven but goes around like a spirit or ghost in this fourth piece. It's an uncanny, eerie, ghostly movement. When I hear it, I feel a chill in my back.

Bars 1-2. It is important to bring out the octave formed by the middle voice in the right hand and the top voice of the left hand in order to give shape to the piece. Crescendo and dimuendo in each bar, each time more as the interval gets bigger and higher. Pedal each bar.

Bar 4. This time crescendo the most. The octave E's are not just a dissonance; they're a warning. The tension increases as the inner voice climbs higher and higher, bar by bar, longing to go somewhere.

Bars 6-7. Play the sixth-beat accent with a full tone. Pedal as I have notated in the score.

Bars 8-9. Accent and pedal similarly to bars 6-7.

Bars 10-15. Here the tension breaks down, as the inner voice descends chromatically bar by bar: G, F♯ F, E, D, and C. Change the pedal on the second beat in bar 10 and hold through the measure. Diminuendo in bars 11 and 12 on the third- and fifth-beat E's. It's very sad here. The grace notes in bars 13-15 are like tears or drops of blood, not just ornaments.

To be able to convince an audience you need to have a strong sense of what such music expresses. A great masterpiece expresses a certain spiritual state. I play it because it says something to me. What I feel may not be right, but I must believe that it is. Another pianist may feel something entirely different with strong conviction. We both are right.

Bars 16-18. Bring out the theme beginning on the second beats. In bar 18 Bartók writes *perdendosi* and stops to catch his breath.

Bar 19. Pause on the eighth rest; great things happen when there is a rest. Shape the eighth notes with crescendo and dimuendo, playing almost *mf*. It's a very warm, human voice. Some sort of consolation is coming.

Bar 21. Diminuendo. The sighs are coming.

Bars 22-23. Diminuendo the two-note slurs in both hands. These slurs are like tiny sighs. Breathe and sigh yourself, bringing out the top notes.

Bars 24-25. In bar 24 the sighs get bigger, becoming in bar 25 a desperate cry.

These terms I'm using to express what I feel — consolation, tears, drop of blood, sighs, a desperate cry, and so on — are nonsense by themselves. Trying to express music in words is as futile as trying to retell a dream. Music, like dreams, has its own logic that is inexpressible in words. Our feelings expressed in words are nonsense for the conscious brain, but not for the dream brain. We must use the dream brain when we play.

Bars 26-27. Again play the chromatic motive with crescendo and diminuendo. In bar 27 Bartók sees that the situation is hopeless and goes on.

Bar 29. Play the octaves very legato.

Bars 30-31. Again, crescendo and diminuendo in each phrase.

Bars 33-35 Bring out the top notes, retarding, playing with crescendo and diminuendo. And in the last two bars, bring out the top notes of the last three dotted-quarter fourths.

No. 3 Allegro Molto

The left hand is technically difficult, but you must forget about the instrument. This is a devilish tide, a flood. You shouldn't be able to distinguish the notes. Non legato is all right, but use the pedal to blur. The blur is made up, if you want to be precise, of lots of tiny things, but the main thing is that it should be something far away, under the earth. You must get the feeling yourself; you must feel from the stage that everyone is afraid.

Bars 49-50. Plunge to these *ff* whole-note chords.

Bars 58-60. Feel the connection from this *fff* tied whole-note chord on to the following chord in the next measure. A long note doesn't always mean the music stops. Go right on.

No. 2 Scherzo

Bars 1-4. No accent on the downbeats until the B♭ of measure 4.

Bar 33. Tranquillo. The right hand is painful — it's more than just a dissonance. Tranquillo here is a term for tempo, not expression. It's not a quiet tranquillo. It should not be aggressive or scherzando but tortured, breathless, a going and holding back. You want to get somewhere and can't. You're not happy, you're disheveled, a monster, really desperate.

Bar 191. The *p* reflects the complete illogic of this nightmare.

Bar 194. This section is surrealistic, like a Dali painting: there are burning giraffes, half bodies, etc. And then comes the whistle of a train — "Whooo!" — with the ♫ ♩.

Bar 207. (Tempo I) This section is searching-like. Beethoven used this same technique, presenting a big question mark before the end of the movement and then suddenly returning with the original idea to finish as in bars 211-216.

Bars 218-end. Go furiously to the end.

No. 4 from Suite Opus 14

Béla Bartók

Rákoskeresztur. 1916. II.

262

TECHNICAL REGIME INTERVIEWS

Cecile Genhart has trained many of the young musicians who have become contest winners over the past few decades. She has also been a judge at various competitions as well as a 20-year member of the National Committee on Fulbright Awards.

interview August 5, 1975

Cecile Genhart *talks to Dean Elder*

ELDER: *A year or so ago you returned to Zürich, supposedly to retire, a flock of your student following you. Now you have returned to Eastman. Why did you leave Zürich so soon?*

GENHART: There are several reasons, the main reason being that there were no facilities for my students: no way for them to practice, to perform, or to live. As living conditions were much too expensive, I taught many of them gratis. My students couldn't afford both to pay and to live. And teaching them was my privilege — I would have died without teaching — for they were such wonderfully gifted, loyal students, like Mark Westcott, who coached with me before his debut in Zürich's *Tonhalle*. Besides, I was very homesick for America and my friends.

ELDER: *Emil Frey (1889-1947), with whom you studied, from all accounts was an extraordinary pianist. Have you read what Arthur Rubinstein writes in his book, "My Young Years," about Emil Frey at a contest of former years, the famous Anton Rubinstein Competition in Moscow in 1910?*

GENHART: No! I would like very much to know.

Rubinstein says "...Frey was quite marvelous. He had impressed the jury with his trio and was considered as the only candidate for the composition prize, but one had never expected him to be the fine pianist he revealed himself to be. His "Hammerklavier" Sonata was technically more perfect than Hoehn's, if not as moving, but the whole program he played was a sheer delight. This Swiss musician appeared to be my most dangerous rival..."

Absolutely thrilling! I am so happy to hear that.

Tell me about your study. I've been told that your father, Gottfried Staub, with whom you first studied, performed the 32 Beethoven Sonatas, frequently in one season.

Yes, he was one of the first to do this. We lived in Basel, where I was born. My sister, a child prodigy, a famous young pianist at 14, was pushed and forced. My mother practiced three hours with her every day. But because my sister did not sustain a career, I was not disciplined very strongly in piano at the beginning. I was brought up freely, almost like a gypsy. My mother used to say, "Don't practice. Go to the zoo." She would give me a little basket filled with stale bread and carrots to bring to my beloved animals. I spent more time at the zoo than I did at the *Töchterschule.*

Later my father began teaching at the Zürich Conservatory, which I entered when I was 16. There I had wonderful training. Very interested in composition and theory, I studied composition with Dr. Volkmar Andreae and counterpoint with Philipp Jarnach, the man who completed Busoni's opera, *"Doktor Faust."*

And I worked very hard at the piano with Emil Frey, an excellent teacher, particularly for technique which I needed desperately. Frey disciplined me — something my father had felt he shouldn't do as he had done with my sister. Frey, who was a wonderful person and a great influence in my life, was definitely responsible for the technique I had. And although I never became a virtuoso, I did play the Brahms B Flat Major and the Beethoven C Major Concertos at one evening concert, later in Münich and in Berlin with Edwin Fischer conducting.

With whom did you study after Frey?

I studied with Pembauer in Münich. As Pembauer was considered the best Liszt player, I had hopes of learning much in studying Liszt with him. But he was not so good a teacher as he was a performer I am sorry to say. His teaching was all imagination and fantasy, with nothing pinpointed, no details analyzed.

So after a half year — I was about 20 — I left for Berlin to study with Edwin Fischer who became the strongest influence in my musical education. Berlin became my home. Edwin Fischer and his wife, Eleanor von Mendelssohn, were wonderful to me.

When I came to Fischer, he was still young. He was inexperienced in conducting, I in concertizing. He admitted using me as his guinea pig, engaging me as his soloist on tour through the *Ruhrgebiet* — Gelsenkirchen, Bochum, and all those places which were at that time tremendously music-conscious. It was a marvelous experience for me and frankly a very good experience for Edwin to practice his conducting, the field in which he was then happiest.

Did you know Busoni?

Yes, I was very fortunate. That goes back to the time when I still lived in Zürich, when I was very young. During the World Wars, we in Switzerland were fortunate to have many great people as refugees.

Through Philip Jarnach, my counterpoint teacher and Busoni's close friend, Busoni became interested in my compositions that I played for him. It was the time when Debussy just began to be known. Busoni — who was then more interested in composition than in piano playing — thought it incredible that I was so avant-garde and yet so young. Being included in his entourage, a very eccentric group of people, was one of my greatest experiences. But I must add that as a composer, I was *ein Backfisch*, young, immature. My composing was just a flash.

Busoni was a stunning man; women were at his feet. Busoni was appalled at the smallness of the Swiss who, of course, followed his every step. In Basel, where he gave master classes, he used to tour through the town in an open-top taxi, his big St. Bernard sitting behind him. Shocked, the very proper Baslers stood and watched, their heads nodding disapproval at such eccentricity.

What other famous musicians did you know?

Carl Friedberg was a friend of our family. My sister studied with him, and I played for him when I was very little. Cortot visited us, as did Kreisler and Schweitzer. I don't know any famous musician or scholar who didn't visit my father, who was tremendously cultured and well-read; as a composer one had to reckon with him. On the other hand, we three children, having not much respect or appreciation, always left the house when these "strange people" came.

Did you know Hans von Bülow?

He had been dead for quite a while when I went to Berlin. But his second wife, his widow, had open salon — *un jour fixe* they called it — and I had the honor to play there frequently. Claudio Arrau played regularly at Madame von Bülow's salon. He played the whole *Well-Tempered Clavier.* Although at that time he was only about 22, he was already a tremendous pianist. Eugene d'Albert, whom we knew very well, had a home with his eighth wife on *Sonnenberg* in Zürich during the War. He and Busoni were rivals: Busoni, the tremendous aesthete, the classicist; d'Albert, the extrovert, the *Fleisch und Blut.* Both were phenomenal though very extreme. Eugene d'Albert came to our home — that again goes back to my youth in Zürich.

When did you go to Matthay?

That was much later, in 1937. I had already been teaching over ten years at the Eastman School. Matthay was a very great teacher and I loved him dearly. I was 25 when I left Berlin for Rochester where I married a student of my father. Mr. Eastman invited me to teach at the Eastman School The Sunday music soirées in his home, where I often played, with international great people present, were unforgettable. Eastman did everything that Rochester stands for, spending millions for the best educational purposes, in other parts of the world too.

I have strong hope that this year the Eastman School will have a re-birth under its new director, Robert Freeman. Still in his thirties, he is a brilliant, enormously gifted, competent, charming man, with a fabulous background. Both his parents are musicians. I can't praise him enough.

Tell me about your teaching at Eastman and that notorious second measure in the Bach D Minor Three-part Invention!

The first year for new students in my studio is a trying one as a rule, sometimes with tears rolling down. Putting students on a Three-part Invention after they've been playing the Tchaikovsky Concerto is not easy for their ego and enthusiam. But if they are strong in talent, they will hold out. And of course it is my duty to keep them interested and to make them understand I do it for their own later good.

The first line of the D Minor Three-part Invention is one of our notorious tests. I insist that students play the second measure faultlessly, in regard to touch and to tone differentiation and duration. In the first measure, if you detach or shorten the first eighth note slightly, in order to emphasize the F — not by tone but by duration — the F becomes more prominent. (Phrasing with no break may not be wrong of course if done musically, with understanding. But from the educational or disciplinary standpoint, it is good to form the habit of detaching before a tied or syncopated note under certain circumstances.)

Inconsistency is delightful at times but in a piece like this, consistency is the test. The separation before the tied note must be carried out wherever it occurs, and that requires coordination, concentration, and control. One must also listen to the end of the long note.

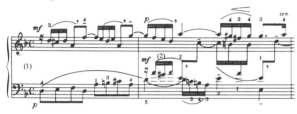

What is especially difficult in the second measure?

It is difficult to make this alto answer sound as if it were played as a solo on a second piano. The spot where you play the second-beat E with the left hand requires arm-weight and finger touches simultaneously. (I recommend either the Busoni or the Mugellini editions. There are some other good editions too. Mugellini and Egon Petri were often co-workers with Busoni.) In the beginning, if you phrase before the tied notes, the tops of the motive in the right hand — the line F, G, and A — stand out without having to force them.

Then the same thing must happen in the alto voice in the second measure. I ask the student, "How long is this alto E in relation to the bass suspension D-C? When do you let the E go? (Naturally, in the beginning one has to play twice as slowly inasmuch as there is so much to think and to hear vertically. Perfecting the line horizontally as a whole will come naturally after everything regarding duration and tonal differentiation is understood.) The D in the bass voice is a suspension which resolves to C, to the third, E-C. Now, if on this second sixteenth, the student doesn't hear the three voices vertically, then his playing is neither correct nor accurate. And the alto E must be released a thirty-second after the C. This is the critical moment:

The fourth beat contains a similar problem: when you play the final soprano A, again you must listen to the sound of the three voices. A violinist would make a crescendo on this A because of its harmonic significance.

Hans Georg Naegeli, Genhart's great-great-grandfather, who wrote many songs to the words of the poet Pfeiffer. Plaster relief.

The A is tonic, an anticipation, while you have dominant harmony. Because we can't sustain or make a crescendo on the A, I have the student pedal the last sixteenth, a very short pedal, half up and rapidly down, giving the A color and harmonic significance, making the two A's legato. A repeated note in the high register can only be played completely legato with the help of the pedal.

So you work through this measure in great detail.

Yes, and that first lesson is torture: a new student thinks, "Heavens, must I be aware of every note and how fussy can one be?" So I tell him, "The greater the artist, the more pains he takes with infinitesimal detail. Taking great pains with detail makes the difference between a dilettante and an artist." If a student masters these problems of coordination and touch, paying attention to such detail will become second nature. His ear will dictate what is right; his instinct will be sharper. I don't insist that every student play this piece, but almost all of my students want it sooner or later, not for performing but for teaching.

Does your Bach interpretation or style stem from tradition?

I think it is partly traditional. My father was a great player, Edwin Fischer too. Speaking of teaching, Bach reminds me how often freshmen are poorly prepared in this regard. How can students learn to play Bach if they haven't played any Bach before they come to college? First of all they have to be exposed to the music. They should know all of the *Well-Tempered Clavier*, in time certainly most of the Three-part Inventions; they should listen to the B Minor Mass, et cetera.

My *Ur-Ur-Grossvater*, my great-great-grandfather, Hans Georg Naegeli (1773-1836), "the forgotten *Sängervater*," first performed the B Minor Mass. And he was the first to publish the *Well-Tempered Clavier* as well as the 32 Beethoven sonatas. My cousins took me to *Rämistrasse* in Zürich to show me his monument this past year. I had to go to Switzerland to re-discover that he was my great-great grandfather.

It is incredible that he is almost forgotten. Our musicologist at Eastman, Dr. Fox, was terribly excited when I brought him news of Naegeli. This being his 200th anniversary, Naegeli will be a major topic. In Swiss school song books, you always find Naegeli songs, and *"Freut euch des Lebens"* is probably the most popular. It's so charming. If I had a piano here, I would play it for you.

Bach performance is in your blood! Would you say that your approach to piano playing — other composers as well as Bach — is more through the music than through the instrument?

Definitely. One reason I want students to learn "voicing" is to achieve orchestral sound. Busoni's greatness lay in his orchestral sound, but students should not want to do splashy things more than anything else. I think, in general, the main fault with teachers is that they give in to students as to what music they want to play. Students should be able to play spashy pieces, bravura and for effect, but not at the expense of solid musicianship.

And you give students the repertoire they should play!

I certainly try, but not without exceptions. And the same with contests. I'm not against contests, providing the students are ready. Contests should not interfere too much with regular, steady, careful study.

What are some basic rules that can be applied to anything as part of this "steady, careful study?"

Awareness is one basic rule: you must know what you do — why, when, and how. And constant listening is extremely important. In polyphonic music, which is a "must" for disciplinary and other reasons, you must listen to the vertical sound as well as the horizontal.

Pedaling, which takes time to develop, is another basic shortcoming of students. I teach four distinctly different types of pedaling. "Pedal is the soul of piano playing" says Chopin! A teacher has to insist upon awareness of the student's pedal use. A teacher cannot be too strict with pedal, mainly its release.

We teachers have to be sympathetic and warm to make up for the suffering our pupils sometimes endure. We must compliment and encourage students whenever they deserve it. On the other hand, I won't give in when it comes to disciplinary detail, so often neglected. Young people, wanting everything right away, too often lack the patience to build brick by brick. They want to start building from the roof. The teacher has to be a good psychologist.

I have heard that you seldom teach by imitation, that your teaching is reasoned so the student understands.

I certainly try. Many times it helps a student enormously if the teacher demonstrates a phrase. It saves time too. But the student doesn't learn to think independently if the teacher plays too much. Analyzing, thinking, and knowing how to practice can never be overemphasized.

This brings me to the point that a teacher can never

Cecile Genhart on balcony of her home in Zurich.

afford to stop practicing. If a teacher doesn't practice, he is no more the best teacher.

One student told me that in studying the Brahms Händel Variations with you, he became aware of every harmonic progression and transposition, that your own playing is notable for the beauty of the harmonies.

I do think that awareness of the harmonies is very much neglected. I am strongly for the student's knowing figured bass. After all, in accompanying a Bach cantata, a musician has to be able to read strict four-part figured bass. That many schools and teachers no longer teach figured bass is a typical sign that students don't want stern discipline. They can never make up what they don't learn when they are very young: *Was Hänschen nicht lernt, lernt Hans nicht mehr.*

I have also heard that you can play Beethoven sonatas in any key. Do you require this work of your students?

No, but I require transposing. Although my absolute pitch is not dependable, my relative pitch is so strongly developed that I can play almost as well in another key, if I don't get in trouble with fingering. If you know a piece thoroughly, you should be able to play it in any key — perhaps, however, not in the same tempo or with the same perfection.

I have found absolute pitch a hindrance in transposing.

Yes. it can be. Some of the greatest musicians have not had it. Wagner didn't. Toscanini often would sing off a fourth or a fifth. The color of D flat major and A flat major, for instance, is to me so related that I can mix them up. But I wish I had a more keen absolute pitch. It's embarrassing to sing off pitch and know it! On the other hand, I've had students with absolute pitch who were unmusical, and vice versa. Absolute pitch is a freakish phenomenon not always connected with musicianship and, in my opin-

Text continued on page 271

Cecile Genhart Exercises

I am indebted to Dr. Gary Wolf, Department of Music, Orlando Florida Techno-logical University, for most of these exercises, taken from his notes when he studied with Mrs. Genhart (and approved by her). They are meant as models, for the teacher and student should create exercises to overcome each individual's problems.

— Dean Elder

The following Keyboard Harmony and Sequence Pattern examples represent Cecile Genhart's vital concern for the total development of a musician-pianist. Unlike harmony classes, which stress written exercises, these require the development of on-the-spot hearing, thinking, and use of theoretical knowledge.

I. KEYBOARD HARMONY

1. Suggested text: *Thoroughbass Method* **by Hermann Keller, translated by Carl Parrish, W.W. Norton and Co., N.Y., 1965.**

2. Emphasize skill in thinking harmonically as well as melodically.

3. Be able to modulate in four strict voices from a given key to any other given key by using various progressions — i.e., augmented sixth chords, diminished sevenths, etc.

4. Harmonize given melodic lines in various styles.

5. Resolve a given chord in several ways.

(All of the above to be done without writing out, in order to develop basic improvisational skills.)

II. SEQUENCE PATTERNS

1. V7 to I.

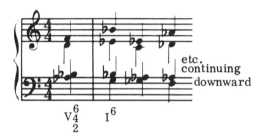

2. Non-simultaneous key release, found in all literature, polyphonic as well as other. Between each two chords in the right hand, two voices remain the same. One voice moves — first the bottom, then the top, and then the middle. Connect the moving voice with the finger, lifting the repeated voices sooner — i.e., emphasize finger legato, non-simultaneous key release, and voice leading.

3. Three-voiced canon in right hand, chromatic scale in left. Practice expanding — left hand three octaves downward, right hand one octave upward — and returning to starting position.

4. Rapid four-voice modulation. The polyphonic nature and non-simultaneous key release are points to stress. The V7 or C (the second chord) should be mentally turned into a German

augmented sixth (F in the soprano becoming E sharp) for proper resolution and modulation. Continue the progression downward until you reach C major.

III. TECHNICAL EXERCISES

5. Five-finger exercise. Slow to fast tempo. Stress absolute evenness.

6. Symmetric inversion of black-white keys to develop and exercise the hands equally. Before the accent, lift the shoulder and float up with the elbow, so the accent is a relaxed but strong arm-weight touch. When playing 2-4, listen to make sure that the fourth finger plays as loudly as the second on the accent. Play hands separately. Also play with rhythmical variants and in single notes instead of double.

Use the same chords as an exercise for the fourth finger. Relax on the long notes, dropping the wrist and shoulder, floating up at the elbow. The finger should spring up rapidly on the staccato notes.

7. Arpeggio exercise. Play each arpeggio four octaves up and back, hands separate and later hands together, two octaves apart. Practice on each note of the chromatic scale, using the same fingering. Slow to fast tempo. Become aware of the weaker fingers and also the black-white key relationship, the black keys being easier to get more tone on, the white being lower — "in the ditch." Absolute evenness of tone requires careful listening.

MM⁷   +6   mM⁷   +6   dim. 7   V7   new key

8. Chromatic scale exercise, symmetric inversion, contrary motion, two octaves up and back, hands together, slow to fast tempo. As the same fingers are used in both hands, both hands are exercised equally. Play six times, using six different fingerings:

1. 123 13 13 123 13 123 13 13 123 123
2. 123 1234 123 13 123 1234 123 123
3. 123 1234 123 123 1234 123 12345
4. 123 1234 1234 123 1234 12345 1
5. 1234 1234 1234 1234 1234 12345
6. 12345 12345 12345 12345 12345

9. Chromatic scale in "blind octaves." Bring out the thumbs to avoid the left hand's being heavier, also creating the illusion of speed even when tempo is the same. Practice four octaves up and return. Also practice beginning with left hand on B and right hand on C. (This exercise is also suggested by Dohnanyi in *Essential Finger Exercises*, E.B. Marks; by T. Matthay in *Musical Interpretation*, Boston Music; and by I. Philipp, *Complete School of Technic*, (Theodore Presser.)

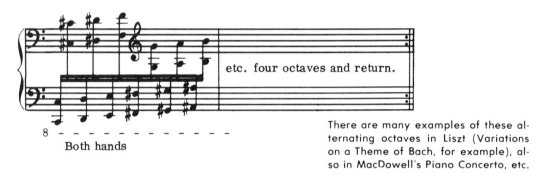

Both hands

There are many examples of these alternating octaves in Liszt (Variations on a Theme of Bach, for example), also in MacDowell's Piano Concerto, etc.

10. Whole-tone scale, same scale in each hand, major third apart. Play up and back four octaves in groupings of six. Also play a minor third apart, each hand playing a different whole-tone scale.

11. Canon exercise. Play on each chromatic tone, first in single notes and later in octaves.

etc. chromatically through all keys

M   m   dim.   New key

12. Chromatic scale with whole-tone scale and chromatic scale with augmented triad. Play four octaves, slow to fast. Then reverse the hands, starting at the top, and go downward. Use different fingerings in the chromatic scales. This exercise is excellent for establishing a strong, steady rhythm, in preparation, e.g., for the chromatic scales in the last movement of the Beethoven Concerto in C Minor

Text of interview continued

ion, is definitely overrated. Relative pitch, however, is indispensable.

Are you concerned about rhythm?

Terribly. I should perhaps have mentioned rhythm first when you asked about principles. Rhythm is very neglected in much of the playing one hears. Many of the new students clip long notes, tied-over syncopated notes, and rests. They must learn to count! In general students aren't aware of the beauty of silence. Why? Because there is very little silence left in this world. All the time the "monster" television is on. I think we must all go deaf sooner or later. Only when there is silence can you hear the angels!

I know you expect your students to have absolute technical command of scales and arpeggios. Do you have your own exercises too?

Yes, I do. That doesn't mean I use only my own. I often recommend the traditional exercises and etudes, but I try to discover and invent exercises for specific shortcomings in an individual. (See technical exercises, pages 268-270.) One of my pet exercises is on the chord E, G, B♭, D, E for the right hand, with the stretch between the third finger on the black key B flat and the fourth finger on the white key D:

I have students do this exercise in double stops, accenting in triplets to vary the accent. It wouldn't make sense to use the same chord in the left hand inasmuch as the the intervals between the fingers would be different, the difficulty would not be the same. But if you use the same intervals inverted — i.e., left hand descending C, A, F sharp, D, C, then you have the same problem between the fingers:

Between the third and fourth fingers you have F sharp-D instead of B flat-D. Of course the hands must not be played together because it would sound absurd. And I use this inverted interval system when I teach whole-tone scales or anything in contrary motion. It's based on contrary motion because the hands

are not built according to the keyboard. So using this system saves time and develops both hands alike.

On those chords you have students play 1-3, 2-4, 3-5 in triplets?

Yes with a chained thumb. Before the accent, you should lift the shoulder a little and float up with the elbow, so that the following accent is a strong arm-weight touch. And then with the left hand:
When the G-D comes in the right hand, for instance, you must listen that the fourth finger plays as loudly as the second on the accent. If you don't listen, and play these exercises mechanically, you will perfect imperfection. Technical exercises require a great deal of concentration. Otherwise, I think they are a waste of time.

Returning to contests — why do the Russians win so many?

The Russian school of piano playing can't be overrated, particularly educationally. May I go back to the children's education where the greatest influence starts and the greatest faults are made? The Russians start disciplining children at the age of four, providing the children have intelligence, vitality, good temperament, good ear, interest, and show talent. If the talent is great, it shows as a rule when children are very little. Then the Russians have their best available teachers teach these little four-year olds every day. And their master pianists — even such a one as Gilels — go to hear these little ones from time to time, to give an overall criticism or praise. So by the time the Russians are 16, they have played the Tchaikovsky Concerto. They are ready for international top contests and beat nearly everyone else.

Would you care to mention some of the students you consider the best you've had, some of the contest winners?

Well, of course, Mark Westcott and John Perry are among the recent contest winners. Barry Snyder, who now teaches here at Eastman, won second place in the Cliburn contest a few years ago. But the list of all the winners I have had the joy of teaching would be very long.

ADELE MARCUS, distinguished faculty member of the Juilliard School in New Yok City has trained many prize-winning students, including Byron Janis, Augustin Anievas, and Horacio Gutierrez, second prize winner in the 1970 Tchaikovsky Competition in Moscow. Miss Marcus studied with Josef Lhevinne and Artur Schnabel and was Josef Lhevinne's assistant for seven years. Besides performing with orchestras and in solo recitals this season, she will give master classes and demonstration lectures in this country, Canada, and Denmark.

The following article, my editing and organization of Adele Marcus' own words, started as a reportage of the lectures she gave at the 1971 University of Maryland International Piano Festival and Competition. But feeling Miss Marcus's concepts important, as well as representing a whole tradition, I wanted to make them complete so that Clavier's readers could put them to use. And subsequently, I interviewed her in her elegant tower apartment near New York City's Lincoln Center. A pleasant, spontaneous, chatty woman — a born teacher who gives unstintingly of her energies to her pupils as well as a pianist who can toss off some of the flashiest scales, both single and double notes, you'll ever hear — she gladly elaborated on and elucidated the original manuscript.

interview August 1971

Adele Marcus

on the

Mechanics of Advanced Technique

When I was 19 I had the great privilege of playing for Gieseking. "What do you want from this audition?" he asked. I had won the Naumburg prize, received fantastic reviews so-to-speak, and been approached by managers. Nevertheless, I felt that as a musician I was somewhat of a fake, that I didn't know enough in depth about music. "I am contemplating studying in Europe," I answered, "and would like to study with you. I want to get a deeper viewpoint of interpretation and technique."

"But there is no difference between interpretation and technique," Gieseking said. "Every dynamic and nuance must be produced simultaneously by a technical means." At the time I was too young to understand the full meaning of his statement. It took me 20 years to analyze it. Gieseking meant that if we have a phrase involving myriad hues of color, dynamics, tone, texture, pedaling, style, or philosophy if you will, we still have to get all this out of the instrument with a physical means. And what we get out of the instrument should be a replica of what we feel.

When I explain this idea to my students, they sometimes ask, "What do you really mean?" And I may say, for example, "If I tell you to start this passage pianissimo, to make a big crescendo at the end, accenting the last three notes, to put your foot on the pedal halfway through, snapping it off in a staccato with the last three notes — and you cannot or don't know how to do these things, then you have mastered neither the interpretative nor the technical requirements of that passage.

Starting with the Mechanics of the Instrument

When a student starts a four years' course of study with me at Juilliard, I usually start him with the mechanics of the instrument. By mechanics I mean the physical movements of the entire body. In expressing music emotionally, intellectually, and spiritually, our physical movements, which have often been neglected, are extremely important. Many talented people with much to say have difficulty in saying it at the piano, not because they lack speed, power, or manipulative ability — which to me is facility and not technique — but because they have not completely analyzed what they must do to a given piece, physically speaking.

We are working with an elusive art that we cannot reproduce in the same way Monday, Tuesday, Wednesday, May, December, or what have you. (I think it was Walt Whitman who said, "Music is created for the aristocratic delight of the moment.") Sometimes I will say to a student, "I know you feel everything about this piece properly, but you must not listen exclusively to what you feel. You must listen to what you hear coming out of the instrument. Are you able to hear objectively and still feel subjectively?" Technique enables us to control that what comes out of the instrument is what we want to come out. And, as we study music and become more involved with the depth, meaning, and grandeur of the more important works, technique is an ever increasing challenge.

Mechanics Can Be Taught

I used to say that mechanics can be taught to a horse. They can't actually, but they can be "taught" to a great degree. When Rosina Lhevinne sent Byron Janis, one of my first pupils, to me — I taught children exclusively for ten years — she said, "You know he has ten fingers like spaghetti." "But," I interjected, "He's only nine and one-half years old and he's enormously musical. This other thing — mechanics — can be built." "Well, try," Madame Lhevinne replied.

Well, I tried and was exceedingly happy with the result, especially when after seven years of work with Byron, he played for Vladimir Horowitz. Mr. Horowitz telephoned me the next day. "You know hees uctaves is faster than mine," he said. "But don't you theenk I sound better?"

Teaching mechanics to Byron was a big challenge: whereas I had always found mechanical ability easy, Byron, more natively musical than pianistically geared, had to build it. I am grateful to Byron for working with the ideas I was evolving some 33 years ago, giving me the opportunity to analyze what I had been doing naturally. Later, of course, in trying to teach these same ideas to everybody else, I didn't always succeed. Through trial and error, however, we develop as teachers.

Concept I: Playing "With" not "At" the Piano

My most important concept in developing a relationship to the instrument — and I'm sure it's not original — is that we play "with" not "at" the piano. The piano has the sound in it; the music hopefully is in us. We do not push sound into the piano; we draw sound out of it. Because the piano is not an instrument with which we have close physical contact, the process of drawing sound out of it is exceedingly difficult. The violinist tucks his instrument under his chin, the cellist wraps himself around his instrument, and the singer has his instrument within his person — every other performer, except the pianist and the organist, has intimate contact with his instrument.

In addition, when the pianist strikes a note on the keyboard, the sound emanates two or three feet away from him. This again is not so with other instruments. Inasmuch as the whole physical relationship is distant, we may see people playing at the piano as if they were typing. They may be involved, but at the same time they are not playing "with" the piano.

Having used the expression, playing "with" the piano, for many years, I jumped for joy when I read in black print — in the biography, *Schumann et l'ame romantique* by Marcel Brion — that Robert Schumann, too, felt we didn't play "at" the piano but that we played "with" the piano.

Now how do we play "with" the piano? Just as when we strike a note we cannot increase the sound, so we cannot diminish it. We can jiggle around with the pedal and try to make a diminuendo or even a crescendo, perhaps being partially successful on some instruments, but we cannot actually do anything after we have struck a note. With the violin you can make a wider or closer vibrato or you can press much more or much less on the bow arm, if you want a bigger or smaller tone. But with the piano you can only control volume of tone in the preparation.

Concept II: Preparation of Sound

Therefore, in piano-playing, the preparation of the sound, not only physically but how we hear, feel, and think it — it all has to work together — is extremely important. Feeling the sound, letting our emotions carry us to a certain degree, is not enough. We must also know how to prepare the sound physically. Any performing artist who has a sustained career has delved into sound preparation very deeply, also taking into consideration adjustment to different instruments in different halls.

Position at the Piano

Before I give some exercises for perfecting the mechanics in building technique, I want to discuss how we should sit at the instrument. We don't sit like robots, nor does everyone have to sit the same way. (We have proof of that with Glenn Gould.) But we have to sit so that we feel comfortable throughout the entire compass of the keyboard. Often a student will say, "I feel comfortable when I play in the center of the piano, but when I play in the high treble I feel as if I'm swimming away from shore."

I usually advocate sitting on half the chair, so that we have the sideways mobility of the torso, the feet flat on the floor. If we sit too far back, we feel as if we're in a lump, reaching out to the extremities of the keyboard; we don't have the same tactile control nor the same distribution of weight which helps sonority.

During a class at the Juilliard School, Adele Marcus explains details of Samuel Barber's Sonata to her student Robert de Gaetano.

The main portion of our physical weight is from our shoulders to our hips. This is where we carry our important organs and where we have our physical power. (I want to reiterate that power can be mental, intellectual, spiritual, or emotional. But here again, I am speaking only of the physical approach.) A student sometimes asks why he should lean forward as he makes a crescendo, for example. When a conductor wants a crescendo he often moves forward, the whole violin section moving forward too. When nine, hearing an orchestra for the first time, I thought this moving was a stunt. "How nice," I said, "They're all moving forward together." When older, I realized that when you want power, you move your torso forward. A singer doesn't sing fortissimo by leaning backwards; he sings pianissimo leaning backwards because that takes less weight.

So the torso is the moderator of our sonority. If we do not have mobility in the torso, we do not have control of the distribution of weight for our sound.

Relaxation

I don't believe in total relaxation. When we're totally relaxed, we are in bed asleep. If I pick up a handkerchief, I don't have to tighten up some other part of my body, but I do have to have some tension in the hand. Very often we will hear someone play who is very involved, but who becomes stymied because all of his feeling goes into his muscles. He is totally involved with what he feels but cannot release his feelings into the instrument. We have to feel free with the piano in order to hear our playing the way an objective listener hears it.

When I think of relaxation, I think of flexibility, like a large rubber band which can stretch this way and that but which is not loose. It has resilience. A student may play in a limp manner, thinking this is relaxation. It is not; it is looseness, which doesn't project anything. Relaxation is in the malleability and pliability of the wrist, the elbow, and the shoul-

der — the three big joints which lead to the torso — and the weight therefrom is the physical moderator of our sound.

I differentiate between tension and intensity. I think of intensity as an emotional quality, whereas tension stifles freedom of feeling. But intensity of feeling can create physical tension and this is where the difficulty lies. You may feel music from the depth of your being but your muscles may be tied up in knots when you're doing it. And therefore, what comes out of the piano is not a duplication of what you feel. My prime concern is to duplicate or match in sound — and that goes for phrasing, punctuation, and everything — what one is trying to express in the music, an elusive process not always achievable.

And where is the tension? The tension should be in the first finger joint, the joint having contact with the key. When we are young, our fingers often cave in due to weakness at this first joint. But weak first joints are ruinous. The first joints must be strengthened by proper exercises, stretching exercises or anything that will help to solidify the total tactile control. Furthermore, the wrist, which has eight bones in it and if not used enough will form small adhesions, must be malleable. I advocate wrist exercises for octaves, which help not only to free the wrist but to strengthen it at the same time. And strengthening and freeing the wrist in turn helps to develop forearm endurance. When we play a great many wrist octaves at high speed, we utilize the muscles just below the elbow, and when we play them enough, as a daily study, we develop tremendous endurance.

Stretching Exercises

I usually start pupils with stretching exercises no matter how large or how small the hand. I believe in these exercises one hundred percent. Some are from Josef Lhevinne, Sergei Rachmaninoff, and Vladimir Horowitz, and some are from me.

Why stretching exercises? In evolving a physical approach to the piano, I often thought of how the body is used in ballet. I would think and ask: "I see a magnificent dancer dancing on her toes for two hours with great technical freedom and expressivity, with a wonderful technique and command of her instrument. Why does she get up the next morning to go to the stretching bar?"

She works out the next morning because her muscles contract during the night while in repose. If I held my arm closed for six or seven hours, I would have difficulty in opening it. It would hurt and pain. Therefore, we must constantly work with the instrument so that our muscles are strong and flexible enough to serve our complete technical aims.

Exercises are very much a part of Mr. Horowitz's daily practice as they were, although to a lesser degree, of Mr. Lhevinne's. When young I was fortunate in having studied in Los Angeles with a remarkable Hungarian pianist, Mr. Vecsei. He insisted upon stretching exercises because my hands were small. But the stretching exercises I am going to give you are not exclusively for stretching the hand horizontally, for developing space between the fingers. They are also for stretching the muscles upward — stretching up with the finger straight and coming down with the finger curved — developing resilience and, if done enough, great endurance.

I. Diminished Seventh Stretching Exercises

Start with the diminished seventh chord on C. Place

the hand on the keys and depress the keys with a firm attack, keeping the elbow close to the body, raising the top knuckles so that there is an arch. Hold on so that you release the weight of the body without tension in the shoulder, the elbow, or the wrist. The finger tips must be strong and have firm contact with the keys, thus allowing the wrist, the elbow, and the shoulder to relax and to be flexible. The entire body should feel as if it were resting on the five fingers. You should have the feeling that you have a body and hands, but no arms.

Horowitz says that you play the piano with the stomach. I once said this and Rosina Lhevinne telephoned me: "What ees this Adele, you say everybody must play wiz the stomach." "This means," I said, "that you play with the entire body." "Just what Josef believed," she said.

Slowly stretch the fifth finger as high as possible, staying in the air the same length of time as on the keyboard. Play four times, forte, counting one "and" two "and," three "and," four "and" (M.M. ♪ = circa 50).

Do the same with the fourth finger which stretches out straight and pulls inward. There should be no

movement from the arm, and keep the elbow close to the body for these stretching exercises.

Then do the same thing with the third and second fingers and the thumb. Each time play from the top knuckle, lifting the finger straight, keeping the wrist low. The lower the wrist, the more pull there is on the muscle. Lift the finger straight but come down with the finger curved which again gives more pull on the muscle. If you lift your third finger, for example, as high as possible and hold your forearm with your other hand, you will feel the pull of the muscle — it moves back and forth. When you curve the finger, the muscle also moves but you tighten the hand unnecessarily. (This is not the way we play; it is purely an exercise. When you play you play close to the keys.)

I reiterate that the body, other than the fingers, should feel as if it doesn't exist. The upward stretching of the fingers is comparable to any kind of stretching — the dancer stretching or the stretching of the arm, for example. Slow stretching exercises give the muscles tremendous resilience and make possible more freedom in playing scales and fast passages. And the endurance which muscles require for continued running notes must be developed through repetition of those same fast passages.

I always start with the fifth and fourth fingers, the violin section of the hand. Without a good violin sec-

tion, you have no orchestra. Furthermore, the fourth and fifth fingers are the weakest because a muscle connects them. Also the fifth finger is usually much shorter, and fourth is difficult to raise because of its connection with the fifth. And yet in most music, up to possibly the avant-garde, the melodic and thematic material is usually written for this outside part of the hand.

It is frequently difficult for students to stretch their fifth and fourth fingers upward, allowing them to remain a given length of time in the air. The reason I say raise the finger as high as possible — it doesn't have to look beautiful — is to have the full length of the muscle in play. You work at stretching exercises in order not to become so tired when you play. But you must realize that the faster the speed, the closer you must get to the keyboard. When you strike any given object slowly, you have a wide leverage; when you strike faster, you have to get closer to the object. And this is exactly the way the fingers work.

You have to be able to mold sound in melodic passages and in thematic material with the two weakest fingers of your hands, the left as well as the right. If you have harmonic or melodic progressions in the bass line which require outlining, you must have strong fourth and fifth fingers. (I realize that this Lhevinne approach, the Russian school, is contrary to schools that believe in rotation in finger work, and I don't say that music should be made Russian school. On the contrary, you can make it American, French, German, Russian, Spanish, or Italian school if you will, and all schools have a way with music which is individual. But I do feel that the Russian School of playing the piano is almost the best from the standpoint of handling the instrument with ease.) In order

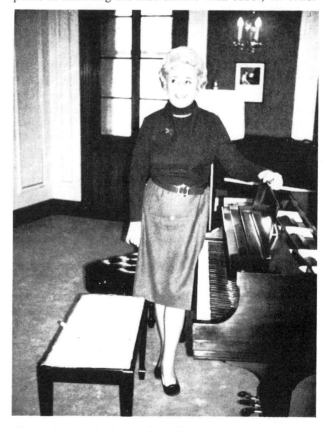

At a workshop at the Jenkins Music Co. in Kansas City, March 1971.

During a television broadcast in New York City (1968), entitled "Master Class Session." The student is Horacio Gutierrez, later (1970) winner of the Tchaikovsky prize in Moscow.

to develop the necessary endurance in the fourth and fifth fingers, I advocate the Chopin "Revolutionary" Etude and various movements such as the last movement of the Chopin B Minor Sonata. In this movement,

an enormous endurance test, the fifth finger is constantly in action for page after page. Repeatedly, through my many years of teaching, I've been asked, "How do you develop the necessary left-hand endurance in this passage?" And I say, "By playing the passage every day slowly, raising the fifth finger, giving it full duty. Then the passage gradually becomes easier and easier until finally you don't get tired."

Occasionally the thumb becomes a melodic finger:

But by nature the thumb is the clumsiest finger. And in playing rapid passages, you have to rest on the second, third, fourth, and fifth fingers much more forcibly than on the thumb. In a passage which covers a span of two or three octaves, the thumb is just a pusher which gets you to another part of the piano. In other words, the thumb must be the lightest finger, the second, third, fourth, and fifth fingers the strongest.

I once read the statement by Leonardo da Vinci that "Structure is the basis of all movement," a potent statement from which I evolved many principles of movement in the hand. By the very structure of the hand, the thumb moves horizontally, the other fingers vertically from the knuckles. Therefore, if someone asks me how to play a scale, I say "Play a scale exactly the way the hand is built: move two, three, four, and five vertically, the thumb horizontally." The hand feels almost like an animal reaching out for two, three, four, and five, the thumb sliding along under the hand.

So play the diminished seventh chord exercise, each hand alone, thinking about how it feels as you play. Stay with one chord until the hand feels the spaces between the fingers and so on. And then change

the chord every four or five days, progressing chromatically. I have children stay on each chord for a week. It's more difficult to raise the second and fourth fingers on A and E flat or F sharp and C than it is on D sharp and A.

Then play again in double notes, using the finger combinations 5-3, 2-4, 1-3, 2-4, 5-3.
Again the wrist should be down, not as far as possible, but not up, to insure greater muscle pull. You should not do this until it pains or anything like that. The entire exercise for the right hand lasts five minutes, not more. Then do the same combinations of single and double notes with the left hand.

We know we can play chords long or short. But this exercise on the diminished seventh chord is not that kind of chord playing. It is a particular type of pulling up and holding, and then relaxing, freeing the rest of the arm. With very small hands it isn't possible. However, when I taught children, I gave them these exercises in small doses just as we give children the same food as an adult, only a smaller quantity.

II. Horowitz Stretching Exercises

Several Vladimir Horowitz stretching exercises came to my attention via Byron and mutual friends. This one is for the five fingers, starting on the second inversion of C major. Again sit as if you didn't have a muscle in your body except in the movement of your fingers. Play slowly, about quarter notes, M.M. ♩ = 60, forte, without moving the wrist. If you were playing faster, you would use your wrist. But this exercise is not playing; it is for the stretching, especially between the fourth and fifth fingers.

The wrist is low but not tight, the fingers go up straight but they come down curved. At first most people turn the hand sideways to help reach the top C. But don't. In playing the span between the fourth and fifth fingers, keep the wrist low to insure greater pull of the muscles, and reach out and up with the fifth finger to strike the C.

Maybe Horowitz doesn't do it exactly this way, but it has been very effective for me and for every student to whom I've given it. The idea is expansion, contraction, expansion, contraction. As DeLarrocha said, "When I'm talking to people, I find myself subconsciously stretching my hands." One is always trying to keep the hands in a flexible state.

Then do the same thing with the left hand, again not raising the wrist, to insure greater pull on the muscles. Also play this exercise starting from the fifth finger, accenting the fifth fingers, again slowly and loudly, without moving the wrist. Stretch sideways and pull upwards. And finally play this exercise faster, M.M. ♩ = circa 112 (or even begin this way as I usually do), in this version:

Mr. Horowitz has another exercise where he puts

his thumb on the wood below the keys, keeps his wrist very low, and crawls up the piano in fourths, striking the fifth finger at a distance as strongly as he can. You will find this puts a considerable pull on the muscles and must not be done endlessly.

III. Rachmaninoff Stretching Exercise

Another wonderful stretching exercise I got vicariously from Rachmaninoff through his grandchild. When Rachmaninoff's grandchild, who had not extraordinary talent, came to study with me, at Mr. Lhevinne's suggestion, he asked if he might warm up. "By all means," I said, and he started playing:

"Where did you learn that?" I asked. "That's my grandfather's exercise," he said. The harmonic framework of the exercise consists of the C major chord with added sixth, the C minor chord with added sixth, the diminished seventh chord, and the next key's dominant seventh chord in first inversion leading to the next key chromatically. In other words, in each succeeding chord, lower the third, the fifth, and the sixth, or their enharmonic equivalents, respectively.

All these exercises are played with the fingers raised up straight, coming down curved on the cushions of the fingers, never coming down flat. Play this exercise very slowly, with the wrist low and the fingers stretched towards the instrument. Also play it fast, repeating each measure four times, accenting the first notes of the measure. Starting from the outer notes prepares you for double-third scales. These three stretching exercises take half an hour.

IV. Lhevinne Stretching Exercise

The last stretching exercise is a fantastic contraction-expansion exercise from Josef Lhevinne which he gave to very few people. I heard him doing it and pestered him until he gave it to me. You play 1, 2, 3, 4, 5 chromatically on C, C sharp, D, D sharp, and E —

putting the thumb *over* the fifth finger on the interval crossing of a second to F; then 1, 2, 3, 4, 5 on the F major chord, using all the fingers — putting the thumb *under* on the skip of a third to the C, and so on. The thumb keeps going over, under, over, under in the right hand ascending and the left hand descending. The elbow sort of weaves. Play it in all keys, chromatically, pulsing in six, M.M. ♩ = circa 80. Of course at first you have to work slowly to insure perfect evenness in tone and rhythm.

I don't use exercise books, because the important thing is not how many exercises you do but how you do them. The four stretching exercises I have given are what I feel should be a setting-up regimen and should be done every day when you are building

muscles. There should not be, however, an invariable formula for practicing. At the beginning of your practice when the mind is fresh, if you feel warm, you can start to memorize or to play music. Exercises such as the mechanics can be done later in the day when the mind is more tired. They do not require the kind of concentration that memorizing does. Practicing is a creating process just as is the building of technique. You have to use your imagination. For example, if you want a certain color of sound, you have to work until you get it. And then work until it becomes a part of your equipment and interpretative scheme. If you get what you want one moment, that doesn't mean you have what you want from then on.

Solid Mechanistic Training Indispensible

If a student wants to play concerts and has the requisite calibre of talent, not only pianistically but musically, and the ability to study intelligently (which I think is one of the prime requisites), I insist that he go through this technical training step by step, so that it's solid. When we are no longer young, we have to rely upon the solid study of our entire technical or mechanical equipment rather than upon the chance-taking of our youth, where one time our playing will be extraordinary and another time less good. Sooner or later you will say, "My arm is weak, I get tight, and this, that, and the third," and then you will realize that solid training in the mechanics of the instrument, hopefully used towards an interpretative end, is indispensible.

Students too frequently don't have the patience to be thorough. They want you to show them how fast; they want to be able to know how by Tuesday. Solid technical training takes time and application, and you have to want to do the work.

I have one student, Horacio Gutierrez, of whom I am very proud, who spends endless time — mostly on these elements — when we are working together. And furthermore, he works on every facet of performance with a patience that will bring him to the heights he seeks. As for myself, I was singularly fortunate in my early training. I had to study the Clementi "Gradus Ad Parnassum," playing all the studies in every key. I did that when I was 11, 12, and 13 years old. At the time I thought it was rather boring, but I realize now what such solid technical training did.

Teaching Scales

Years ago a friend of mine from Australia visited Mr. Kutner Solomon, one of my favorite pianists, who unfortunately is quite ill now, in London. She asked to study with him. "I will teach you," he said, "if for five weeks you will practice scales five hours daily." This woman was a very good pianist, a remarkable technician, and a very fine musician. "You don't really mean that!" she exclaimed. "Well, if you can't do that," Solomon, who is not essentially a virtuoso pianist, replied, "then you cannot enter the fold. I require this kind of discipline." When she told me this story, I realized what Solomon meant.

A scale is not just a scale, or moving your fingers to warm up, or stretching exercises. A scale is already music — Mozart or early Beethoven let us say. You can play scales forte, mezzo forte, piano, pianissimo, staccato, legato, portamento. You can make crescendos; you can start at the top.

In teaching scales — and you should all teach scales — you should have students, when big and advanced enough, play scales in four octaves in four ways, accenting the bottom and top notes of the scale, in octaves, in thirds, in tenths, and in sixths.

Light Thumb. The thumb should be the lightest finger, only a pusher, like an animal crawling. Besides being light, the thumb should play on the end and be placed under the hand — as we have all heard since we were children — simultaneously with the dropping of the second finger, with no movement in the wrist.

Torso moves with the arms. Young people, in playing scales, often sit with their torso immobile, reaching out as they play high or low. You should not have the same position of the upper body when you are playing at the bottom or the top of the piano as when you are playing in the center. The upper part of the body should move with the arms. When you get to the top of the piano, your hands should feel as if they're the same distance from the body — they should not be reaching out — as when you are playing the center of the piano. In other words, in practicing scales it is important to have the hands an equal distance from the body in every register of the piano as you ascend and descend four octaves. In this way the distribution of the weight to the hands from the torso creates an evenness of sound.

And whether you play forte or piano, you should be able to play at a certain predetermined tempo, eventually without accents except on the bottom and the top notes, in octaves, in tenths, in thirds, and in sixths.

Teaching Arpeggios

In putting the thumb under the hand in arpeggios, similarly as in scales, there should be no bump in the wrist. Mr. Lhevinne had us practice arpeggios in contrary motion, closing the hand on the end note, raising the fifth finger.
Just that little extra grabbing of the fifth finger develops the pocket-sized muscle on the fifth-finger side of the hand upon which we have to depend.

When the hand is properly developed, you should have the feeling that each hand is two hands: the fourth and fifth fingers are the stronger of the two hands; and the thumb, second, and third fingers, which feel less important, are an adjunct to the outer part of the hand. You have four hands with which to work, so-to-speak.

The Importance of the Outside of the Hand

It is important to have the feeling that the thumb can reach out and still be light and that most of the weight, balance, and facility is in the outside of the hand. For example, in playing the third Etude from the Schumann *Symphonic Etudes*, you should feel as if you have first and second fingers but that your fourth and fifth fingers are the important fingers and are pointed up:

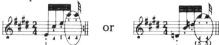

Or, in the left hand of Variation IX:

In Variation V (Etude VI), the hand seems to feel as if it must be geared toward the outside of the hand.

In all of these Schumann Studies, in order to get the lightness and to be able to get off the keys quickly, the fingers should be pointed towards the instrument, always with the feeling of lightness in the thumb and weight in the outside of the hand. The hand is fixed, but not too tight, because it revolves on the wrist.

An Hour and a Half Daily on Technique

It is very important for a student, seriously geared towards a career, to devote a minimum of an hour and a half every day to stretching exercises, scales, arpeggios, scales in double thirds and double sixths, octaves, and chords. This is what I had to do; I did it with Mr. Lhevinne. When I went to Mr. Lhevinne at the age of fifteen and a half, he said, "Play a scale." I played a scale in double thirds because I had played double-third scales all my life. "Where did you learn that?" he asked astonished. "Learn what?" I asked. "Doesn't everybody play scales this way?" "No," he said. All kinds of scales were part of my very early training.

Scales in Double Thirds

In double-third scales too, you should work up to a very high speed, four octaves, but still within a rhythmic pulse.
The work is all on the outside of the hand, in the third, fourth, and fifth fingers, the thumb just tagging along for the ride. Usually I teach double-third scales after the student has had a good grounding in single-note scales, after I feel that the outside part of his hand is developed enough for control.

I don't use 1-2 in the fingering. I use the Moszkowski "Scales in Double Notes," Book II of his "School of Scales and Double Notes for the Pianoforte," distributed in this country by Boosey & Hawkes. Moszkowski gives special fingerings for two, three, and four octaves, but I use only his "General Fingering" which he gives at the beginning of each scale and which may be employed for any compass.

The fingering is not the same for all the scales, but some of them — C major for example — use 1-3, 2-4, 3-5 in the right hand (5-3, 4-2, 3-1 in the left hand), on the tonic triad part of the scale. And you use this same fingering on the top five notes of the scale. In between you use 1-3, 2-4, 1-3, 2-4 in the right hand (2-4, 3-1, 2-4, 3-1 in the left hand), except before the top five notes of the scale where you have 1-3, 2-4 in the right hand (2-4, 3-1 in the left hand) only once.

The third, fourth, and fifth fingers are almost always legato. If you play 1-3, 2-4, 3-5 and are crossing over to 1-3, you put the third finger over the fifth, the thumb sliding under the hand. In other words, keep the thumb tip close to the keyboard and reach over with the outside of the hand, without moving the wrist up and down. Always keep one voice legato and play the finger playing the nonlegato part of the third, lighter. Again you have the feeling of having two hands in one.

Furthermore, when the hand is going over 3, 4, 5, the hand points. The hand must be pointed in the direction it is going. Coming down I don't point so much.

I insist that students play double-third scales four octaves up and back, sometimes (but not generally) two octaves apart, listening to the right hand ascending and the left hand descending. The left hand must not know what the right hand is doing.

Scales in Double Sixths

The same things apply to scales in double sixths. Again I use the Moszkowski general fingerings. If you have played 3, 4, 5 and you want to cross over with four, keep your thumb tip close to the keyboard and reach over with outside of your hand, without moving the wrist up and down. Again always keep one voice legato and play the less-connected voice lighter than the connected voice. Also in scales in double sixths, keep the wrists elevated a little so that the knuckles are up. You will then be able to move the hands more easily.

Important Final Suggestions for Scales

In exercises, the elbows are close to the body, but not rigid. But with scales, the elbow is removed from the body, so that the elbow leads. For very talented people, when they have achieved high speed in scales, I suggest that the left-hand wrist be a little higher than the right, ascending; the right-hand wrist a little higher than the left, descending. In double-third scales this seems more difficult, but it is the same thing, but always with the thumb going under the hand light, always stressing the third, fourth, and fifth fingers.

Using the Whole Instrument and Listening

I stress using the whole instrument, thinking of the piano as an orchestral entity, listening melodically and thinking harmonically. By doing this we have greater sonority in our sound and never lose sight of a constant melodic or thematic flow in the music.

I've had some fascinating teachers. My principal teacher, of course, was Josef Lhevinne, a great man and master — I think he could have stuck everybody into his vest pocket when it came to pianistic wizardry. My several years of study with Artur Schnabel in Berlin opened new vistas of thought and understanding about a musician's responsibility to the music. And my encounters from time to time with Vladimir Horowitz have been very exciting. In a conversation one evening, Mr. Horowitz and I were talking about sonority and pianistic things. "Where does pianism come from?" he asked. "I suppose," I said, "it comes from the music." "Good," he replied.

We like to categorize. We say this one is a musician; this one is a pianist; this one is musical. But categorizing is inaccurate because everything we do at the instrument is motivated by the music. For what we want to say and express, for everything pianistic, musical, and musicianly can be valid only if it is motivated by the source: the score.

If Rubinstein, Horowitz, Richter, Gilels, or Serkin — five of the greats — all look at the music, naturally they will all come out with a different interpretation, the music's having gone through their entire metabolism, their entire responses, their kinds of temperament. But still they evaluate and re-evaluate everything in the music. There is nothing they do which does not emanate from the score.

Understanding how to illuminate the score is of paramount importance and also has to do with pianism and our individual technique as well as our musicianship and interpretative concepts. Students often say, "It's dry to sit and practice scales and all of it." And I say, "Yes, it is if you do it that way. But it isn't if you are trying to achieve different qualities of touch, speed, control, and endurance." If you are working towards an evenness or a legato, for example, you are developing your ear at the same time. Students don't listen to themselves enough. They play and whatever goes out — well, that's the listener's business. Violinists and singers *have* to listen carefully because they are closer to their instruments. Music is still an aural art, and ears are the greatest teachers.

Octaves

The elbows, in playing octaves, should be close to the body, the feet flat on the floor. Raise the hand as high as possible, without moving the arm, keeping the fingers free — the fifth finger straight, the thumb light, the second finger curved. That's all you have to remember! The hand is geared primarily toward the fifth finger — a straight fifth finger from the knuckle — throwing the hand back, the fingers free and reaching towards the keyboard.

I suggest doing octaves at first very slowly (later in different speeds), chromatically, four times on each key, the fourth finger on the black notes.
Then, using the same pattern, but playing six notes, then eight notes, the left hand two octaves below the right.

I never practice these exercises hands together; I begin with the left hand. I also work the left hand alone in all pieces. Josef Hofmann said, "By their left hand, you know them." If you don't have a comfortable left hand, you will never have the right sonority in passages that require holding up of the harmonic line.

You get over octave passages much faster with the fourth and the fifth fingers firm, the thumb light. Speed is augmented by what I call a streamlined feeling in the hand — like today's low cars that go fast. When octaves feel bumpy, you neither have contact with the keys nor do you have speed and clarity.

And then a very important exercise for developing virtuoso octaves is playing the whole circle of scales, going through all the keys counter-clockwise, major-relative harmonic minor, in octaves daily. The order of the keys is C major-A minor, F major-D minor, B flat major-G minor, E flat major-C minor, A flat major-F minor, D flat major-B flat minor, G flat major-E flat minor, B major-G sharp minor, E major-C sharp minor, A major-F sharp minor, D major-B minor, G major-E minor, and back to C major.

Starting on the next-to-top octave C, play the scale of C in octaves one octave up and back. The left hand plays the same thing one octave lower throughout. In making the transition to the relative harmonic minor, A minor, play up one whole step and then down the scale to A.

Then play the scale of A harmonic minor in octaves one octave up and back. In making the transition to the next major key, in this case F Major, play up one *half* step and then down the scale to F.

Proceed downward toward the circle of keys, always going up a *whole* step in making the transition to the relative minor, a *half* step in making the transition to the next major key, until you reach A flat major. After playing A flat major one octave up and back, jump to the next-to-top B flat octave on the piano, and make the transition to F minor.

Continue downward again through the circle of keys until you reach G sharp minor. After playing G sharp minor, jump to the next-to-top A octave on the piano, and make the transition to E major. Continue downward until you've completed C major.

When students can get through this whole circle at very good speed, without the right arm practically falling off, they already have some specific endurance. When Byron Janis was studying with me, he lived in back of another pupil of mine, Cy Coleman, who has become a well-known figure in the Jazz world. Cy, without a doubt, had the fastest octaves in the world. They sounded like a whrrrr, like glissandi. Byron's octaves, on the other hand, although sharper and more exciting, were a little slower. To annoy Byron, Cy would start this whole circle of octaves terribly, incredibly fast. And Byron would retaliate by banging on the wall and playing some part of *Rhapsody in Blue* or something expressive.

In playing octaves, if possible, play in on the white keys and out on the black keys, so there is very little in and out movement of the hand. Excessive motion retards your speed. In playing chromatic octaves, the fourth and fifth fingers should be firm, straight down from the knuckle. If you keep the thumb light, the hand will feel larger. Small hands usually hold the thumb tight but they shouldn't. People with small hands should keep their wrists a little higher.

I: Arm-Weight Chords

I have students practice arm-weight chords on the pattern — major, minor, diminished, dominant first inversion of the next key — dropping the whole arm, very slowly:

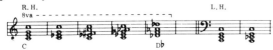

Arm-weight practice is wonderful for the hands and the sonority, but you lose all your neighbors — they stop talking to you. Keep the elbow low, just hanging like a hammock between your shoulder and your finger tips. Mr. Lhevinne had me play these arm-weight chords. At first your fingers sting. And by the time you get calluses you almost know how to play them. Use the total weight of the body, dropping the wrist — the wrist straight down — and try to get the right notes.

Count slowly: one, two, three, four. On four raise your hand very slowly — your fingers feel as if they have wet sand on the ends — with the wrist high, proceed to the minor, and so on. Use the heaviness of the hand and the whole weight of the body.

In the beginning of the Brahms F Minor Sonata,

for instance, you want resonance and weight. But if you don't use the whole weight of the body and the arm, the fingers firm, and you slap with the forearm, you get that kind of hard, lacking-in-resonance sound which I dislike — a sound with fewer overtones because it's done with the forearm.

I used to practice the opening chords of the Brahms E Flat Rhapsody slowly, with the fingers pointed and firm:

If you use the forearm, you get a less resonant sound. You should use the weight of the whole body for these chords.

If you play the opening octaves of Brahms's Intermezzo in A Minor, Opus 118, No. 1, with the forearm — which I call slapping — you do not get the required resonant sonority.

Towards the end of the Brahms E Flat Rhapsody, you play the chords and the octaves very close to

the keys with a pizzicato staccato; otherwise the jumps would be too clumsy. But if you're playing chords such as the arm-weight harmonic progressions I gave you, it's a legato that's done with the same pulling up as the diminished-seventh chord stretching exercise I gave.

These things are difficult to teach because students don't have the patience to do them long enough. They do them one day, wanting to see miraculous results. You have to work at these things for months and years in order to make them part of your working equipment.

II. Short Chords

Short chords, as in the Variation III of Schumann's *Symphonic Etudes*, are played from the stomach muscles, but much more with the fingers, the wrist pulling up. It's pizzicati with all the fingers:

Trills

If you play scales well, you can play trills well. Often students find trills difficult because they don't have sufficient endurance. Rudolf Firkusny has fantastic trills. Backstage, after his performance of the Beethoven Third Concerto in Westchester, New York, I said to him, "I've never before in my life heard such trills." "You spotted a specialty of the house," he said. "How did you develop them?" I asked. "When I was young," he said, "there was not a passage that I didn't practice in trills." Such work know-how is what achieves total evenness, and the evenness of the trill is very important. Remember that an even trill is not only more expressive, but that out in a hall, it also sounds faster.

I don't think it's very interesting to practice an exercise made of a chain of trills. I think it is more interesting and beneficial to practice trills in music. If I am working on Variation 4, for example, of the Brahms Paganini Variations, Book I:

I make it far more difficult than it is, playing the left hand slowly with lots of trills in the right hand. Making a passage more difficult than it is, is like hitting your head against the wall: it feels so good when you stop. In this Variation, practice more trills than written until it feels easy when you play it as written.

Most trills are in the music for expressive purposes. In the beginning of the slow movement of the Chopin F Minor Concerto, many people trill right away fast. I feel this trill is part of the melodic line; it is not just

a trill. In other words, you should go into the trill a little slowly. I say to students: "Find out what kind of trill you have. Is it lyric, heroic, expressive, dynamic?" But the ability to move the fingers evenly and fast in trills, believe me, can be developed by practicing scales in all forms, at the highest speed.

Working for Endurance

You should work for endurance by practicing the same passage at various speeds. Mr. Lhevinne insisted that we practice a fast piece in four different tempi. It is easy to play very slowly. You can possibly play part of the Liszt Sonata in the right hand and part of the Tchaikovsky Concerto in the left. But when you begin to play faster, the difficulties begin to appear. You begin to find the uneasinesses, not only of fingerings, but also of your approach to the instrument. This is one reason why you should decide upon proper fingerings in difficult technical passages when playing at fast tempo. Any fingering feels comfortable when you are playing the passage slowly.

It is important to find the most uncomfortable tempo and practice in that tempo until it becomes comfortable, not necessarily playing very slowly and then very fast as many students do. Students often play a passage in different rhythms, and then start to play very fast. Then they still have the same problems because control comes not only with the actual tactile feeling but also with the listening and the thinking. I advocate slow practicing, but it is also important to practice in a moving tempo in order to know how the hand feels and how the entire passage feels within a given space of notes.

Anticipating Difficult Passages

A student often says, "This place troubles me." And I say, "It isn't that place; it's what precedes that is causing the difficulty." You have to prepare yourself — whether it is the way the hand lies, the way you hear or think the passage, or possibly a fingering that needs changing.

Practicing in Different Rhythms

I believe in practicing in different rhythms, but not as a cure-all for all technical problems. After you've practiced something which has a phrase feeling, for example, in various rhythms, the phrase comes out with accentuated notes not belonging to its meaning. (I am speaking about students who are not yet cultivated or developed.)

Rather than practice in different rhythms, I prefer to make positive that which is negative in a fast passage by accenting the notes which lack clarity. Furthermore, we must work for color, nuance, pedaling, dynamics, punctuating, to try to bring to light a phrase's exact musical meaning as we understand it.

In closing, let me reiterate that our ultimate goal in developing the mechanics of advanced technique is to serve interpretation. And I can never emphasize enough that all of this takes time. Someone, hearing myriad hues of beauty in a phrase Horowitz played, asked him how he does it. "Oh, it's simple," he answered. "It took me my whole life."

Revision Comments on

ADELE MARCUS'S TECHNICAL REGIME

In her teaching at the Juilliard School as well as in her master classes in this country and abroad Miss Marcus has found considerable misunderstanding as to how these exercises should be practiced. Consequently, we met in her studio on July 10, 1980 and she elucidated:

Diminished Seventh Stretching Exercise:

Start this exercise with your feet under the pedals, the shoulders relaxed, and the elbows close to the body. Sit on only one half of the bench so that you are leaning into the piano and have horizontal mobility.

Raise the finger straight out as high as possible and come down curved on its pad. The fifth finger will be a little less curved because of its shortness. By putting the finger out straight, you can pull it towards you to curve it with a tremendous amount of energy. I advocate stretching the thumb — which does not stem from the same point as do the other fingers but which comes from the arm — horizontally as far as you can, then raising it and coming down on the tip end of it.

When you grab vigorously the first diminished chord, the fingers are flat on the keys at first, but as you play the chord the fingers pull towards you. If your fingers aren't able to play at the ends of the keys, then slide them to the outside end. At that moment, the wrist is almost stiff. There should be reaction in the bottom stomach muscles; you should feel the stomach jump.

When you begin raising the fifth finger straight out, nothing else moves. Play extremely slowly, holding the finger down, then raising it straight out as high as possible four times. Pull the finger down curved each time.

Horowitz Stretching Exercise:

Again raise the fingers straight, but come down curved. When you see Horowitz on television, you may think he's coming down with straight fingers but he isn't. Keep the thumb open, no movement in the wrist.

Scales

Only accent the bottom and top notes of a four-octave scale when playing very fast. Otherwise, and this means in most scale practice, accent every ninth note: in the scale of C, accent C, then after eight notes the D, then the E, then the F et cetera. You have to feel this rhythm without accents in order to build up to a fast speed. Exercises should always be played feeling a pulse.

Chromatic Repeated Octaves:

The arm is relaxed and anchored to the side of the body. In throwing the hand back from the wrist, you are summoning tension without moving any other part of the arm. You move the hand, not the wrist. Stay in the air the same length of time that you stay on the key. Contract the hand, let the fingers come together when the hand is in the air between each octave., When the hand is way back, there is no tension in the fingers. And then when you play the octave, the hand opens up like an umbrella.

The second finger should be curved; the thumb should play on its tip. The whole arch of the hand is firm. When you play a diminished seventh arpeggio in octaves, or any octave passage, the fifth finger side of the hand has to be like steel. The thumb side of the hand just tags along.

Setting Up Exercises

The Regimen **Adele Marcus** Suggests for her Students

Stretching Exercises

Diminished Seventh Stretching Exercise

Change chromatically to the next chord every five days. M.M. ♩ = 50. Also play three octaves lower with the left hand.

1 & 2 & 3 & 4 &   1 & 2 & 3 & 4 &   1 & 2 & 3 & 4 &   1 & 2 & 3 & 4 &   1 & 2 & 3 & 4 &

Also:

Vladimir Horowitz Stretching Exercise   M.M. ♩ = circa 60

Right hand:

etc. chromatically

Also (keeping the thumb on the wood below the keys):

etc.

Similarly with the left hand:

etc. and

etc.

Also in this version, slowly, loudly, without moving the wrist, lifting the fingers high and straight, coming down hard and curved:

etc.

Also faster, M.M. ♩ = circa 112, or sometimes begin with this version:

etc.

Sergei Rachmaninoff

Stretching Exercise

Josef Lhevinne Stretching Exercise

Put the thumb over the fifth finger on the interval crossing of a second, under on the skip of a third. M.M. ♩ = ca. 80.

etc. in all keys

Scales

Practice all major and minor scales, four octaves, in octaves, thirds, tenths, and sixths. Play rhythmically, accenting after every eight notes.

In octaves

For example, E major (but play four octaves):

In thirds

In tenths

In sixths

In double thirds

Use the Moszkowski general fingering. For example, D major (but play four octaves):

In double sixths

Moszkowski fingering. For example, B major (except play four octaves):

Arpeggios

Four octaves, loud, fast, strongly accenting after every four notes; up and back twice in all major and minor keys.

Root position

First inversion

Second inversion

In contrary motion

Close the hand on the end note, raising and grabbing with the fifth finger:

Octaves

Very slow, the arm immobile, the hand raised up and down as far as possible, chromatically, four times on each key, then six, then eight. Use the fourth finger on the black notes. Later play at different speeds.

Then: And:

Circle of keys

The left hand one octave lower throughout; work up as fast as possible:

286

Arm-Weight Chords

Mark Westcott's Technical Regime

interview June 6, 1978

We know the scene. The artist, asked why and how he creates, sighs, shrugs, and says, "Ah, that is another matter," and gestures toward the beyond. His eyebrows play a variation of " Beauty is truth, truth beauty - that is all / Ye know on earth, and all ye need to know," and we are left with a vague vision of a muse in the corner.

But many of us want to know more about beauty and how it is achieved and can only be frustrated by inarticulate artists. On the other hand, there is Mark Westcott. Hailed by critics as a virtuoso whose "name may soon join those of the keyboard giants," he also happens to strike interesting chords in conversation. As a superb technician he knows the shapes and angles as well as the texture, color, and meaning of music. He can express why and how he achieves his virtuosity.

As a child he studied with Aurora Underwood, later with John Perry, Frank Mannheimer, and Cecile Genhart, and coached with Vladimir Ashkenazy, Van Cliburn, Claude Frank, and Eugene List. Winner of at least half a dozen competitions, he has embarked on a fast-growing career. This past year he gave over 50 recitals and master classes in Europe, South America,

Mexico, and the U.S.; appeared on TV and radio programs; made recordings; and performed with more than 15 American orchestras.

"After gulping down a piece of pastry, drinking a cup of black coffee, and gathering the courage to go to the piano," Westcott said as we began a three-hour taped interview devoted to his extraordinary technical regime, "I work first on a rather slow piece or movement from the standpoint of ear and heart - to get my best juices flowing. I try to get my heart warmed up and my ear attentive to sound qualities.[1] Then I concentrate on keyboard feel, what I call 'walking on the key bottoms.' "

Basic Warm-up Exercises

Exercise 1. Fingertips. I establish the feel of the fingertips resting on the bottoms of the keys. (The concept is to begin technical work with the smallest joint, the fingertip, then go to the hand and then the arm.) Depress five white keys in each hand - G A B C D, for example - holding the fingers down by resting the weight freely on the fingertips, not in a slouched position but supporting the weight at the knuckles.

[1]Here's a way to practice slow movements to achieve ultra-accuracy. At a tempo slightly under your performance tempo, set the metronome to tick to sixteenth or thirty-second notes. Practice to perfect every detail, changing pedal on every note to acquire sonority control. Then at a tempo much faster than your performance tempo, set the metronome to tick to quarter or eighth notes. Try to perfect *every* musical and pianistic detail. Technical hitches--little hidden faults that can ruin your line and tone control--may show up only at a faster than normal tempo. Playing a slow movement is as difficult technically as playing a fast movement.

Relax until the elbows, forearms, and shoulders have little tension in them. Then play two coordinated fingers like the second fingers but do not let the fingertips off the keys. Go halfway down into the keys, fast enough to produce sound but not deep enough to hit the bottom. The weight or force of the key pushes the finger up. Repeat as in eighth notes followed by eighth rests: "Down, up, down, up."

Then play the third, fourth, and fifth fingers, doing the thumb last. Don't let any finger joints collapse. After establishing that each finger is working properly, double and quadruple the tempo and number of repetitions, always playing just halfway down, letting the key push the finger up.

Exercise 2. Legato. The next exercise is valuable for establishing the fingers going to the bottom of the keys without forearm tension. Walk from key bottom to key bottom hands together: G A B C D, A B C D E, B C D E F, etc., the weight resting gently in each fingertip, passing from finger to finger so that each overlaps half into the next. Start rather slow in eighth notes, then work up to a rather fast-moving tempo. Concentrate on legato and relaxation.

Exercise 3. Individual Fingers. Each part of this two-part exercise focuses on one finger at a time, saving the thumb for last. Play the left hand in contrary motion, using the same fingering as the right hand.

Part 1: Rest the arm weight on the held finger with no collapsed joints.

Make sure that your weight does not vary in intensity on the held note as you play the moving legato voice. The weight of the arm is passive, transferring from one connected, supporting fingertip to the next. Play *mp* to *mf*, slow to moderate, in sixteenths as well as eighths.

When you've mastered the problem of a held finger with a moving line, proceed to a repeated finger with a moving line:

Here the weight problem is concerned with the moving voice, not the repeated finger. As you increase tempo, let the hand float, do not push. Achieve absolute legato in both voices, with the notes going down exactly together. Then move to the next finger, and so on.

Part 2: Using the same basic pattern as Part 1, Part 2 is designed to liberate each finger one by one from the hand. Make sure the grace notes are very fast, the moving voice legato.

The hand should be poised, not stiff. If you have problems with the repeated staccato grace notes, you are probably pushing with weight. Work slow to fast.

Practice schedule. After one or more of these basic warm-up exercises, I will go to some difficult passage in my pieces. There is always one to sweat about. Busoni believed in first practicing a piece from the hardest part - the hardest measure or half-measure. Starting with the most difficult part eliminates the bad practice of playing from the beginning straight through to the end.

When I'm on tour and cyclically practicing a 90-minute program, every day I work on about one-third of that program. In the morning I concentrate on a long work - the *"Appassionata"* or the Brahms *Sonata in F minor.* Then I break for lunch and a walk. I like to keep my afternoons light. As long as I have worked well in the morning I see no reason to stay in all day. I like to practice at night.

My technical work, which I separate from the rest of my practice, is the only thing I'll do in the afternoon. Together with work on a difficult etude, the rest of my technical regime takes an hour or so.

Scale Exercises[2]

Exercise 1. Double notes. Each day I emphasize only one scale, first for perfecting melodic and tonal continuity, then for speed. The scales of B♭, D, F, G, and C are the hardest. Remember that scale playing is only as good as one's best legato--the basis for balance and coordination. Play each two notes of the scale together, two octaves up and back, always maintaining the scale fingering, overlapping each pair of notes. Hang the hand from the wrist. Keep the repeated note partway down so there are no holes.

Pay special attention to 3-4 to 4-1 and 4-1 to 2-1. Think of disengaging the hand and the wrist, relaxing each time you play the interval of a second so that when you get to a fast tempo, you're playing with a vibrating hand, not a tense arm. Coordination and balance of the hand are extremely important in scale playing.

You cannot manipulate this exercise by crowding the bottoms of the keys, nor can you keep it legato by playing at the tops. So play in the middle of the key descent. This is one of the most useful exercises I've found for developing evenness in scale playing. Great pianists have sweat blood over that.

Exercise 2. Walking on key bottoms. Now break the seconds and overlap every note half by walking quietly on the key bottoms with equal weight and tone on each finger. Feel the hand rest on every finger's key bottom including the thumb's. This approach is for a legato, melodic scale, not a virtuoso scale.

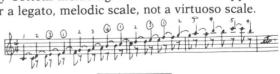

[2]A good preparatory exercise for scales is to practice C major using just 1-4, then 1-5. Play melodically with some arm weight, insisting on total evenness and legato. Work slow to fast. When you get tired, make sure your elbow is relaxed and practice throwing the fingers slow to fast. Make sure your thumb is working independently, not as an extension of the arm. Then practice B and D major two octaves up and down using 1-2, then 1-3, using the same demands as above.

Make sure to transfer equal weight from the thumb to the fourth finger. If the tone is not equal at a slow speed, it will become less and less so at faster speeds.

It is generally bad to talk about wrist manipulation because most people will tense their arms or shoulders when you do. But for a perfect legato, the elbow must be flexible, especially when the fourth finger crosses over the thumb, descending. Playing with an inflexible elbow will make your approach to the keyboard static.

Exercise 3. Trilling. Achieve speed by alternating two notes at a time, no overlapping, with different touches. Surprisingly, kids love to practice scales this way; working on each little bit instead of on endless long strings of notes produces immediate improvement of the whole.

Be sure that the fourth finger is working independently from the knuckle and is extending fully down into the key:

Go up to the top of the scale:

Then turn back down, doubling the tempo. Work for complete evenness in timing and tone:

Next take all the notes in groups of three, repeating each group as often as necessary. Also double the tempo, working through in sixteenths, or alternate measures of eighths and sixteenths.

When going around the thumb, be careful not to accent the B's and D's, the wrist moving very quickly and in advance at a slow tempo:

Sometimes hold the thumb and practice the cross-over:

Then take four notes, then five, and so on. Keep changing the dynamics, using *crescendo, diminuendo, ppp, fff:*

Elder: Would you apply this kind of practice to say the B♭ minor scale in the Chopin Polonaise in A♭?

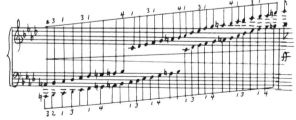

Westcott: Perhaps, if I was having trouble with it. Make sure in this scale that you hear the half-step

from A to B♭ in each octave all the way up. If the half-step isn't in the ear, the left hand will probably slide over it. Many hands-together problems are actually listening problems.

A scale problem usually consists of one note passing incorrectly to another. As soon as you can figure out the culprit note, you have the problem solved.

Exercise 4. Add-a-note. In this process I go up nine notes, then come down eight. Each new rising scale is always a third higher than the previous one.

Continue through two octaves to arrive at the tonic, then come back down. This exercise is marvelous for endurance, fingering, and sight-reading. You use the scale fingering no matter where you are. If it's four on B, you play four on B no matter which note you start from.

I use the fourth finger on F♯ in all my left-hand sharp scales (G, D, and A are the only ones that are different from the traditional fingerings). This left-hand fingering is then analogous to the right-hand fingering for flat scales (4th on B♭). For me this fingering is far more comfortable.

Leggiero Touch

A leggiero touch is important because if offers much dynamic and tonal variety. You can always mix a bit of pedal with it. To acquire a beautiful leggiero touch, practice slowly with a hand position that requires the fingers to be fully extended down to reach the key surface. Strike the keys shallowly, so that the dampers don't get far off the strings.

Start by holding the thumb down with no weight, the wrist poised, not drooped. In both hands, the hardest part in any scale is usually 3-4-1-2. Hold on to the thumb, raising the hand to the point where four is stretched straight down to its maximum.

The fingers are high; four is going straight down and coming up into a curve.

Hang the hand much higher in this exercise than you would for normal playing. Holding the thumb, alternate between B with four and D with two:

Four will be at its fullest extension, just barely hitting the key. Now add the note above D and the note below B. Don't think of lifting the fingers but of "throwing" them with vitality to the key surface with no arm weight. Now practice all the 1-2's, the 1-3's, and the 1-2-4's that fall in a scale.

Practice just the 2-3-1's:

Make up difficult patterns such as:

Would you give some examples where you would use leggiero touch?

In the "Corrente" of the Bach *Partita* in E minor.

I use a leggiero touch a great deal in Bach. In the fugue of the *Chromatic Fantasy and Fugue*, I like the leggiero sixteenth-notes running against the long legatissimo melodic notes of the theme:

In Bach, Mozart, and Schubert, getting air between the notes is important. Comparatively few pianists have a fine leggiero technique. Serkin and John Perry have it: it gives their playing a buoyant, beautiful quality, especially important for clarity in large halls.

In the Mozart *Sonata* in A minor, I play measures 23-27 leggiero, then measures 28-29 melodic, then back to leggiero:

What's the difference between leggiero and "jeu perlé"?

Perlé is a light, even, but not detached scale. In leggiero the notes are separated and the piano sings beautifully with air in the sound, like sunlight through the leaves of a tree.

Arpeggios-Stretching

Next I'll work on one set of arpeggios, perhaps dominant sevenths, to stretch out the hand, four octaves up and back, overlapping with dropping fingers, slow to fast. Attack each arpeggio's special technical problem. Or work every type of seventh-chord arpeggio you can think of with C at the bottom: C major, C minor, C diminished, and C augmented triads with major, minor, and diminished sevenths.

In slow playing try to get the hand motivated at the bottom of the key, supporting with arm weight on the knuckle. All I'm concerned about is relaxation and walking from one key bottom to the next.

Walk with the knuckles supporting, no saggy wrists. When accuracy and security at one tempo are established, double the tempo and repeat, no longer overlapping. Work with digging fingertips.

As I go faster, I drag my hand across the keyboard as in a glissando, carrying my hand with a floating forearm. The elbow does not prepare so much because there is not enough time to overlap and turn the elbow. What used to be transfer is now a quick slide. (Illustrates by playing C-B, C-B, C-B, crossing over with 1-4, 1-4, 1-4.)

I find students have trouble getting speed in that arpeggio in Chopin's A♭ Polonaise because they hold the notes down, overlapping.

Speed in such a passage is not so much a problem of holding down the notes as of pressing with the arm instead of keeping it in motion. If the fingers are not thoroughly trained, one tries to compensate by pushing with more arm weight, making the arm static, crushing the fingers.

Going from a white to a black key presents a special problem, as in the C dominant seventh arpeggio. The spacing from 3 to 4 on G to B♭ is difficult. It helps to practice over-preparing the fourth finger, lifting it straight out parallel with the black key, then playing it with an accent. The literature abounds with arpeggios presenting this spacing problem as in the last movement of Beethoven's Sonata in C major, op. 2 no. 3:

Playing with a sweeping motion comes from the hand's being carried on the bottom of the keys by a mobile arm. The fingers distribute the weight and eventually rip off the arpeggio with the help of the tips. In the *tutta forza* page of arpeggios near the end of Liszt's *Mephisto Waltz* the hand must be in line, *en face* as the French say, and pulled to the top.

However, certain arpeggios must be connected and legato, as in Beethoven's Fourth Concerto.

Scales in Thirds

I like to do double-thirds[3] scales next. They are good for the wrists, help the whole technique, and are not as difficult as some people think. I practice by the fingering groups. Every scale played in thirds usually has three groups of fingerings. In D major there is a long group of 3-4-5 (for the top notes of the thirds), plus two short groups of 3-4, and then you are back where you started.

[3]Editor's note: The term "double thirds" can be misleading. If both hands are playing thirds then we do indeed have two sets of thirds. However, if only one hand is playing we then have consecutive thirds.

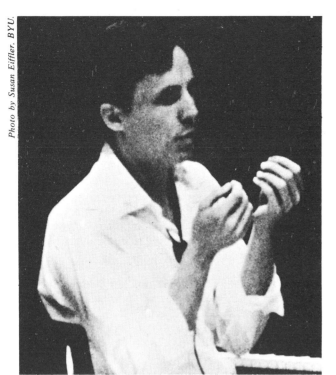

Westcott giving a master class at the Brigham Young University Piano Festival.

1. Practice starting with each group going up and back only an octave at the beginning:

Don't try for speed yet. Get a relaxed, legato feel in your hand, every pair of notes coming absolutely together.

The left hand fingering is the same idea in reverse—two short groups and a long. Drill the left hand the same way as the right:

2. Practice these same groups and prepare each finger movement in advance; when resting on the first pair of fingers 1-3, think of 4; resting on 2-4 think of 5, etc. Going from a white to a black note (B-C♯) with 3-4 is a vertical as well as a horizontal problem. Raise the fourth finger higher than the third and over-compensate by lifting the fourth finger straight out, parallel with the key.

3. Also play with a sort of flopping, arm staccato motion. The hand sits in the keys of its own weight on each pair of keys. Make sure your hand is always relaxed. Keep working over the various groups, watching where the fourth finger should be prepared.

4. To get these thirds going smoothly and fast, take hold of every third with the fingertips. My hand rocks forward a little on each attack. Then try a finger staccato. You can't play everything legato. Also practice staccato from the wrist, sloping sideways to the next notes, so the arm weight is elevated and loose. Another good way to practice thirds is staccatissimo, leggiero, not going to the bottom of the keys. Every time I play one third, the fingers are instantaneously on the next third, with the hand dragging from one note to the

next. As the speed increases, the staccato falls out. Keep the wrist super-relaxed. As I come away from the thumb to cross, the hand tilts slightly towards the fifth finger, and then turns back toward the thumb after the crossing. The hand doesn't stay static but rotates slightly.

In the first bar of Debussy's *Etude pour les tierces*, there is the problem of coming up to 3-1 on two black keys. If you use unorthodox fingerings, it's easy; if you use the "right" ones, it's awful!

When playing scales in thirds would you say the outside fingers do the work and the thumb just comes along?

Well, that is somewhat true, but I think consecutive thirds playing is greatest when it's clean and you hear all the notes, even with less speed. Horowitz rarely takes consecutive thirds very fast, but you hear every note.

For the consecutive thirds D major scale in the Brahms B♭ Concerto, do you start with the fingering 1-2?

This is a trick passage. You can't hear every third at any fast speed. The thing to do is to learn how to get over the passage. Start with one for nothing, the D-F♯; then play six upbeats, always aiming for the F♯'s on the beats, making a four-octave scale into a one-octave scale. Rebound from one D-F♯ to the next, using a long fingering. I suspect that in Brahms' time this allegretto movement wasn't taken at the tempo that many pianists use today. Any tempo faster than a true allegretto turns the movement into a bit of a romp. If you take a sweeter, more leisurely tempo, you can play this thirds passage. Brahms wanted a bubble coming up out of the water.

Mrs. Genhart feels that if the passage is unmanageable for you, you should play the thirds with two hands, as written the first time. The second time when the right hand is supposed to play the thirds, the left hand is doubling harmonically what the orchestra is doing anyway and could be used on the thirds instead. Arrau plays the passage the second time as written and does it very well. Serkin plays the second time like the first:

Thumb Exercises

I have a rather short thumb compared to the length of my other fingers and have to compensate. Many times the problem in scale playing is that the thumb does not work as effectively as the other fingers; this necessitates lowering the hand and the wrist. The thumb is not working from the joint back at the wrist.

Exercise 1. One of my favorite exercises uses the plain chromatic scale. This not only helps your chromatic scales and your thumbs immensely, but also gets your fourth and fifth fingers working Practice the chromatic scale with these fingerings:

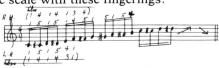

Every time you play the thumb, roll forward towards the fallboard, digging in with the last joints of the fourth and fifth fingers.

You're rolling upwards on the tip of your thumb.

The thumb is pushing the hand up and toward the fallboard. This is for practice, not how you actually play. Walk on every key bottom, transferring your weight from 5 to 1 to 4 to 5 to 1. Believe me your thumb will get tired and so will your fifth finger. Keep your fifth finger high to relieve tension and fatigue. The elbow must be out to relieve strain.

When you have finished working 1515145, use 1414132, and then practice the left hand until you can play two octaves fast up and back. Chromatic scales in *La Campanella* or the *Mephisto Waltz* are a snap after this workout.

Exercise 2. Another good thumb exercise, which I got from John Perry, I call "chromatic cross-overs." Work first with the thumb and second finger, alternating between D and C♯, moving the second finger up by half steps:

Play slow to fast with a light rotation of the forearm supported with the elbow. Do it hands separately and together and with the fingerings 1-3, 1-4, and 1-5. It is a marvelous exercise for the whole anatomy of the hand as well as for the muscles used in forearm rotation.

Hand Development

The following is a good developmental exercise for the whole hand. Play slow to fast, legato, *mf*, resting the weight on the fifth finger. Dig with the fingertips. Raise the shoulder and drop it into the third and fourth fingers when playing slowly to create accents on the first note of each triplet. Keep the elbow light.

Chords

A very good chord exercise is to play hands together, starting with the C octave and a C major triad filling out the middle. Then move those two inside notes up to play the fifth and the minor seventh. Play the IV $\frac{6}{4}$ (F and A) triad, then a minor triad (F, A♭), and then move up a half step:

Here is a pattern for going down:

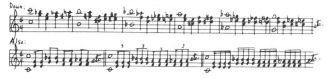

Your hand should be relaxed and flat, weight poised on your fifth and first fingers. Every time the middle fingers play their notes, the elbow should thrust slightly toward the fallboard. As you go faster, the wrist provides mobility.

Repeat the middle notes in eighths, triplets, and sixteenths, working from slow to a fast vibration. The arms should be relaxed with the forearms and elbows rather close to the sides. In playing most chords, except the quiet ones in Brahms and Debussy, the elbow thrusts inward, the wrist bends and drives the fingers directly into the keys, evenly. If you need to bring out the top note, just lean or thrust toward the fifth finger. This method produces volume for playing powerful chords. Concentrate on economy, voicing, and relaxation.

Remember that in chord work the longer you sit in a chord before playing the next one, the bigger and more rhythmic the sound will be. The fingers must play the chord, with the arm or wrist being agents for speed and weight. As soon as the hand becomes static or immobile, you cannot voice the chord. In the first page of the Tschaikowsky *Concerto* in B♭ minor you must thrust forward at the points of attack to produce the most beautiful sound.

In the opening of Brahms' *Sonata* in F minor many pianists cannot play the thirty-second note pickups cleanly with the following chord:

They come up-down for the chord. But if you come from within-up, using the elbow, you avoid being static and can manage the thirty-seconds.

For the very soft chord work in Brahms and Debussy the hand should be fixed as a unit, the tone being created by playing the chord from the shoulders or from the body itself. When you need a slow descent into the keys, it is good to use big parts of the anatomy. Gieseking played and taught soft chords in this manner.

The more one can bring out the top notes while keeping the others only as color, the greater the illusion of softness despite the fact that the top itself may actually be *forte*. Remember, half of dynamics is voicing!

The more I teach, the more I find that students lack keen appreciation of simultaneous dynamic levels. Too often chords and intervals are played without a prior decision about which note or notes should dominate. The more extreme the balance between one note and another becomes, the more the instrument seems to sustain. Also, the more prudently one delineates important melodies–subduing inner fourths, fifths, and tritones, warmly playing inner thirds and sixths, and punctuating important bass notes—the more freedom and imagination one can employ in the pedaling.

The great teacher at Oberlin, Jack Radunsky, often said that to achieve just six truly different levels of dynamics at the piano is difficult. One might also say that nearly all six levels should be at work all the time. Horowitz claims to have 14 levels—Busoni had dozens!

Crawl-Stretch Exercises

Exercise 1. This is good for the outer part of the hand. I think Adele Marcus got it from Horowitz. I do it hands together in symmetric inversion:

Practice slow-fast, elbows out, hands relaxed. The thumb slides in front of the keys or on the wood; the fingers are straight with the weight hanging in the keys. Lift each finger until parallel with the key surface.

Exercise 2. I do the same exercise with the third and fourth fingers on a major third:

Exercise 3. Take all this one step further, again working slow to fast:

Two-Note Slurs

Exercise 1. These are marvelous exercises for improving repeated notes, trills, and scales. Go up and back an octave, à la Liszt, using all the finger combi-

nations, not releasing one key all the way before starting the next one. Play legato when going slow, and let the wrist come in a bit when going fast. Accent the second note sometimes to assure evenness.

Exercise 2. Also play chromatically, using every finger combination. In slow playing, poise weight above; in a moderate tempo use some wrist roll; in fast, dig into the keys; and when playing presto play close to the keys.

Repeat the exercise in a dotted rhythm:

Repeated Notes

1. It is important to begin repeated-note practice slowly, not letting the key all the way down or up. Poise the weight above from the elbow. At a fast tempo dig more from the fingertips, keeping the accents strong.

Also repeat each finger, bouncing a bit with the wrist:

2. Repeated notes are a problem because inevitably half of the hand (fingers 1, 2, 3) is better at them than the other half (3, 4, 5). Here's a great preparatory exercise: keep repeating 5, 4, 3 at the top in groups of four sixteenth notes, accenting the first note of each group. Underneath, the thumb and second finger alternate as legato quarter notes:

The repeated note goes up by half steps: B♭ ,B,C,C♯ , up to F. When the repeated note gets to C♯ , move the second finger up to A♮ and so on. When you get tired, slow down, going to a higher finger action for relief.

You find that when your fingers get tired, it's good to go to a higher finger action?

Yes, extend the fingers, just dropping or "throwing" them. This is a wonderful exercise for music in which you have to pick up groups of repeated notes from the top of the hand, as in *La Campanella:* or in the *Piu vivo* (measure 137) of the Scriabin *Ninth Sonata* which demands two different voicings. This exercise will help increase flexibility at the top of the hand.

3. At a slow tempo, throw the fingers; at moderate speeds, bounce from the wrist; and at a fast tempo, rotate with shallow descent. Use all pairs of fingerings: 1-2, 1-3, 1-4, 1-5, 2-3, 3-4, 4-5, 2-4, 2-5, and 3-5.

4. The following exercise is based on Liszt's *Mephisto Waltz*:

Octaves

Three separate parts of the anatomy are involved in octave work: 1) the fingers which grip the key and support the octave, 2) the wrist which requires as much work as the fingers, and 3) the arms and shoulders which need to cooperate lightly and flexibly with the wrist and fingers.

Problems in octave playing usually result from too much arm weight crushing the hand and immobilizing the wrist. Use full, dropping arm weight only in rather slow fortissimo octaves; otherwise use the fingers and wrist in difficult, fast octave passages.

Remember these rules: 1) Keep your thumb at the outer tip of the black keys; don't move it in and out when playing from white to black or black to white. 2) Train your wrist and fingers to lift up and down from the wrist, with speed and suppleness, starting from a position relatively near the key bottom. 3) Overcompensate for the black keys being higher by lifting the wrist a little before playing them.

The following is a good 20-minute, three-stage octave routine coupled with a difficult octave passage from the standard repertoire.

1. To set the hand and fingers, play all scales, progressing chromatically in broken octaves, slow to moderate speed, overlapping both the top and bottom notes. Rest the arm weight gently on each note, playing legato, and gripping the notes with the thumb and fourth and fifth fingers. The arms should feel as if they are hanging, not pushing, with the hands perched independently on the outer fingers.

2. To train the wrist, practice a scale routine slowly and *pp*, plucking the octaves from the key surface by lifting the hand at the wrist as high as possible. Don't move the arm. Drop to the next octave key surface. Always rest on the key surface before plucking the octave and lifting from the wrist.

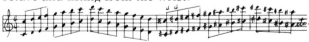

Practice the same scale routine starting the hand from its highest raised-wrist position. Snap the hand toward the key surface, playing the octave staccatissimo, instantly bouncing back up to the high suspended position. Throw just the wrist, not the arm weight, working slow to fast and bouncing from note to note like a rubber ball. The faster you play, the less you can bounce.

Practice the same scale routine with a feather-light hand, staying in the keys as long as possible, dragging the hand from one key to the next. Work up to a fast tempo.

3. Using the same scale routine, practice just the thumbs. Grip each note with the tip of the thumb, not crooking the thumb toward the palm. The thumb should operate independently from the joint nearest the wrist. Work slowly and legato, then faster and more detached with a bounce.

Then practice just the fourth and fifth fingers, *ff*, digging mercilessly with the fingertips, legato. Keep the thumb side of the hands free, the arms loose. Work slow to fast.

Sometimes if you feel your arms are lazy about getting out of the keys, practice arpeggios staccato, snapping up from a relaxed elbow. The forearm snaps up and immediately drops to the next octave.

After practicing this three-stage octave routine (or at another time of the day) work on a difficult octave passage such as the one at the *poco piu mosso* in the last movement of Tschaikowsky's *Concerto* in B♭ minor.

Practice the sides of the hand separately. First drop on the fifth (or fourth) finger, repeating the thumb twice. Drop the weight on the top note while the thumb plays short repeated notes. Add more repetitions until the thumb is quite brilliant. Then reverse the process, making the thumb the long note carrying the hand weight and repeat the top notes. Work up the speed of the repeated notes until you reach the tempo of the passage. Compensate for the black keys by lifting the hand from the wrist.

Do you think Cliburn practiced those octaves that way?

With his huge meat hooks it would be like me playing sixths. How you practice depends upon the size of your hand. We all have different problems. If your hand gets tired, don't put it in your lap. Put it up alongside the music rack or hang it on the fallboard.

If the hand gets tired, is it better to put it on top rather than hang it relaxed, loose?

It's better to let the acids and toxins from tired muscles get out of the arm. Let the arm get free of the blood rather than holding it in by letting the arm hang.

Then work the left hand an octave lower the same way. You see I'm working the sides of the hands separately. The right hand by this time will feel fabulous because it's rested. The problem with this passage is that it doesn't go up in a straight line but goes up in groups:

So practice in this rhythm ♪.♪.♪.♪. etc., so you feel you are always ascending. Use first the arm then the wrist on the dotted eighth notes for impulse.

After this kind of octave work, it's all I can do to play slowly. I just sit back and let the octaves take me for a ride."

MARK WESTCOTT'S TECHNICAL REGIME

As you work through each exercise, read the corresponding directions in the article on pages 289-296. All exercises are also to be played with the left hand, usually in contrary motion, using a mirror fingering.

I. Basic Warmup Exercises

1. Keeping the chord depressed silently, play halfway down into the key, letting the key push the finger up, the finger tip never leaving the key, the arms relaxed. Also play in 8ths and 16ths, playing each finger 8 and 16 times respectively, with no caved in finger joints!

2. Starting in slow eighth notes, gradually working up faster, walk from key bottom to key bottom, hands together, overlapping each note, with no tension in the forearm. The key pushes the finger up, the finger tip never leaving the key.

3. Play each held-finger and repeated-finger exercise in 16ths as well as 8ths. In the grace-note exercise, play the grace notes forte, staccato, fast with poised hand, not missing any repetitions; play the upper voice *mp*, legato, not fast. Play the left hand in contrary motion, using the same fingering as the right hand.

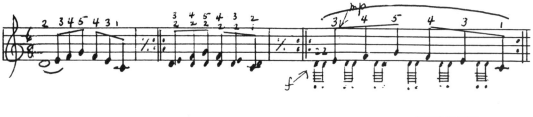

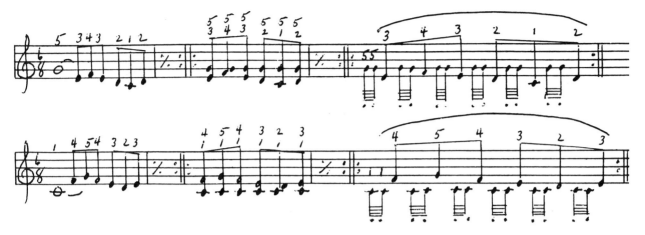

II. Scale Exercises

1. Each day emphasize one scale. Play two octaves up and back, blocking, legato, not letting the keys all the way up, the wrist hanging, the arm relaxed. Work between two pairs as needed, slow to fast, the notes exactly together and even in tone.

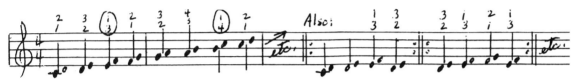

2. Work from slow to fast, overlapping, walking quietly on the key bottoms with equal weight and tone on each finger, the elbow flexible and prepared. Also play the scale regular in two, three, and four octaves.

3. Trill each two notes of the scale, playing half down in the key, no overlapping:

Each three notes, repeating each measure 4 times:

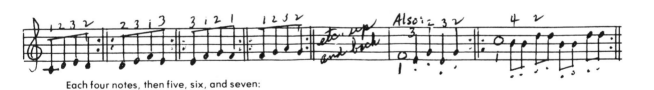

Each four notes, then five, six, and seven:

Then each four, five, six, and seven notes. Concentrate on the area at 3, 4, 1, 2 and exhaust only one scale a day, running through others once slowly, then moderato — legato.

When you get to eight notes, play:

Leggiero Scale Exercises

Hold the hand high. Play with high fingers and don't go to the bottoms of the keys.

III. Arpeggios-Stretching

Work all dominant seventh arpeggios chromatically or work on such arpeggios as the following, four octaves, overlapping at slow tempo, the hand motivated at the bottom of the key, supported with arm weight on the knuckle, the wrists not saggy. Also work for speed, taking weight out of the bottom of the key, carrying the hand with a floating forearm.

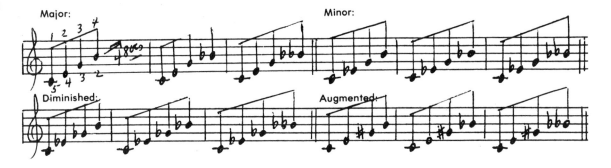

Dropping fingers from high position, overlapping:

Also trill various sets of fingers in one octave form:

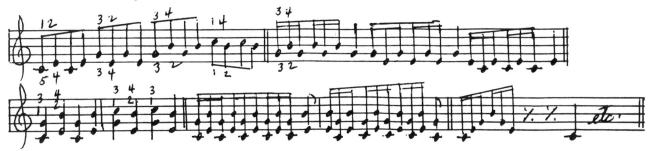

IV. Double Thirds Scales

Practice one octave up and back, starting with each finger grouping: 1) slowly with relaxed hand, every third coming together; 2) preparing the top finger of each pair — i.e., resting on 1-3, think of 4, etc; 3) working for some speed with arm staccato; 4) taking hold with the finger tips, playing finger staccato, going instantly to the next two keys to be played; 5) working for speed, up and back, up and back. Then play four octaves. Also practice all possible pairs of thirds legato, fingers digging.

299

V. Thumb Exercises

Play slow to fast, checking that thumb works freely, finger tips digging, wrist rolling. Also try light, leggiero touch, two octaves up and back.

1. Also use the fingering 1-2-3-4-5, 1-2-3-4-5, etc. up and back two octaves, in triplets and in sixteenths. When using high fingers, drop the fifth from a curved, not a straight position. Also start on D, playing hands together in contrary motion.

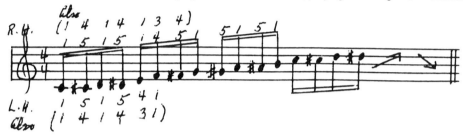

2. Play slow to fast, high fingers, very free thumb and rotation. Practice both legato and brilliant, also with 1-3, 1-4, and 1-5.

3. Play slow to fast, legato, *mf*, resting weight on the fifth finger. Check that the fourth finger extends "into" the key from its knuckle. Dig with the finger tips. Raise the shoulder and drop it into the third and fourth fingers to accent the first note of each triplet, keeping the elbow light.

VI. Chord Exercise

Play hands together, the inner notes from the wrist, resting on each note as long as possible.

VII. 4-5 and 3-4 Stretching-Strengthening Exercises

1.

Play slow, legato, with flat fingers straight in descent, digging with the finger tips. Also play with fast bounce, always keeping the thumb below the hand resting in front of the wood, the elbow suspended and flexible.

3. Check legato and avoid arm tension.

VIII. Two-Note Slur Exercises

Use every finger combination: 12, 23, 34, 45, 13, 24, 35, 14, and 25. Also play in dotted rhythms. At slow tempo, poise weight above; at moderate, use some wrist roll; at fast, dig into the keys; and at presto, play close to the keys. Make sure the second note of each slur is as loud as the first.

IX. Repeated-Note Exercises

1. Slow: push the key only half down, never letting the key fully up, posing the weight above from the elbow. Moderate: Bounce with the wrist. Fast: dig more from the finger tips. Keep the accents strong and make sure every joint in the finger works.

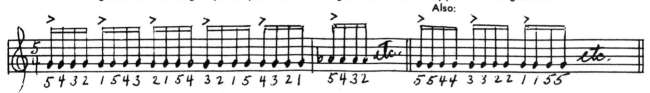

2. Play with light hand, tips digging, slow to fast; also play with some wrist bounce.

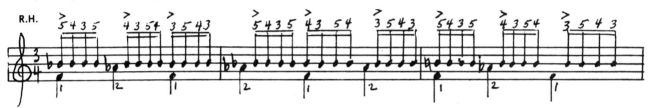

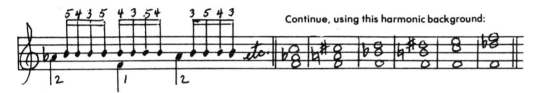

Continue, using this harmonic background:

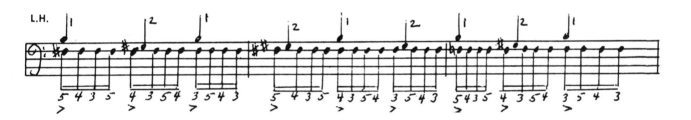

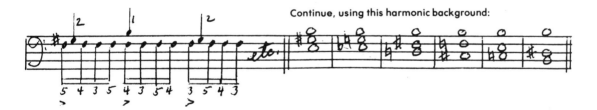

Continue, using this harmonic background:

3. Slow: throw fingers. Moderate: bounce from wrist. Fast: rotate with shallow descent. Also practice the same thing with the major scales. Also use the fingerings 1-3, 1-4, 1-5, 2-3, 3-4, 4-5, 2-4, 2-5, and 3-5.

4. (Liszt) Slow: play legato, dig. Moderate: Use high fingers, bouncing the wrist.

Also:

X. Octaves

1. Play all scales in broken octaves from slow to moderate tempo, overlapping the top and bottom notes. Rest the arm weight on each note. The arms should hang, the hands perched upon well-supported outer fingers.

2. a) Starting on the key surface, pluck the octave, lifting the hand high from the wrist, dropping to the next key surface and so on; b) starting with the hand raised high at the wrist, play the octave staccatissimo, instantly bouncing back to the high suspended position; and c) staying at the key bottoms as long as possible, slop or drag — don't lift much — the hand from one key bottom to the next. Also practice the thumbs alone and the fourth or fifth fingers alone.

3. Snap the forearm up from the elbow, dropping immediately to the next octave.

4. Practice the octaves in the last movement of the Tchaikowsky B♭ Minor Concerto: 1) the sides of the hand separately, repeating the bottom notes twice, then four times; then similarly the top notes, dropping the weight on and holding the note not being repeated; 2) in the rhythm   etc.; 3) also finger staccato, rebounding horizontally to the next note.

5. For fast, light octaves, think of the fourth and fifth fingers as melodic, the thumb as light, bouncing. Also play finger staccato, rebounding to the next note:

How a Young Virtuoso Practices

Santiago Rodriguez

interview 1977

Santiago Rodriguez has won prizes in 10 national competitions including the Dealey, the MTNA, and the Naumburg. In international competitions he has been a semi-finalist in the 1973 Cliburn and the 1974 Tchaikovsky, first-prize winner in the 1975 Maryland, and a finalist in the 1976 Leventritt. To crown his competition career, he has recently won second prize in the much-publicized and televised 1981 Cliburn Competition.

Rodriguez was born in Cárdenas, Cuba, in 1952, and he came to this country in 1961. "After Fidel Castro took over, my parents sent my brother and me to the United States," he says. "As we had no relatives to meet us, we marched around Miami Airport yelling, 'Catholic Charities!' hoping someone would take us there. An airline hostess did. We spent three years in a Catholic orphanage. From there we were shuttled to different foster homes or orphanages and wound up in New Orleans. My parents were unable to emigrate to this country for six years."

Rodriguez started piano study when he was five. "By the time I left Cuba, I had played all the Bach Two-part Inventions in recital, had studied all the Three-part Inventions and had begun some Chopin. When I was nine the nuns at the orphanage in New Orleans thought I would have a chance to win the symphony competition. I did win, so I played the Mozart Concerto K. 595 with the New Orleans Symphony."

After his debut, Santiago Rodriguez studied with various teachers until he entered the University of Texas to study with William Race for four years. Then from 1973 to 1977 he was a scholarship pupil of Adele Marcus at the Juilliard School. The Cliburn Competition resulted in a full concert schedule for Rodriguez, who now has 56 concertos in his repertoire. When he is not performing, he teaches at the University of Maryland.

Santiago, how do you start your day's practicing?

To be perfectly honest with you, I first sit down and feel the piano out, playing a few chords in popular style.

In the early morning I'm cranky and usually half asleep. I may start a popular song to get myself into the mood to play, or I may play a little jazz — improvisation on a theme or on a chord progression — to get my mind started.

I practice almost everything very slowly so that I can hear what is happening and can concentrate on the troublesome part.

After that I start my technical regime: playing the first 30 Hanon exercises and all the scales and arpeggios. I practice about seven hours a day and try to devote one hour at the beginning to technique. I want to warm up my fingers and not get very involved emotionally.

How do you practice the Hanon?

Slowly! I set the metronome at 100 or slower and play with very high dropping fingers to build endurance. The good thing about the Hanon exercises is that they are simple and all the fingers get to work. For me Czerny is not good because you work the fingers only one hand at a time.

After playing the 30 Hanon exercises, I continue into scales. I got this procedure from David Bar-Illan, who practices his exercises for half an hour without stopping. He claims this regimen builds endurance, and it has done so for me.

You play 30 Hanon exercises with high fingers all the way through?

Yes, but you have to keep the wrist loose. You are going to be a little tight when you begin, so keep the mind working on relaxation except for the finger stroke which must be precise. Don't stiffen the wrist or the forearm when you are doing the finger stroke. Play slowly, looking at each finger as it goes down, and trying to keep all five fingers as even as possible. Of course there is going to be one weaker finger that you will work on for the rest of your life. Hanon number 30 is especially good for the fourth and fifth fingers:

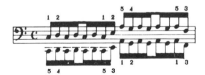

Have your muscles ever tired going through these 30 exercises in this manner?

The first time I played through them I thought my forearm, wrist, and body were going to cave in and fall off the piano by number 5. In the beginning the process was extremely tensing.

Let's say you practice seven hours a day for a performance that may last half an hour. In that half hour you have to maintain great tension. You expend a lot of sweat and guts. Having this kind of regimen behind you reassures that you aren't going to get tired and break down in the middle. You are confident you will be able to do whatever you want. Endurance is one of the most important things in piano playing.

Some people's muscles won't take such a grueling regimen.

You have to know when to quit. The first time I did these exercises, I didn't push myself too far. The last thing I wanted was to get tendonitis. You can ruin your hand by pushing yourself too far. Sometimes it is better to sit back and think, or come back to the piano after you are rested. Start little by little, gradually building up endurance as you would build up muscles for anything else. It takes about half an hour to play the first 30 Hanon exercises at this slow speed. Then I spend another 20 minutes on scales.

How do you practice scales?

I play all the major and the melodic and harmonic minor scales, four octaves, keeping the same principle of high, very articulated fingers and even stroke, setting the metronome at $\downarrow$ =108 or 112. If I want to work on speed, I lower the finger stroke and try to get a flowing feeling out of the scale. Mozart and Beethoven are full of scales. I try to perfect scales in a manner to fit the pieces I am playing.

Sometimes when I am preparing a recital, I start cold on the first piece to see how it is going to work. When you walk out on stage, you don't get a chance to play a couple of scales beforehand. Or, if I am going to play a concerto, I play the beginning of that. Once I have the necessary confidence, I don't lose it.

The first time I played through them I thought my forearm, wrist, and body were going to cave in and fall off the piano by number 5.

And then you start on repertoire?

I decide what piece needs most work. I don't like to play a piece all the way through 150 times, hoping that one time it is going to be good. I work on passages that are hard for me — possibly a slow part, not necessarily a technical part. I may work on either the

sound or the shape of the passage, practicing very slowly so that I can hear what is happening and can concentrate on the troublesome part. I practice almost everything very slowly.

Could we take some examples?

Let's begin with something slow like the Schubert *Impromptu* in Gb, op. 90 no. 3. The problem is to keep this rolling motion Ave-Maria-type middle voice quiet while making the melody sing. So I begin the piece very slowly, about ♩=69, playing the melody strongly and the inner eighth notes softly and evenly. Some people might think this a cruel and inhuman thing to do to a piece, but it is the only way I can find out exactly what the middle voice is doing. I would use this method to practice just the passages that give me a problem.

The beginning and the ending of any piece are the hardest parts. If I can begin a piece correctly, it usually ends correctly. Sometimes I have played the beginning of this piece with blocked accompaniment to decide where I wanted the melody to go and how I wanted to shape, phrase, and color it. Then I worked technically on that middle voice to make it quiet with as little finger stroke as possible. This piece is difficult because of this technical challenge. Yet it must sound like a piece of music and not a technical challenge.

Another passage I practice is the opening of the Fugue of the Bach *Chromatic Fantasy and Fugue*. The Fantasy ends softly, and I like to continue that soft mood into the Fugue. The problem is to play the opening of the Fugue softly with finger legato and as little pedal as possible. I practice slowly and carefully to get the touch I want and to observe my fingers. I work on the shape of the theme and how it ends. The fingery passages in the Fugue don't trouble me as much as this opening.

In the Fantasy there is huge run which I often practice a few times slowly, like an exercise, to get a good feeling in my fingers:

I don't want to be known only as a person who has fast fingers, octaves, or wrists. I want people to listen to the music and forget about the technique. Of course, if the piece I am playing — like some of Liszt — is basically a show piece, I am also going to show the technique. I will work hard to make the piece as flashy and exciting as possible.

The beginning of the Fantasy, which must go very fast and have guts, also requires very clean fingers. I would be easy to sit back and play it lightly, but to achieve a really important-sounding opening you have to practice deep into the keys. Bringing out what you and the music have inside is what technique is about. Practicing slowly so I can hear what is going on has worked for me.

309

You seldom have to practice finger work?

Don't get me wrong. I do practice much finger work. But I find it more difficult to get out of the piano what I feel in warm, mellow passages than I do in technical passages. I find the Schubert *Impromptus* op. 90, for example, hard because they demand this warm quality.

Let's return to the Schubert Impromptus.

The first Impromptu, a gorgeous piece, immediately presents a theme which repeats many times:

The concluding part of the theme follows:

The many repetitions which follow make the piece difficult. It should not sound like "here's the theme" and "here's the theme again." The phrasing and color must be varied: one phrase opens, one closes. As the interpreter, I have to show all the different lights into which the theme is cast. I have to figure out what Schubert is trying to do and where he's going.

In the middle Schubert throws in another theme, the only thematic change in the whole piece.

So I work for the direction of the piece, seeing where the high points are and what I have to do technically and musically to reach them. You have to seek out the right touches, how to change the character of each section depending on whether it's going into major or minor. You have to take time with it.

And the second Impromptu?

The second Impromptu is more of a finger piece than the others, except perhaps number four. The first section is basically the E♭ major scale going up and down the piano. You have to know what you want to do with it to avoid making it sound like just a scale.

First I practice the right hand slowly and very articulated to get the fingers to know where they are going. Then I try to see how legato I can get it without using much pedal.

There is a gorgeous little middle section in this same passage which is hard to get properly musical. It is crucial to bring out the melody and give the whole line a musical shape.

This Impromptu needs to have a very flowing motion, with the middle section a little warmer. I think of the whole as a Viennese waltz — very light, clean, and classically pure. I play it straight and as warm as possible within its classical framework. It's a very simple piece that must sound simple. You have to shape your technique to that interpretative end. The piece must sound clean and articulated but not technically oriented. It shouldn't be played too fast.

Do you listen to recordings as part of your practice?

I have a nice record collection, which is not limited to piano music. I listen to orchestral music of the composer I'm playing. When I'm getting acquainted with a piece, I may get a recording by someone I respect and listen to see how the piece comes across and see if I think I could put it across.

But after I begin working on a piece, I don't listen to recordings. I want to figure out myself how the piece should go. After I have worked it out and feel that my interpretation is valid, I will listen to different interpretations, either agreeing or disagreeing. I have a keen ear and listening to records could be a cheap way of getting ideas. I strive to get my own.

Your tone is one of the things I found beautiful in your Chopin. Do you work especially on tone?

I've worked a lot on tone ever since I studied with Adele Marcus. At the University of Texas I worked mostly on my fingers. I'm still working on my fingers but I've expanded. I'm also working a great deal on projection. In projection you have to have tone: the tone has to carry and it has to say something. The piano has to sound beautiful.

How have you worked on the Chopin Sonata in B♭ minor?

When I first began the piece I wasn't careful enough how I played it. Although I felt the music, I wasn't sure what I was doing. I knew the phrases had to "go somewhere," but feeling something and actually putting what you feel across are two different things. As I have marked in the score, I work on getting the second theme to go somewhere:

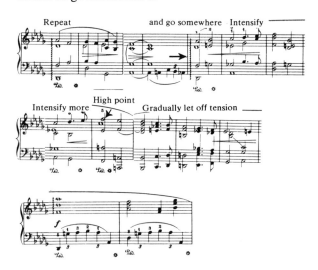

Studying and concentrating on the composer's markings are of course two basic principles. Chopin wrote those phrasings and dynamics in the music. If I follow his "road signs," I can figure out how to play the music. I don't want to recreate or redo Chopin's phrasing and dynamics.

I see you have a repertoire sheet on your piano.

I list the pieces I am working on. Whenever I've practiced hard on a piece or played it all the way through, I write a check. In working on a lot of repertory, I find I need to know what I have worked on and what needs the most work. I also want to keep track of pieces I have to keep in my fingers. I don't want to leave any out.

Let's talk about Petrouchka, a specialty of yours.

Because I like to come out and grab the audience with this piece, I have worked tremendously on the opening five-note chords that go up and down the keyboard. This opening must sound technically brilliant and at the same time like a Russian dance:

To begin close to the keyboard for me is committing suicide. Coming down in the keyboard with an arm-stroke produces a better sound, creates an immediate beginning to the dance and is great fun to watch. Then, too, if you play these opening chords close to the keys, the accents won't be there. By beginning above the keys, the accents come out wonderfully. This beginning shows something essential in real music making: you have to take chances. It would be easier to play more cautiously, but my whole concept is based on taking chances.

Petrouchka requires great endurance. Color, too, is of the utmost importance. You can beat yourself through *Petrouchka*, playing all the notes, and not accomplish anything. In ending the glissando, I go right to the following E, even though it is dangerous to land on the little finger. I may miss sometimes but usually I am successful because I practice it.

Petrouchka is a "knuckle cruncher!" The hand positions are extremely wide and uncomfortable. Especially in the last movement, you are constantly doing technical feats that must sound like music. Stravinsky asks you to jump up and down the piano constantly. There is one part where you keep reaching for two E's at the extremes of the keyboard and diving back to a chord in the middle, all at a rapid tempo:

You don't play the E's, then jump, go back to the E's, and then jump. You play the E's and the minute you release them you are here in the middle; and as soon as you release again, you are back at the high E's, et cetera. You have to get to the notes fast in a perfectly straight line. I may miss sometimes, but I prefer to take that chance for the whole effect.

At the same time you are going back and forth between the middle and the extremes of the keyboard, you are building up to a big fortissimo. I could keep it mezzo forte and get through easily, but those octaves must keep coming out, growing and growing. The immediate dropping to a subito pianissimo at the Agitato is a wonderfully effective part.

Being of Spanish ancestry, do you play Spanish music?

I'm performing three selections from *Iberia* by Albeniz and the *Baby's Family* of Villa-Lobos this year in recital. The Spanish repertoire is a recent addition to my programs.

Overall, how would you say that you spend the six hours of your practice after the technical work?

I'd say I work mostly on the slow, meditative parts of the repertoire that are the most difficult for me. I have only recently realized that this approach is extremely important. I used to think, "If it is slow, it is bound to be easy."

In many performances the fast passages are terrifically clean and you are amazed at how great the fingers are. And that is exactly what you say about the performance, how fast the fingers are. I think the worst compliment backstage would be for someone to say, "You've got the best octaves I've ever heard." Pianists can talk to each other about such things, but I don't want to leave just the impression that my octaves in the *Hungarian Rhapsody* or *Petrouchka,* that my repeated notes in *Carnaval,* or whatever, were fantastic. I want the whole effect to come through.

For example, I spend my time tying the first section of the *Hungarian Rhapsody* into the next part, making a gradual progression into the showy part. If I didn't practice the beginning, it would be as if I had decided, "I'll sleep during the first part and wake up during the ocatves."

So you are constantly working on phrasing, architecture, projection, and tone?

And these things are all technique to me. Holding a piece together is the hardest thing. When I first heard Vladimir Horowitz some people just talked about how fast his octaves were. His octaves certainly *are* fast, but for me, the effect was also that I had been through a great musical experience. The music and the technique were tied together. He and Artur Rubinstein are two of my favorite pianists.

Your approach seems closer to Rubinstein's than to Horowitz's.

I find Rubinstein's approach to his audience close to my ideal. I want to go onstage and project "Here I am and here's this gorgeous piece of music. I think it's wonderful and that's why I am playing it." I practice a lot because I want to be good. But more important, I want to have something to say and to give pleasure. I want people to like the music, my playing, and me.

312

PETER ORTH
on the Chopin Etudes

interview 1979

Blessed with hands that can strike a stretch of 13 notes, absolute pitch and marvelous ear memory, Peter Orth began playing by ear at four years old. Raised near Philadelphia by a musical family, he became a scholarship pupil of Adele Marcus at the Juilliard School from which he graduated in 1976. He has since worked with Rudolf Serkin, won the 1979 Naumburg Competition, toured with a Music from Marlboro group, and give recitals and appeared with leading orchestras throughout the country. His dazzling technique, rich vibrant tone, and gripping communicative qualities are ensuring him an ascendant place among the world's great pianists.

I first heard Orth in a concerto performance five years ago. Afterwards, I asked him if he had a technical regime.

"Yes," he responded, "Chopin Etudes, Chopin Etudes. The more I play them, the more secure I feel on the stage. When I read that Alicia DeLarrocha is 'always doing Chopin etudes' to keep up her technique, I felt I must not be crazy."

Recently I heard Orth perform the 12 Chopin *Etudes*, op. 25 as the second half of a solo program. That afternoon, practicing in the hall, he had worked through them after having played the Beethoven "Appassionata" and op. 109 *Sonatas*, the Franck *Prelude Chorale & Fugue*, and the Brahms D minor *Concerto* and *Handel Variations*. He had his fingers working so well that when he finally played the etudes (the "Aeolian Harp," for example) his fingers were fluttering almost automatically with a very "oiled-mechanism" sound. "By then," Orth recounted, "I was relaxed and had much better control of sound."

Great artists in their prime mostly no longer remember or aren't interested in recalling how they practiced in earlier years; but this information is of great help to teachers and students delving into the piano literature. I asked Orth to recall how he first practiced the Chopin Etudes.

"Adele Marcus gave everybody the 'Black Key' and the 'Revolutionary' first. She taught me how to practice them very slowly, triple forte. She used the expression 'as if you wanted to disturb your neighbors.' Every day for about four years, as an initial warmup in the morning, I first practiced the 'Chromatic,' the 'Sixths,' and the 'Thirds.' They take a lot of time and slow practice to perfect. There's not one muscle, one finger, one knuckle in the right hand that isn't put to the royal test in these three pieces. Then for the left hand, I used the 'Revolutionary,' and after that I practiced the 'Winter Winds' and the 'Octave.'

Etude in D♭, Op. 25 No. 8

Bar 1. "Let's begin with the *Etude* in double sixths. I use a peculiar fingering which fits my large hand and helps me play legato. Now that 4-2 is uncomfortable unless you can stretch it easily; but if you can,

it makes all the difference in the world. The more legato you can play with your fingers, the less pedal you will need.

"I practice with the outer voices as legato, pronounced, and pointed as I possibly can, the inner voices staccato. I practice the inner voices staccato because when you go for the most musical tempo, you want to be able to play them very light.

"In the first and second measures I pedal through the first and second beats and release on the third. I find you get more excitement, more of an undulating quality, if you leave the pedal off in the second half of the measure. After the beginning, you can find your own way with the pedaling.

Bars 9-13. "Beginning here, in the second section, I would work keeping the wrist low, firm but not stiff, not letting it bounce around. Practice accenting the first of every triplet strongly to get your bearings.

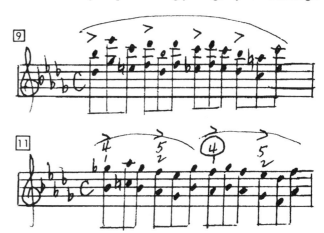

For example, on the third beat of measure 11 you will come down on a fourth finger which is uncomfortable. Accenting will give you the security to play that F comfortably. The only way you can make this section come off with continuity and not have it sound all chopped up is to play very legato, bringing out mostly the top voice, keeping the thumb very light.

"Practicing this piece in rhythms can help. For instance in the first measures, use the rhythm:

 playing the first notes of the first and third beats staccato. Raise your hands up into the air and let them come down freely to play the second note of the triplet. Doing this helps your security. Or, play very sharply the rhythm:

. In this etude legato is the most important thing because it stretches. Stretching makes your fingers very malleable, as Miss Marcus would say.

Bars 32-35. "The way that gets me to the top of this final chromatic run accurately is to follow my hand with my body. Also work the entire piece at a deliberate, determined tempo, without pedal, as evenly as possible, forte and without expression, with an edge of sound on the top of the sixths and the bottom of the bass.

Etude in A minor, Op. 10 No. 2

Bar 1. "I recommend two ways of practicing this etude. One is to keep your wrist firm and low, playing the two chordal under-notes on each beat staccato, pointing your fingers. Lift the fingers high enough

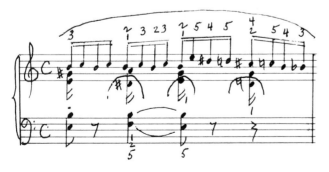

so that they can push the keys down again; that is, the fingers are neither very high nor very close. With a firm wrist, the sound and the energy to the fingers becomes more channeled. Many people let their wrists move too much, so that their fingers don't do their share of the work; they never get the strength they need for big playing. If the wrist wields too much power, the fingers become mushy. The tone won't be firm, even, and pearly.

"The other way is to practice slow, forte, very close to the keys, super-legato with a lot of finger pressure, like bubble gum sticking on. Some people say this way of practicing isn't right, but I have to do it often.

Bar 4. "On the second, third, and fourth beats, I take the bottom notes of the right-hand chords with the left hand and use 2-3 on the second-beat 16th

notes. This arrangement gives the fourth and fifth fingers a rest. You can make a little crescendo on the B-C trilling without getting tired and using up energy.

Bar 9. "Here, the second time around, I play very quiet with almost no pedal.

Bars 19-20. "These etudes take time. You have to examine every tie, eighth note, anything there is any question about. You can't slough over things. For example, these thumb notes are here for a reason: they balance the other side of the hand. If you don't play

them out, the piece doesn't do the hand much good.

Bars 25-26. "Going from the fourth beat of measure 25 to the first of measure 26 to me is terror. So I practice going from the fourth to the first beat. And as much as I hate to practice in rhythms, I find that

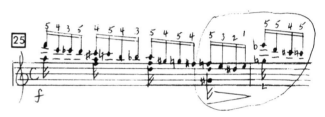

playing the following rhythm helps here:

Etude in G♯ minor, Op. 25 No. 6

Bar 1. "The 'double thirds' etude is a very light piece, and you only get that lightness by practicing very slowly with emphasis on the fourth and fifth fingers, playing the thumb and second finger staccato. That is, you practice double thirds the same way as

double sixths: staccato in the quiet part of the hand where there is no melody. After you do this for a thousand years and you get some articulation in the trilling double thirds, you can get beautiful evenness. You can go fast and light to the end.

"I would also practice this piece very 'sticky-into-the-keys' as in the A minor 'chromatic' etude, releasing the thumb each time, keeping the wrist low. Go through the whole piece like this, accenting the first note of each group of 16ths.

Bar 4. "Use a fingering on the last 16th to put your hand in position to play the following ascending chromatic scale. Some people omit the bottom A♯ and use the second finger on the remaining top C double sharp (similarly in measure 8).

Bars 23-24. "I use $\frac{3}{2}$ and $\frac{1}{5}$ for the trill all through the measure. Then on the last 16th ($\frac{1}{5}$) I let go of the thumb to play the next measure with the fingering shown.

Bars 39-40. See fingering shown.

Bars 47-48. "This scale is rough as the devil. You have to work out most of the fingerings yourself, fitting them to your hand according to how your technique works. My fingering is shown with the printed measures.

Bars 49-50. See fingering shown.

The left hand and pedaling. "After the first two measures I put the soft pedal down until the last 16th of measure four. The left hand has to be practiced very legato. In measures five and six, for example, some people pedal only every few beats. But I think you should pedal every beat or even every eighth note. The pedaling depends upon the person, the foot, how sensitive the ear is to the harmonies, what you want to be heard, how articulate the fingers are.

"Whenever the right hand bumps, it's often the thumb's fault. So you have to practice the thumb very light, always releasing it. I don't practice this piece in strange rhythms. I practice it in straight, slow tempi forever.

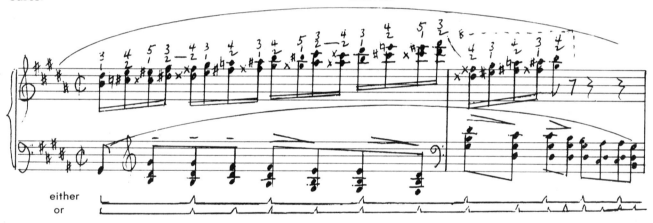

either
or

Etude in C minor, Op. 10 No. 12

Bars 2-3. "As soon as you come down on the chord on A♭, put down the pedal and raise your arm. Then come down in one motion for the 16th G octave and the first-beat chord of measure three. Release the pedal for the 16th and take it again for the following chord. If you come off the keys as you play the first chord,

you will give it a better accent. By coming up, your arm is free to play the two following chords in one

motion. My reason for doing this is to be able to make the jump and to make the accent without having it sound punched.

Bar 9. "Practice the left hand of the 'Revolutionary' using the same principle as in the A minor 'chromatic': wrists low, fingers doing the work. Make sure the thumb crosses under as soon as it finishes playing. Coming down, you've got to have it under to get the necessary smoothness and agility.

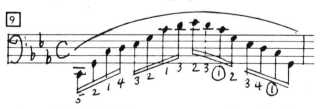

Bars 29-37. "I find this passage marvelous for oiling up the left hand. Practice it slowly with high fingers, low wrist, then with close fingers — as many ways as possible to give the fingers a real workout.

Bar 66. "When you come down the home stretch on the last page, cut the pedal off cleanly before playing the first beat of measure 67.

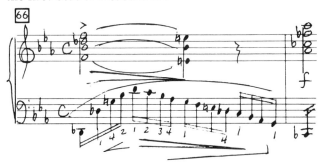

Bar 68. "Bring out the thumb for greater sonority in the chord and to keep it from sounding as if the left hand is taking over.

Bar 70. "The same thing here: bring out the thumb G's in the right hand. I keep measures 71 and 72 mezzo forte.

Bars 75-76. "I sometimes hold the right-hand D in measure 75 through measure 76, so that there is a continuity of line, so you don't hear this 'chunka, chunka, chunk' of the left hand.

Bars 80-81. "And I make a crescendo in measure 80 to the fortissimo chord of measure 81.

Etude in A minor, Op. 25 No. 11 ("Winter Wind")

"Practicing an isolated section in various rhythms is fine if you can't resolve the problem by other means. But in general I've found that when I've been practicing with different rhythmic patterns, my playing doesn't get the pearly evenness that I get when I practice plain old slow with a firm, low, 'nonbouncing' wrist, making the fingers do the work. It wasn't until I worked this etude slowly, evenly, determinedly that it came out with some kind of evenness and quality.

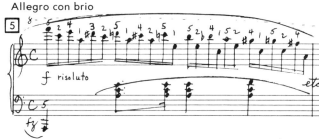

"And after doing that kind of work, I've found that the best way to play it is with an emphasis on melody. Don't think, 'There are all of these notes here. It goes from this difficult section to that difficult section.' Play it as a melody, then the right hand become less difficult.

"With Serkin I worked on the *Etudes* from the very first Breitkopf edition edited by Ernst Rudorff. Chopin approved and liked this edition and gave a copy to Felix Mendelssohn. Mendelssohn's grandson was a friend of Adolf Busch and gave it to him. Serkin has it now.

Etude in E minor, Op. 25 No. 5

Bars 42-45. "I've learned something recently about relaxation which has been a big help. In these jumps, if you lift your hands after each one and stretch your arms out completely, all your muscles will relax.

"Serkin said, 'Make the jump in one motion. As soon as you play it, extend your arms, relax, and start over again.'

"Whether I'm practicing the Chopin Etudes or other works, I've learned that when I think of something musically, it becomes a musical, not a technical problem. When you solve the musical problem, you can play the piece better regardless of its technical difficulty. And if you think someone is right, consider following his advice; but if you think he's not right, don't. The more I play the piano, the more I like my playing when I trust myself."

INDEX*

*Dates and places of birth and death are given for pianists only.